House of MYSTERY

DESOLATION

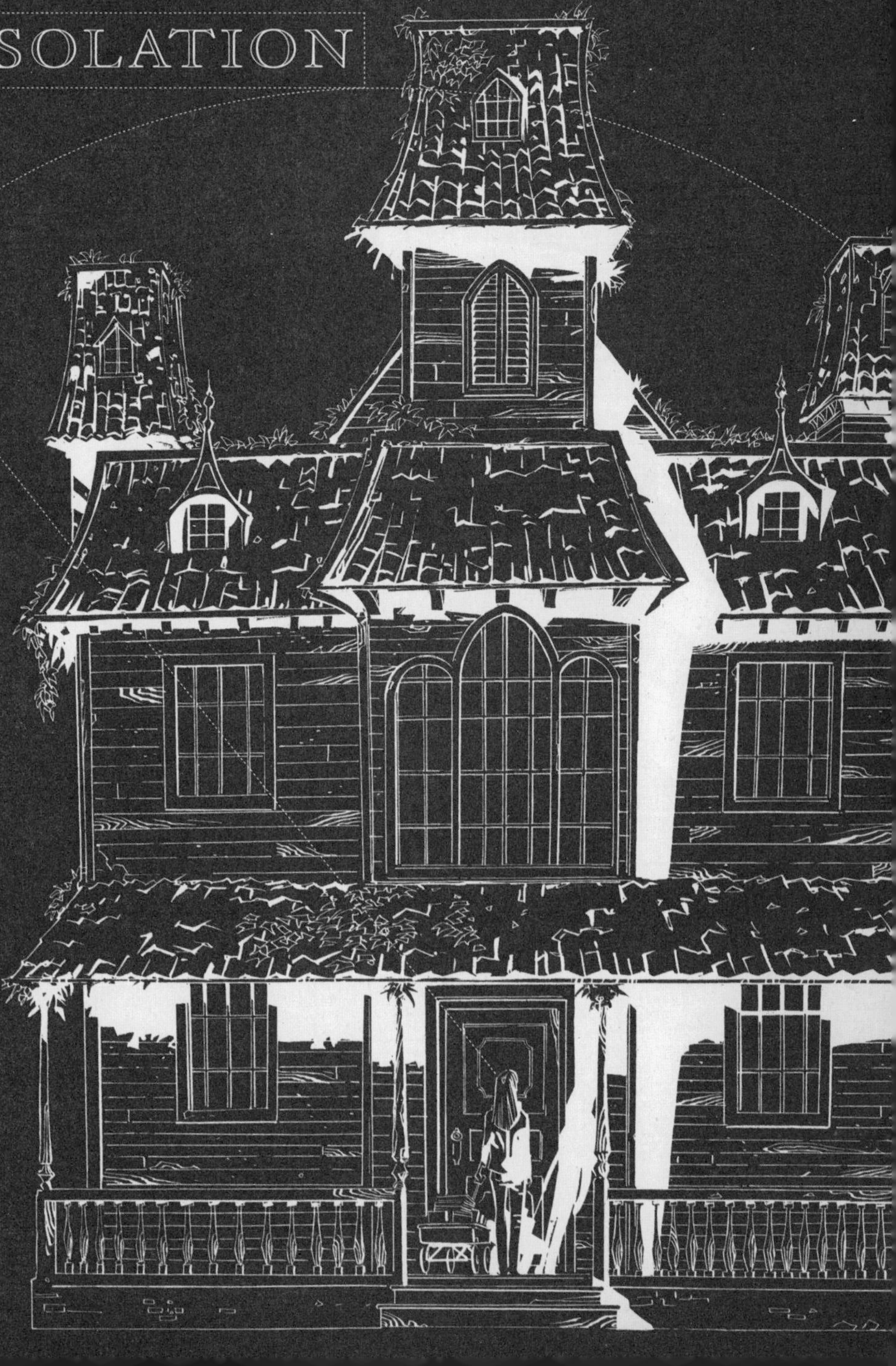

MATTHEW STURGES WRITER

LUCA ROSSI PENCILLER

JOSÉ MARZÁN, JR. INKER

LEE LOUGHRIDGE • DAVE STEWART

EVA DE LA CRUZ COLORISTS

TODD KLEIN LETTERER

ESAO ANDREWS COLLECTION & ORIGINAL SERIES COVERS

MATTHEW STURGES • BILL WILLINGHAM
STEVEN T. SEAGLE SHORT STORY WRITERS

DARWYN COOKE • AARON CAMPBELL • DAVID LAPHAM • PETER SNEJBJERG
ANNIE WU • TONY AKINS • TEDDY KRISTIANSEN • INAKI MIRANDA SHORT STORY ARTISTS

SPECIAL THANKS TO DAVE JUSTUS

House of MYSTERY

DESOLATION

SHELLY BOND — EDITOR – ORIGINAL SERIES
GREGORY LOCKARD — ASSISTANT EDITOR – ORIGINAL SERIES
ROBIN WILDMAN — EDITOR
ROBBIN BROSTERMAN — DESIGN DIRECTOR – BOOKS

KAREN BERGER — SENIOR VP – EXECUTIVE EDITOR, VERTIGO
BOB HARRAS — VP – EDITOR-IN-CHIEF

DIANE NELSON — PRESIDENT
DAN DIDIO AND JIM LEE — CO-PUBLISHERS
GEOFF JOHNS — CHIEF CREATIVE OFFICER
JOHN ROOD — EXECUTIVE VP – SALES, MARKETING AND BUSINESS DEVELOPMENT
AMY GENKINS — SENIOR VP – BUSINESS AND LEGAL AFFAIRS
NAIRI GARDINER — SENIOR VP – FINANCE
JEFF BOISON — VP – PUBLISHING OPERATIONS
MARK CHIARELLO — VP – ART DIRECTION AND DESIGN
JOHN CUNNINGHAM — VP – MARKETING
TERRI CUNNINGHAM — VP – TALENT RELATIONS AND SERVICES
ALISON GILL — SENIOR VP – MANUFACTURING AND OPERATIONS
HANK KANALZ — SENIOR VP – DIGITAL
JAY KOGAN — VP – BUSINESS AND LEGAL AFFAIRS, PUBLISHING
JACK MAHAN — VP – BUSINESS AFFAIRS, TALENT
NICK NAPOLITANO — VP – MANUFACTURING ADMINISTRATION
SUE POHJA — VP – BOOK SALES
COURTNEY SIMMONS — SENIOR VP – PUBLICITY
BOB WAYNE — SENIOR VP – SALES

HOUSE OF MYSTERY: DESOLATION

DC COMICS, 1700 BROADWAY, NEW YORK, NY 10019
A WARNER BROS. ENTERTAINMENT COMPANY.
PRINTED BY RR DONNELLEY, WILLARD, OH.
6/29/12. FIRST PRINTING. ISBN: 978-1-4012-3495-9

SUSTAINABLE FORESTRY INITIATIVE   Certified Sourcing
www.sfiprogram.org
SFI-01042
APPLIES TO TEXT STOCK ONLY

LIBRARY OF CONGRESS CATALOGING-IN-PUBLICATION DATA

STURGES, MATTHEW.
 HOUSE OF MYSTERY: DESOLATION / MATTHEW STURGES, LUCA ROSSI, JOSÉ MARZÁN, JR.
  P. CM. — (HOUSE OF MYSTERY; V. 8)
"ORIGINALLY PUBLISHED IN SINGLE MAGAZINE FORM IN HOUSE OF MYSTERY 36-42."
 ISBN 978-1-4012-3495-9 (ALK. PAPER)
 1. GRAPHIC NOVELS. I. ROSSI, LUCA. II. MARZÁN, JOSE. III. TITLE.
 PN6727.S786H656 2012
 741.5'973—DC23
                    2012015590

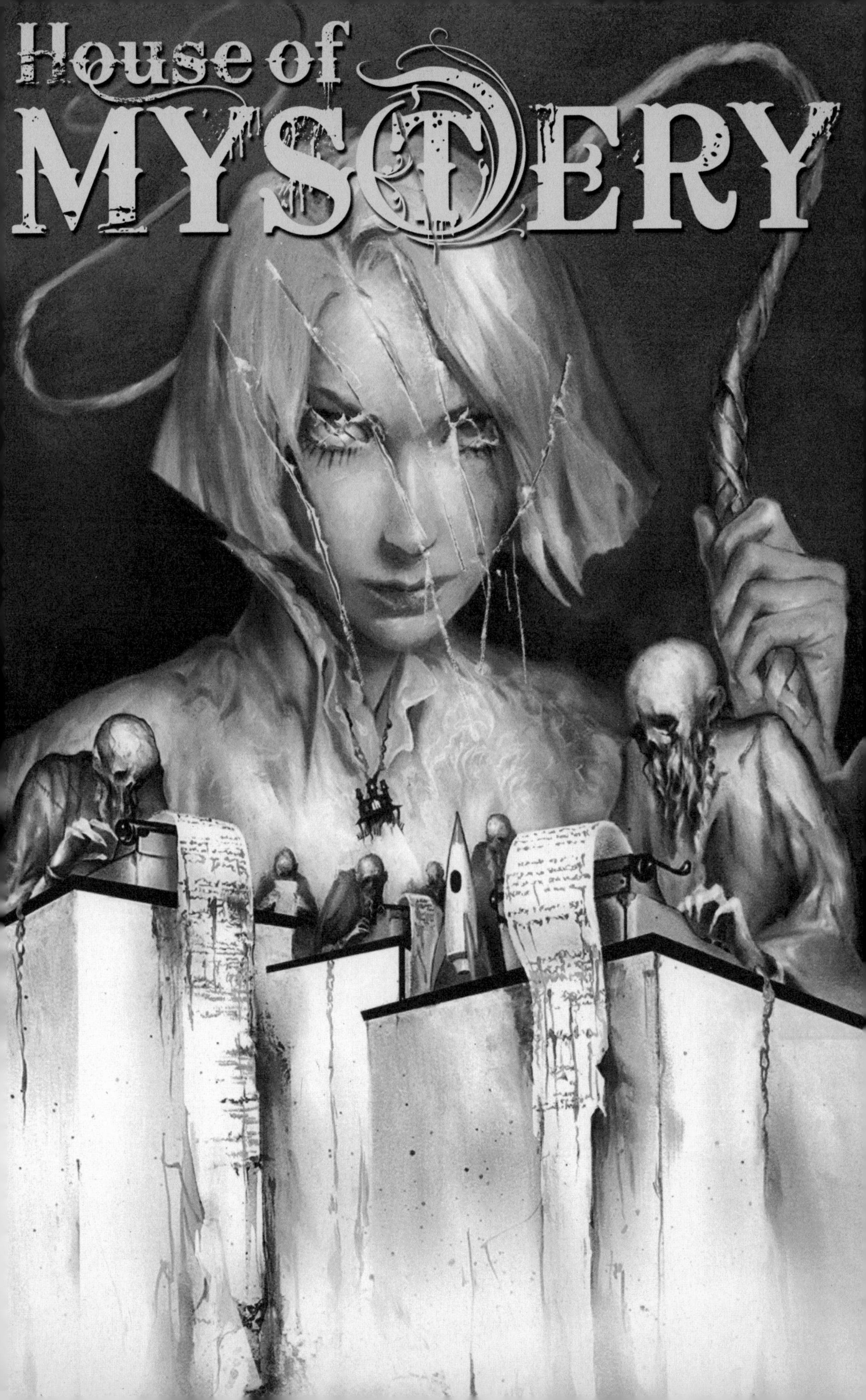
House of
MYSTERY

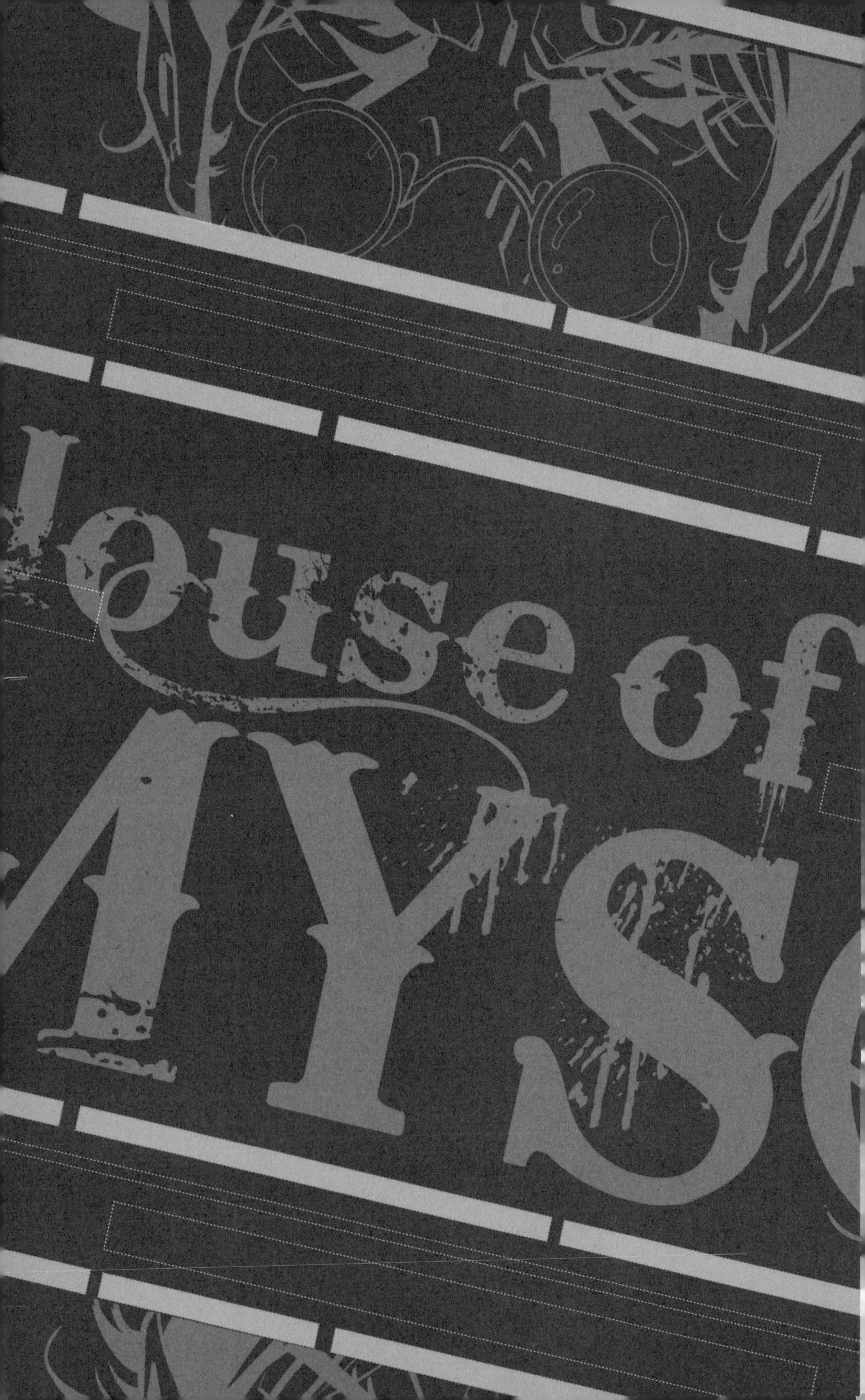
ouse of
YS

THESIS

CHAPTER ONE: ROOM AND BOREDOM

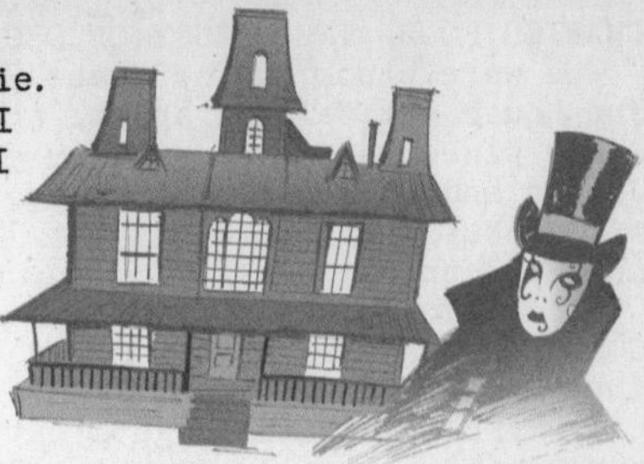

I was just a regular girl. No, that's a lie. I wasn't regular, but I tricked myself into believing I was. I was an architecture student, failing out of my senior year. I was unhappy with my life. Also, I liked to draw pictures of an odd old house.

One night, a strange couple broke into my house trying to abduct me. When they grabbed me, the house literally collapsed. I ran, they pursued, and I ended up in a place called The House of Mystery.

The House of Mystery was a bar located at a crossroads between the many worlds. It was also the odd old house I kept drawing. People came and went and they paid for their food and drinks by telling stories. There was a catch, of course: the people who worked at the house, the staff, couldn't leave. And guess what--I was the newest employee.

There was Harry the bartender, who I just fell for like a ton of smitten bricks. There was Cress the waitress who was a giant bitch who'd sleep with just about anyone. There was Ann the lady pirate, who was the bouncer, and then there was Poet, poor, poor Poet, who cooked.

I tried everything I could to escape, but no dice. When I couldn't escape I flipped out and fell apart--and so did the House. Again, literally. I ran out of the House only to be met by my asshole father--and that strange couple, The Pair of the Conception, waiting for me. So I stayed.

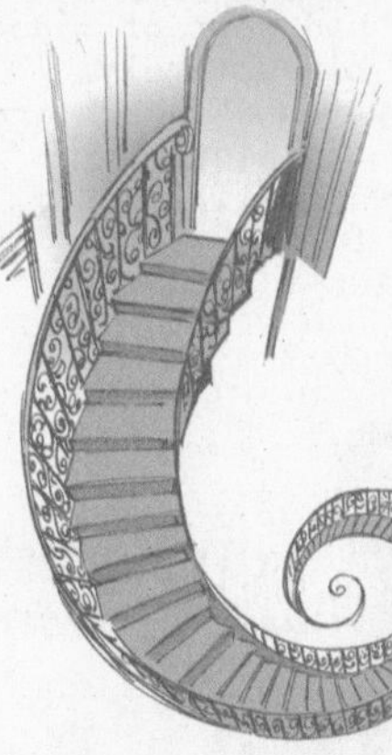

CHAPTER TWO: LOVE STORIES FOR DEAD PEOPLE

I got this crazy idea that we could escape through the basement. But, this house being what it was, the basement was perhaps the scariest place that you could possibly imagine. Seriously--other basements were afraid of this thing. It was also impossibly big; it went on for what seemed like forever.

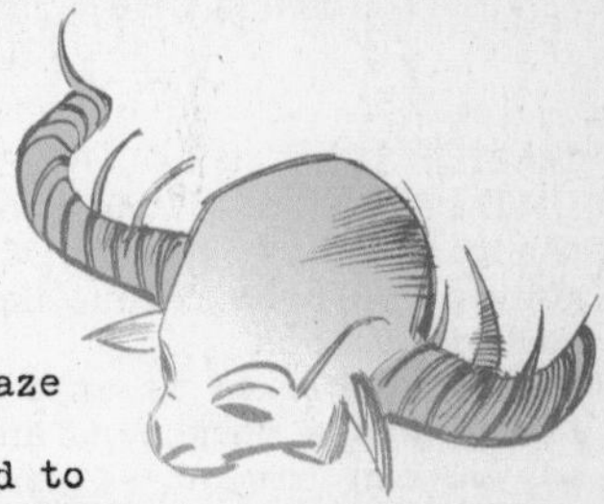

And the basement wasn't empty, either. There were these, um, weird deer baby things, which were creepy and sad. And there was Miranda, a gal who used to have my job upstairs, who had since gone totally batshit crazy and was married to an evil nightmare (literally--it was a living nightmare, and it was evil).

I did manage to find my way out of the maze of the basement, and at the end was a door leading into the real world. It actually led to my dad's study, which was weird. My dad was there waiting for me. But my friends had been attacked by the evil nightmare dealie and I had to run back to help them. My dad followed. Chaos, as they say, ensued. So there I was, right back where I started, except now my asshole dad was there, too.

CHAPTER THREE: THE SPACE BETWEEN

Okay, back up a little. There was this gal named Rina, who left the House of Mystery right before I showed up. She was carted off by this mysterious Coachman fellow and delivered to the Conception, who are the villains of the piece. Sort of. They wanted to use her to get at me, for reasons I had yet to understand.

Anyway, here's my dad at the House, and he tells this wild story about how he and I are descended from these people in The City in The Space Between, and that we have special powers that allow us to "fold," meaning we can make the world go all squishy and then end up someplace else. Like you do.

Harry and my dad got in this big fight because of me, and my dad did his "folding" trick, and they ended up out in the ruins of a Goblin Market near the House. Harry immediately became very ill, and that's when my dad sprung the news on Harry that Harry wasn't actually a real person, and was actually part of the House, and that he'd die if he didn't get back to it. Just to be clear: my boyfriend? Not an actual person. Can I get an amen, ladies?

Easier said than done because between them and the House were various monsters and some nasty goblins. There was some fighting and so forth and they made it back to the House, just in time for the Conception to attack! Fortunately, my friend Overhill turned out to be a dragon and he dragoned them long enough for me to try my hand at "folding," which was a big clusterfuck because the whole House ended up stuck in The Space Between, which is where my dad said we were from.

Also, it turned out that this Coachman guy was actually Cain--the House's original owner--all along. It was a big deal at the time.

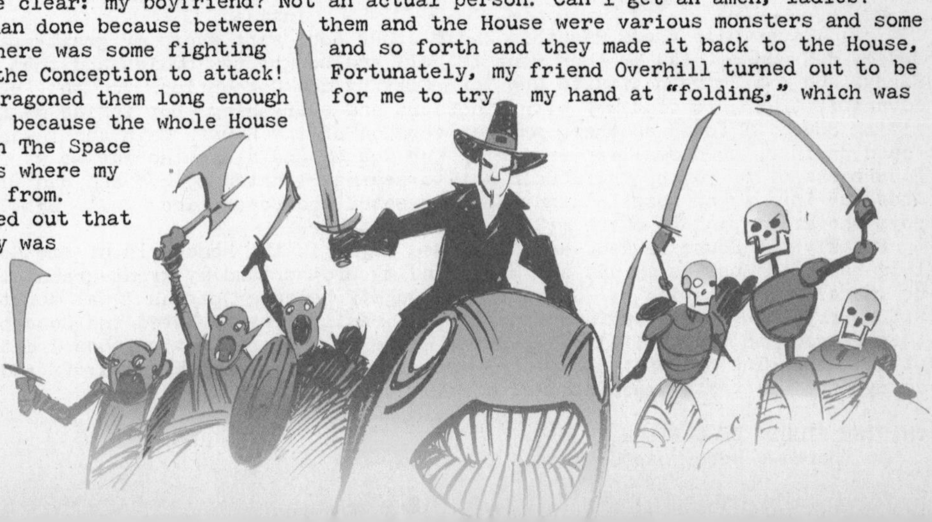

CHAPTER FOUR: THE BEAUTY OF DECAY

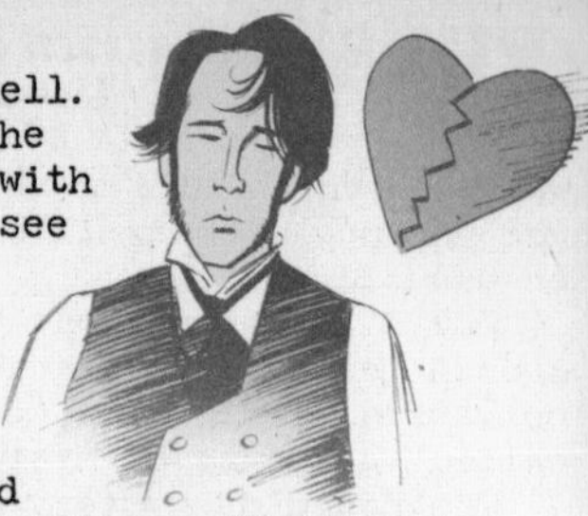

We were stuck in The Space Between, and everything had gone to hell. The House was falling apart, and Harry was turning into wood, and the whole place was surrounded by ghosts that wanted to eat us. I went with Jordan and my dad to this place called the Pathfinder's Academy to see if we couldn't find a way out. But that sucked because my dad went nuts and tried to kill Jordan, who I kind of liked.

And then, wouldn't you know it? Cain showed up with this creepy Conception Administrator named Ceorel, who wanted to catch me. So they're after me, my dad is nuts, my friend Poet accidentally gets killed, and Rod Cannon gets eaten and Simon the punk rocker dies and everything basically is shit. Finally the Pair of the Conception showed up and told me that they'd let us go if I made a deal with them. The deal was that I would have to give up everything I loved--including Harry--and then come join them willingly after a time. I reluctantly agreed, and the House disappeared again, this time reappearing in the Goblin Market.

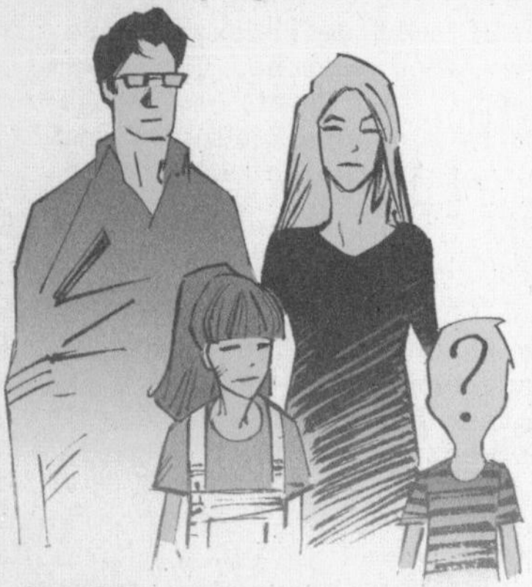

CHAPTER FIVE: UNDER NEW MANAGEMENT

So now Cain and I were sort of co-managing the House of Mystery, and I was using Jordan as rebound guy, which wasn't really fair to him. And things were at least tolerable...until my brother Strawberry showed up. The thing was, I didn't even remember having a brother.

Strawberry was kind of a psycho who had some creepy pseudo-incestuous ideas about me, and as a result I had sort of made him disappear and made everyone forget about him entirely. That may sound harsh, but if you knew the guy you'd understand. He attacked me, and we had to lock him up in the liquor cabinet. Where he was murdered. I didn't know who killed him, even though Cain's brother Abel took the rap for it. (It turned out it was Jordan who did it, but I didn't find that out until later. Poor Jordan.)

CHAPTER SIX: SAFE AS HOUSES

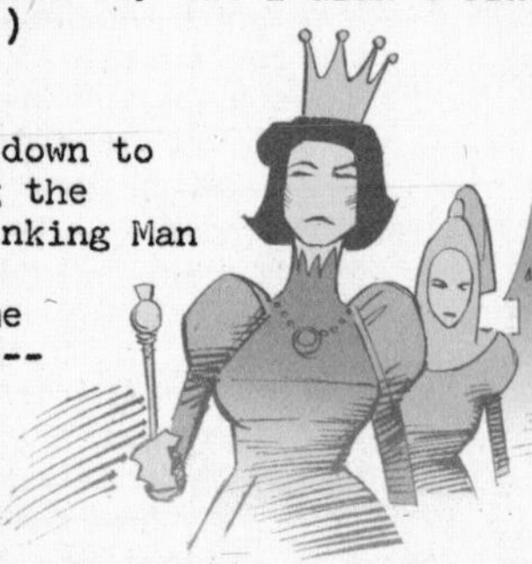

This one is a long story, so I'm just going to boil it down to the gist of it. A witch queen named Diana showed up asking the goblins to help retake her witch kingdom back from the Thinking Man and his robots.

Diana tricked me into believing that she really liked me like I was a daughter, and I wanted to believe her because--as you can imagine--I was pretty fucked up by this point, and my real mother was a frigid bitch.

Long story short: we went to the witch kingdom, got captured, got rescued by my childhood stuffed rabbit named Walden, and then I killed a monster with a big flying roll of toilet paper that came from a little universe I created with my brain. That helped the witches and the goblins win the fight with the robots. Plus, also my friend Tursig became the first gay Goblin King, which was nice.

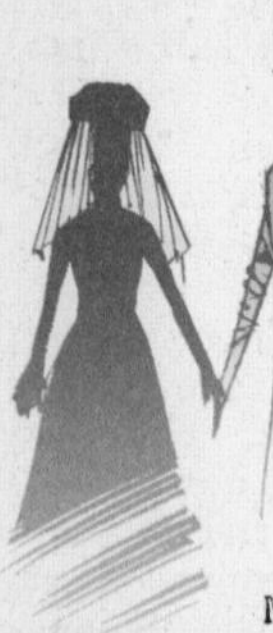

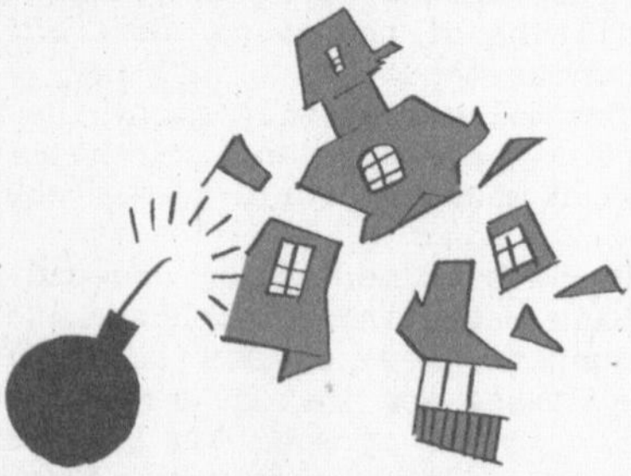

CHAPTER SEVEN: CONCEPTION

But it was only a matter of time before everything went to shit again. The Pair of the Conception showed up in the Goblin Market, telling me it was time to go with them. But I wasn't really into that, so I hauled ass out of there and ran and hid in the House. And to just about everyone's surprise, the House jumped up off its foundation and leapt out into space, with just me and Cain inside.

Meanwhile there was this whole other cool part where my great-grandfather Keele and my dad and my dead brother went to hell and bought new bodies and then came and found Harry, who'd been relocated to New York City by the Conception. And they had a grand adventure trying to find me, with dinosaurs and everything. But inside my bedroom in the flying House, I found another, smaller version of the House. Cain and I went inside and we found another, even smaller version of the House. And along the way we were treated to flashbacks of my youth, where Cain got to see how I hated my mom and had fits and then ended up in a psych hospital and then I created the Conception. Wait. What? I created the guys who are trying to catch me? How does that work?

Finally the House landed, and it landed right in the homeworld of the Conception. And this happened just as my dad and Harry and my brother and my great-grandfather also showed up there trying to find me. Or so they thought, because just as I was about to be reunited with Harry, my great-grandfather Keele (who really, really hated the Conception because they ruined his whole life) blew up the House of Mystery, for reasons I didn't understand at the time. The Conception captured all of us, and we were dragged off and it looked like everything was pretty much screwed at that point.

CHAPTER EIGHT: DESOLATION

So there we were, captured. And I had to

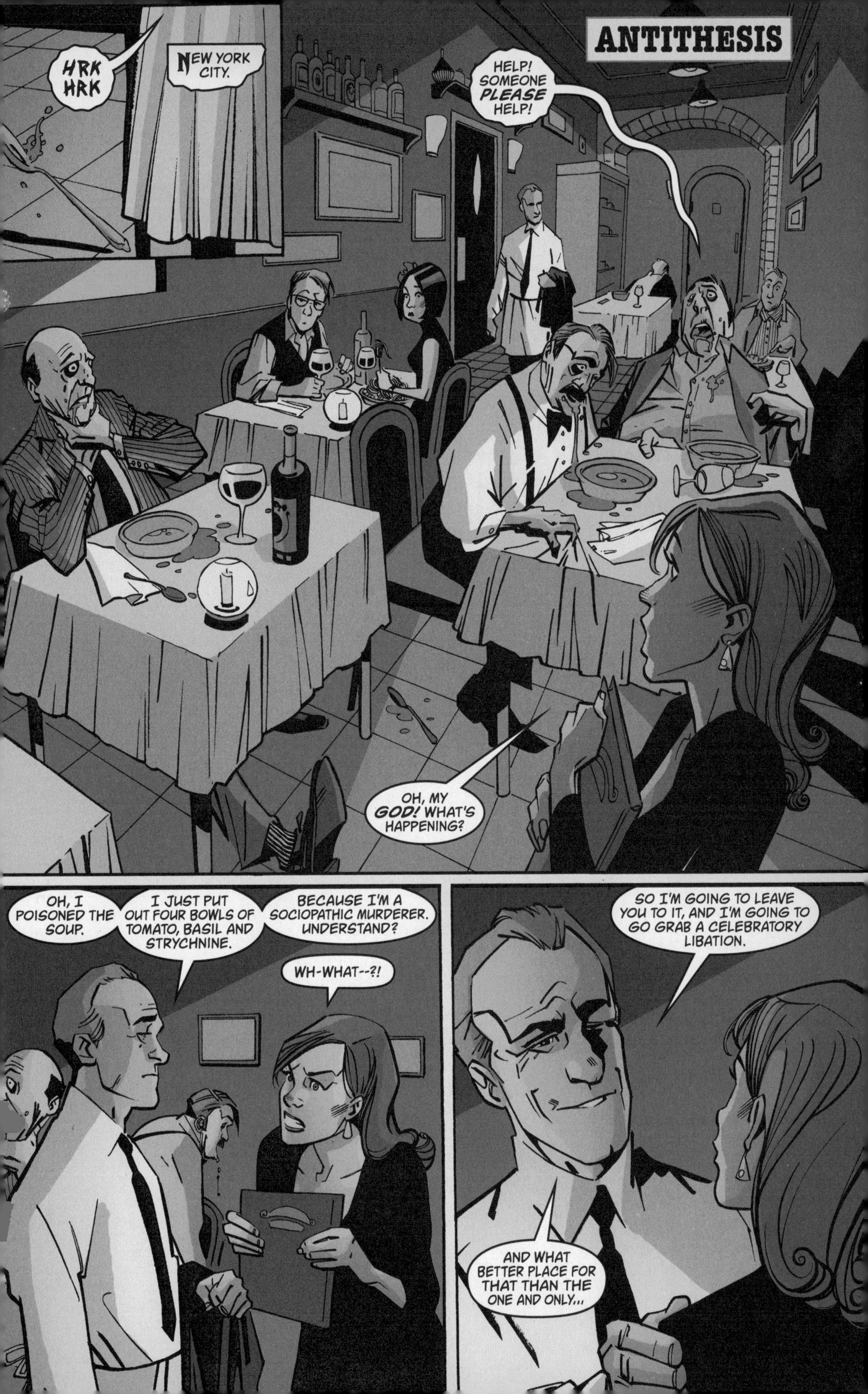
ANTITHESIS
HRK HRK
NEW YORK CITY.
HELP! SOMEONE PLEASE HELP!
OH, MY GOD! WHAT'S HAPPENING?
OH, I POISONED THE SOUP.
I JUST PUT OUT FOUR BOWLS OF TOMATO, BASIL AND STRYCHNINE.
BECAUSE I'M A SOCIOPATHIC MURDERER. UNDERSTAND?
WH-WHAT--?!
SO I'M GOING TO LEAVE YOU TO IT, AND I'M GOING TO GO GRAB A CELEBRATORY LIBATION.
AND WHAT BETTER PLACE FOR THAT THAN THE ONE AND ONLY...

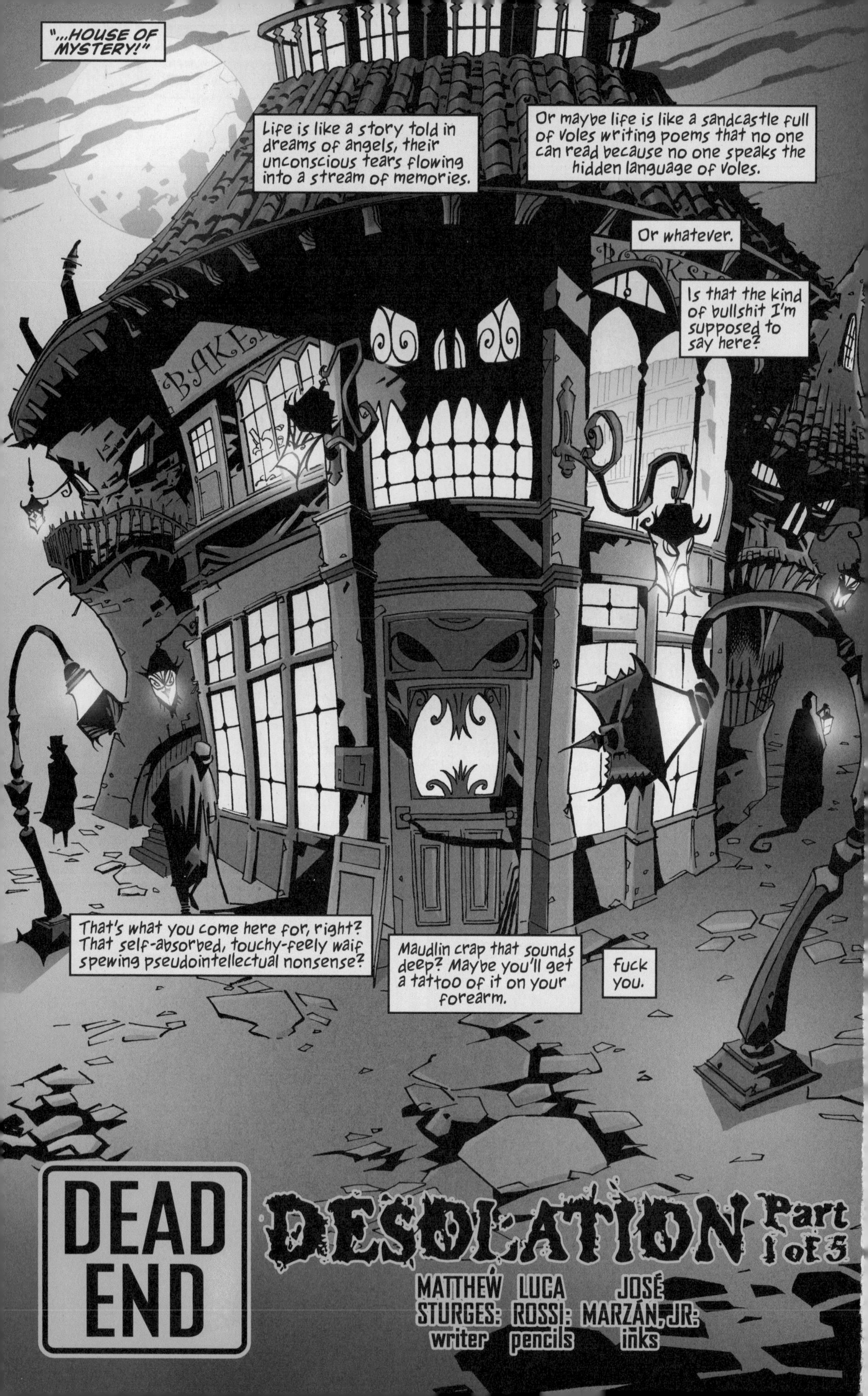
"...HOUSE OF MYSTERY!"
Life is like a story told in dreams of angels, their unconscious tears flowing into a stream of memories.
Or maybe life is like a sandcastle full of voles writing poems that no one can read because no one speaks the hidden language of voles.
Or whatever.
Is that the kind of bullshit I'm supposed to say here?
That's what you come here for, right? That self-absorbed, touchy-feely waif spewing pseudointellectual nonsense?
Maudlin crap that sounds deep? Maybe you'll get a tattoo of it on your forearm.
Fuck you.
DEAD END
DESOLATION Part 1 of 5
MATTHEW STURGES: writer
LUCA ROSSI: pencils
JOSÉ MARZÁN, JR.: inks

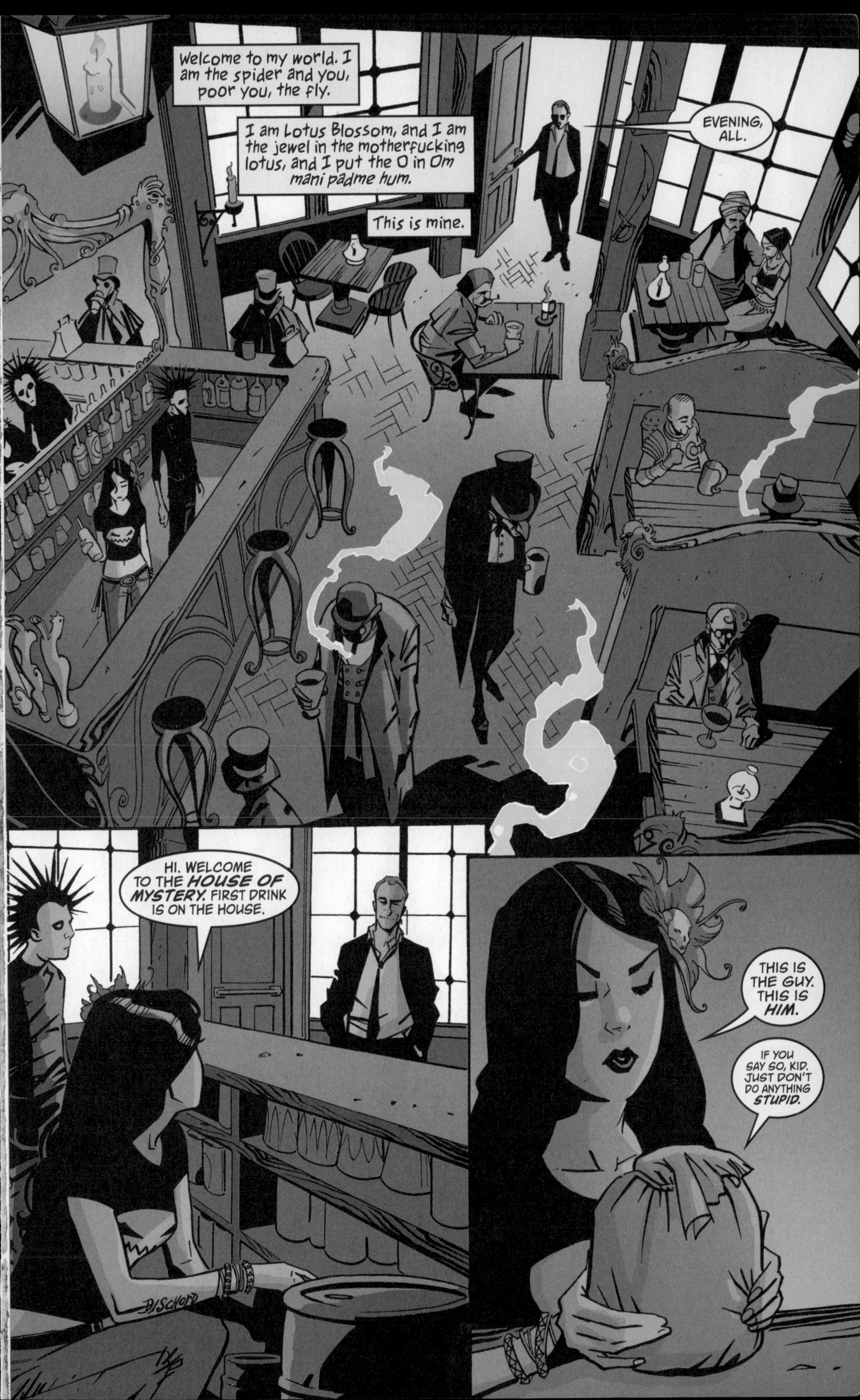

Welcome to my world. I am the spider and you, poor you, the fly.
I am Lotus Blossom, and I am the jewel in the motherfucking lotus, and I put the O in Om mani padme hum.
This is mine.
EVENING, ALL.
HI. WELCOME TO THE HOUSE OF MYSTERY. FIRST DRINK IS ON THE HOUSE.
THIS IS THE GUY. THIS IS HIM.
IF YOU SAY SO, KID. JUST DON'T DO ANYTHING STUPID.
BISCHOFF

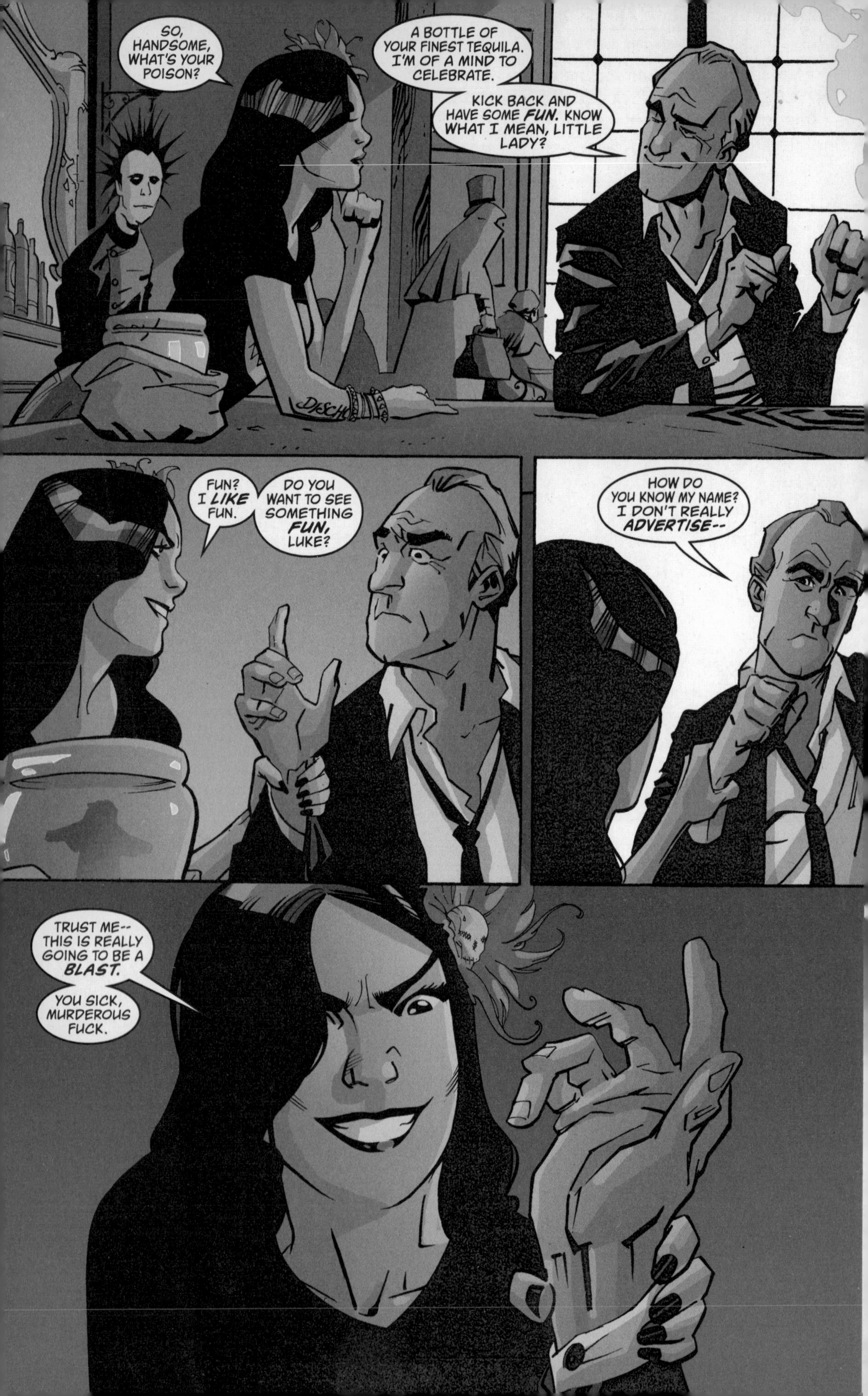
SO, HANDSOME, WHAT'S YOUR POISON?
A BOTTLE OF YOUR FINEST TEQUILA. I'M OF A MIND TO CELEBRATE.
KICK BACK AND HAVE SOME FUN. KNOW WHAT I MEAN, LITTLE LADY?
FUN? I LIKE FUN.
DO YOU WANT TO SEE SOMETHING FUN, LUKE?
HOW DO YOU KNOW MY NAME? I DON'T REALLY ADVERTISE--
TRUST ME-- THIS IS REALLY GOING TO BE A BLAST.
YOU SICK, MURDEROUS FUCK.

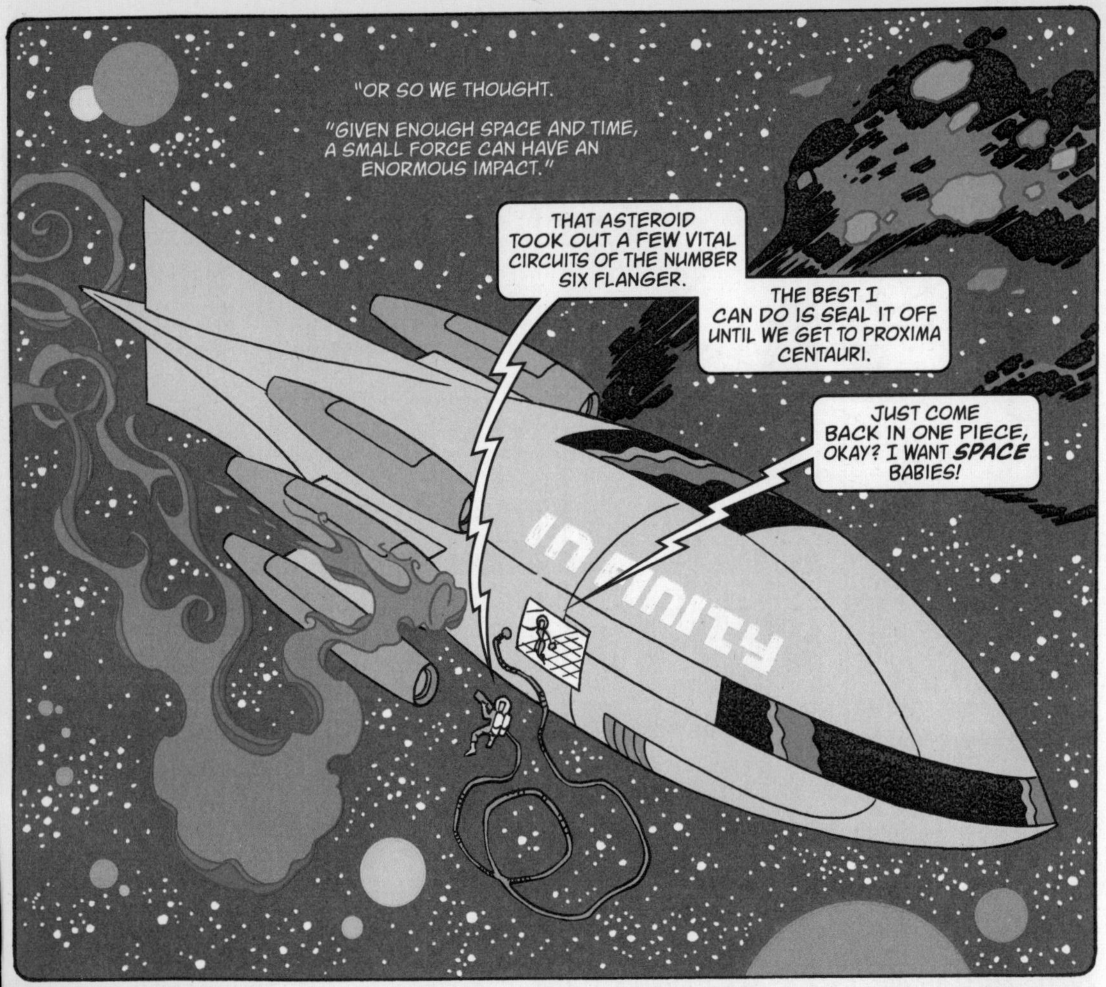
"OR SO WE THOUGHT.
"GIVEN ENOUGH SPACE AND TIME, A SMALL FORCE CAN HAVE AN ENORMOUS IMPACT."
THAT ASTEROID TOOK OUT A FEW VITAL CIRCUITS OF THE NUMBER SIX FLANGER.
THE BEST I CAN DO IS SEAL IT OFF UNTIL WE GET TO PROXIMA CENTAURI.
JUST COME BACK IN ONE PIECE, OKAY? I WANT *SPACE* BABIES!
INFINITY

THE LAWS OF MOTION

Matthew Sturges: writer
Darwyn Cooke: artist

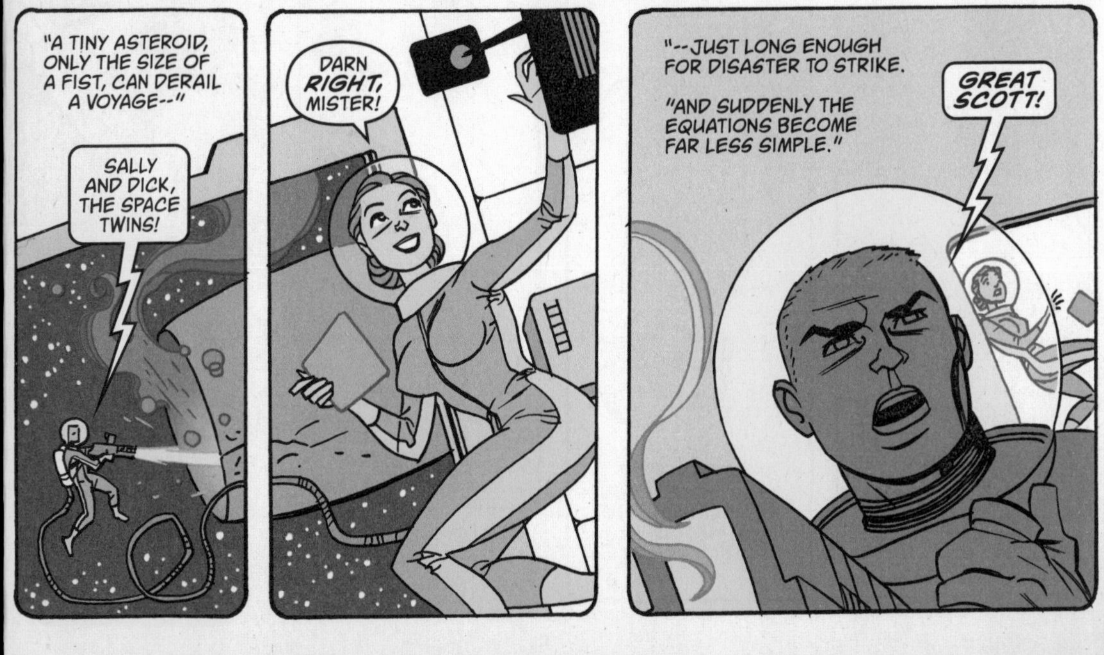
"A TINY ASTEROID, ONLY THE SIZE OF A FIST, CAN DERAIL A VOYAGE--"
SALLY AND DICK, THE SPACE TWINS!
DARN *RIGHT,* MISTER!
"--JUST LONG ENOUGH FOR DISASTER TO STRIKE.
"AND SUDDENLY THE EQUATIONS BECOME FAR LESS SIMPLE."
GREAT SCOTT!

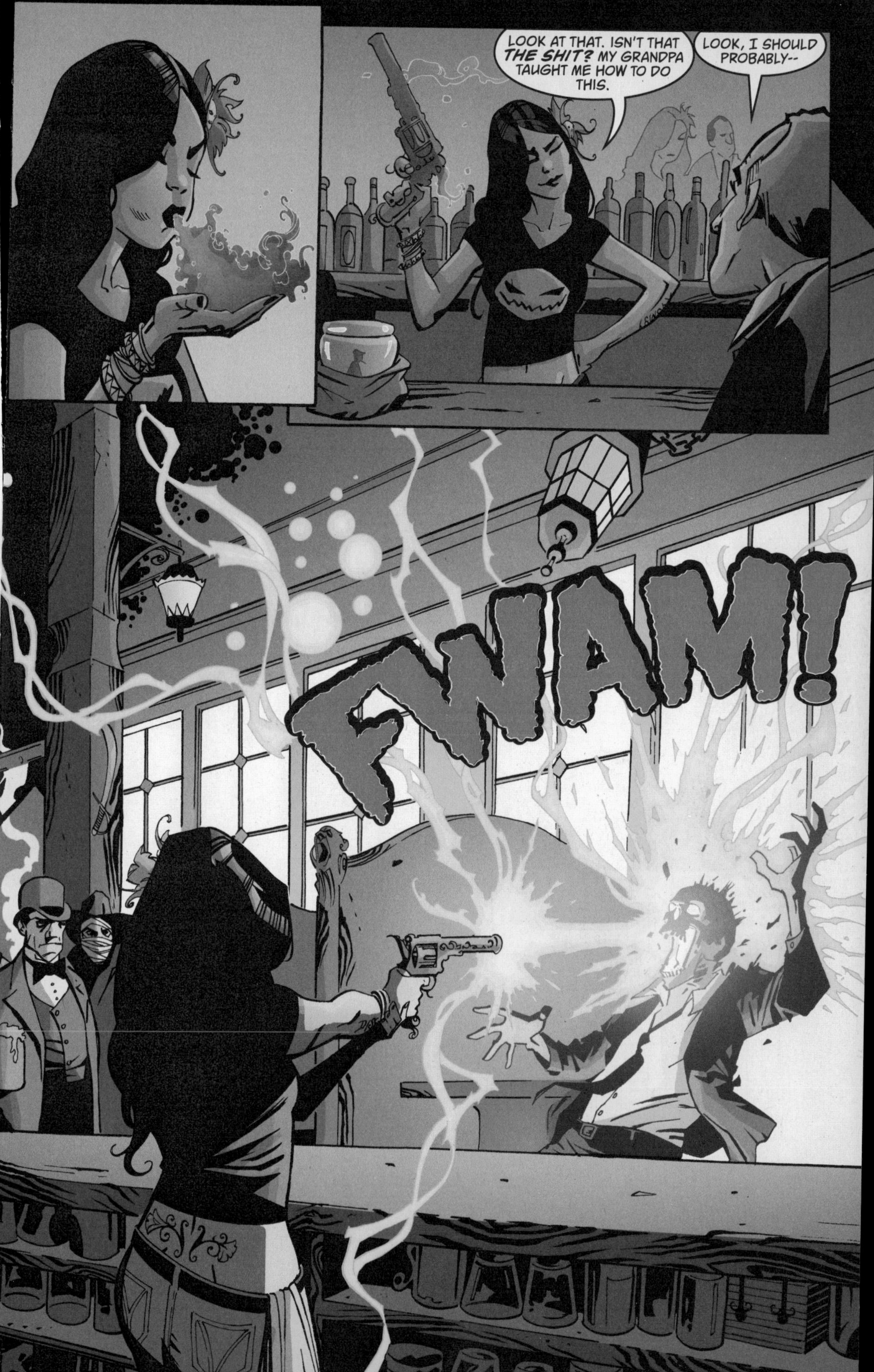
LOOK AT THAT. ISN'T THAT *THE SHIT?* MY GRANDPA TAUGHT ME HOW TO DO THIS.
LOOK, I SHOULD PROBABLY--
FWAM!

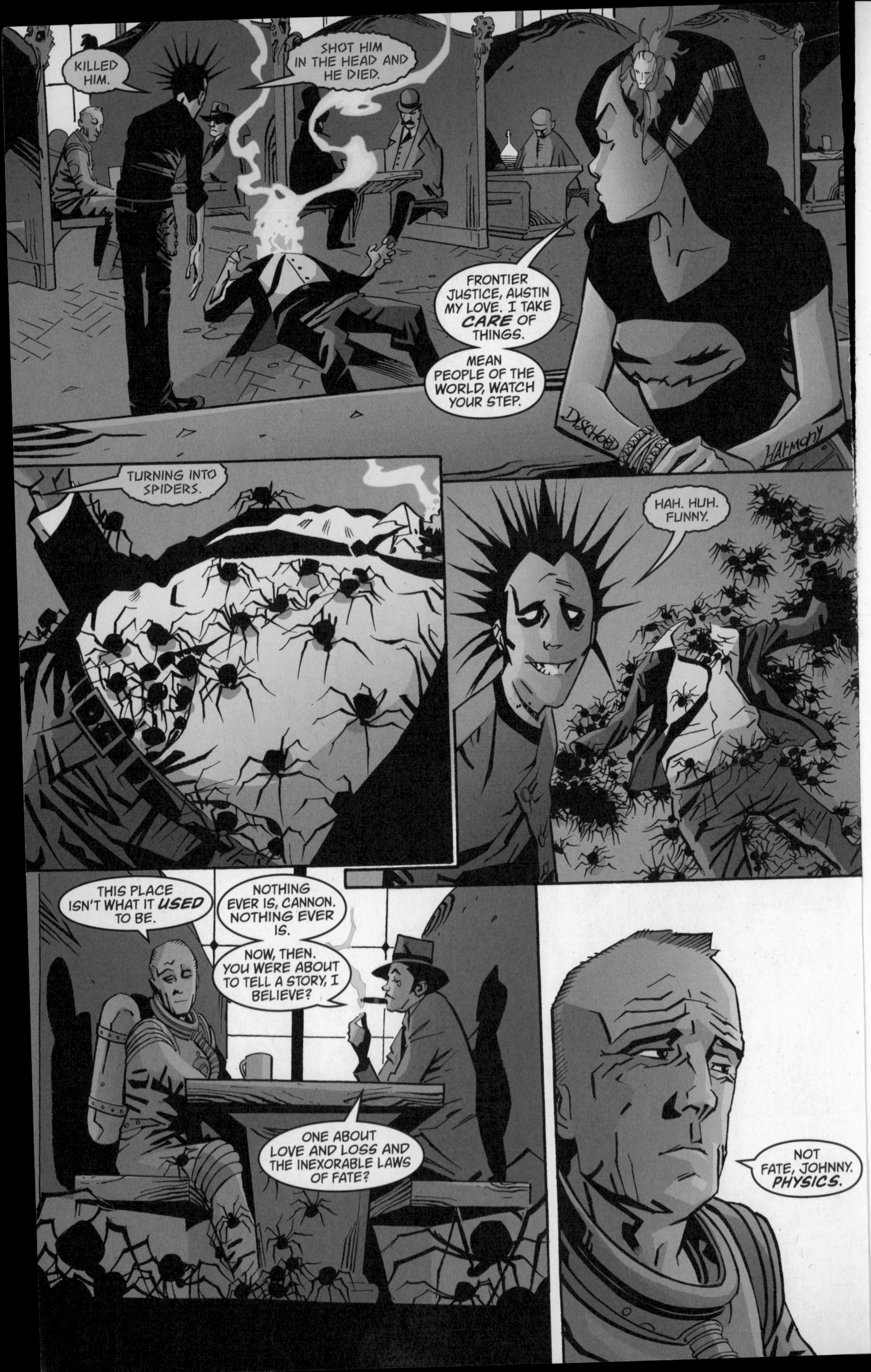
KILLED HIM.
SHOT HIM IN THE HEAD AND HE DIED.
FRONTIER JUSTICE, AUSTIN MY LOVE. I TAKE *CARE* OF THINGS.
MEAN PEOPLE OF THE WORLD, WATCH YOUR STEP.
TURNING INTO SPIDERS.
HAH. HUH. FUNNY.
THIS PLACE ISN'T WHAT IT *USED* TO BE.
NOTHING EVER IS, CANNON. NOTHING EVER IS.
NOW, THEN. YOU WERE ABOUT TO TELL A STORY, I BELIEVE?
ONE ABOUT LOVE AND LOSS AND THE INEXORABLE LAWS OF FATE?
NOT FATE, JOHNNY. ***PHYSICS.***

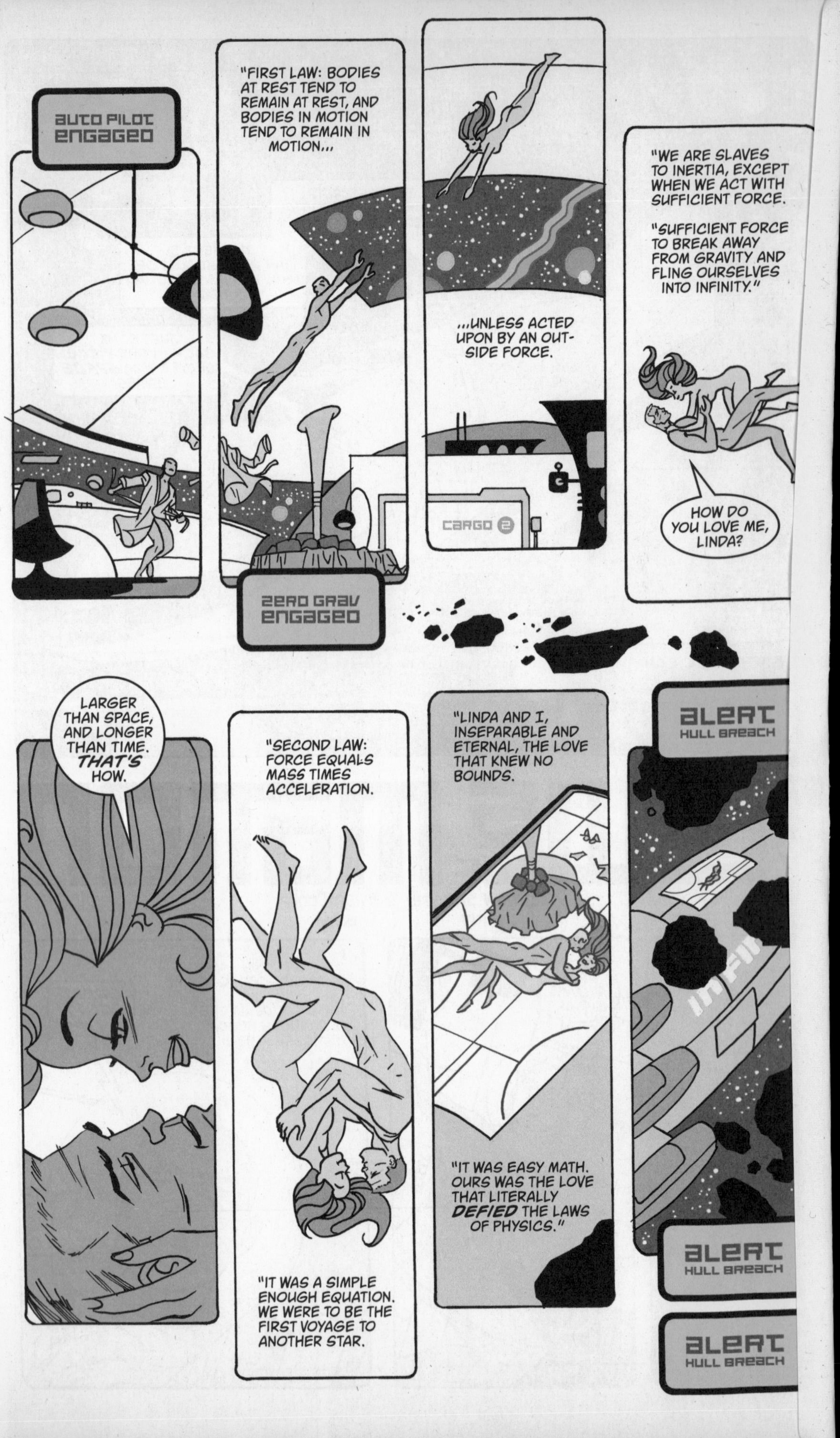
AUTO PILOT ENGAGED
"FIRST LAW: BODIES AT REST TEND TO REMAIN AT REST, AND BODIES IN MOTION TEND TO REMAIN IN MOTION...
ZERO GRAV ENGAGED
...UNLESS ACTED UPON BY AN OUT-SIDE FORCE.
CARGO 2
"WE ARE SLAVES TO INERTIA, EXCEPT WHEN WE ACT WITH SUFFICIENT FORCE.
"SUFFICIENT FORCE TO BREAK AWAY FROM GRAVITY AND FLING OURSELVES INTO INFINITY."
HOW DO YOU LOVE ME, LINDA?
LARGER THAN SPACE, AND LONGER THAN TIME. ***THAT'S*** HOW.
"SECOND LAW: FORCE EQUALS MASS TIMES ACCELERATION.
"IT WAS A SIMPLE ENOUGH EQUATION. WE WERE TO BE THE FIRST VOYAGE TO ANOTHER STAR.
"LINDA AND I, INSEPARABLE AND ETERNAL, THE LOVE THAT KNEW NO BOUNDS.
"IT WAS EASY MATH. OURS WAS THE LOVE THAT LITERALLY ***DEFIED*** THE LAWS OF PHYSICS."
ALERT HULL BREACH
ALERT HULL BREACH
ALERT HULL BREACH

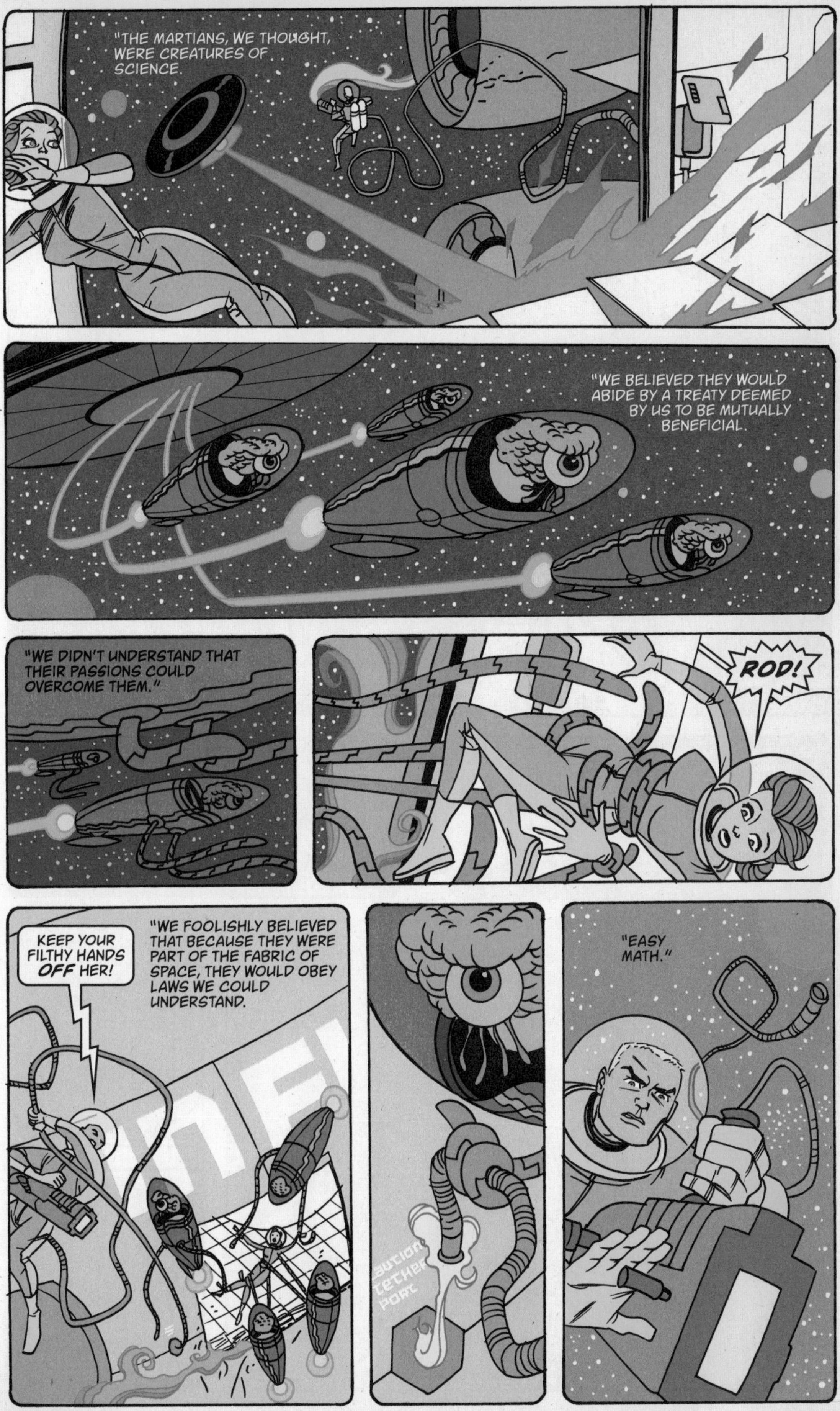
"THE MARTIANS, WE THOUGHT, WERE CREATURES OF SCIENCE.
"WE BELIEVED THEY WOULD ABIDE BY A TREATY DEEMED BY US TO BE MUTUALLY BENEFICIAL.
"WE DIDN'T UNDERSTAND THAT THEIR PASSIONS COULD OVERCOME THEM."
ROD!
KEEP YOUR FILTHY HANDS OFF HER!
"WE FOOLISHLY BELIEVED THAT BECAUSE THEY WERE PART OF THE FABRIC OF SPACE, THEY WOULD OBEY LAWS WE COULD UNDERSTAND.
"EASY MATH."

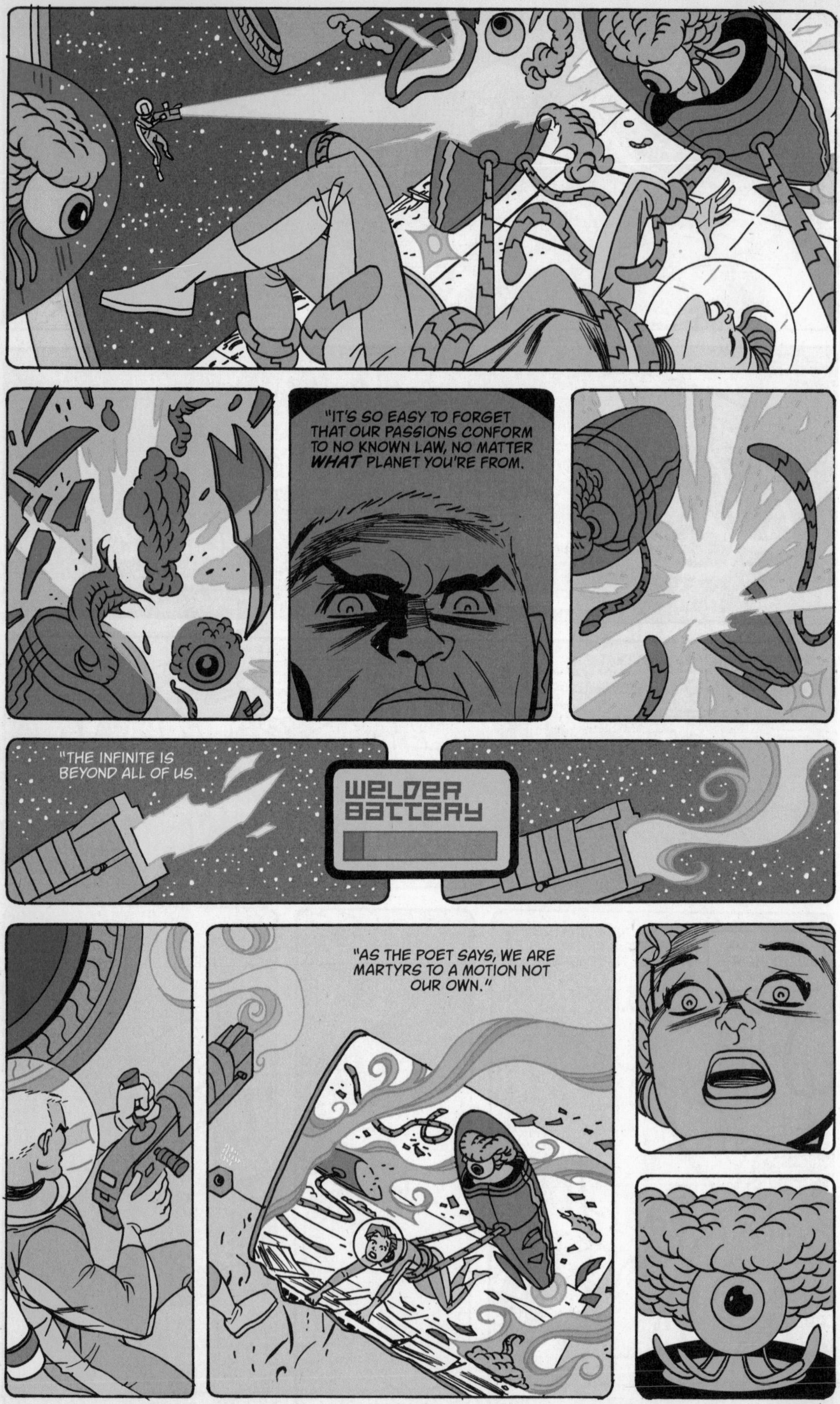
"IT'S SO EASY TO FORGET THAT OUR PASSIONS CONFORM TO NO KNOWN LAW, NO MATTER *WHAT* PLANET YOU'RE FROM.
"THE INFINITE IS BEYOND ALL OF US.
WELDER BATTERY
"AS THE POET SAYS, WE ARE MARTYRS TO A MOTION NOT OUR OWN."

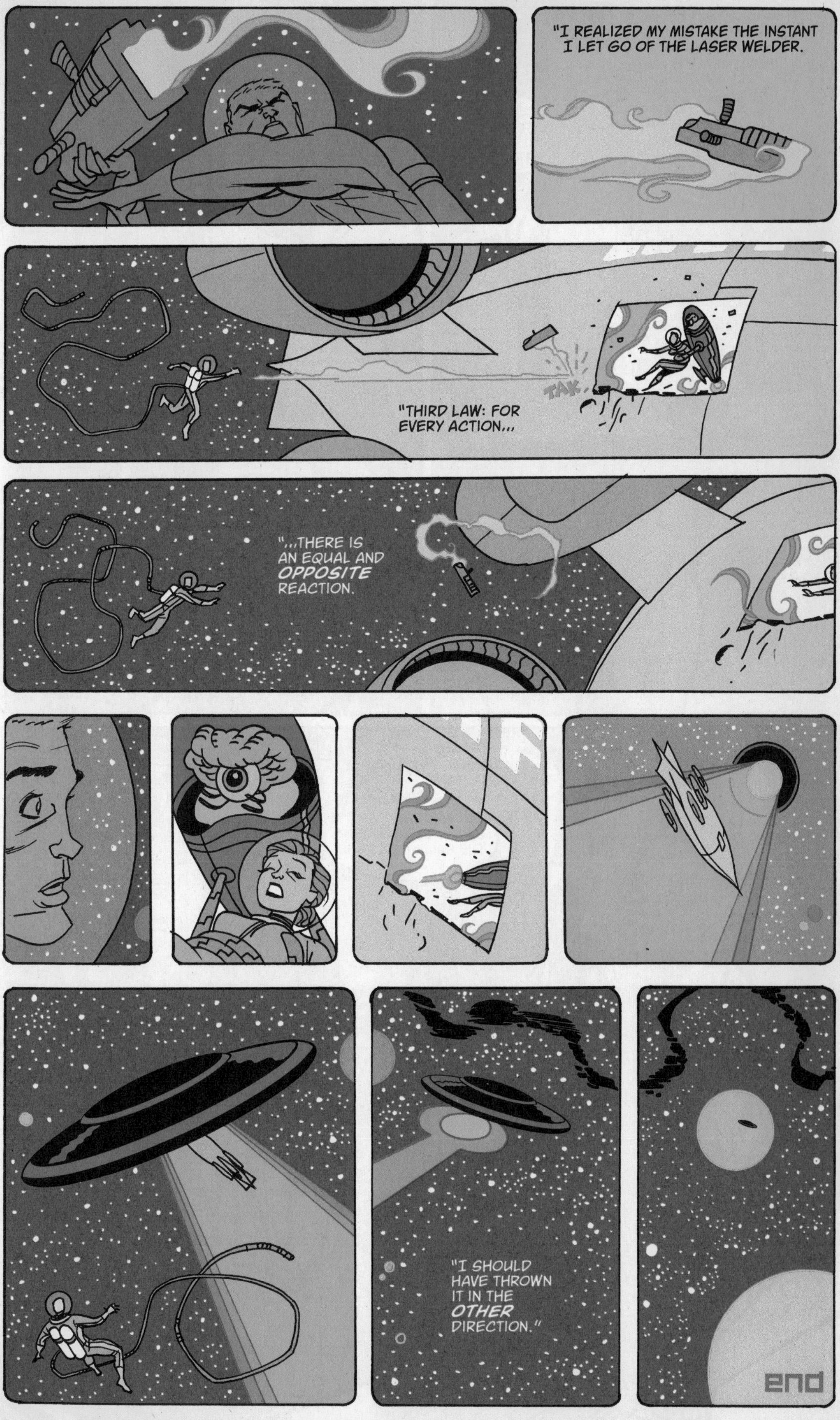
"I REALIZED MY MISTAKE THE INSTANT I LET GO OF THE LASER WELDER.
TAK
"THIRD LAW: FOR EVERY ACTION...
"...THERE IS AN EQUAL AND OPPOSITE REACTION.
"I SHOULD HAVE THROWN IT IN THE OTHER DIRECTION."
end

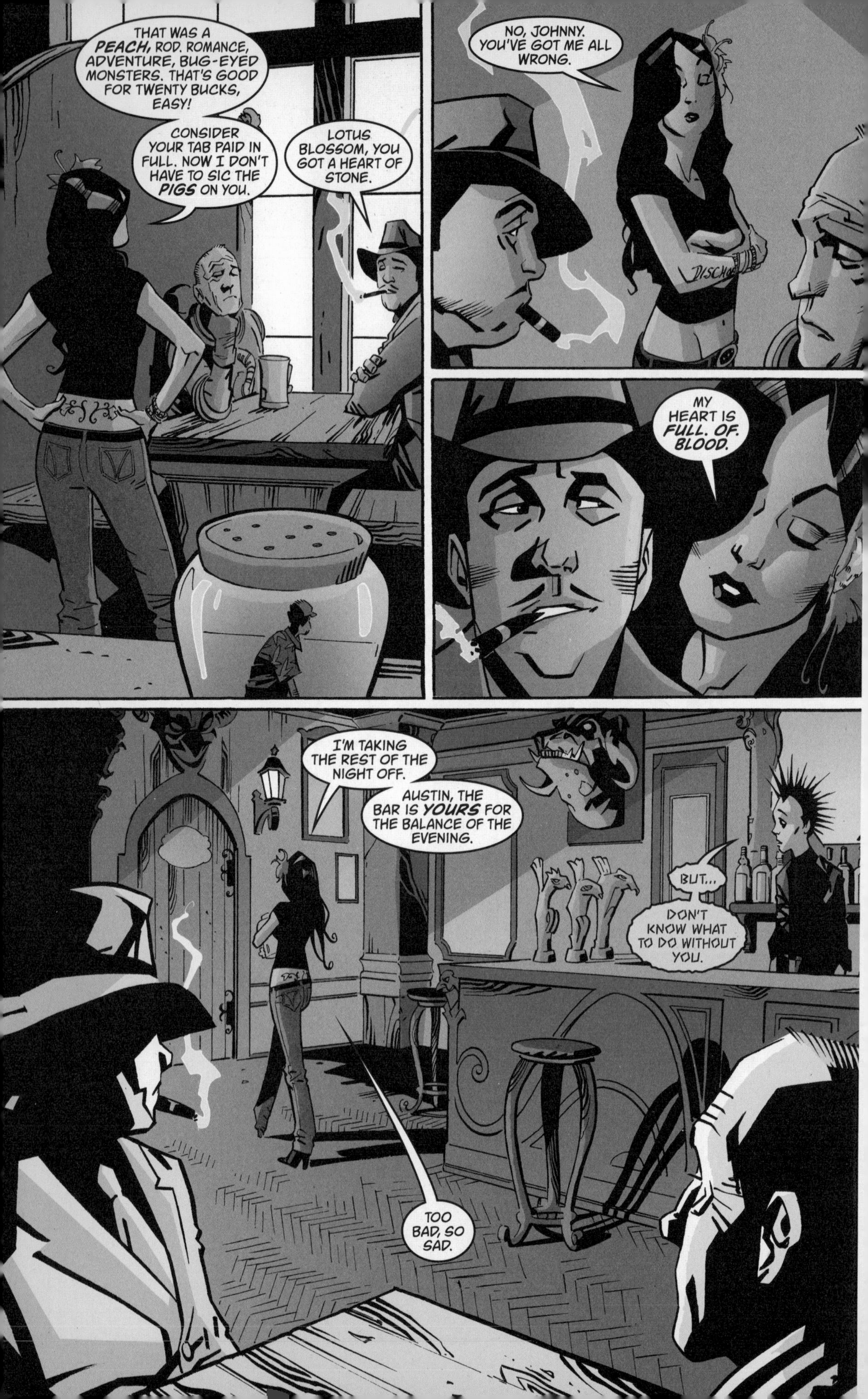
THAT WAS A PEACH, ROD. ROMANCE, ADVENTURE, BUG-EYED MONSTERS. THAT'S GOOD FOR TWENTY BUCKS, EASY!
CONSIDER YOUR TAB PAID IN FULL. NOW I DON'T HAVE TO SIC THE PIGS ON YOU.
LOTUS BLOSSOM, YOU GOT A HEART OF STONE.
NO, JOHNNY. YOU'VE GOT ME ALL WRONG.
MY HEART IS FULL. OF. BLOOD.
I'M TAKING THE REST OF THE NIGHT OFF.
AUSTIN, THE BAR IS YOURS FOR THE BALANCE OF THE EVENING.
BUT...
DON'T KNOW WHAT TO DO WITHOUT YOU.
TOO BAD, SO SAD.

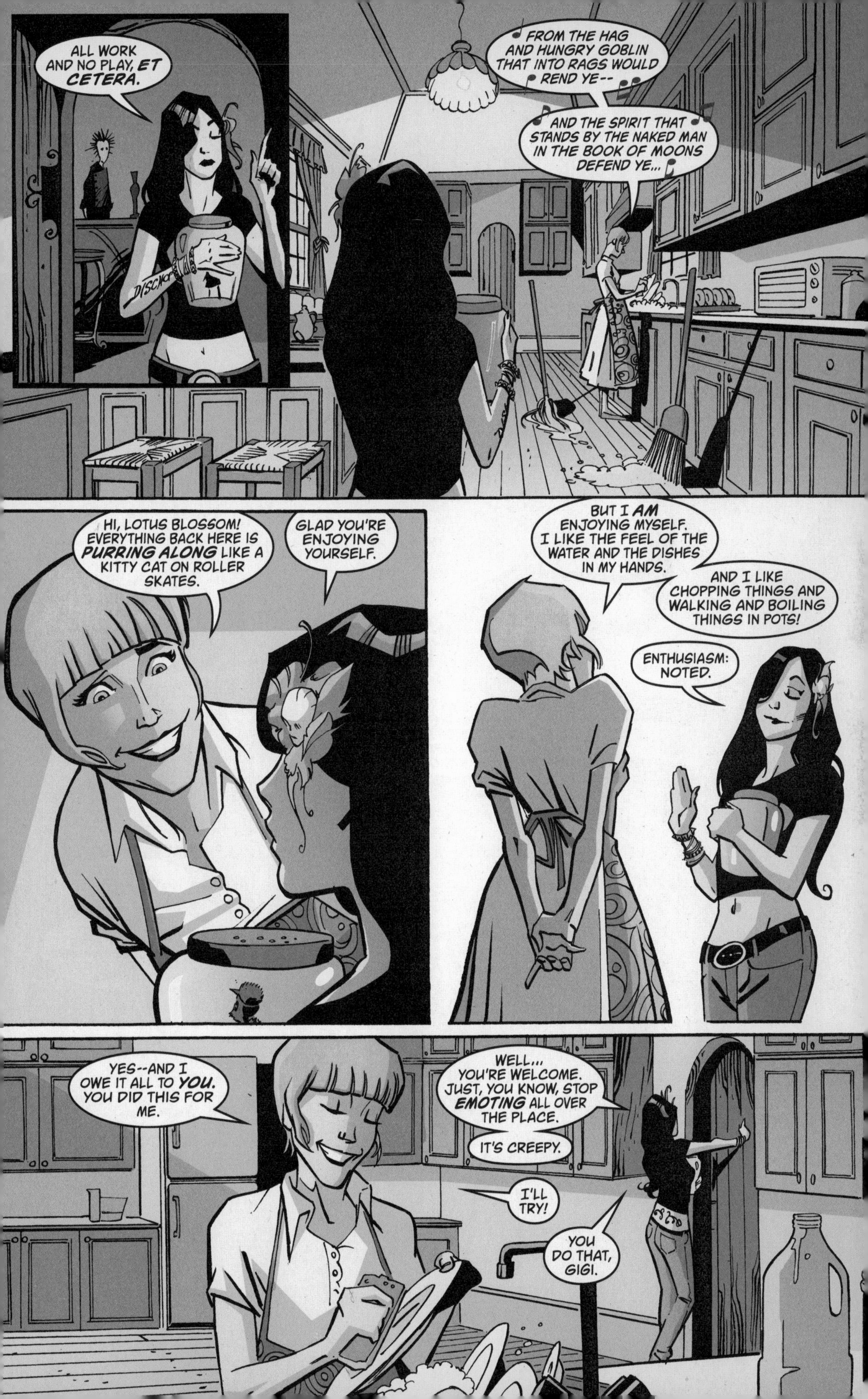

ALL WORK AND NO PLAY, ET CETERA.
FROM THE HAG AND HUNGRY GOBLIN THAT INTO RAGS WOULD REND YE--
AND THE SPIRIT THAT STANDS BY THE NAKED MAN IN THE BOOK OF MOONS DEFEND YE...
HI, LOTUS BLOSSOM! EVERYTHING BACK HERE IS PURRING ALONG LIKE A KITTY CAT ON ROLLER SKATES.
GLAD YOU'RE ENJOYING YOURSELF.
BUT I AM ENJOYING MYSELF. I LIKE THE FEEL OF THE WATER AND THE DISHES IN MY HANDS.
AND I LIKE CHOPPING THINGS AND WALKING AND BOILING THINGS IN POTS!
ENTHUSIASM: NOTED.
YES--AND I OWE IT ALL TO YOU. YOU DID THIS FOR ME.
WELL... YOU'RE WELCOME. JUST, YOU KNOW, STOP EMOTING ALL OVER THE PLACE.
IT'S CREEPY.
I'LL TRY!
YOU DO THAT, GIGI.

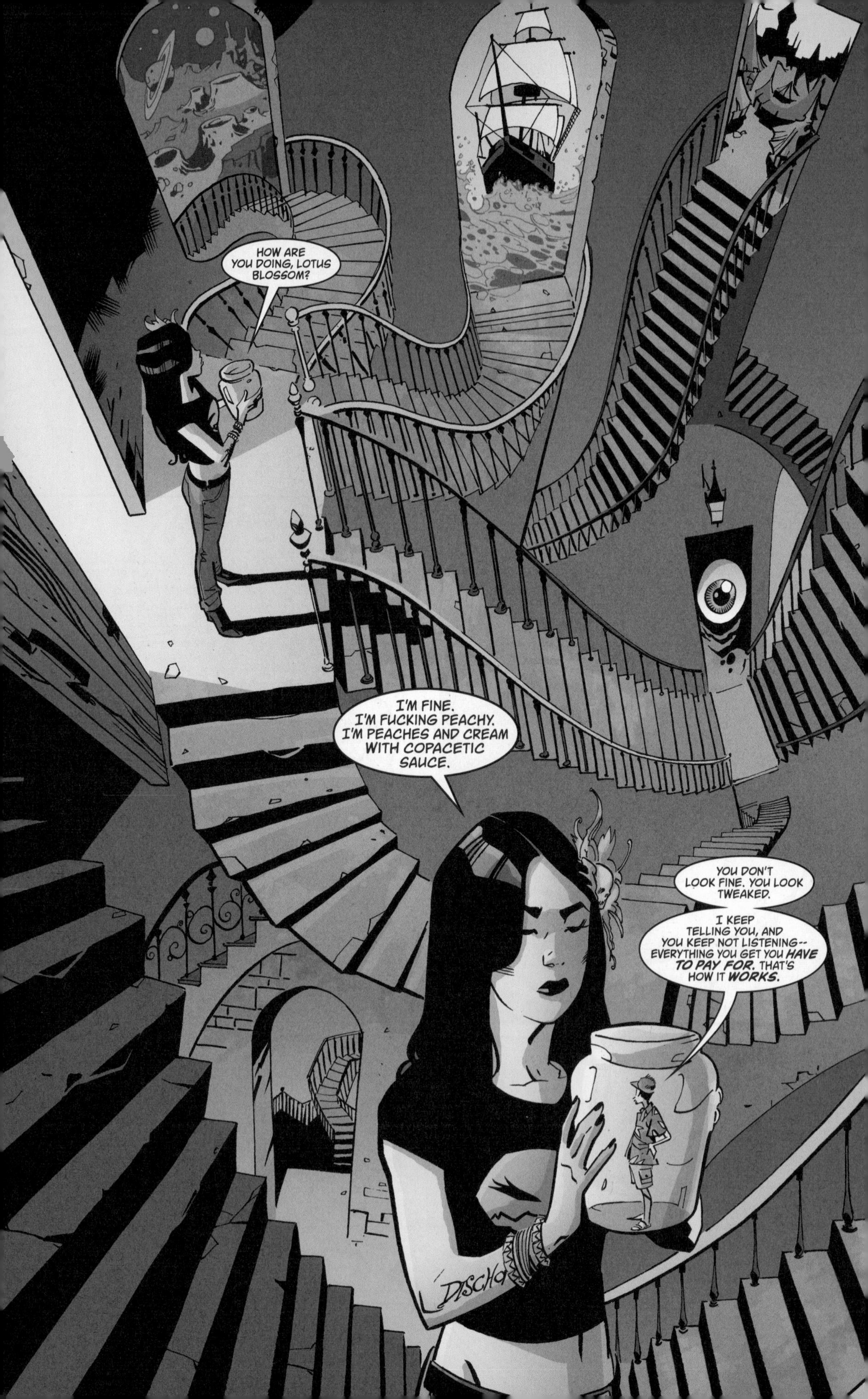
HOW ARE YOU DOING, LOTUS BLOSSOM?
I'M FINE. I'M FUCKING PEACHY. I'M PEACHES AND CREAM WITH COPACETIC SAUCE.
YOU DON'T LOOK FINE. YOU LOOK TWEAKED.
I KEEP TELLING YOU, AND YOU KEEP NOT LISTENING-- EVERYTHING YOU GET YOU *HAVE TO PAY FOR*. THAT'S HOW IT *WORKS*.
DISCHO

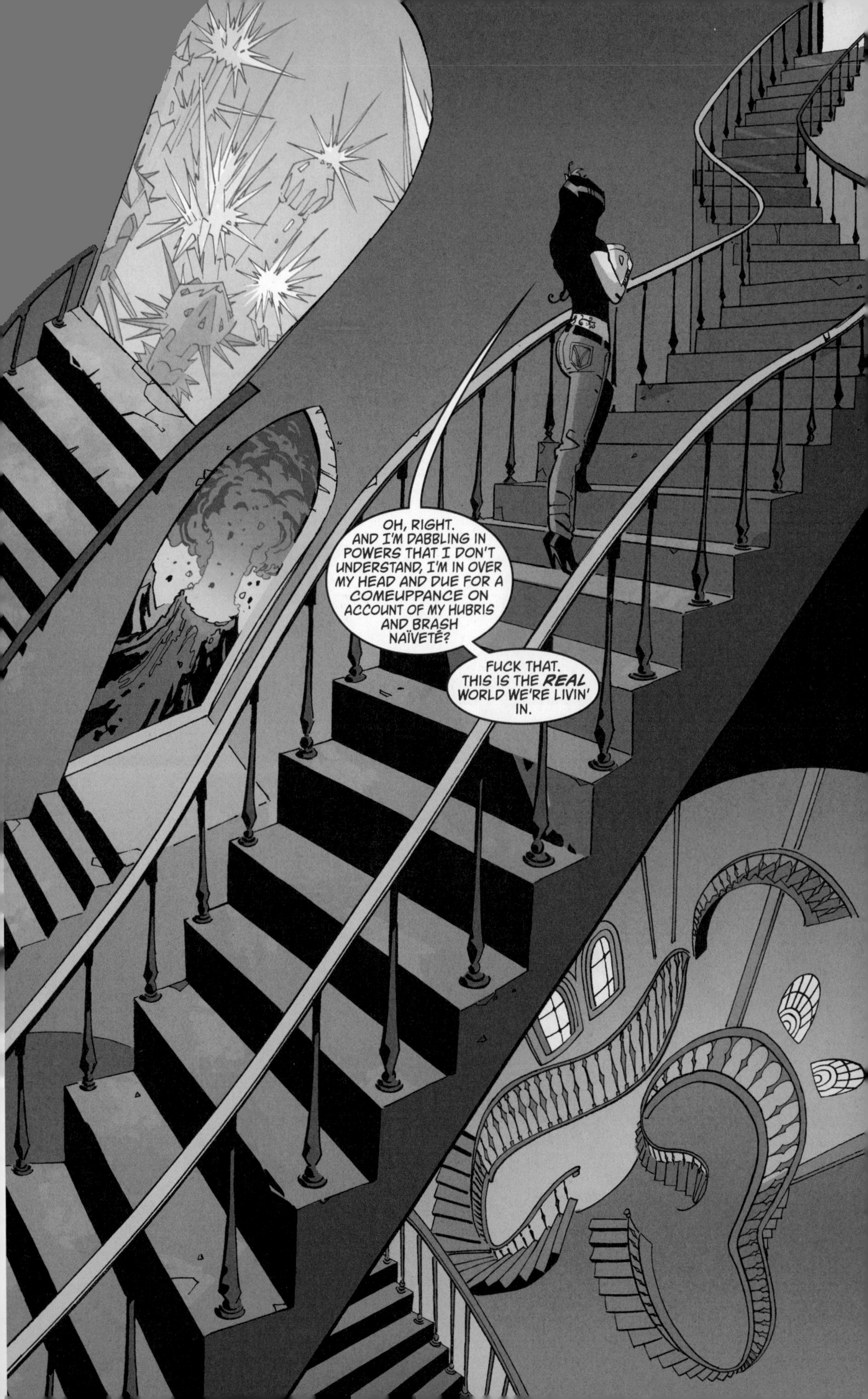
OH, RIGHT. AND I'M DABBLING IN POWERS THAT I DON'T UNDERSTAND, I'M IN OVER MY HEAD AND DUE FOR A COMEUPPANCE ON ACCOUNT OF MY HUBRIS AND BRASH NAÏVETÉ?
FUCK THAT. THIS IS THE ***REAL*** WORLD WE'RE LIVIN' IN.

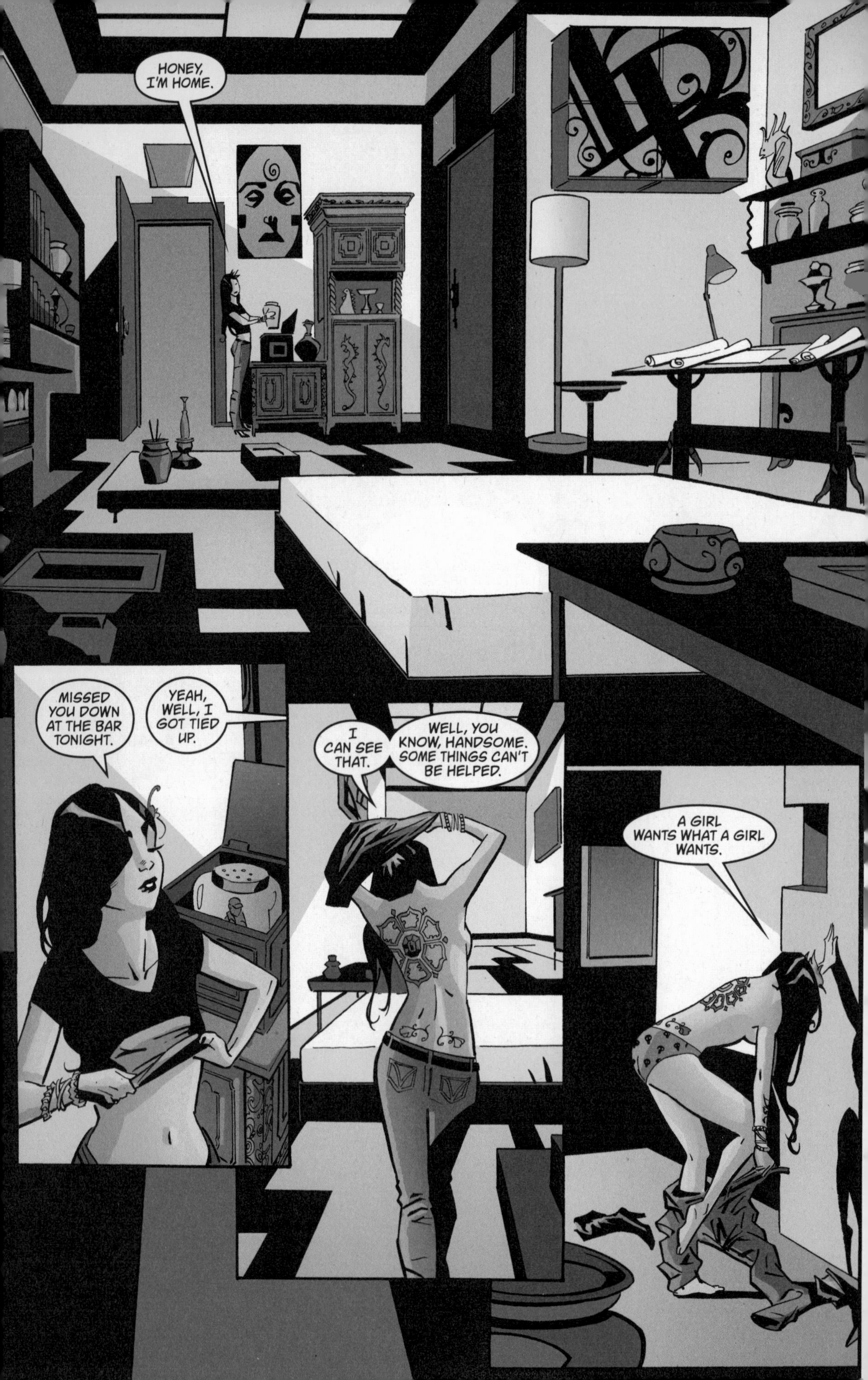
HONEY, I'M HOME.
MISSED YOU DOWN AT THE BAR TONIGHT.
YEAH, WELL, I GOT TIED UP.
I CAN SEE THAT.
WELL, YOU KNOW, HANDSOME. SOME THINGS CAN'T BE HELPED.
A GIRL WANTS WHAT A GIRL WANTS.

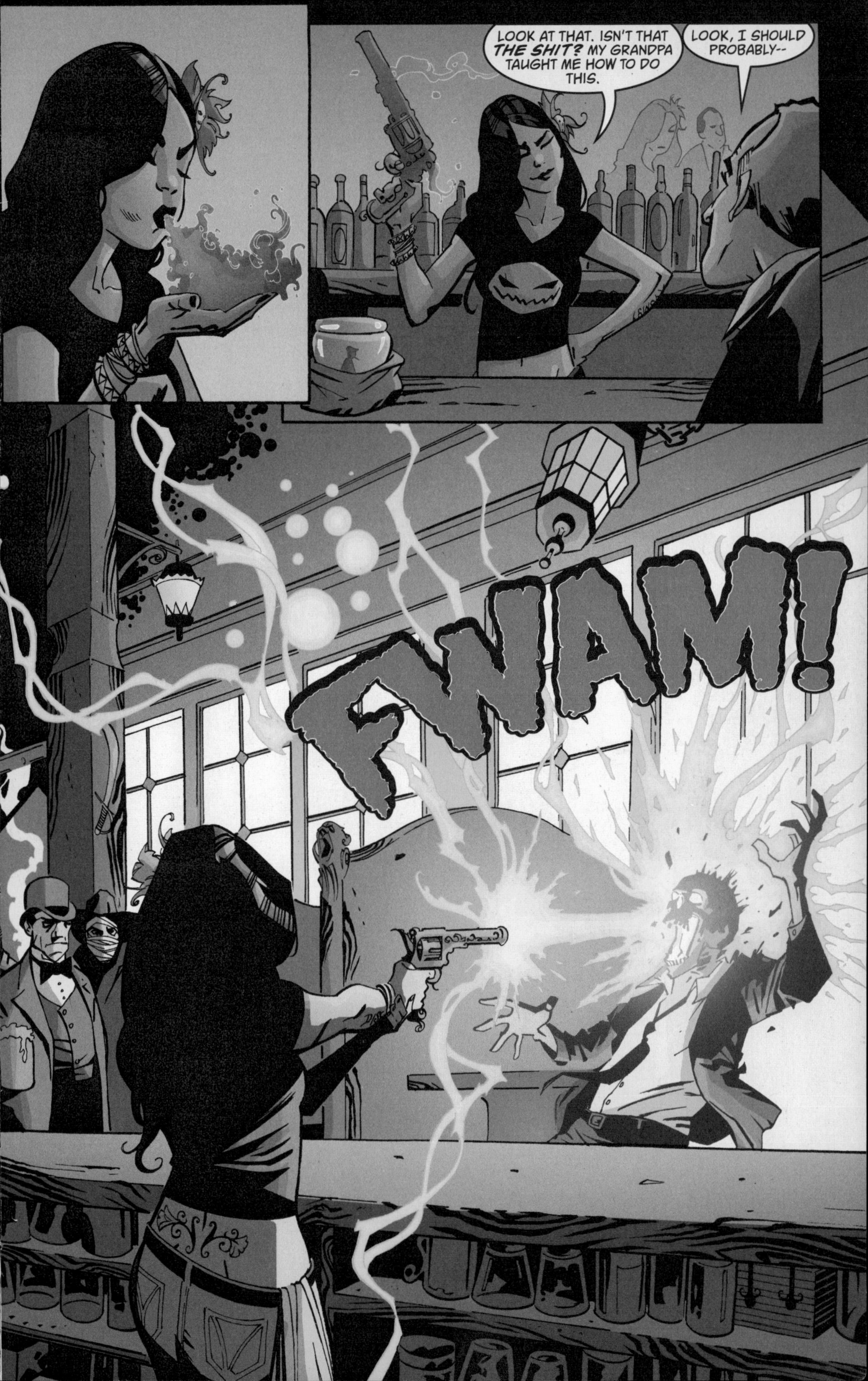
LOOK AT THAT. ISN'T THAT *THE SHIT?* MY GRANDPA TAUGHT ME HOW TO DO THIS.
LOOK, I SHOULD PROBABLY--
FWAM!

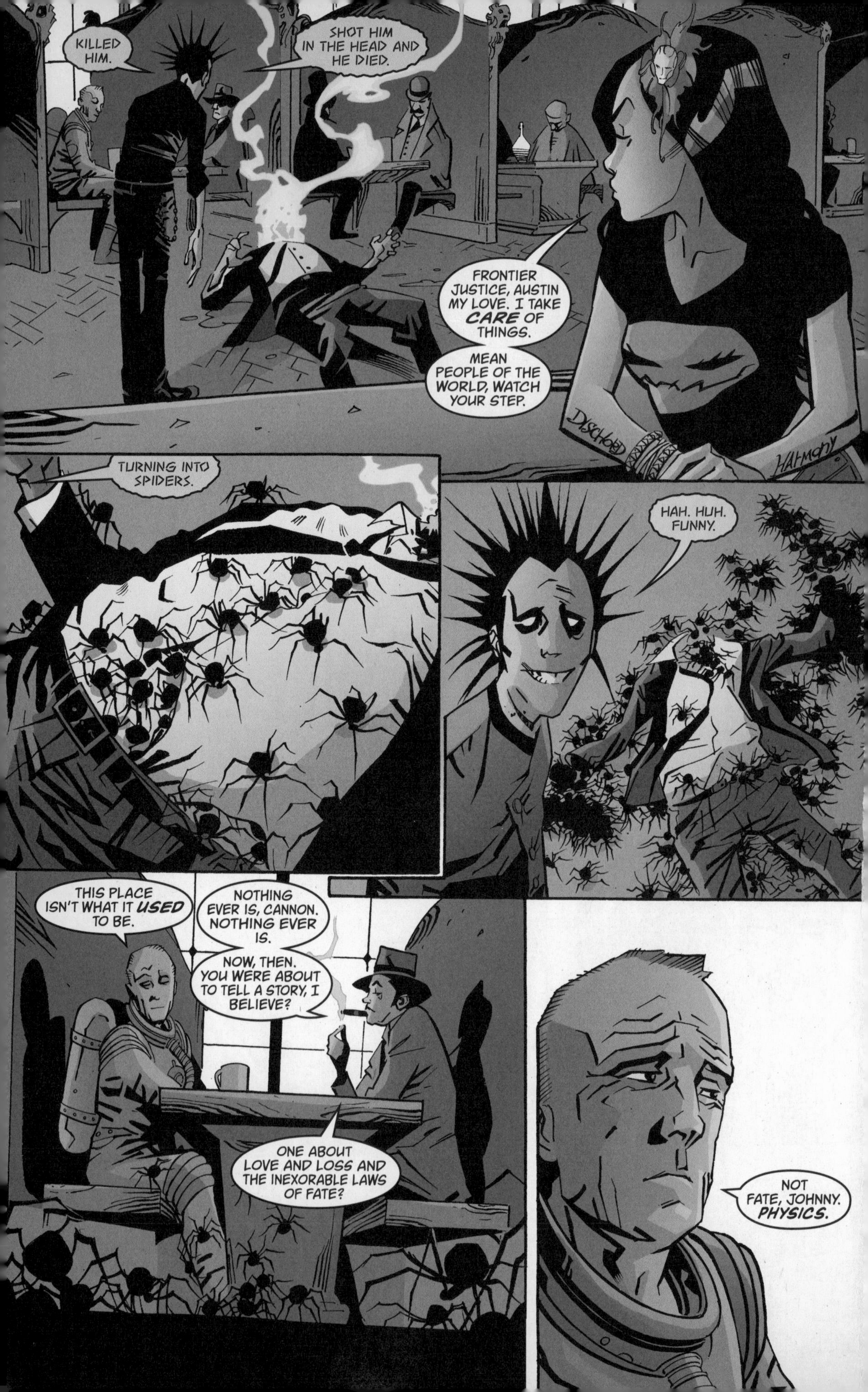
KILLED HIM.
SHOT HIM IN THE HEAD AND HE DIED.
FRONTIER JUSTICE, AUSTIN MY LOVE. I TAKE CARE OF THINGS.
MEAN PEOPLE OF THE WORLD, WATCH YOUR STEP.
DISCHORD
HARMONY
TURNING INTO SPIDERS.
HAH. HUH. FUNNY.
THIS PLACE ISN'T WHAT IT USED TO BE.
NOTHING EVER IS, CANNON. NOTHING EVER IS.
NOW, THEN. YOU WERE ABOUT TO TELL A STORY, I BELIEVE?
ONE ABOUT LOVE AND LOSS AND THE INEXORABLE LAWS OF FATE?
NOT FATE, JOHNNY. PHYSICS.

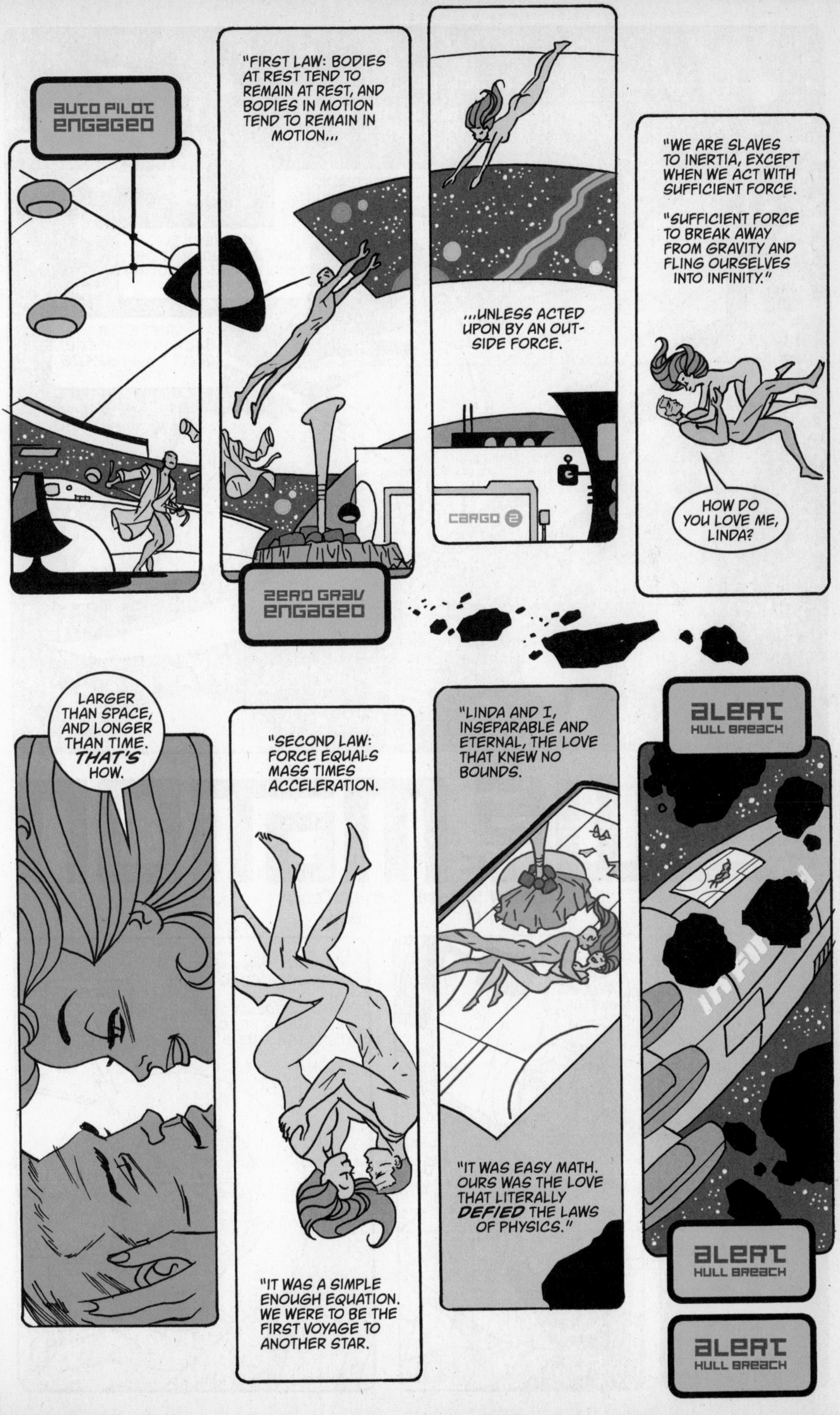
AUTO PILOT ENGAGED
"FIRST LAW: BODIES AT REST TEND TO REMAIN AT REST, AND BODIES IN MOTION TEND TO REMAIN IN MOTION...
ZERO GRAV ENGAGED
...UNLESS ACTED UPON BY AN OUT-SIDE FORCE.
CARGO 2
"WE ARE SLAVES TO INERTIA, EXCEPT WHEN WE ACT WITH SUFFICIENT FORCE.
"SUFFICIENT FORCE TO BREAK AWAY FROM GRAVITY AND FLING OURSELVES INTO INFINITY."
HOW DO YOU LOVE ME, LINDA?
LARGER THAN SPACE, AND LONGER THAN TIME. THAT'S HOW.
"SECOND LAW: FORCE EQUALS MASS TIMES ACCELERATION.
"IT WAS A SIMPLE ENOUGH EQUATION. WE WERE TO BE THE FIRST VOYAGE TO ANOTHER STAR.
"LINDA AND I, INSEPARABLE AND ETERNAL, THE LOVE THAT KNEW NO BOUNDS.
"IT WAS EASY MATH. OURS WAS THE LOVE THAT LITERALLY DEFIED THE LAWS OF PHYSICS."
ALERT HULL BREACH
ALERT HULL BREACH
ALERT HULL BREACH

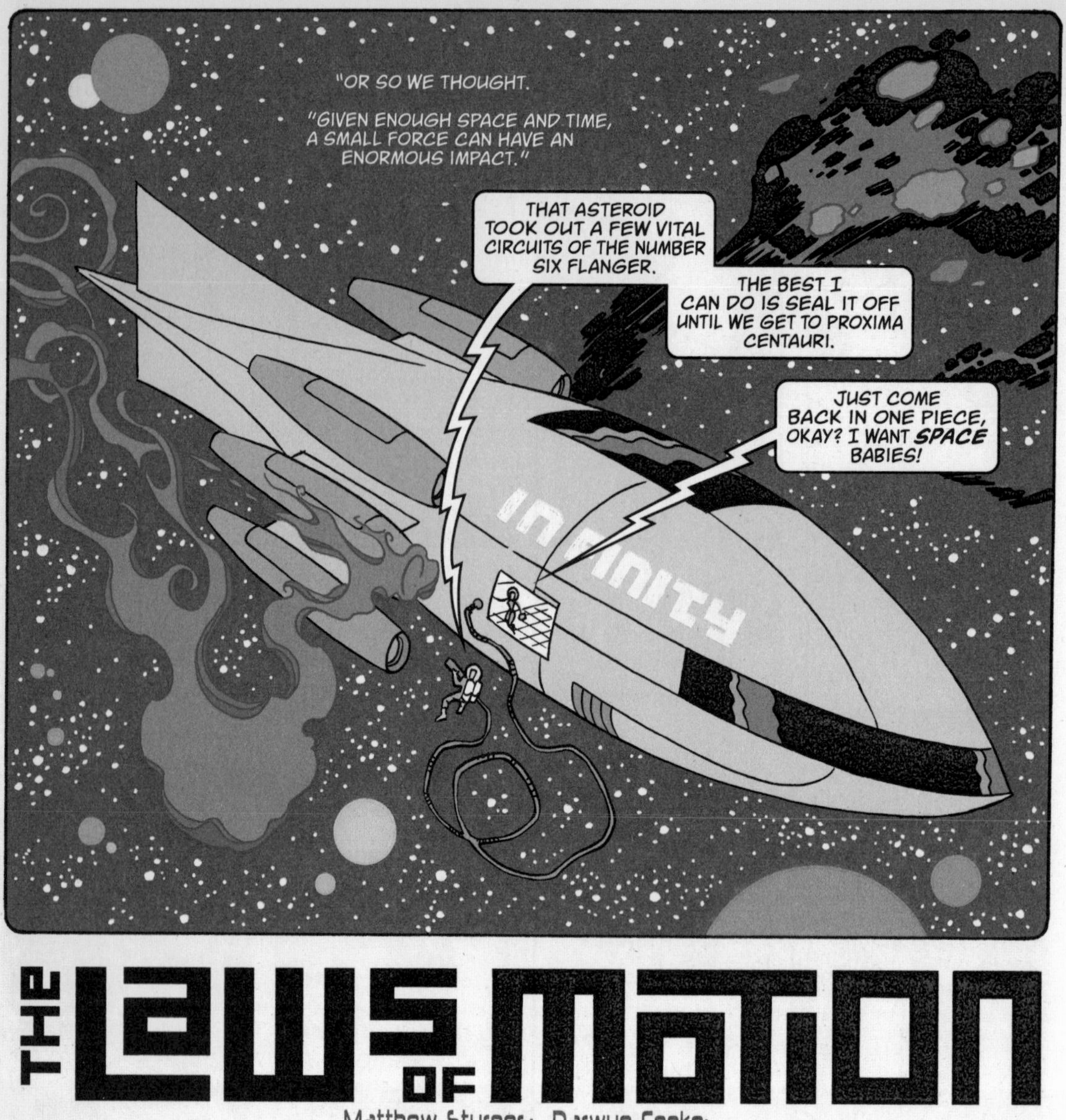
"OR SO WE THOUGHT.
"GIVEN ENOUGH SPACE AND TIME, A SMALL FORCE CAN HAVE AN ENORMOUS IMPACT."
THAT ASTEROID TOOK OUT A FEW VITAL CIRCUITS OF THE NUMBER SIX FLANGER.
THE BEST I CAN DO IS SEAL IT OFF UNTIL WE GET TO PROXIMA CENTAURI.
JUST COME BACK IN ONE PIECE, OKAY? I WANT *SPACE* BABIES!
INFINITY

THE LAWS OF MOTION

Matthew Sturges: writer
Darwyn Cooke: artist

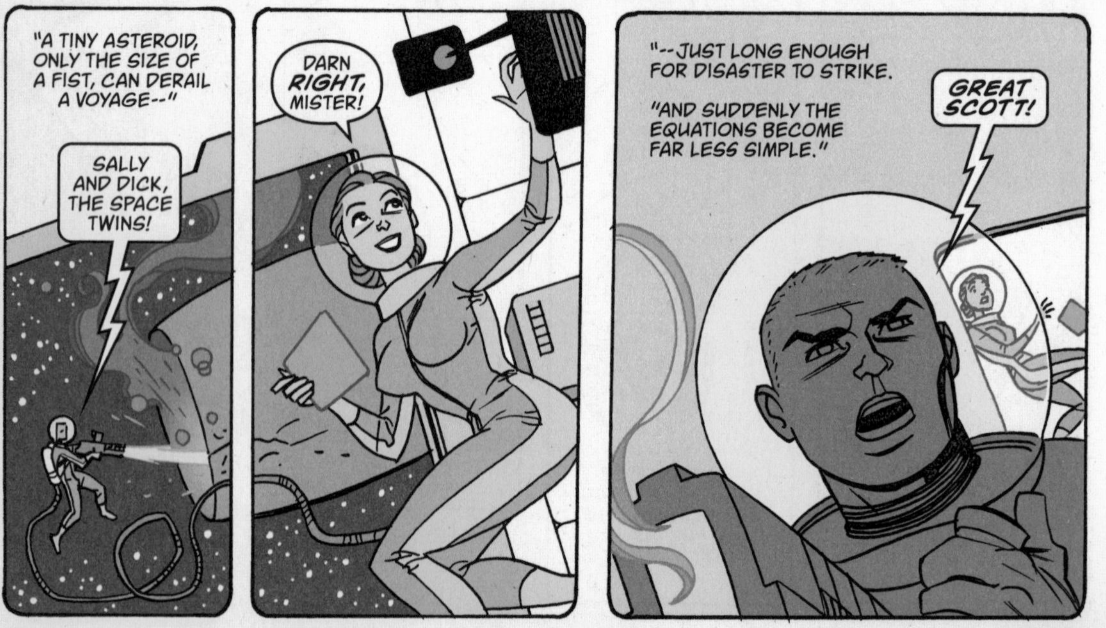
"A TINY ASTEROID, ONLY THE SIZE OF A FIST, CAN DERAIL A VOYAGE--"
SALLY AND DICK, THE SPACE TWINS!
DARN *RIGHT,* MISTER!
"--JUST LONG ENOUGH FOR DISASTER TO STRIKE.
"AND SUDDENLY THE EQUATIONS BECOME FAR LESS SIMPLE."
GREAT SCOTT!

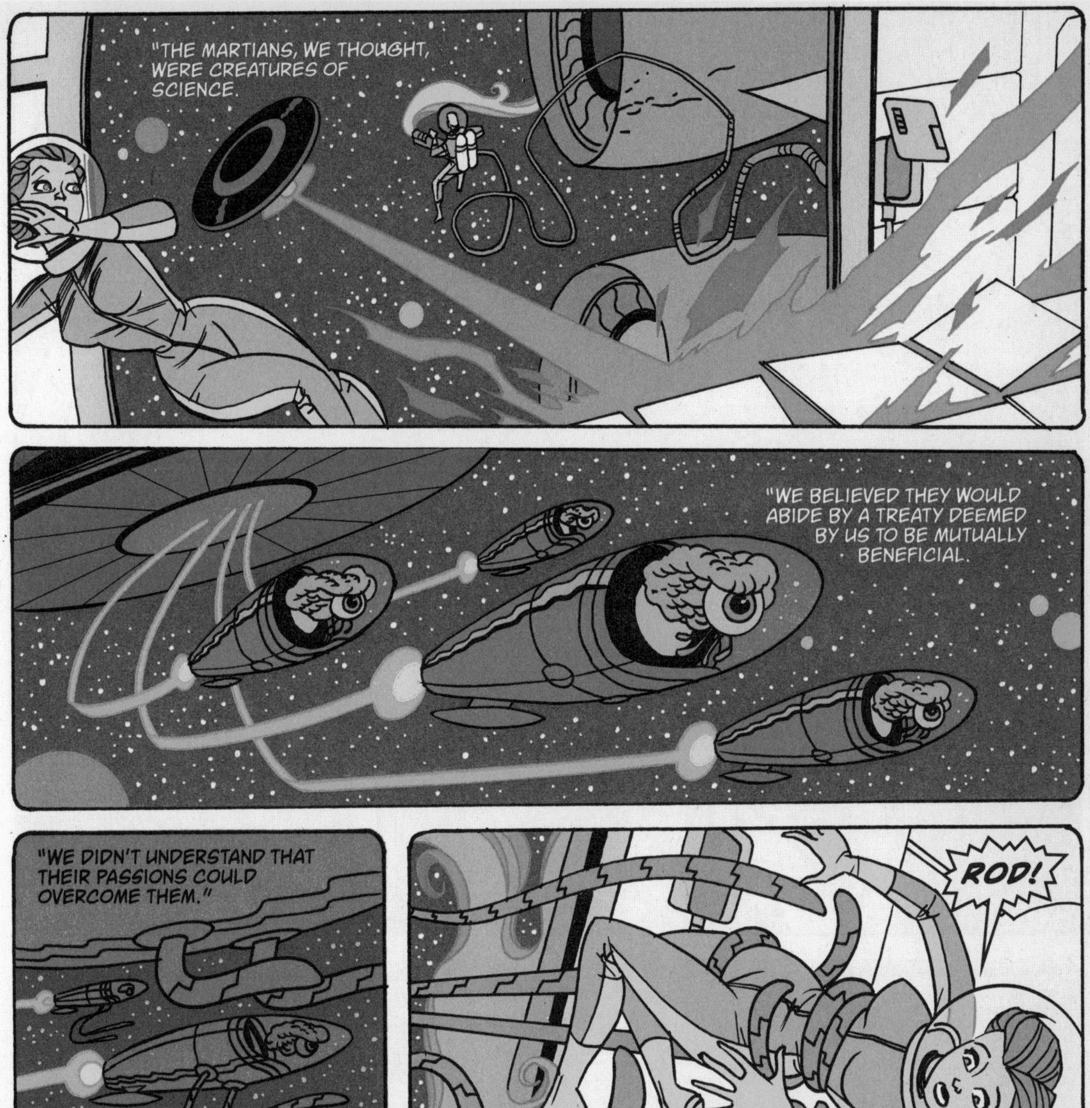
"THE MARTIANS, WE THOUGHT, WERE CREATURES OF SCIENCE.
"WE BELIEVED THEY WOULD ABIDE BY A TREATY DEEMED BY US TO BE MUTUALLY BENEFICIAL.
"WE DIDN'T UNDERSTAND THAT THEIR PASSIONS COULD OVERCOME THEM."
ROD!
KEEP YOUR FILTHY HANDS OFF HER!
"WE FOOLISHLY BELIEVED THAT BECAUSE THEY WERE PART OF THE FABRIC OF SPACE, THEY WOULD OBEY LAWS WE COULD UNDERSTAND.
TETHER PORT
"EASY MATH."

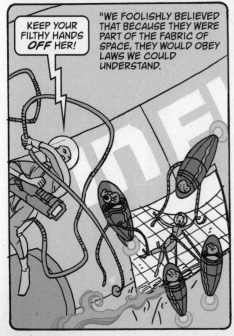

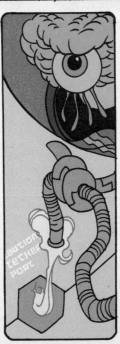

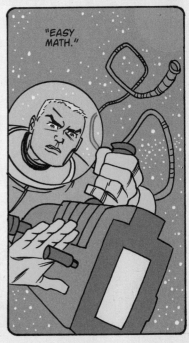

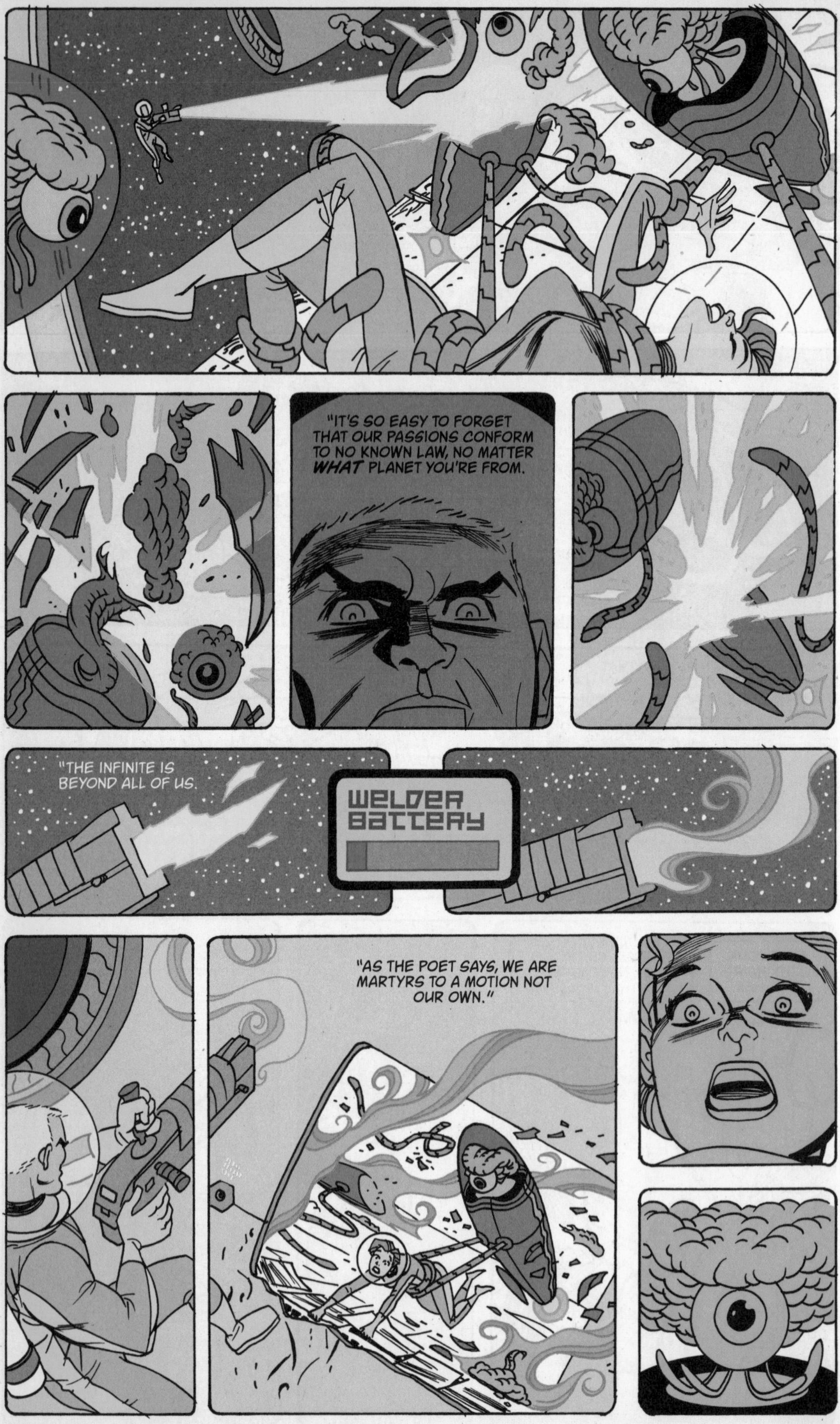
"IT'S SO EASY TO FORGET THAT OUR PASSIONS CONFORM TO NO KNOWN LAW, NO MATTER WHAT PLANET YOU'RE FROM.
"THE INFINITE IS BEYOND ALL OF US.
WELDER BATTERY
"AS THE POET SAYS, WE ARE MARTYRS TO A MOTION NOT OUR OWN."

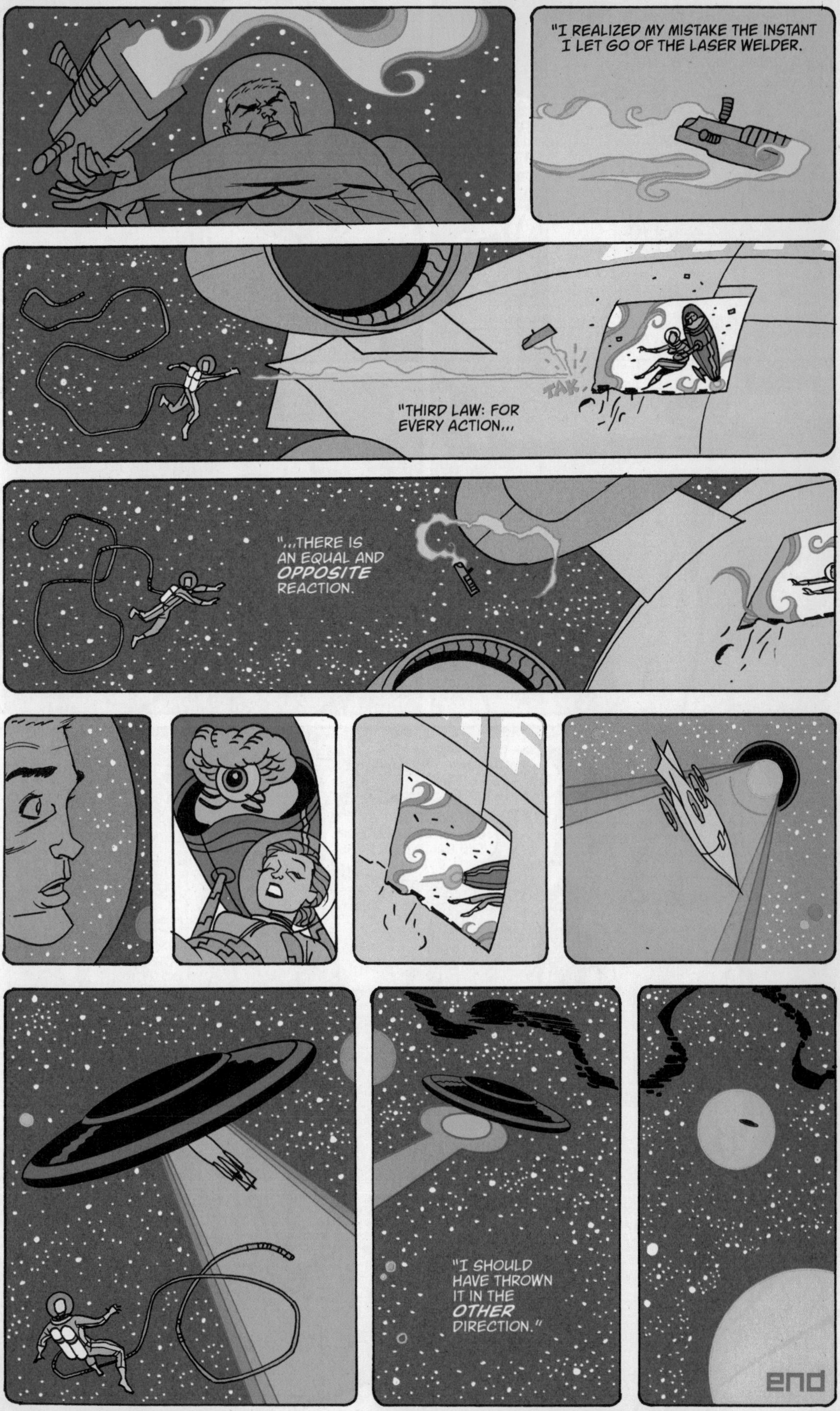

"I REALIZED MY MISTAKE THE INSTANT I LET GO OF THE LASER WELDER.
TAK
"THIRD LAW: FOR EVERY ACTION...
"...THERE IS AN EQUAL AND *OPPOSITE* REACTION.
"I SHOULD HAVE THROWN IT IN THE *OTHER* DIRECTION."
end

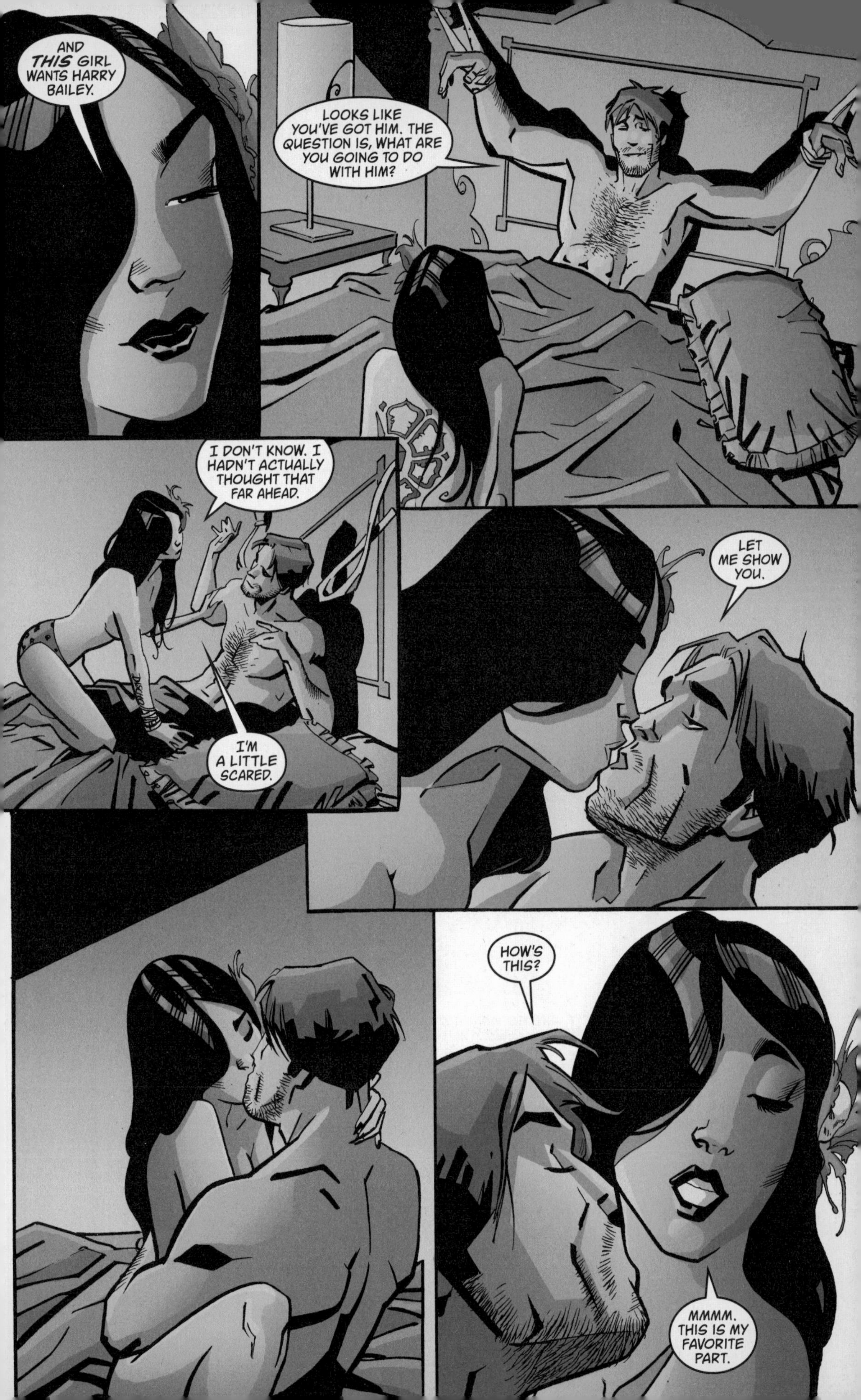
AND THIS GIRL WANTS HARRY BAILEY.
LOOKS LIKE YOU'VE GOT HIM. THE QUESTION IS, WHAT ARE YOU GOING TO DO WITH HIM?
I DON'T KNOW. I HADN'T ACTUALLY THOUGHT THAT FAR AHEAD.
I'M A LITTLE SCARED.
LET ME SHOW YOU.
HOW'S THIS?
MMMM. THIS IS MY FAVORITE PART.

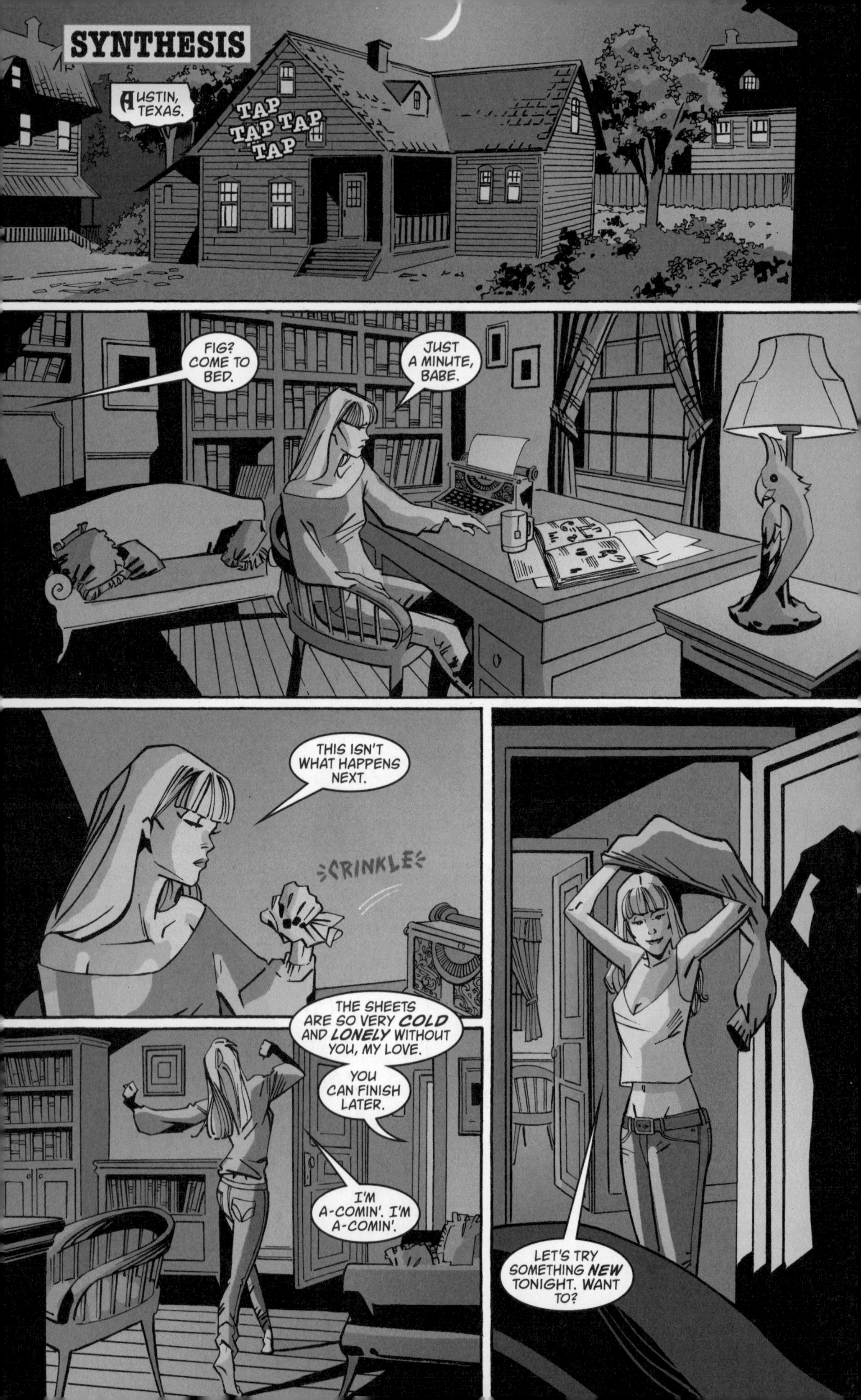
SYNTHESIS
AUSTIN, TEXAS.
TAP TAP TAP TAP
FIG? COME TO BED.
JUST A MINUTE, BABE.
THIS ISN'T WHAT HAPPENS NEXT.
CRINKLE
THE SHEETS ARE SO VERY COLD AND LONELY WITHOUT YOU, MY LOVE.
YOU CAN FINISH LATER.
I'M A-COMIN'. I'M A-COMIN'.
LET'S TRY SOMETHING NEW TONIGHT. WANT TO?

House of MYSTERY

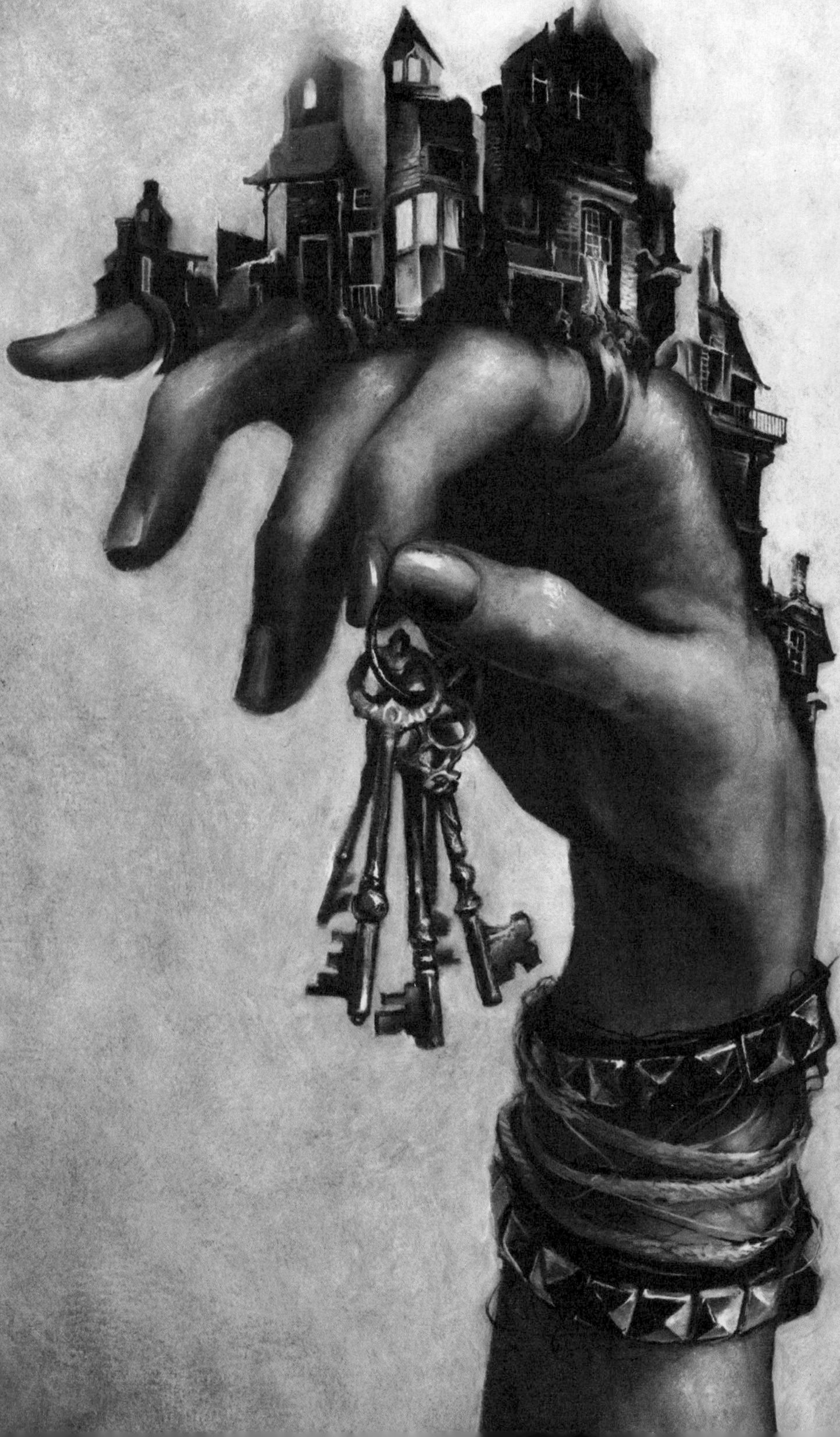

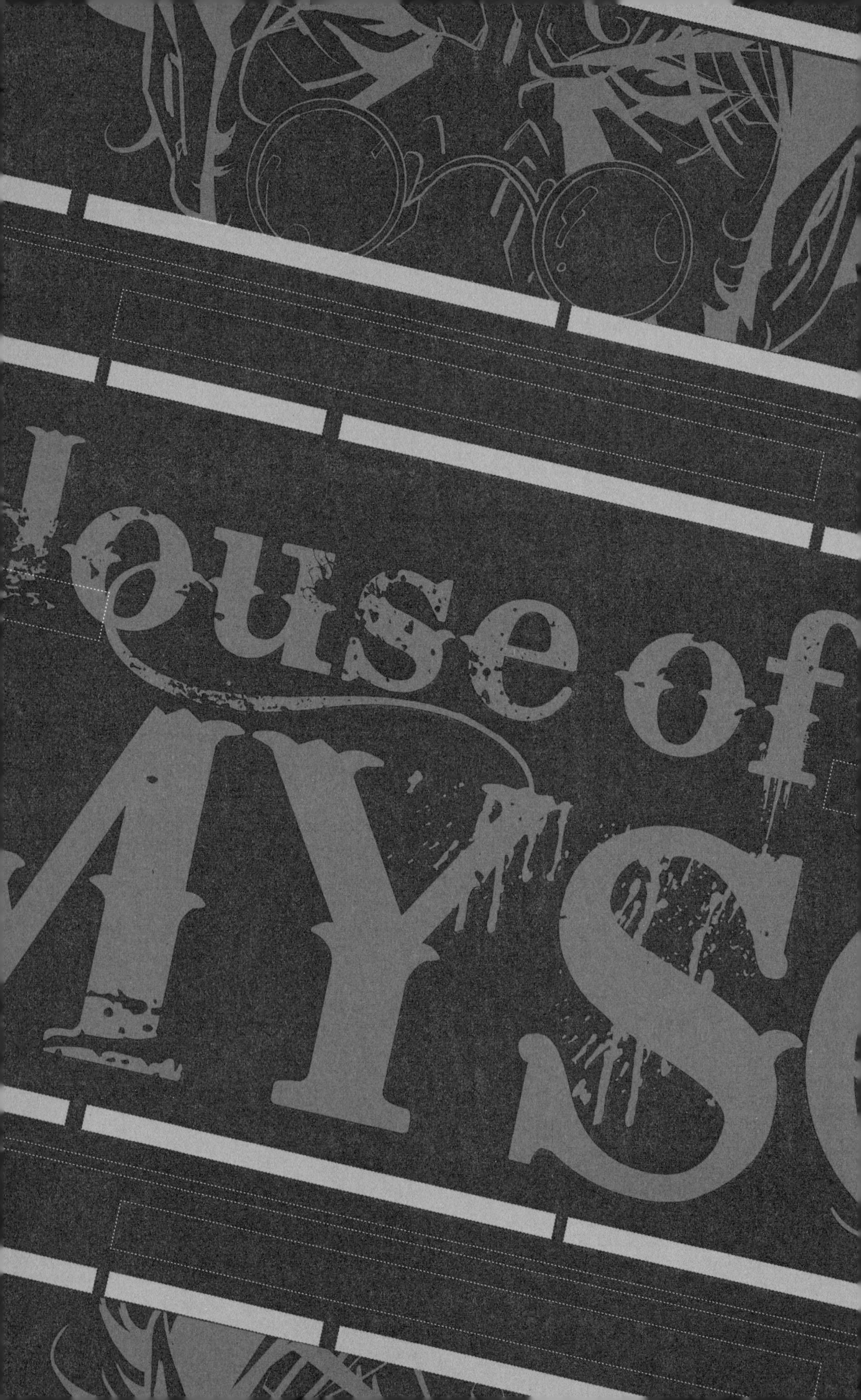
ouse of

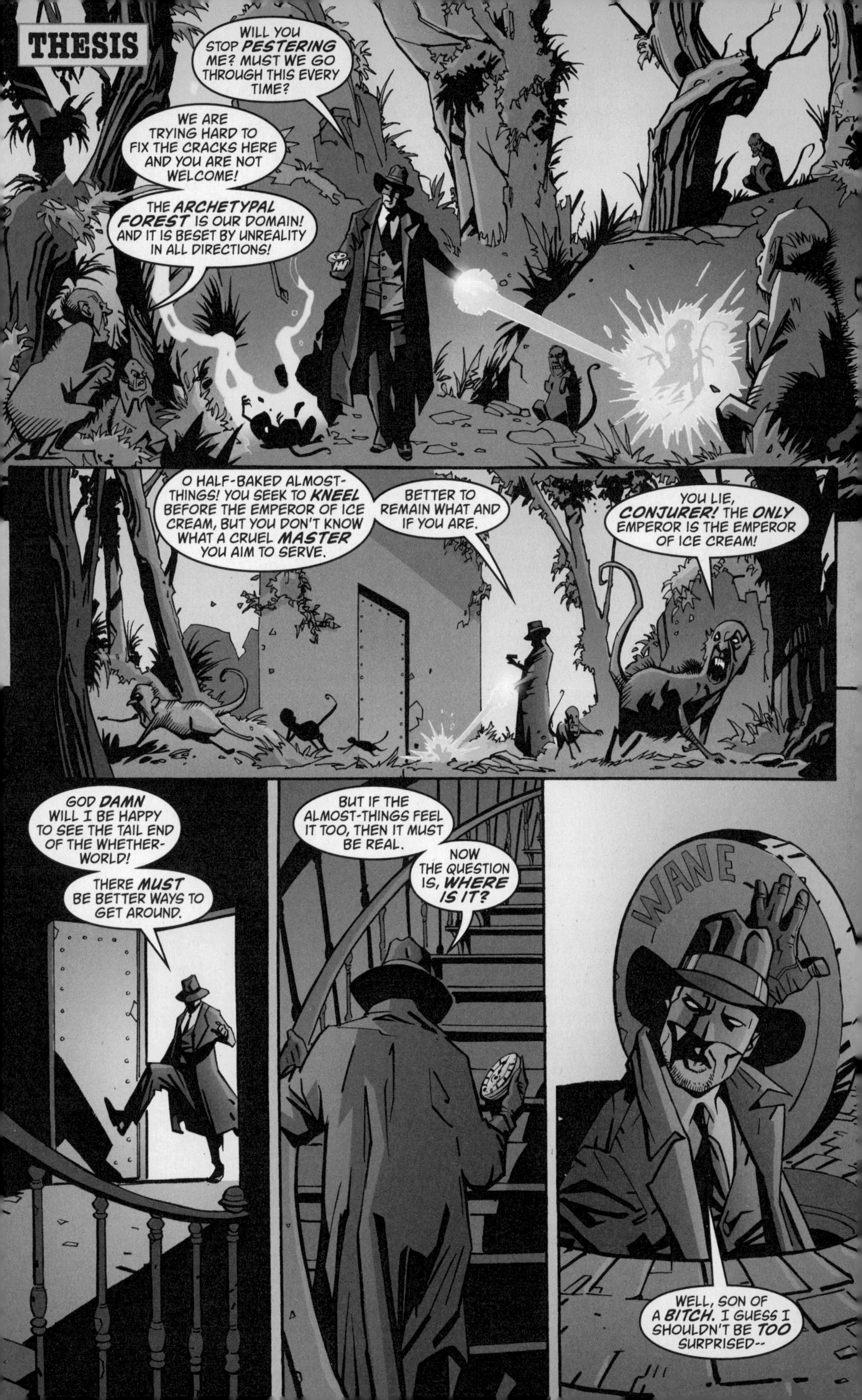
THESIS
WILL YOU STOP PESTERING ME? MUST WE GO THROUGH THIS EVERY TIME?
WE ARE TRYING HARD TO FIX THE CRACKS HERE AND YOU ARE NOT WELCOME!
THE ARCHETYPAL FOREST IS OUR DOMAIN! AND IT IS BESET BY UNREALITY IN ALL DIRECTIONS!
O HALF-BAKED ALMOST-THINGS! YOU SEEK TO KNEEL BEFORE THE EMPEROR OF ICE CREAM, BUT YOU DON'T KNOW WHAT A CRUEL MASTER YOU AIM TO SERVE.
BETTER TO REMAIN WHAT AND IF YOU ARE.
YOU LIE, CONJURER! THE ONLY EMPEROR IS THE EMPEROR OF ICE CREAM!
GOD DAMN WILL I BE HAPPY TO SEE THE TAIL END OF THE WHETHER-WORLD!
THERE MUST BE BETTER WAYS TO GET AROUND.
BUT IF THE ALMOST-THINGS FEEL IT TOO, THEN IT MUST BE REAL.
NOW THE QUESTION IS, WHERE IS IT?
WANE
WELL, SON OF A BITCH. I GUESS I SHOULDN'T BE TOO SURPRISED--

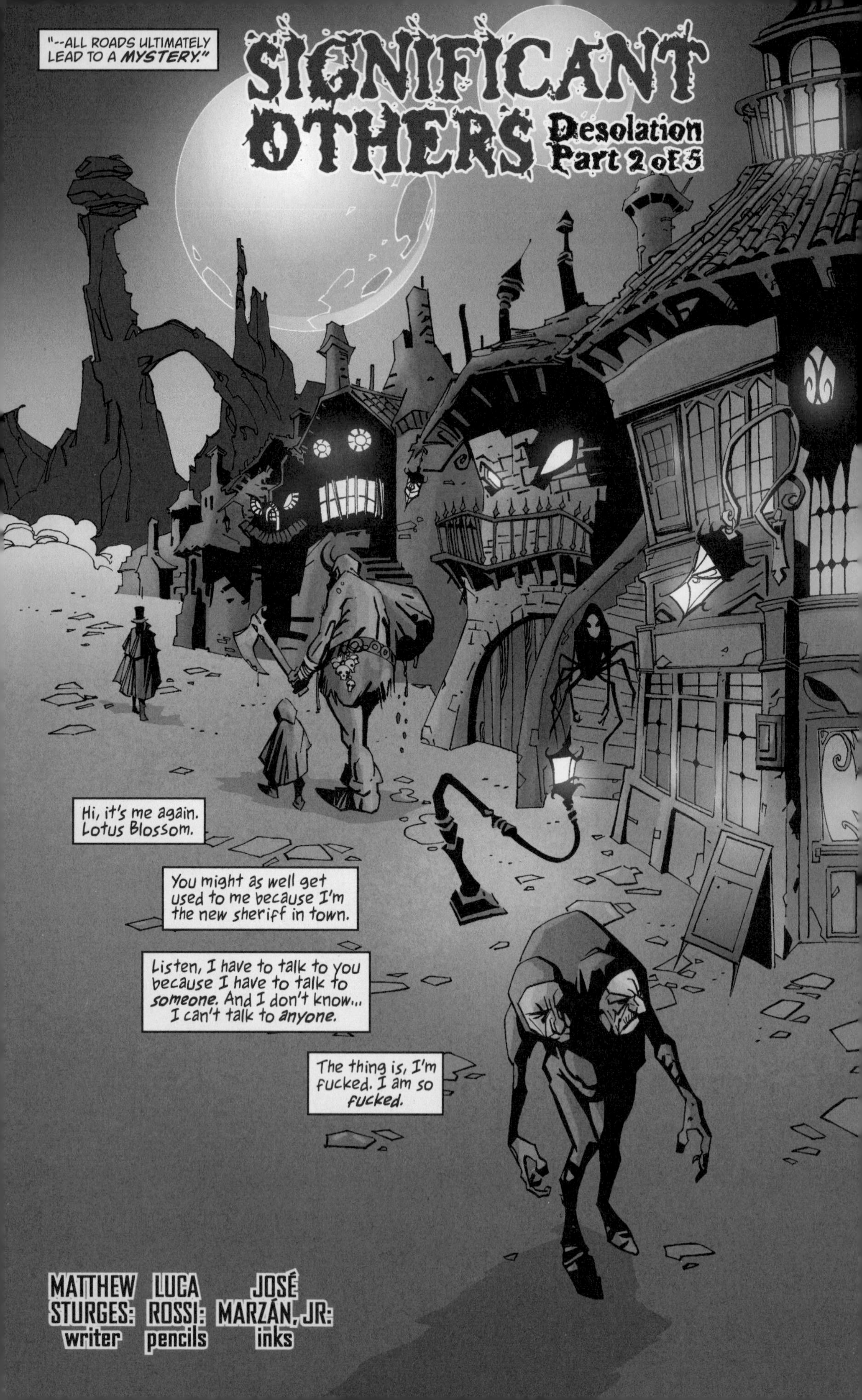
"--ALL ROADS ULTIMATELY LEAD TO A MYSTERY."
SIGNIFICANT OTHERS
Desolation Part 2 of 5
Hi, it's me again. Lotus Blossom.
You might as well get used to me because I'm the new sheriff in town.
Listen, I have to talk to you because I have to talk to someone. And I don't know... I can't talk to anyone.
The thing is, I'm fucked. I am so fucked.
MATTHEW STURGES: writer
LUCA ROSSI: pencils
JOSÉ MARZÁN, JR: inks

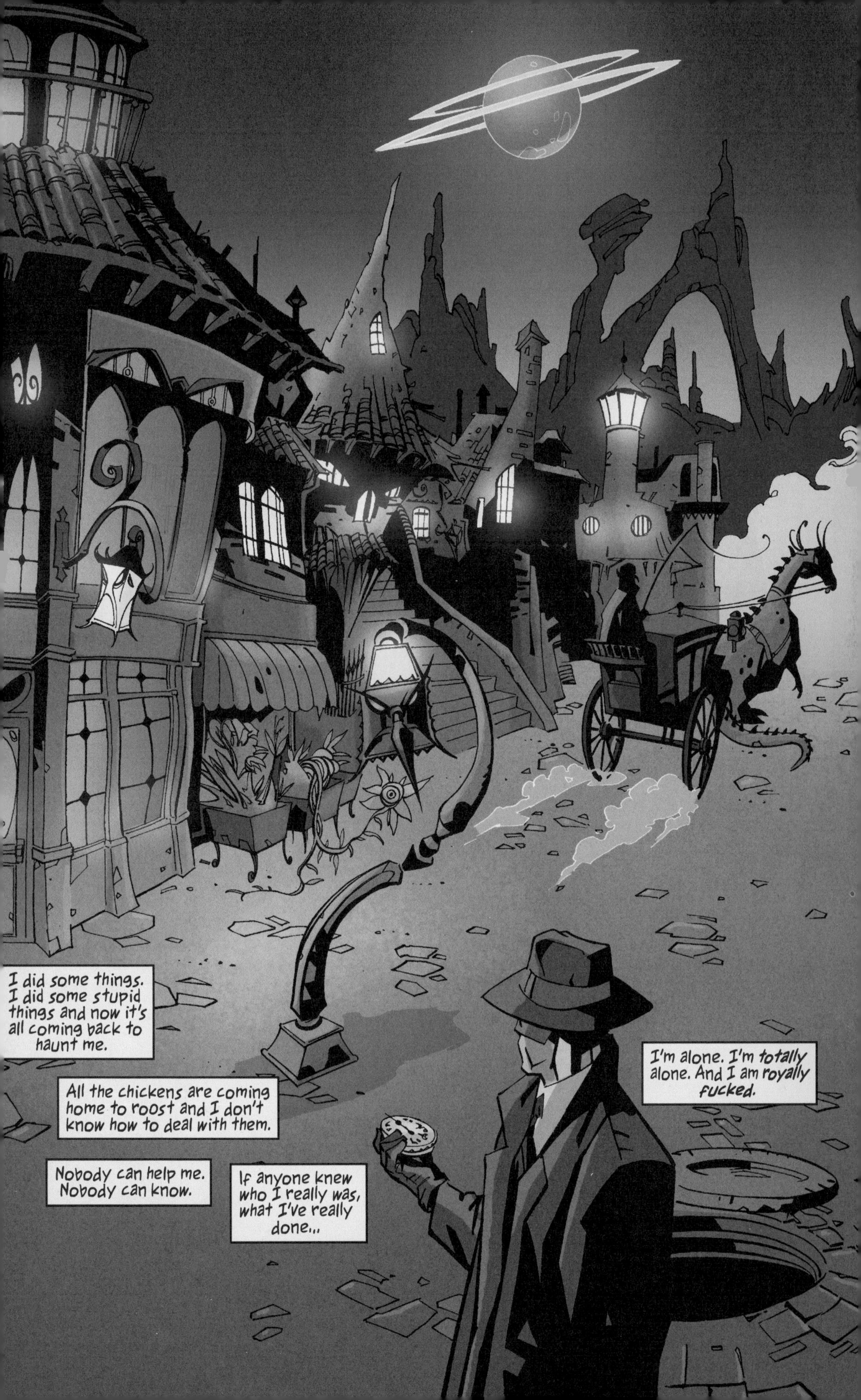
I did some things. I did some stupid things and now it's all coming back to haunt me.
All the chickens are coming home to roost and I don't know how to deal with them.
Nobody can help me. Nobody can know.
If anyone knew who I really was, what I've really done...
I'm alone. I'm *totally* alone. And I am *royally* ***fucked***.

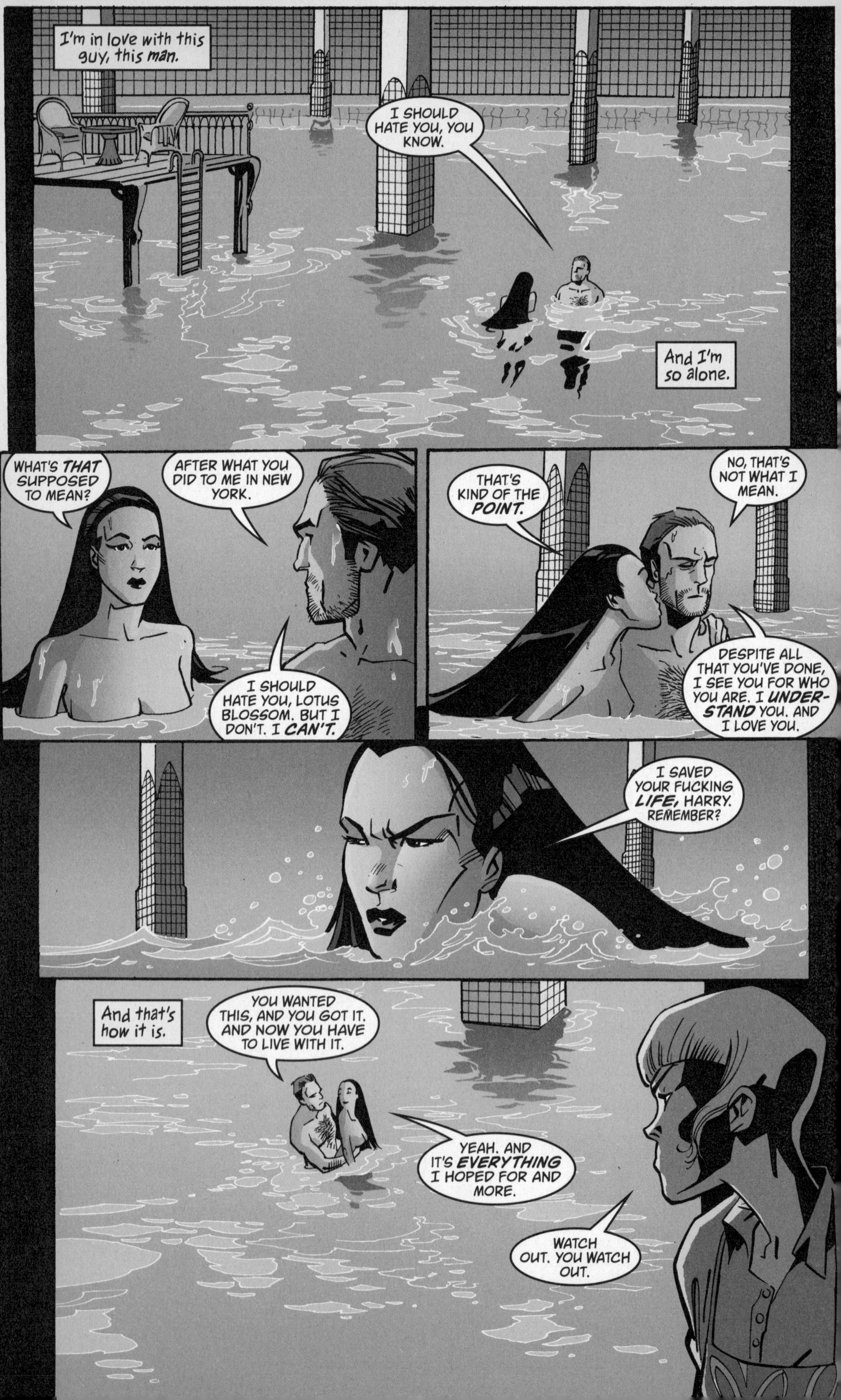
I'm in love with this guy, this *man.*
I SHOULD HATE YOU, YOU KNOW.
And I'm so alone.
WHAT'S **THAT** SUPPOSED TO MEAN?
AFTER WHAT YOU DID TO ME IN NEW YORK.
I SHOULD HATE YOU, LOTUS BLOSSOM. BUT I DON'T. I **CAN'T.**
THAT'S KIND OF THE **POINT.**
NO, THAT'S NOT WHAT I MEAN.
DESPITE ALL THAT YOU'VE DONE, I SEE YOU FOR WHO YOU ARE. I **UNDER-STAND** YOU. AND I LOVE YOU.
I SAVED YOUR FUCKING **LIFE,** HARRY. REMEMBER?
And that's how it is.
YOU WANTED THIS, AND YOU GOT IT. AND NOW YOU HAVE TO LIVE WITH IT.
YEAH. AND IT'S **EVERYTHING** I HOPED FOR AND MORE.
WATCH OUT. YOU WATCH OUT.

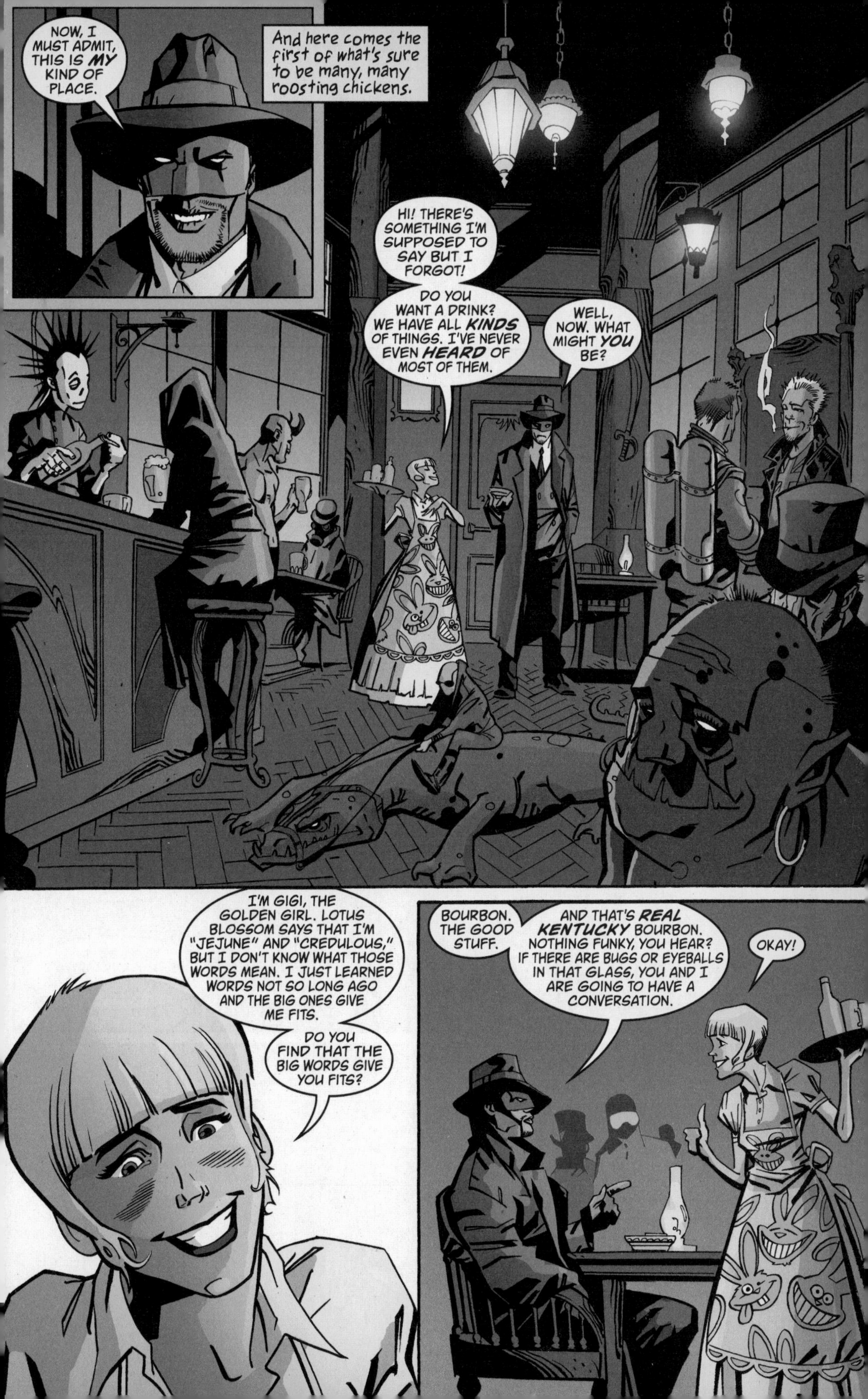

NOW, I MUST ADMIT, THIS IS MY KIND OF PLACE.
And here comes the first of what's sure to be many, many roosting chickens.
HI! THERE'S SOMETHING I'M SUPPOSED TO SAY BUT I FORGOT!
DO YOU WANT A DRINK? WE HAVE ALL KINDS OF THINGS. I'VE NEVER EVEN HEARD OF MOST OF THEM.
WELL, NOW. WHAT MIGHT YOU BE?
I'M GIGI, THE GOLDEN GIRL. LOTUS BLOSSOM SAYS THAT I'M "JEJUNE" AND "CREDULOUS," BUT I DON'T KNOW WHAT THOSE WORDS MEAN. I JUST LEARNED WORDS NOT SO LONG AGO AND THE BIG ONES GIVE ME FITS.
DO YOU FIND THAT THE BIG WORDS GIVE YOU FITS?
BOURBON. THE GOOD STUFF.
AND THAT'S REAL KENTUCKY BOURBON. NOTHING FUNKY, YOU HEAR? IF THERE ARE BUGS OR EYEBALLS IN THAT GLASS, YOU AND I ARE GOING TO HAVE A CONVERSATION.
OKAY!

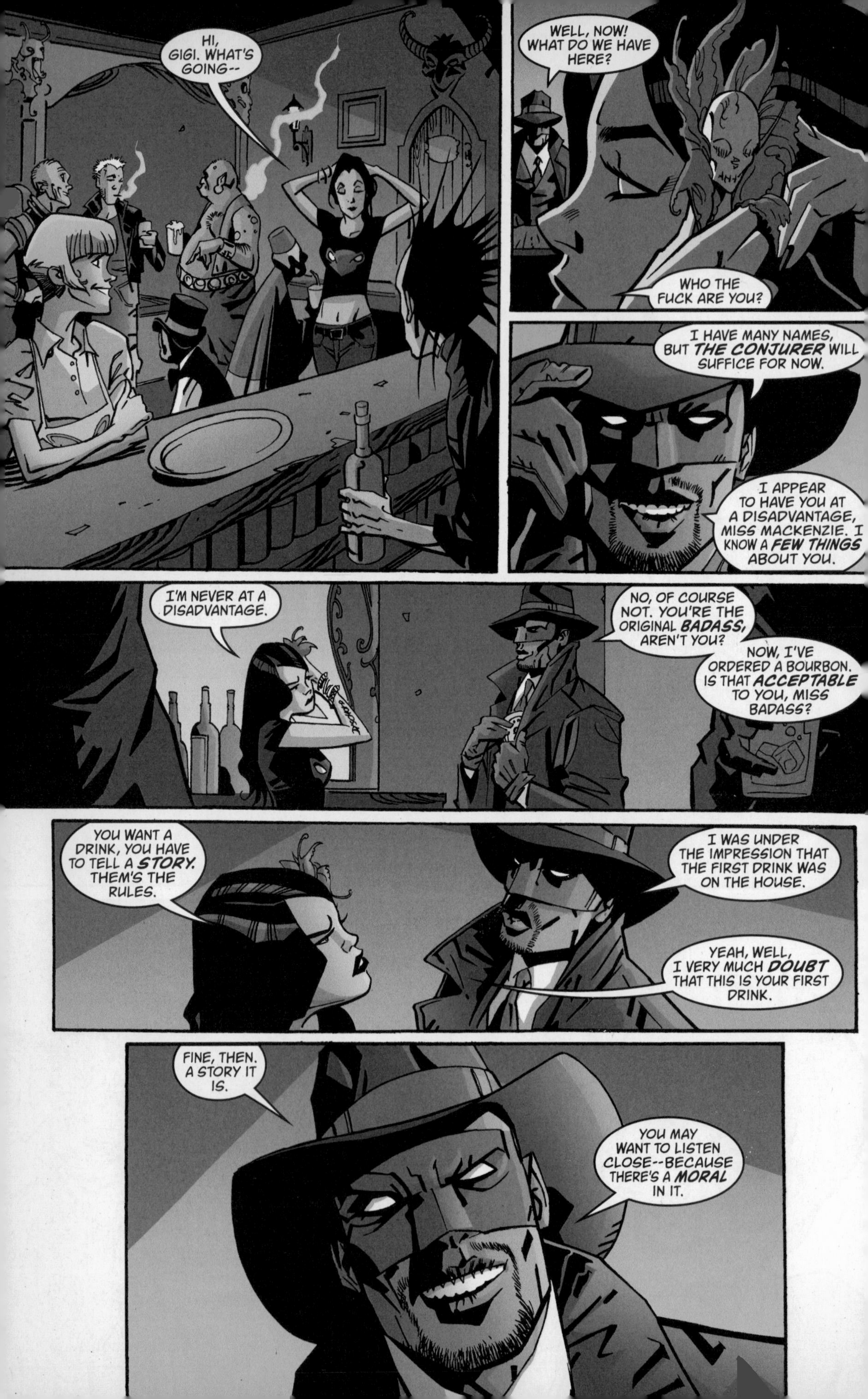
HI, GIGI. WHAT'S GOING--
WELL, NOW! WHAT DO WE HAVE HERE?
WHO THE FUCK ARE YOU?
I HAVE MANY NAMES, BUT THE CONJURER WILL SUFFICE FOR NOW.
I APPEAR TO HAVE YOU AT A DISADVANTAGE, MISS MACKENZIE. I KNOW A FEW THINGS ABOUT YOU.
I'M NEVER AT A DISADVANTAGE.
NO, OF COURSE NOT. YOU'RE THE ORIGINAL BADASS, AREN'T YOU?
NOW, I'VE ORDERED A BOURBON. IS THAT ACCEPTABLE TO YOU, MISS BADASS?
YOU WANT A DRINK, YOU HAVE TO TELL A STORY. THEM'S THE RULES.
I WAS UNDER THE IMPRESSION THAT THE FIRST DRINK WAS ON THE HOUSE.
YEAH, WELL, I VERY MUCH DOUBT THAT THIS IS YOUR FIRST DRINK.
FINE, THEN. A STORY IT IS.
YOU MAY WANT TO LISTEN CLOSE--BECAUSE THERE'S A MORAL IN IT.

EARL LITTLE WAS A HARDENED CRIMINAL.

IT'S A *BEAUTIFUL* DAY IN NEW YORK CITY, LADIES AND GENTLEMEN!

BUT ONE STRANGE NIGHT HE FOUND HIMSELF GRANTED MYSTERIOUS MAGICAL POWERS!

AND WHEN HE FELL IN LOVE WITH THE BEAUTIFUL MARIA VELERIO, THE DAUGHTER OF A PROMINENT BANKER, EARL DECIDED TO GIVE UP HIS LIFE OF CRIME.

NOW UNBEKNOWNST TO ALL-- INCLUDING THE WOMAN HE LOVES--HE PROTECTS THE CITY UPON WHICH HE ONCE PREYED IN THE GUISE OF...

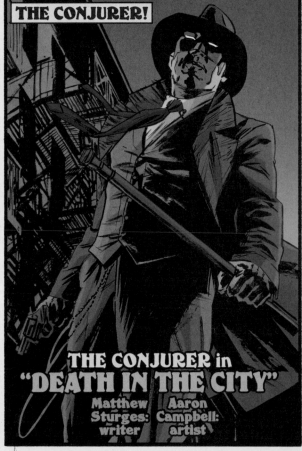

THE CONJURER!

THE CONJURER in "DEATH IN THE CITY"

Matthew Sturges: writer

Aaron Campbell: artist

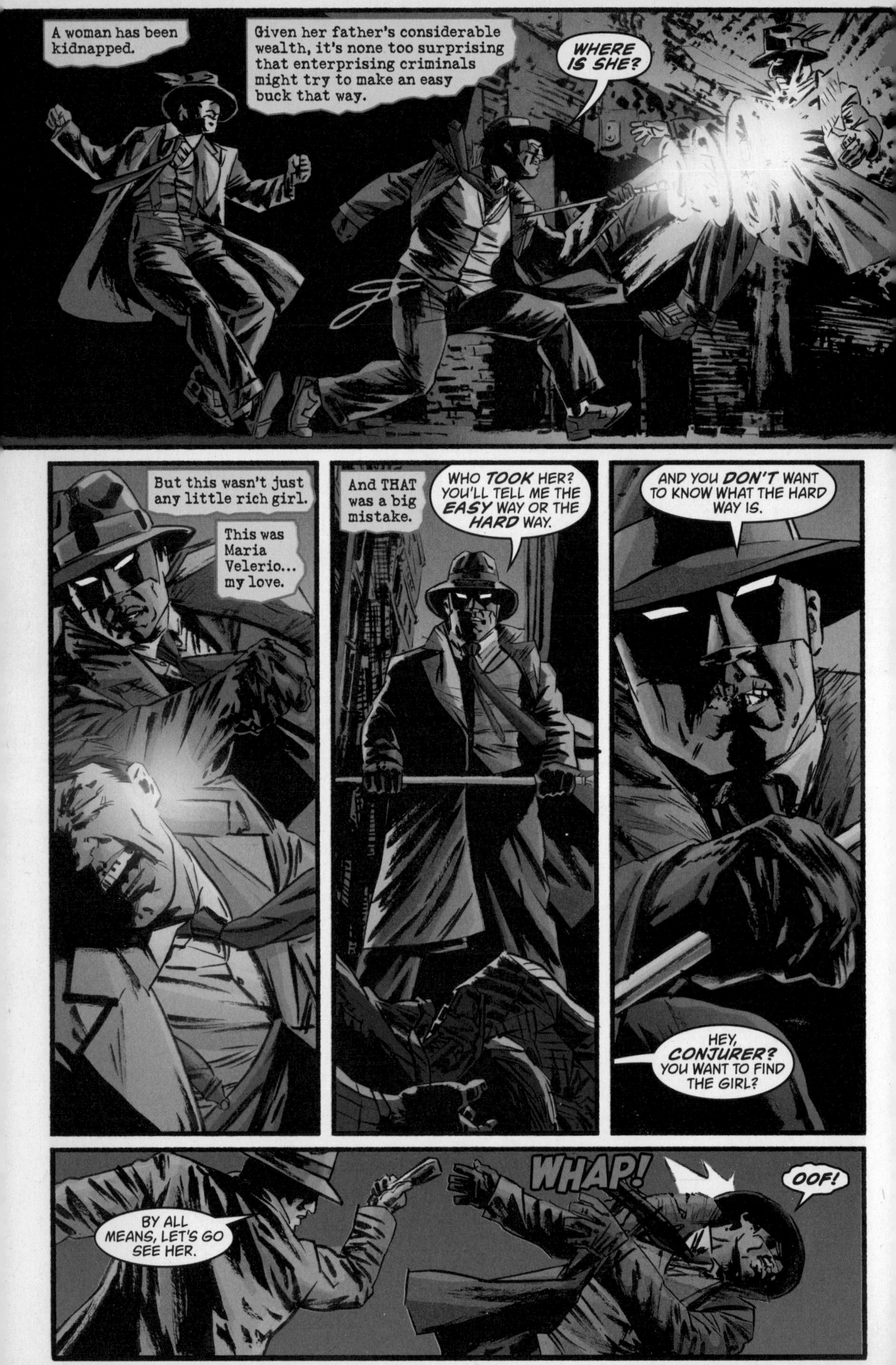
A woman has been kidnapped.
Given her father's considerable wealth, it's none too surprising that enterprising criminals might try to make an easy buck that way.
WHERE IS SHE?
But this wasn't just any little rich girl.
This was Maria Velerio... my love.
And THAT was a big mistake.
WHO TOOK HER? YOU'LL TELL ME THE EASY WAY OR THE HARD WAY.
AND YOU DON'T WANT TO KNOW WHAT THE HARD WAY IS.
HEY, CONJURER? YOU WANT TO FIND THE GIRL?
BY ALL MEANS, LET'S GO SEE HER.
WHAP!
OOF!

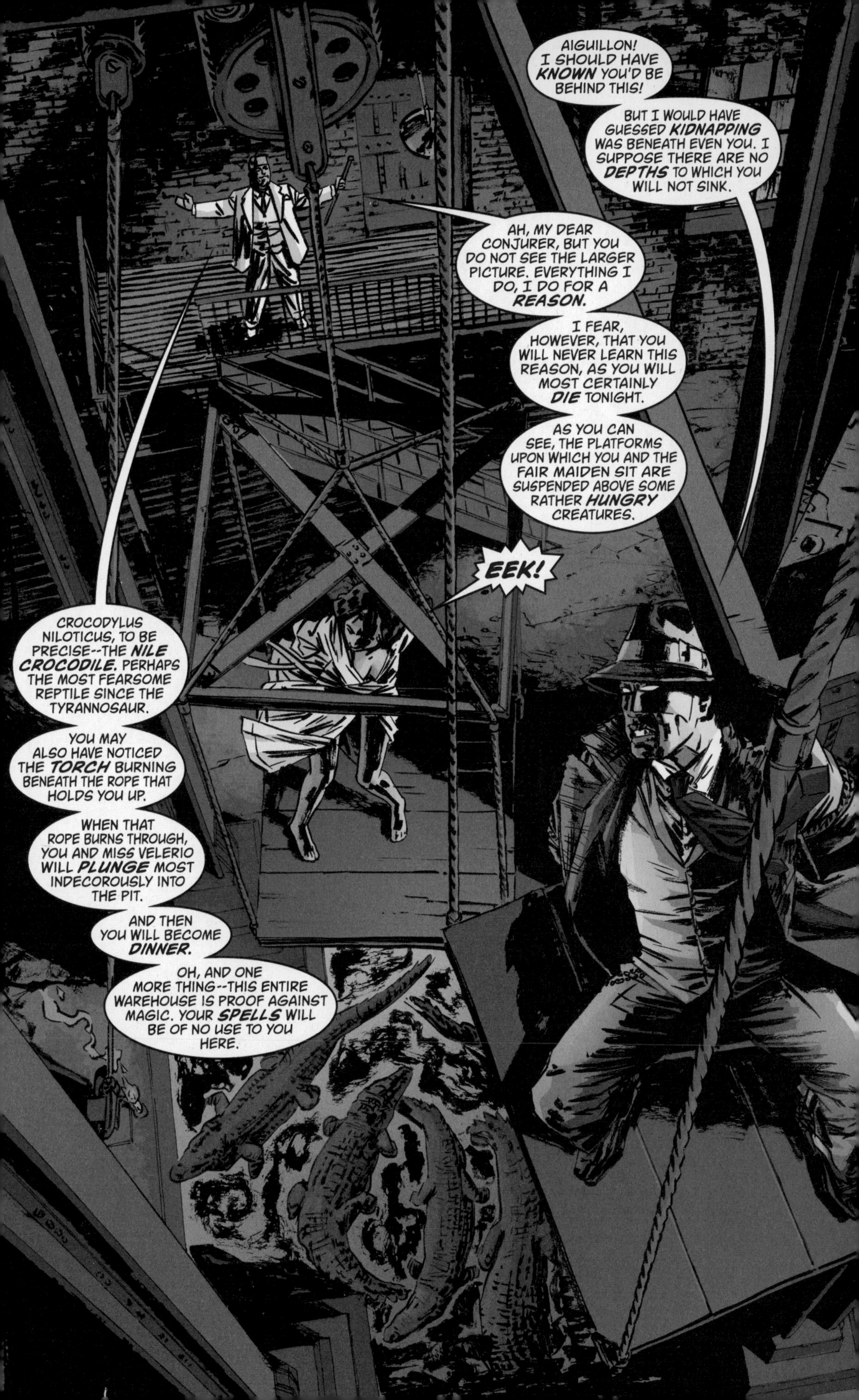
AIGUILLON! I SHOULD HAVE **KNOWN** YOU'D BE BEHIND THIS!
BUT I WOULD HAVE GUESSED **KIDNAPPING** WAS BENEATH EVEN YOU. I SUPPOSE THERE ARE NO **DEPTHS** TO WHICH YOU WILL NOT SINK.
AH, MY DEAR CONJURER, BUT YOU DO NOT SEE THE LARGER PICTURE. EVERYTHING I DO, I DO FOR A **REASON.**
I FEAR, HOWEVER, THAT YOU WILL NEVER LEARN THIS REASON, AS YOU WILL MOST CERTAINLY **DIE** TONIGHT.
AS YOU CAN SEE, THE PLATFORMS UPON WHICH YOU AND THE FAIR MAIDEN SIT ARE SUSPENDED ABOVE SOME RATHER **HUNGRY** CREATURES.
EEK!
CROCODYLUS NILOTICUS, TO BE PRECISE--THE **NILE CROCODILE.** PERHAPS THE MOST FEARSOME REPTILE SINCE THE TYRANNOSAUR.
YOU MAY ALSO HAVE NOTICED THE **TORCH** BURNING BENEATH THE ROPE THAT HOLDS YOU UP.
WHEN THAT ROPE BURNS THROUGH, YOU AND MISS VELERIO WILL **PLUNGE** MOST INDECOROUSLY INTO THE PIT.
AND THEN YOU WILL BECOME **DINNER.**
OH, AND ONE MORE THING--THIS ENTIRE WAREHOUSE IS PROOF AGAINST MAGIC. YOUR **SPELLS** WILL BE OF NO USE TO YOU HERE.

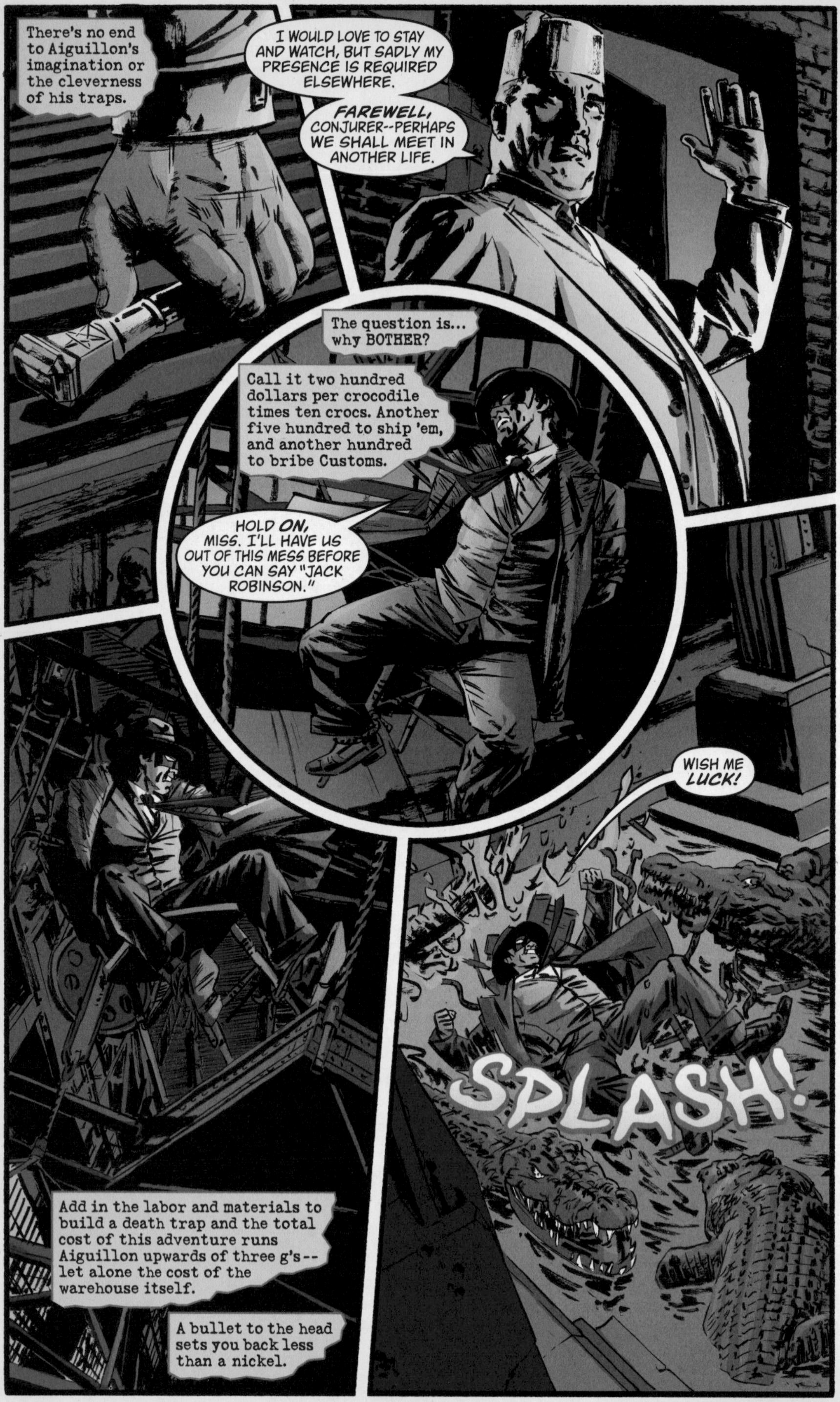

There's no end to Aiguillon's imagination or the cleverness of his traps.
I WOULD LOVE TO STAY AND WATCH, BUT SADLY MY PRESENCE IS REQUIRED ELSEWHERE.
FAREWELL, CONJURER--PERHAPS WE SHALL MEET IN ANOTHER LIFE.
The question is... why BOTHER?
Call it two hundred dollars per crocodile times ten crocs. Another five hundred to ship 'em, and another hundred to bribe Customs.
HOLD ON, MISS. I'LL HAVE US OUT OF THIS MESS BEFORE YOU CAN SAY "JACK ROBINSON."
Add in the labor and materials to build a death trap and the total cost of this adventure runs Aiguillon upwards of three g's--let alone the cost of the warehouse itself.
A bullet to the head sets you back less than a nickel.
WISH ME LUCK!
SPLASH!

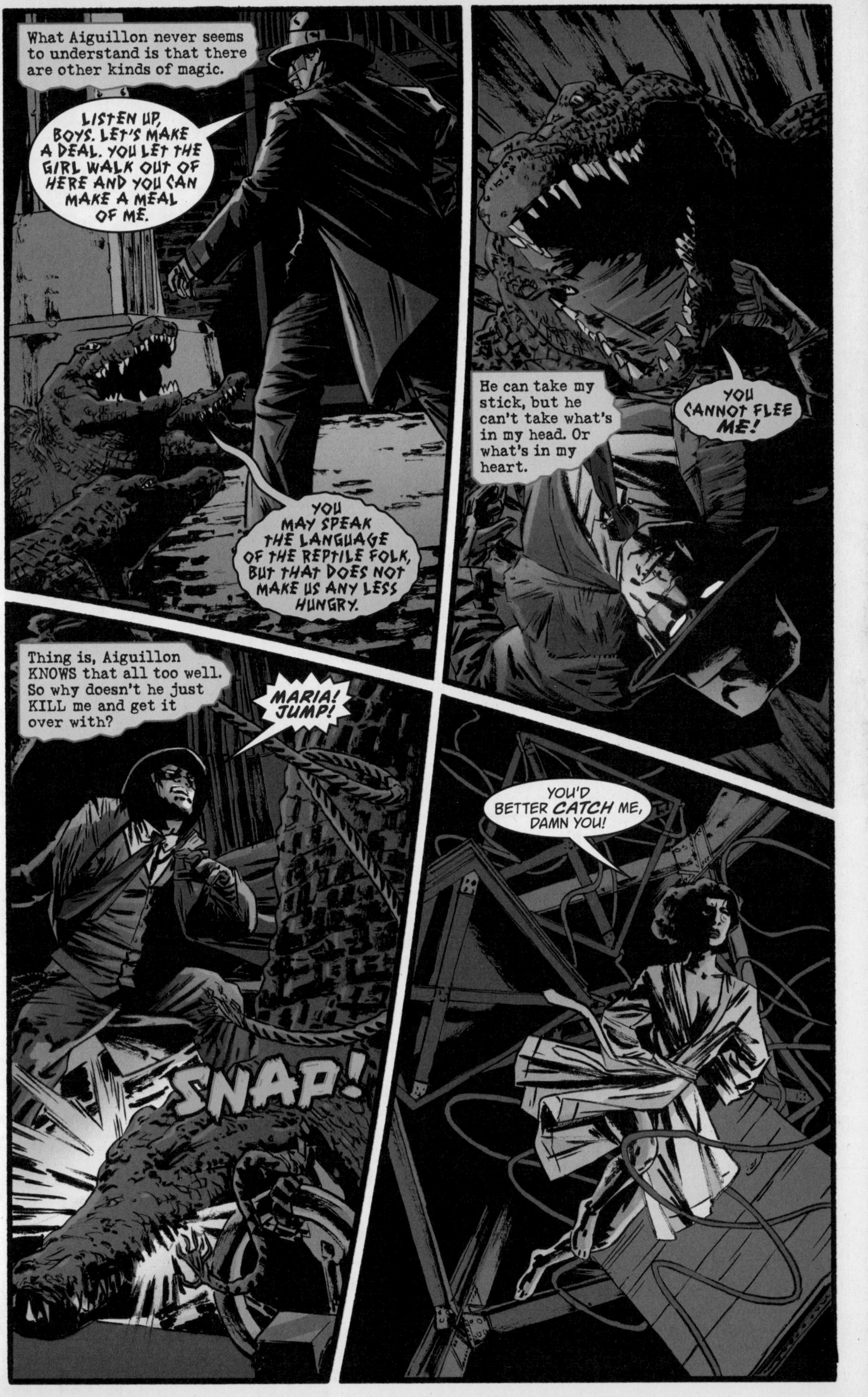

What Aiguillon never seems to understand is that there are other kinds of magic.
LISTEN UP, BOYS. LET'S MAKE A DEAL. YOU LET THE GIRL WALK OUT OF HERE AND YOU CAN MAKE A MEAL OF ME.
YOU MAY SPEAK THE LANGUAGE OF THE REPTILE FOLK, BUT THAT DOES NOT MAKE US ANY LESS HUNGRY.
He can take my stick, but he can't take what's in my head. Or what's in my heart.
YOU CANNOT FLEE ME!
Thing is, Aiguillon KNOWS that all too well. So why doesn't he just KILL me and get it over with?
MARIA! JUMP!
SNAP!
YOU'D BETTER CATCH ME, DAMN YOU!

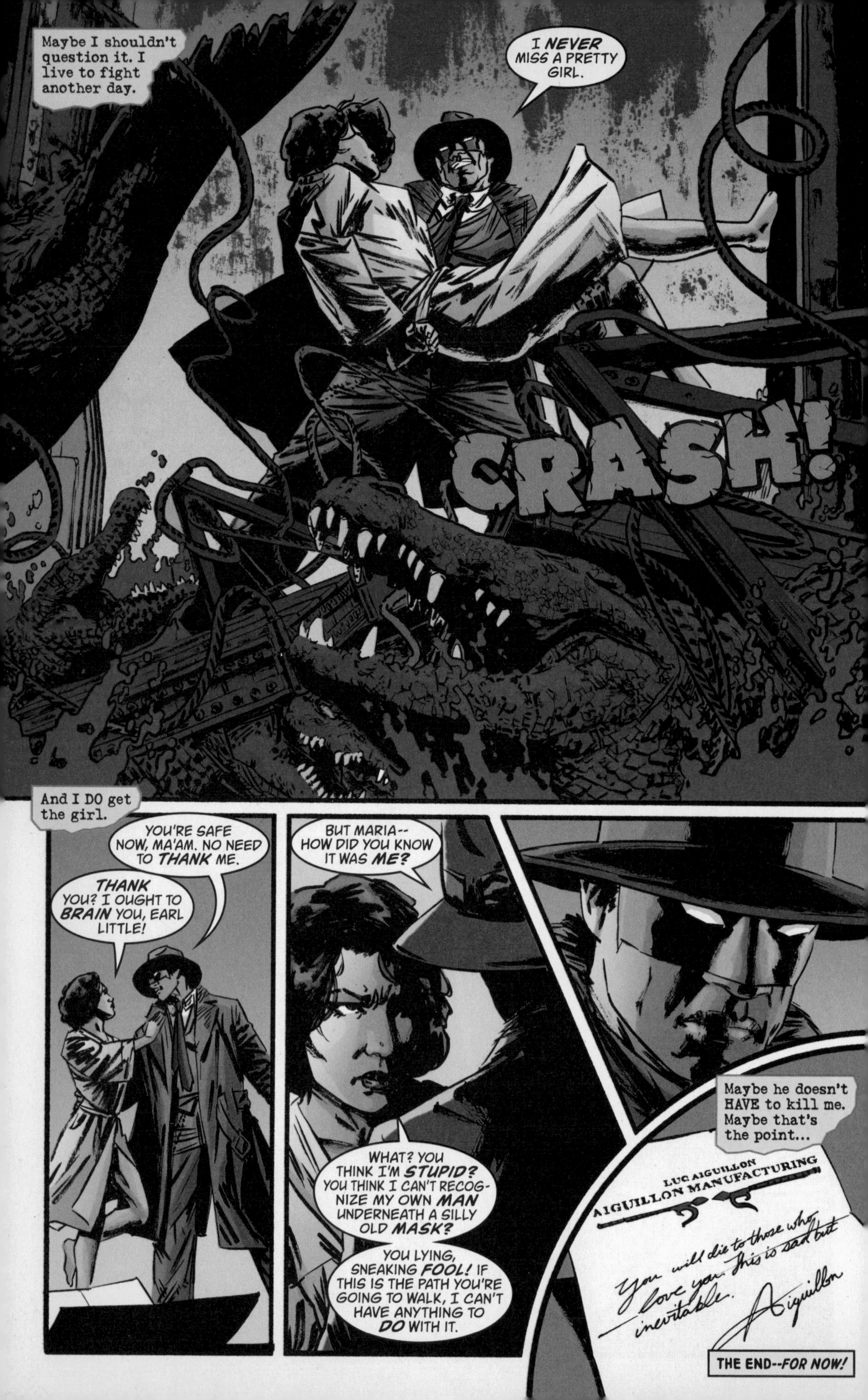
Maybe I shouldn't question it. I live to fight another day.
I NEVER MISS A PRETTY GIRL.
CRASH!
And I DO get the girl.
YOU'RE SAFE NOW, MA'AM. NO NEED TO THANK ME.
THANK YOU? I OUGHT TO BRAIN YOU, EARL LITTLE!
BUT MARIA-- HOW DID YOU KNOW IT WAS ME?
WHAT? YOU THINK I'M STUPID? YOU THINK I CAN'T RECOGNIZE MY OWN MAN UNDERNEATH A SILLY OLD MASK?
YOU LYING, SNEAKING FOOL! IF THIS IS THE PATH YOU'RE GOING TO WALK, I CAN'T HAVE ANYTHING TO DO WITH IT.
Maybe he doesn't HAVE to kill me. Maybe that's the point...
LUC AIGUILLON
AIGUILLON MANUFACTURING
You will die to those who love you. This is sad but inevitable.
Aiguillon
THE END--FOR NOW!

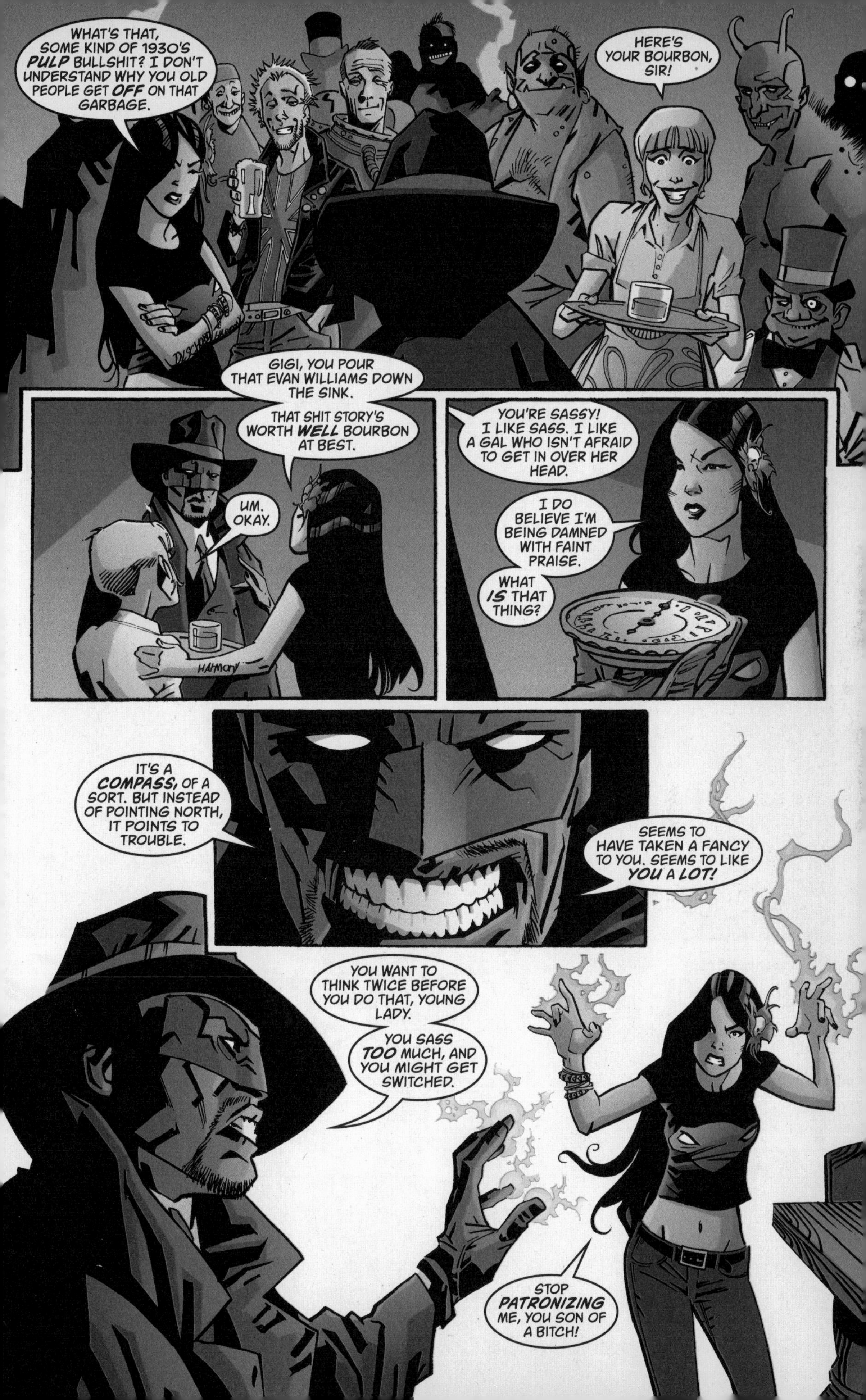
WHAT'S THAT, SOME KIND OF 1930'S PULP BULLSHIT? I DON'T UNDERSTAND WHY YOU OLD PEOPLE GET OFF ON THAT GARBAGE.
HERE'S YOUR BOURBON, SIR!
GIGI, YOU POUR THAT EVAN WILLIAMS DOWN THE SINK.
THAT SHIT STORY'S WORTH WELL BOURBON AT BEST.
UM. OKAY.
YOU'RE SASSY! I LIKE SASS. I LIKE A GAL WHO ISN'T AFRAID TO GET IN OVER HER HEAD.
I DO BELIEVE I'M BEING DAMNED WITH FAINT PRAISE.
WHAT IS THAT THING?
IT'S A COMPASS, OF A SORT. BUT INSTEAD OF POINTING NORTH, IT POINTS TO TROUBLE.
SEEMS TO HAVE TAKEN A FANCY TO YOU. SEEMS TO LIKE YOU A LOT!
YOU WANT TO THINK TWICE BEFORE YOU DO THAT, YOUNG LADY.
YOU SASS TOO MUCH, AND YOU MIGHT GET SWITCHED.
STOP PATRONIZING ME, YOU SON OF A BITCH!

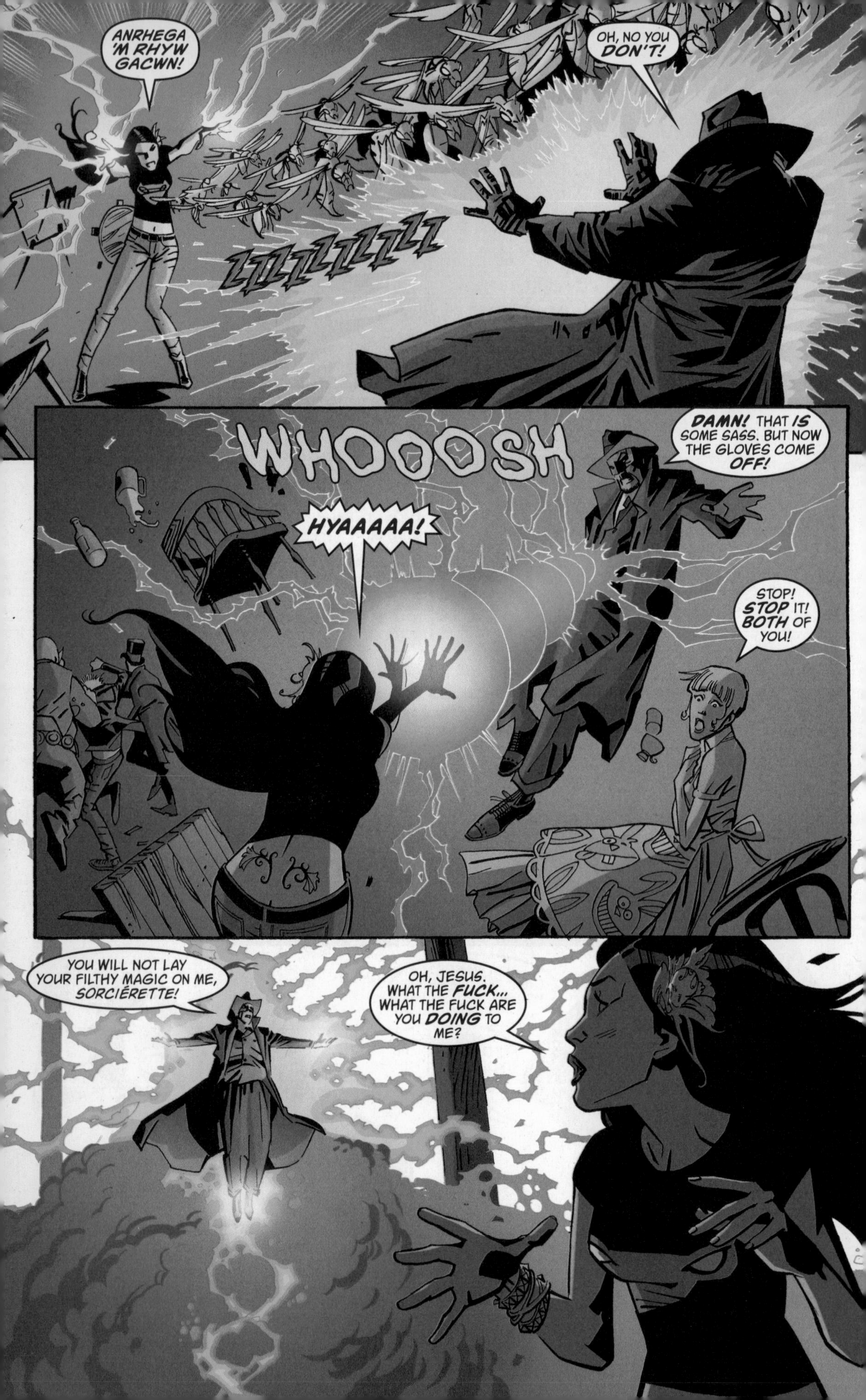
ANRHEGA 'M RHYW GACWN!
OH, NO YOU DON'T!
ZZZZZZZZZZ
WHOOOSH
DAMN! THAT IS SOME SASS. BUT NOW THE GLOVES COME OFF!
HYAAAAAA!
STOP! STOP IT! BOTH OF YOU!
YOU WILL NOT LAY YOUR FILTHY MAGIC ON ME, SORCIÉRETTE!
OH, JESUS. WHAT THE FUCK... WHAT THE FUCK ARE YOU DOING TO ME?

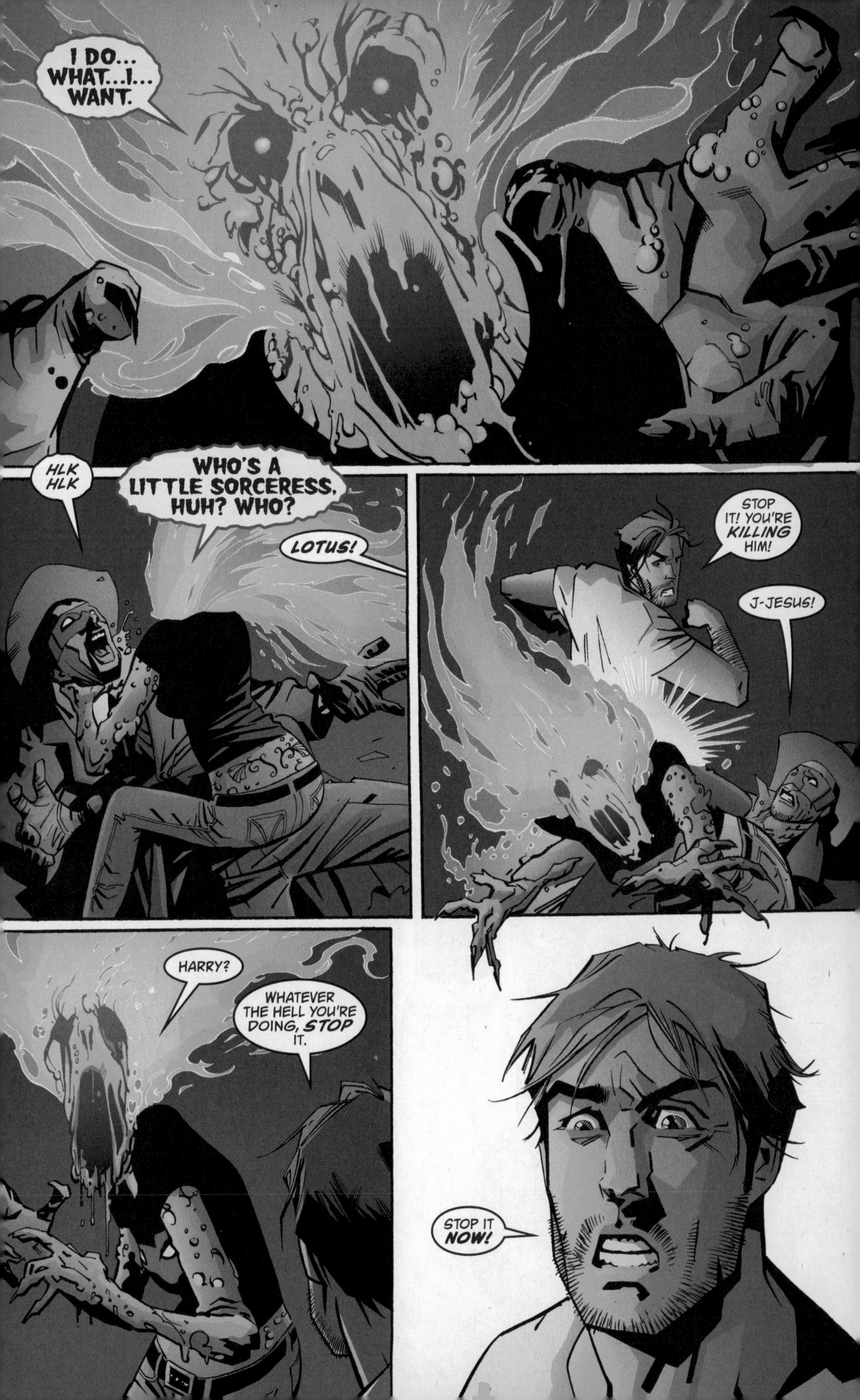
I DO... WHAT...I... WANT.
HLK HLK
WHO'S A LITTLE SORCERESS, HUH? WHO?
LOTUS!
STOP IT! YOU'RE KILLING HIM!
J-JESUS!
HARRY?
WHATEVER THE HELL YOU'RE DOING, STOP IT.
STOP IT NOW!

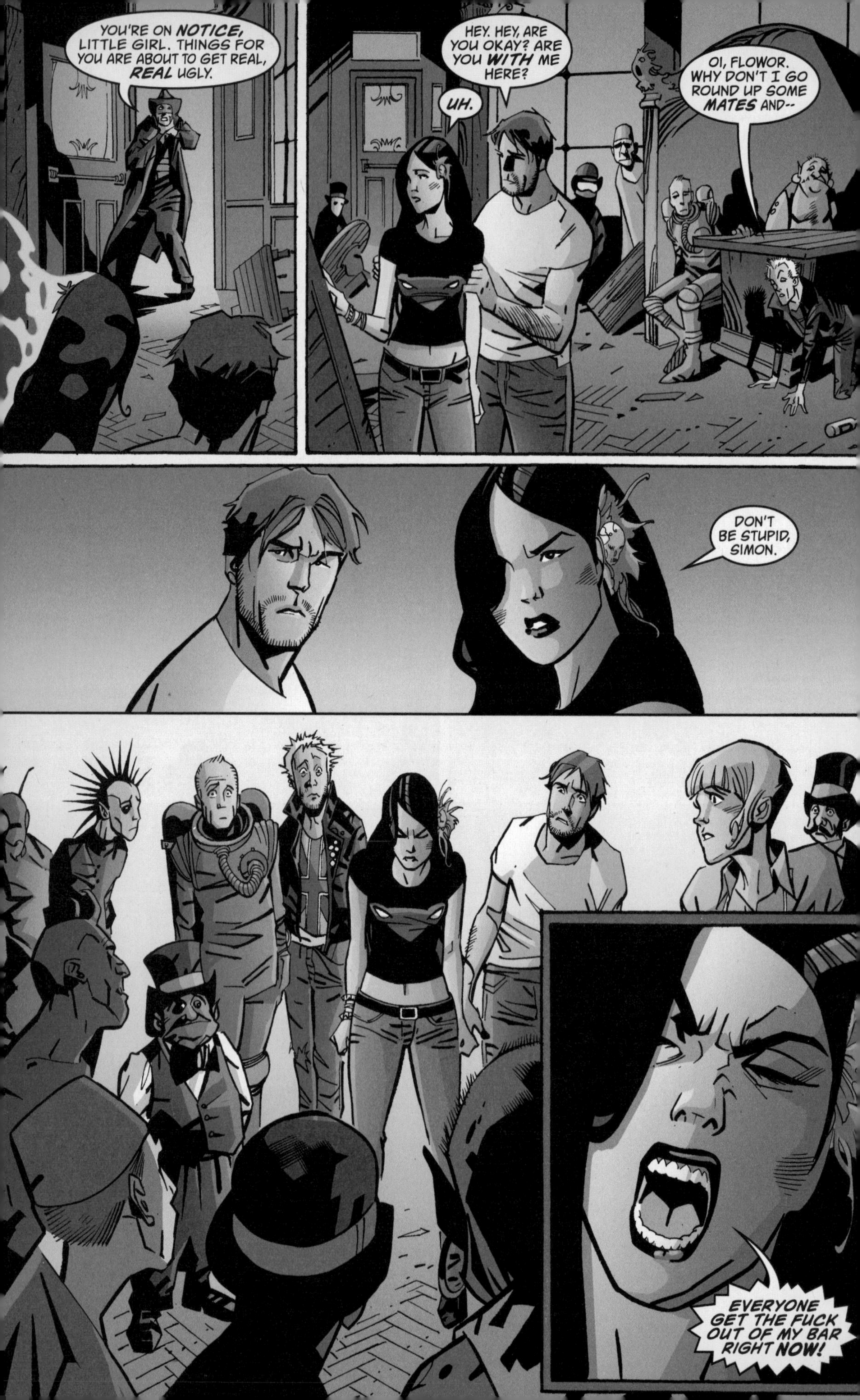
YOU'RE ON NOTICE, LITTLE GIRL. THINGS FOR YOU ARE ABOUT TO GET REAL, REAL UGLY.
HEY. HEY, ARE YOU OKAY? ARE YOU WITH ME HERE?
UH.
OI, FLOWOR. WHY DON'T I GO ROUND UP SOME MATES AND--
DON'T BE STUPID, SIMON.
EVERYONE GET THE FUCK OUT OF MY BAR RIGHT NOW!

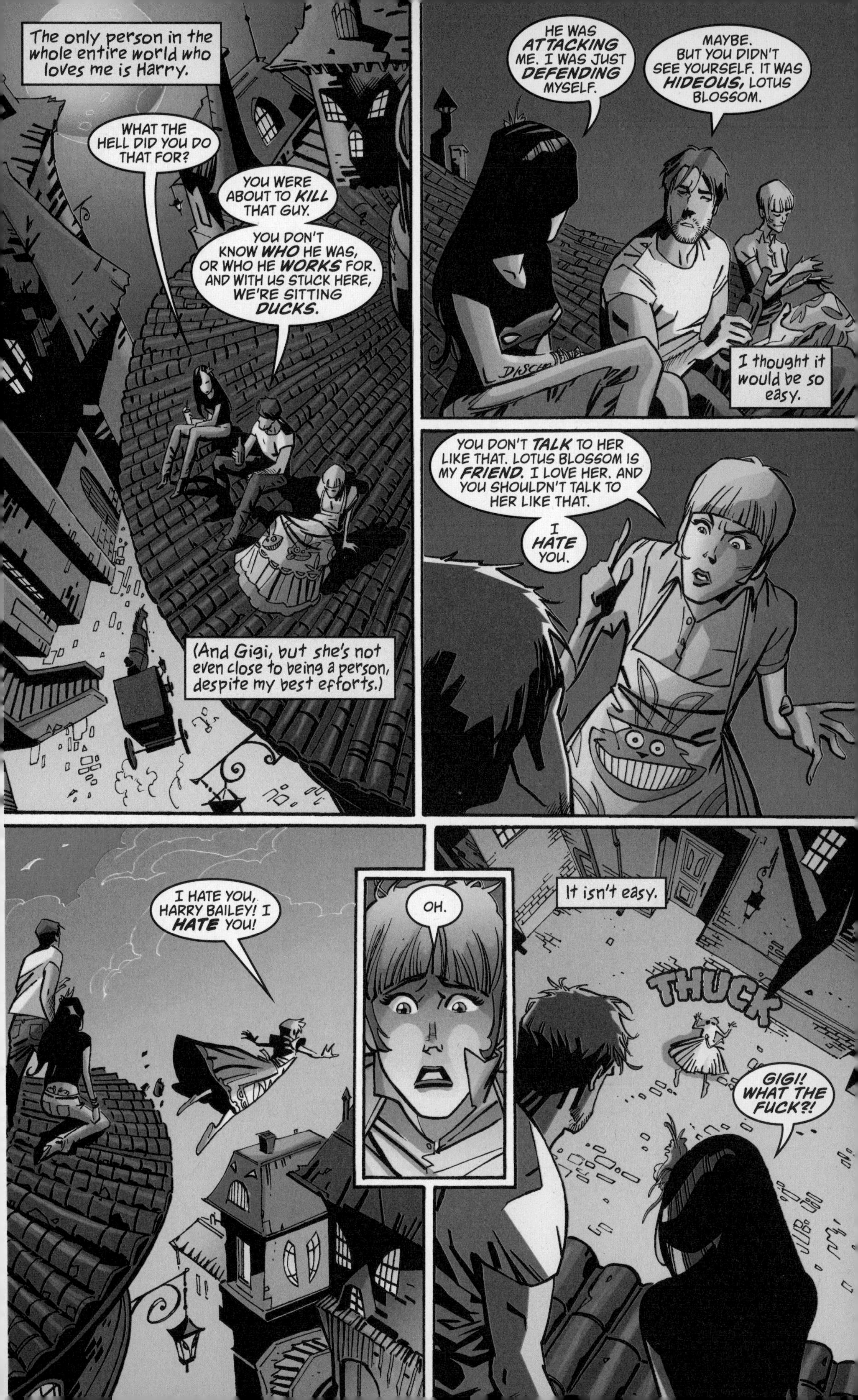

The only person in the whole entire world who loves me is Harry.
WHAT THE HELL DID YOU DO THAT FOR?
YOU WERE ABOUT TO KILL THAT GUY.
YOU DON'T KNOW WHO HE WAS, OR WHO HE WORKS FOR. AND WITH US STUCK HERE, WE'RE SITTING DUCKS.
(And Gigi, but she's not even close to being a person, despite my best efforts.)
HE WAS ATTACKING ME. I WAS JUST DEFENDING MYSELF.
MAYBE. BUT YOU DIDN'T SEE YOURSELF. IT WAS HIDEOUS, LOTUS BLOSSOM.
I thought it would be so easy.
YOU DON'T TALK TO HER LIKE THAT. LOTUS BLOSSOM IS MY FRIEND. I LOVE HER. AND YOU SHOULDN'T TALK TO HER LIKE THAT.
I HATE YOU.
I HATE YOU, HARRY BAILEY! I HATE YOU!
OH.
It isn't easy.
THUCK
GIGI! WHAT THE FUCK?!

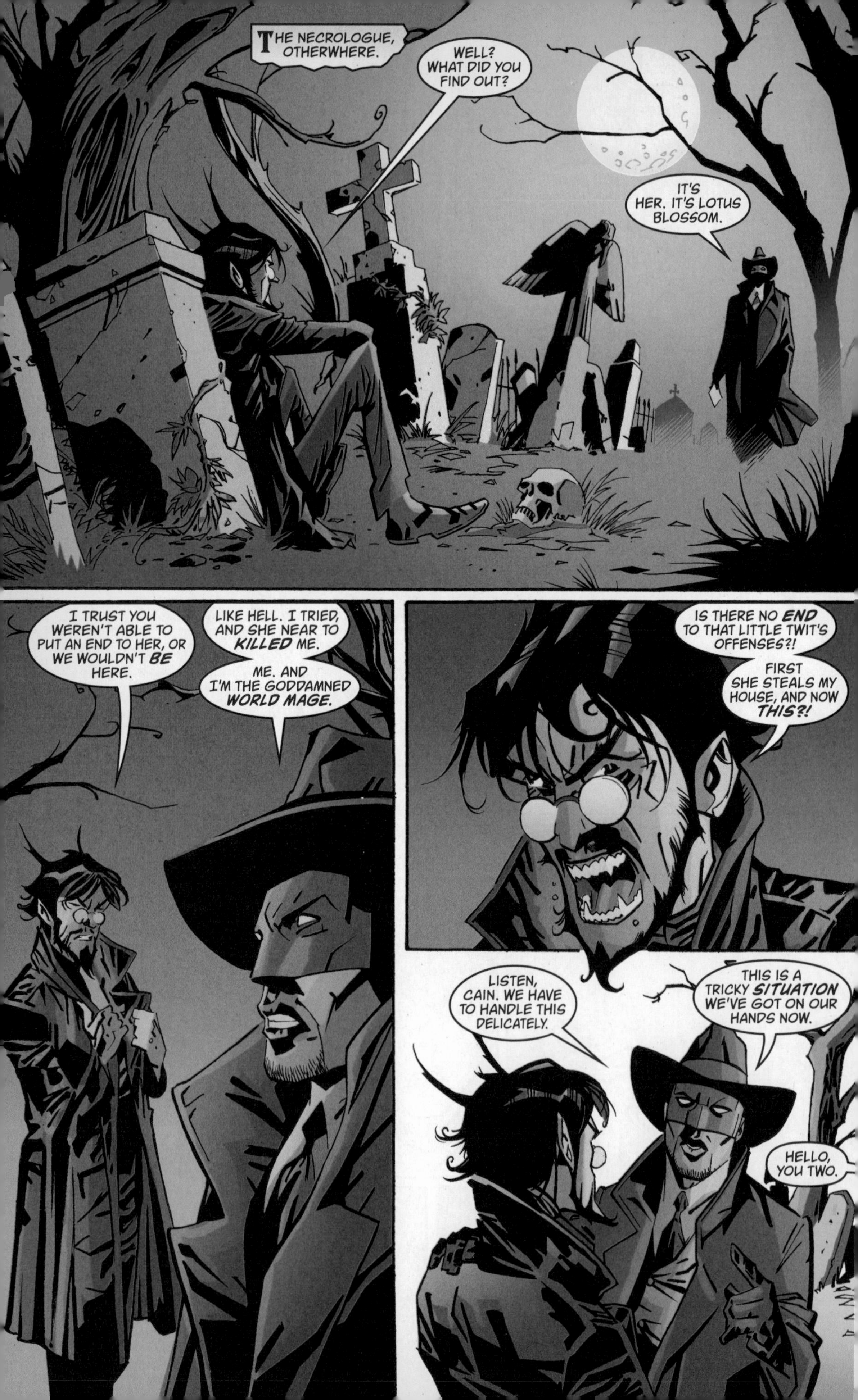
THE NECROLOGUE, OTHERWHERE.
WELL? WHAT DID YOU FIND OUT?
IT'S HER. IT'S LOTUS BLOSSOM.
I TRUST YOU WEREN'T ABLE TO PUT AN END TO HER, OR WE WOULDN'T BE HERE.
LIKE HELL. I TRIED, AND SHE NEAR TO KILLED ME.
ME. AND I'M THE GODDAMNED WORLD MAGE.
IS THERE NO END TO THAT LITTLE TWIT'S OFFENSES?!
FIRST SHE STEALS MY HOUSE, AND NOW THIS?!
LISTEN, CAIN. WE HAVE TO HANDLE THIS DELICATELY.
THIS IS A TRICKY SITUATION WE'VE GOT ON OUR HANDS NOW.
HELLO, YOU TWO.

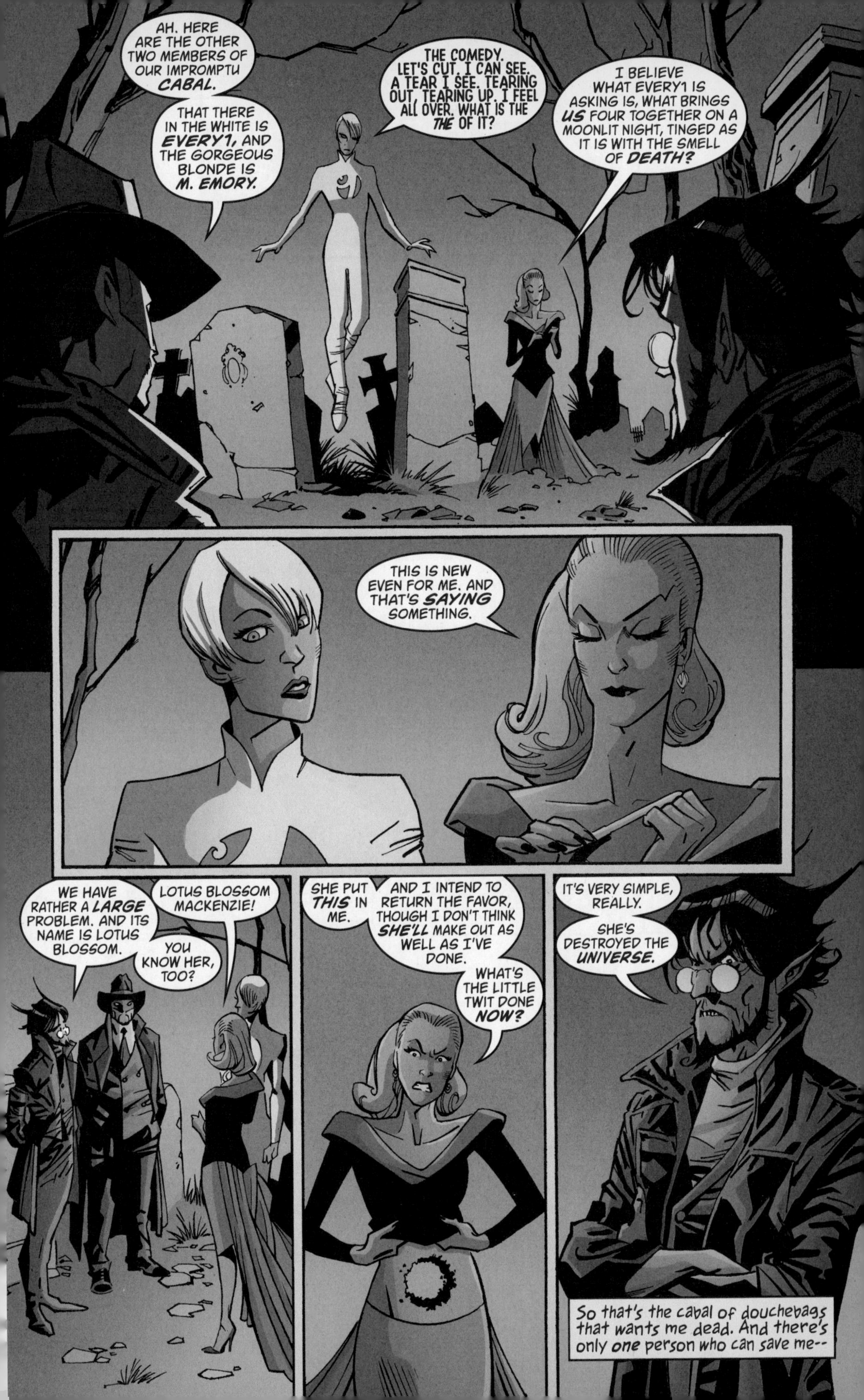
AH. HERE ARE THE OTHER TWO MEMBERS OF OUR IMPROMPTU CABAL.
THAT THERE IN THE WHITE IS EVERY1, AND THE GORGEOUS BLONDE IS M. EMORY.
THE COMEDY. LET'S CUT. I CAN SEE. A TEAR I SEE. TEARING OUT, TEARING UP. I FEEL ALL OVER. WHAT IS THE THE OF IT?
I BELIEVE WHAT EVERY1 IS ASKING IS, WHAT BRINGS US FOUR TOGETHER ON A MOONLIT NIGHT, TINGED AS IT IS WITH THE SMELL OF DEATH?
THIS IS NEW EVEN FOR ME. AND THAT'S SAYING SOMETHING.
WE HAVE RATHER A LARGE PROBLEM. AND ITS NAME IS LOTUS BLOSSOM.
LOTUS BLOSSOM MACKENZIE!
YOU KNOW HER, TOO?
SHE PUT THIS IN ME.
AND I INTEND TO RETURN THE FAVOR, THOUGH I DON'T THINK SHE'LL MAKE OUT AS WELL AS I'VE DONE.
WHAT'S THE LITTLE TWIT DONE NOW?
IT'S VERY SIMPLE, REALLY.
SHE'S DESTROYED THE UNIVERSE.
So that's the cabal of douchebags that wants me dead. And there's only one person who can save me--

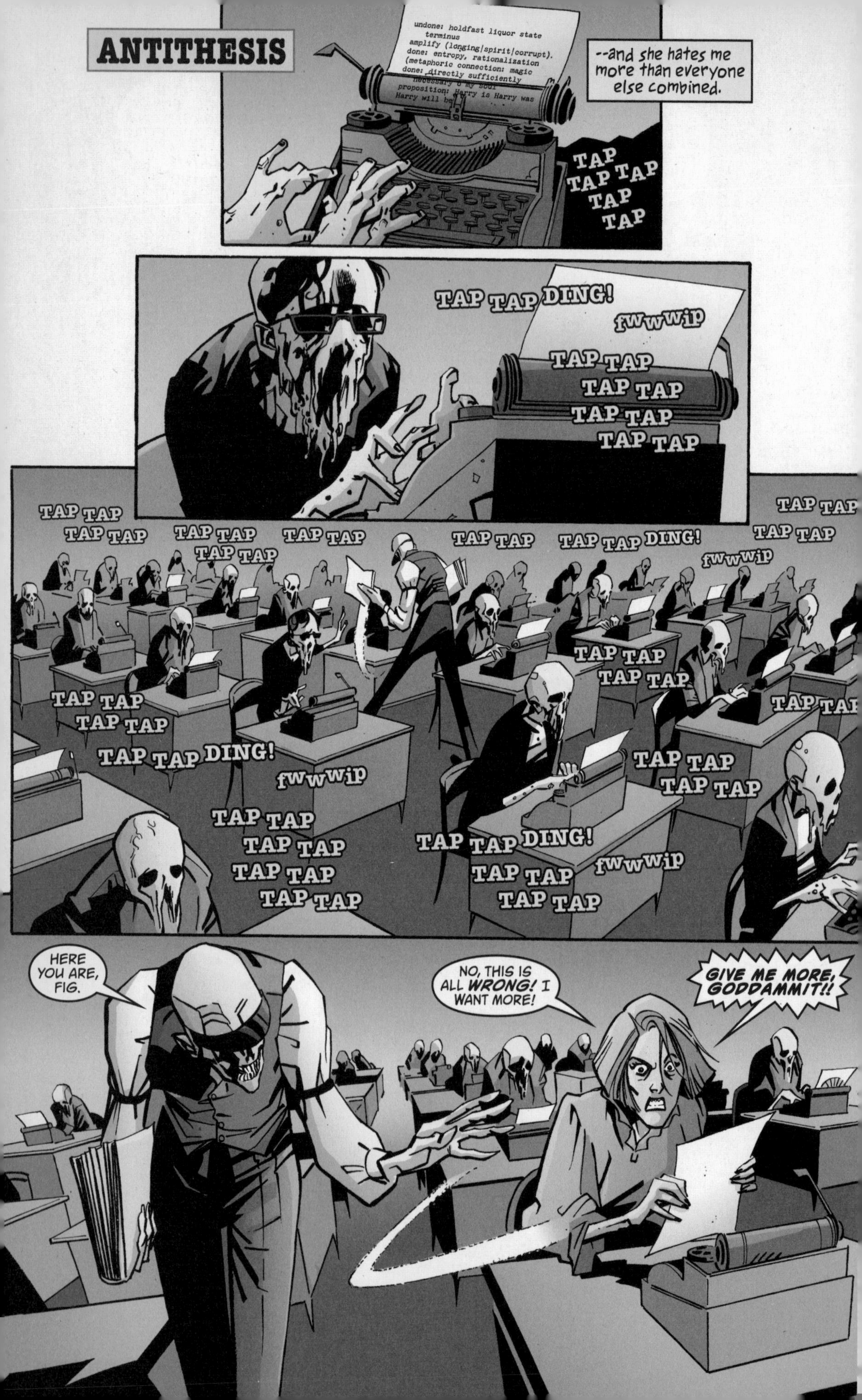
ANTITHESIS
undone: holdfast liquor state
terminus
amplify (longing|spirit|corrupt).
done: entropy, rationalization
(metaphoric connection: magic
done: directly sufficiently
necessary o my soul
proposition: Harry is Harry was
Harry will be . . .
--and she hates me more than everyone else combined.
TAP
TAP TAP
TAP
TAP
TAP TAP DING!
fwwwip
TAP TAP
TAP TAP
TAP TAP
TAP TAP
TAP TAP
TAP TAP
TAP TAP
TAP TAP
TAP TAP
TAP TAP
TAP TAP
TAP TAP
TAP TAP DING!
TAP TAP
TAP TAP
fwwwip
TAP TAP
TAP TAP
TAP TAP
TAP TAP
TAP TAP DING!
fwwwip
TAP TAP
TAP TAP
TAP TAP
TAP TAP
TAP TAP DING!
fwwwip
TAP TAP
TAP TAP
TAP TAP
TAP TAP
HERE YOU ARE, FIG.
NO, THIS IS ALL WRONG! I WANT MORE!
GIVE ME MORE, GODDAMMIT!!

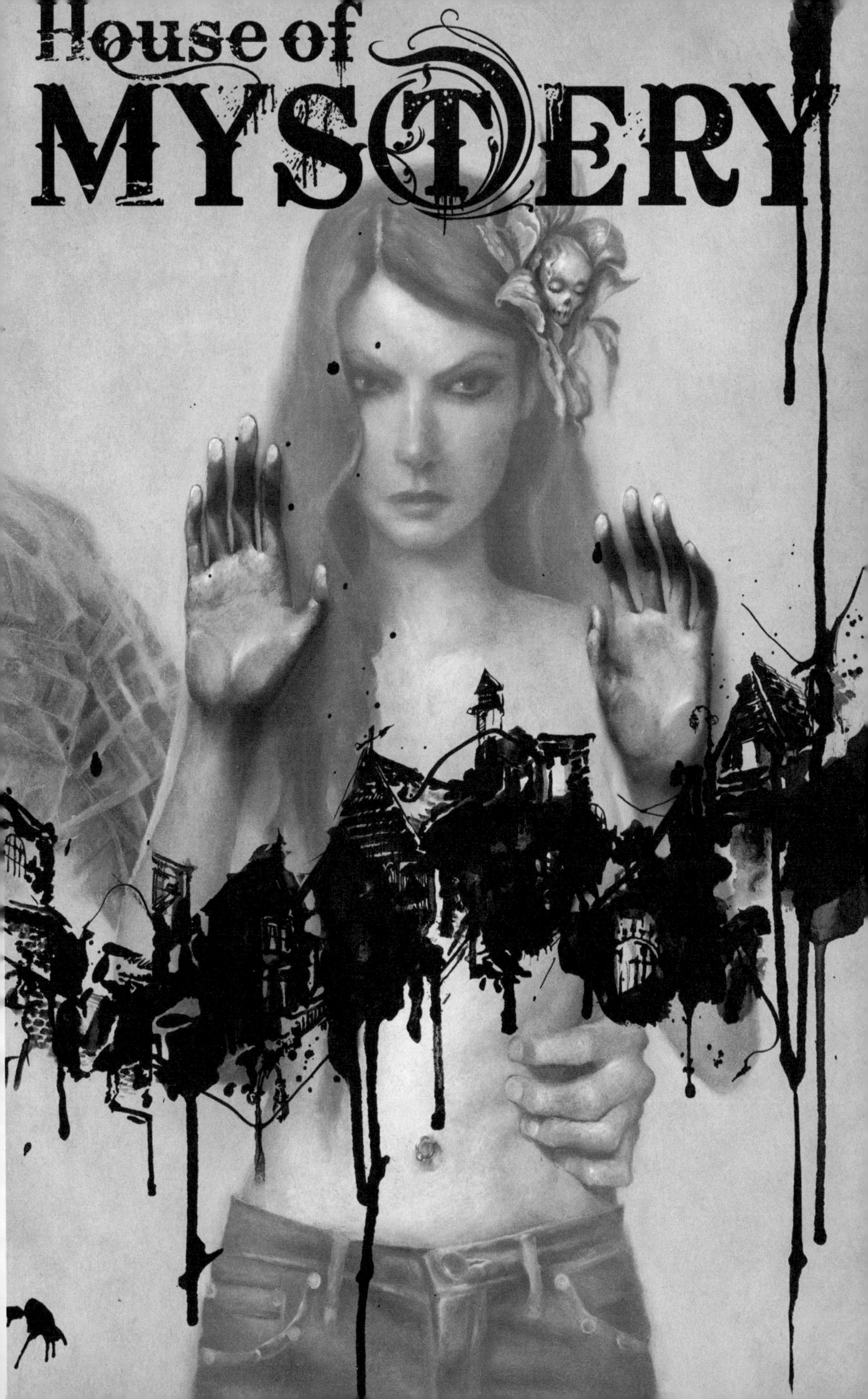
House of
MYSTERY

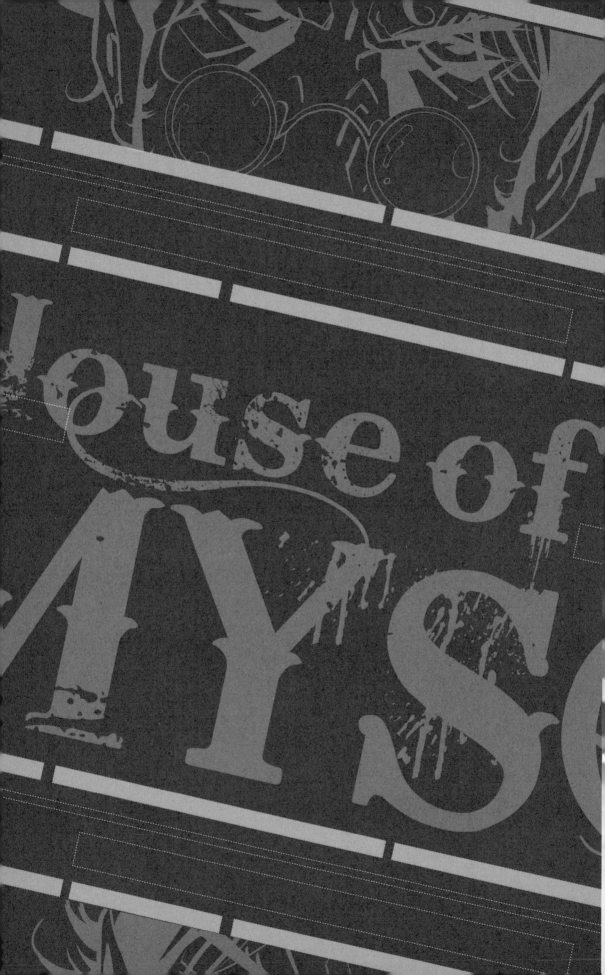

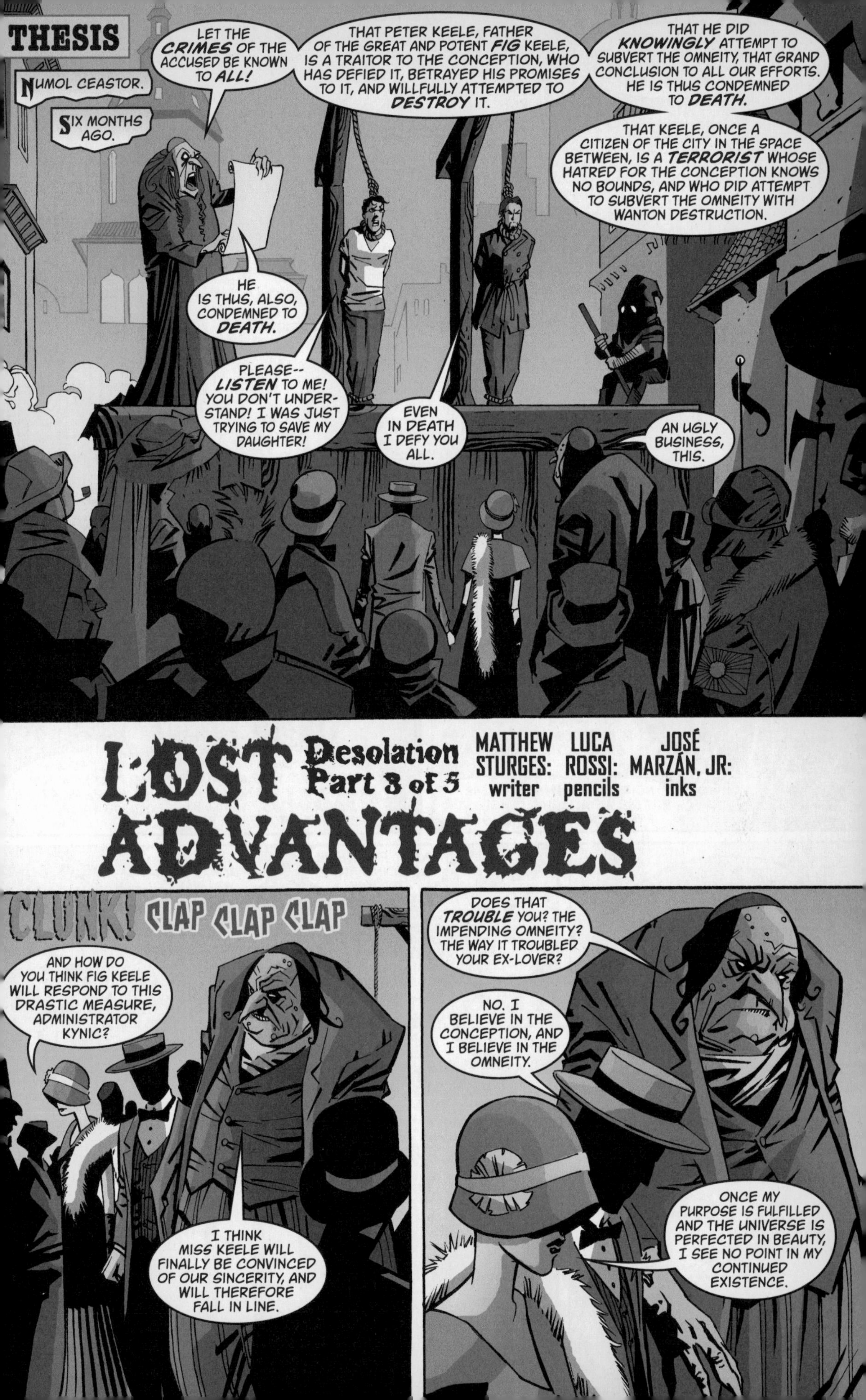
THESIS
NUMOL CEASTOR.
SIX MONTHS AGO.
LET THE CRIMES OF THE ACCUSED BE KNOWN TO ALL!
THAT PETER KEELE, FATHER OF THE GREAT AND POTENT FIG KEELE, IS A TRAITOR TO THE CONCEPTION, WHO HAS DEFIED IT, BETRAYED HIS PROMISES TO IT, AND WILLFULLY ATTEMPTED TO DESTROY IT.
THAT HE DID KNOWINGLY ATTEMPT TO SUBVERT THE OMNEITY, THAT GRAND CONCLUSION TO ALL OUR EFFORTS. HE IS THUS CONDEMNED TO DEATH.
THAT KEELE, ONCE A CITIZEN OF THE CITY IN THE SPACE BETWEEN, IS A TERRORIST WHOSE HATRED FOR THE CONCEPTION KNOWS NO BOUNDS, AND WHO DID ATTEMPT TO SUBVERT THE OMNEITY WITH WANTON DESTRUCTION.
HE IS THUS, ALSO, CONDEMNED TO DEATH.
PLEASE-- LISTEN TO ME! YOU DON'T UNDERSTAND! I WAS JUST TRYING TO SAVE MY DAUGHTER!
EVEN IN DEATH I DEFY YOU ALL.
AN UGLY BUSINESS, THIS.
LOST ADVANTAGES
Desolation Part 3 of 5
MATTHEW STURGES: writer
LUCA ROSSI: pencils
JOSÉ MARZÁN, JR: inks
CLUNK! CLAP CLAP CLAP
AND HOW DO YOU THINK FIG KEELE WILL RESPOND TO THIS DRASTIC MEASURE, ADMINISTRATOR KYNIC?
I THINK MISS KEELE WILL FINALLY BE CONVINCED OF OUR SINCERITY, AND WILL THEREFORE FALL IN LINE.
DOES THAT TROUBLE YOU? THE IMPENDING OMNEITY? THE WAY IT TROUBLED YOUR EX-LOVER?
NO. I BELIEVE IN THE CONCEPTION, AND I BELIEVE IN THE OMNEITY.
ONCE MY PURPOSE IS FULFILLED AND THE UNIVERSE IS PERFECTED IN BEAUTY, I SEE NO POINT IN MY CONTINUED EXISTENCE.

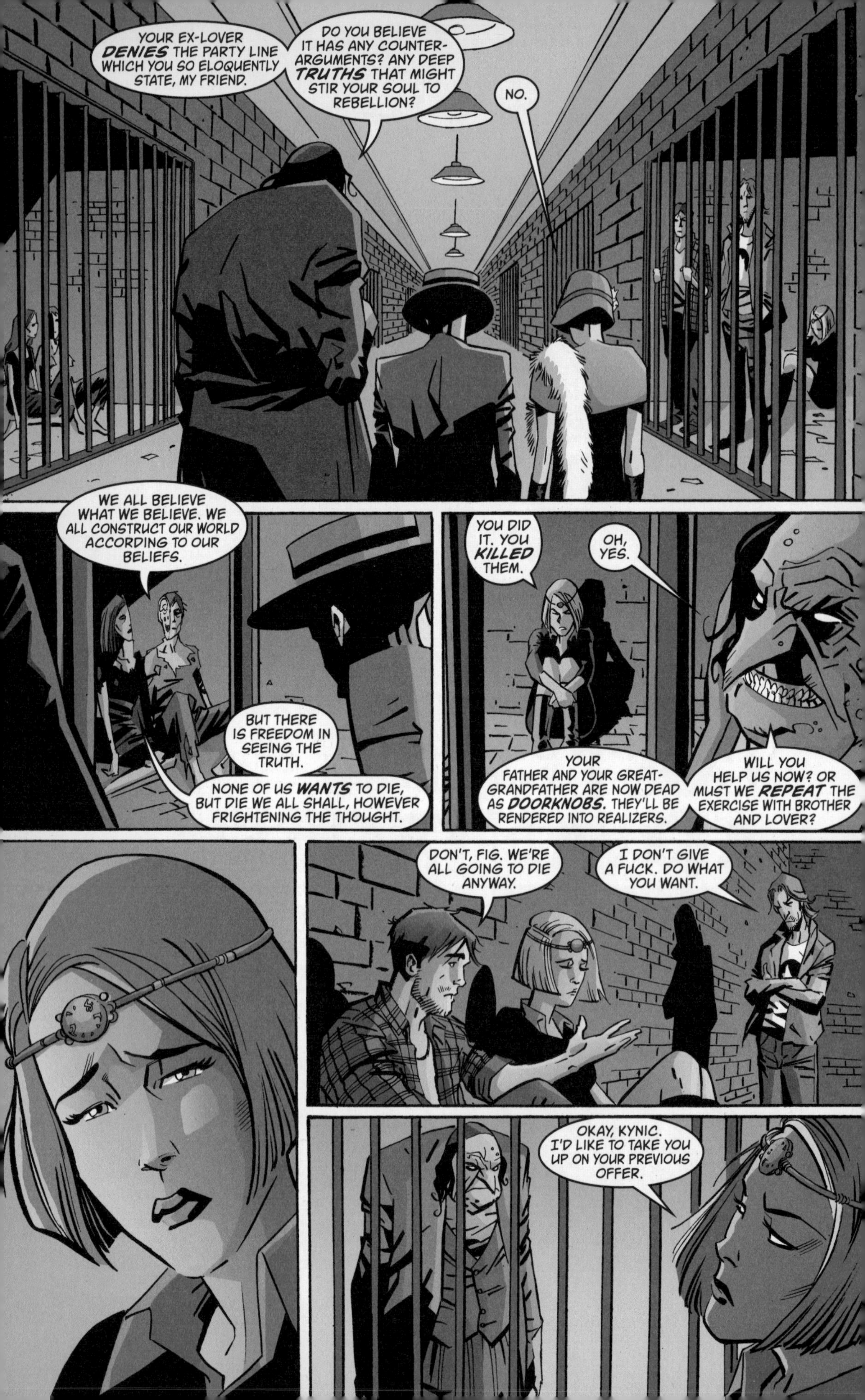
YOUR EX-LOVER DENIES THE PARTY LINE WHICH YOU SO ELOQUENTLY STATE, MY FRIEND.
DO YOU BELIEVE IT HAS ANY COUNTER-ARGUMENTS? ANY DEEP TRUTHS THAT MIGHT STIR YOUR SOUL TO REBELLION?
NO.
WE ALL BELIEVE WHAT WE BELIEVE. WE ALL CONSTRUCT OUR WORLD ACCORDING TO OUR BELIEFS.
BUT THERE IS FREEDOM IN SEEING THE TRUTH.
NONE OF US WANTS TO DIE, BUT DIE WE ALL SHALL, HOWEVER FRIGHTENING THE THOUGHT.
YOU DID IT. YOU KILLED THEM.
OH, YES.
YOUR FATHER AND YOUR GREAT-GRANDFATHER ARE NOW DEAD AS DOORKNOBS. THEY'LL BE RENDERED INTO REALIZERS.
WILL YOU HELP US NOW? OR MUST WE REPEAT THE EXERCISE WITH BROTHER AND LOVER?
DON'T, FIG. WE'RE ALL GOING TO DIE ANYWAY.
I DON'T GIVE A FUCK. DO WHAT YOU WANT.
OKAY, KYNIC. I'D LIKE TO TAKE YOU UP ON YOUR PREVIOUS OFFER.

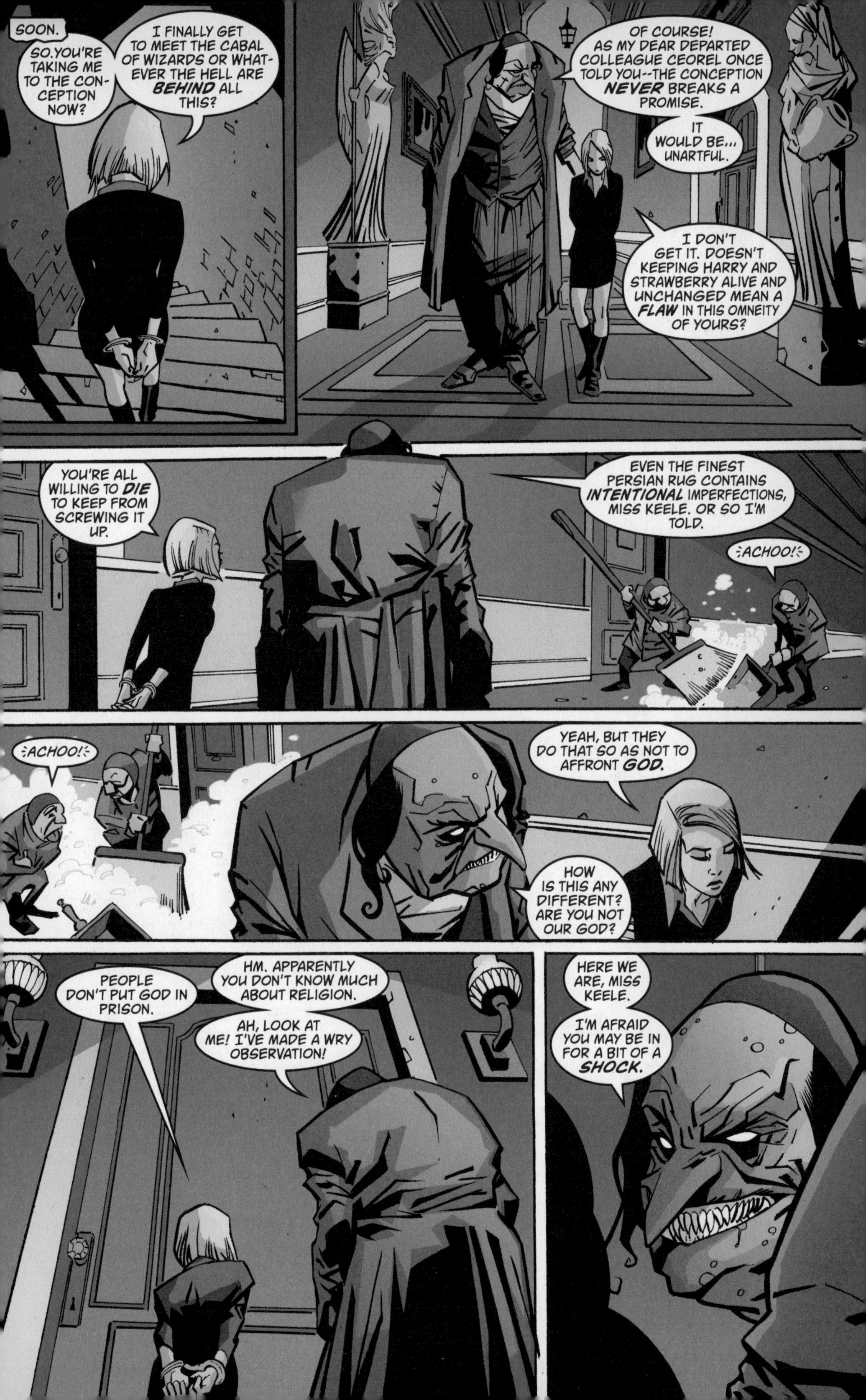
SOON.
SO.YOU'RE TAKING ME TO THE CONCEPTION NOW?
I FINALLY GET TO MEET THE CABAL OF WIZARDS OR WHATEVER THE HELL ARE BEHIND ALL THIS?
OF COURSE! AS MY DEAR DEPARTED COLLEAGUE CEOREL ONCE TOLD YOU--THE CONCEPTION NEVER BREAKS A PROMISE.
IT WOULD BE... UNARTFUL.
I DON'T GET IT. DOESN'T KEEPING HARRY AND STRAWBERRY ALIVE AND UNCHANGED MEAN A FLAW IN THIS OMNEITY OF YOURS?
YOU'RE ALL WILLING TO DIE TO KEEP FROM SCREWING IT UP.
EVEN THE FINEST PERSIAN RUG CONTAINS INTENTIONAL IMPERFECTIONS, MISS KEELE. OR SO I'M TOLD.
ACHOO!
ACHOO!
YEAH, BUT THEY DO THAT SO AS NOT TO AFFRONT GOD.
HOW IS THIS ANY DIFFERENT? ARE YOU NOT OUR GOD?
PEOPLE DON'T PUT GOD IN PRISON.
HM. APPARENTLY YOU DON'T KNOW MUCH ABOUT RELIGION.
AH, LOOK AT ME! I'VE MADE A WRY OBSERVATION!
HERE WE ARE, MISS KEELE.
I'M AFRAID YOU MAY BE IN FOR A BIT OF A SHOCK.

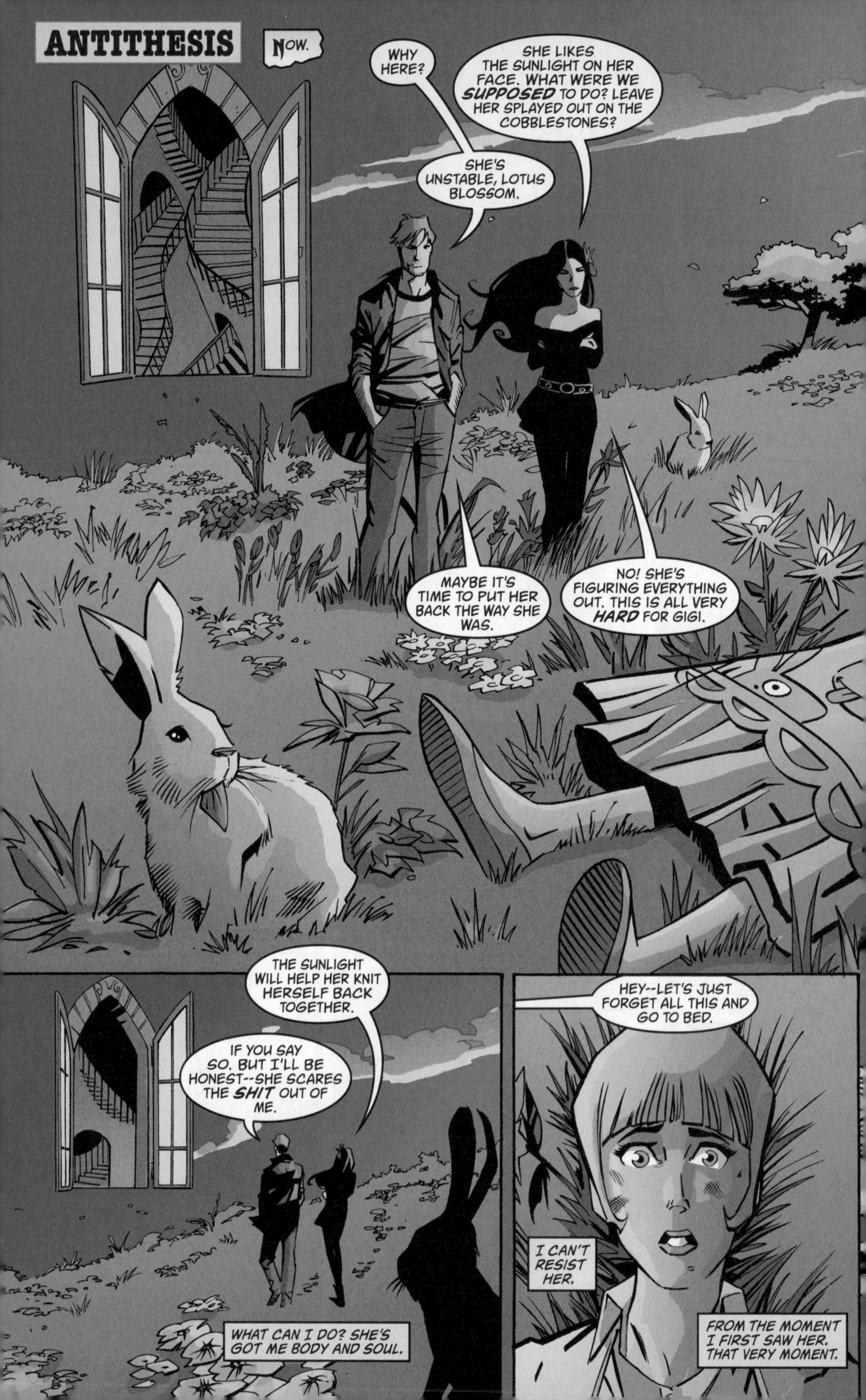
ANTITHESIS
NOW.
WHY HERE?
SHE LIKES THE SUNLIGHT ON HER FACE. WHAT WERE WE SUPPOSED TO DO? LEAVE HER SPLAYED OUT ON THE COBBLESTONES?
SHE'S UNSTABLE, LOTUS BLOSSOM.
MAYBE IT'S TIME TO PUT HER BACK THE WAY SHE WAS.
NO! SHE'S FIGURING EVERYTHING OUT. THIS IS ALL VERY HARD FOR GIGI.
THE SUNLIGHT WILL HELP HER KNIT HERSELF BACK TOGETHER.
IF YOU SAY SO. BUT I'LL BE HONEST--SHE SCARES THE SHIT OUT OF ME.
WHAT CAN I DO? SHE'S GOT ME BODY AND SOUL.
HEY--LET'S JUST FORGET ALL THIS AND GO TO BED.
I CAN'T RESIST HER.
FROM THE MOMENT I FIRST SAW HER. THAT VERY MOMENT.

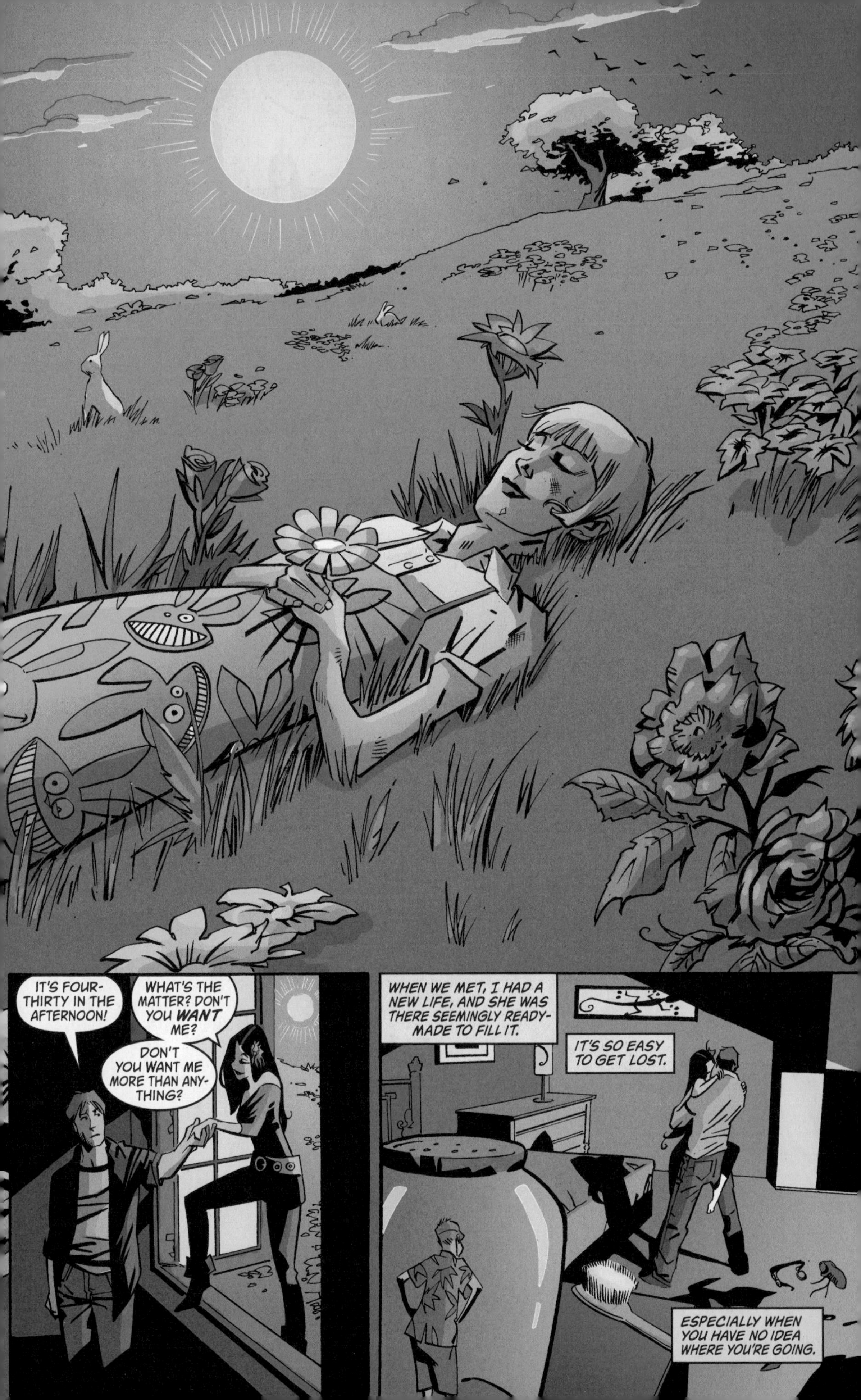

IT'S FOUR-THIRTY IN THE AFTERNOON!
WHAT'S THE MATTER? DON'T YOU WANT ME?
DON'T YOU WANT ME MORE THAN ANYTHING?
WHEN WE MET, I HAD A NEW LIFE, AND SHE WAS THERE SEEMINGLY READY-MADE TO FILL IT.
IT'S SO EASY TO GET LOST.
ESPECIALLY WHEN YOU HAVE NO IDEA WHERE YOU'RE GOING.

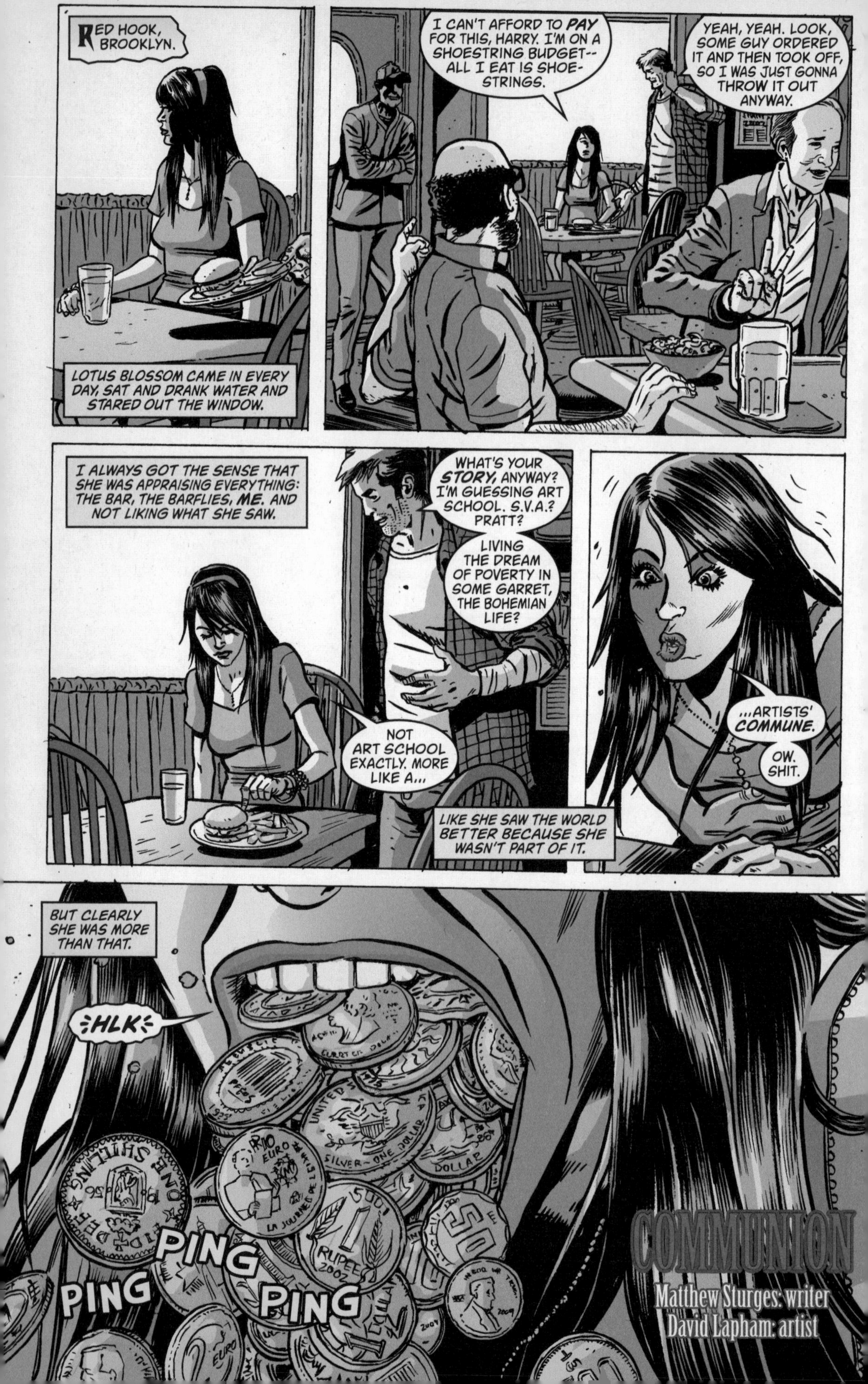
RED HOOK, BROOKLYN.
LOTUS BLOSSOM CAME IN EVERY DAY, SAT AND DRANK WATER AND STARED OUT THE WINDOW.
I CAN'T AFFORD TO PAY FOR THIS, HARRY. I'M ON A SHOESTRING BUDGET-- ALL I EAT IS SHOE-STRINGS.
YEAH, YEAH. LOOK, SOME GUY ORDERED IT AND THEN TOOK OFF, SO I WAS JUST GONNA THROW IT OUT ANYWAY.
I ALWAYS GOT THE SENSE THAT SHE WAS APPRAISING EVERYTHING: THE BAR, THE BARFLIES, ME. AND NOT LIKING WHAT SHE SAW.
WHAT'S YOUR STORY, ANYWAY? I'M GUESSING ART SCHOOL. S.V.A.? PRATT?
LIVING THE DREAM OF POVERTY IN SOME GARRET, THE BOHEMIAN LIFE?
NOT ART SCHOOL EXACTLY. MORE LIKE A...
LIKE SHE SAW THE WORLD BETTER BECAUSE SHE WASN'T PART OF IT.
...ARTISTS' COMMUNE.
OW. SHIT.
BUT CLEARLY SHE WAS MORE THAN THAT.
HLK
PING PING PING PING
COMMUNION
Matthew Sturges: writer
David Lapham: artist

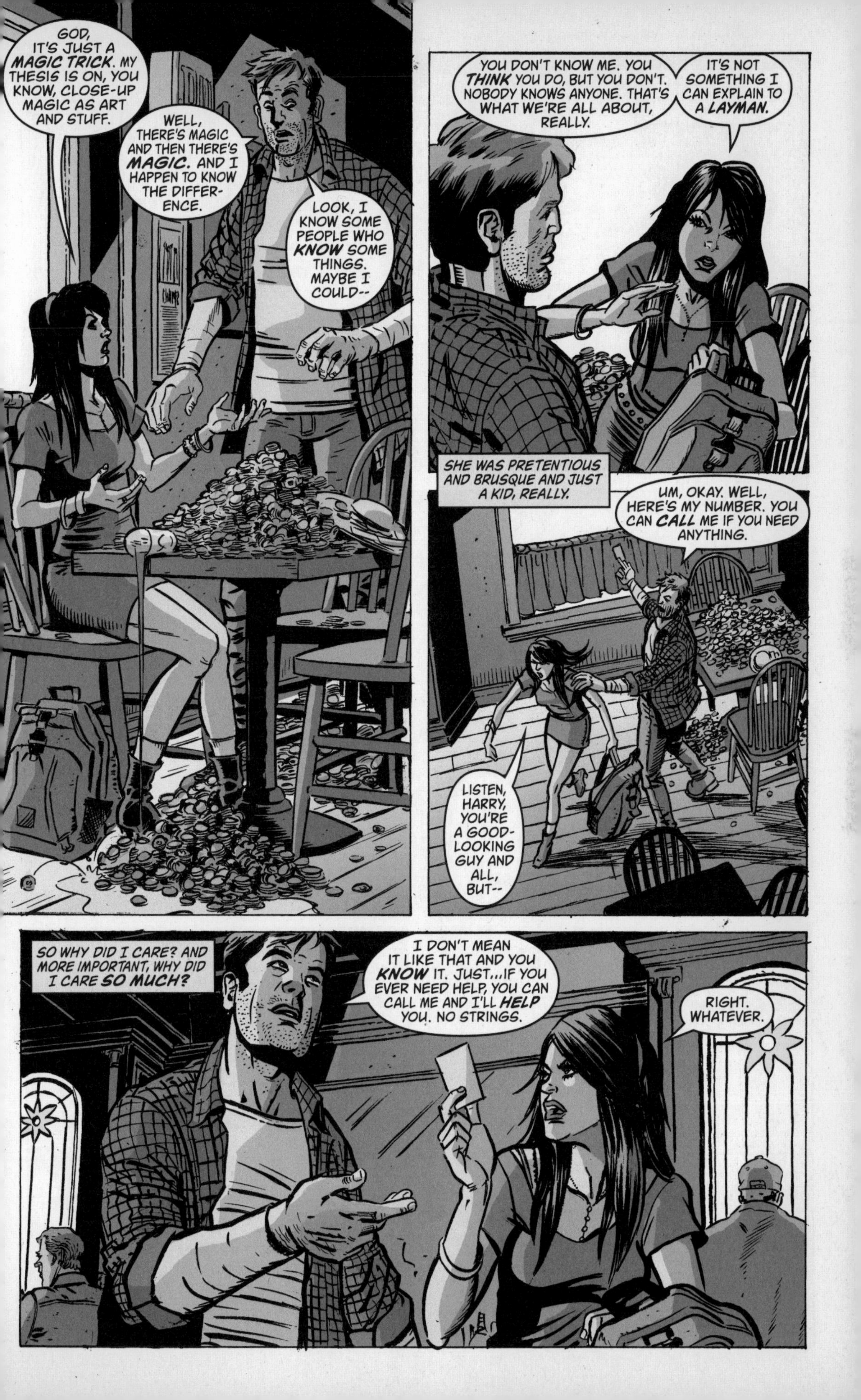
GOD, IT'S JUST A MAGIC TRICK. MY THESIS IS ON, YOU KNOW, CLOSE-UP MAGIC AS ART AND STUFF.
WELL, THERE'S MAGIC AND THEN THERE'S MAGIC. AND I HAPPEN TO KNOW THE DIFFERENCE.
LOOK, I KNOW SOME PEOPLE WHO KNOW SOME THINGS. MAYBE I COULD--
YOU DON'T KNOW ME. YOU THINK YOU DO, BUT YOU DON'T. NOBODY KNOWS ANYONE. THAT'S WHAT WE'RE ALL ABOUT, REALLY.
IT'S NOT SOMETHING I CAN EXPLAIN TO A LAYMAN.
SHE WAS PRETENTIOUS AND BRUSQUE AND JUST A KID, REALLY.
UM, OKAY. WELL, HERE'S MY NUMBER. YOU CAN CALL ME IF YOU NEED ANYTHING.
LISTEN, HARRY, YOU'RE A GOOD-LOOKING GUY AND ALL, BUT--
SO WHY DID I CARE? AND MORE IMPORTANT, WHY DID I CARE SO MUCH?
I DON'T MEAN IT LIKE THAT AND YOU KNOW IT. JUST...IF YOU EVER NEED HELP, YOU CAN CALL ME AND I'LL HELP YOU. NO STRINGS.
RIGHT. WHATEVER.

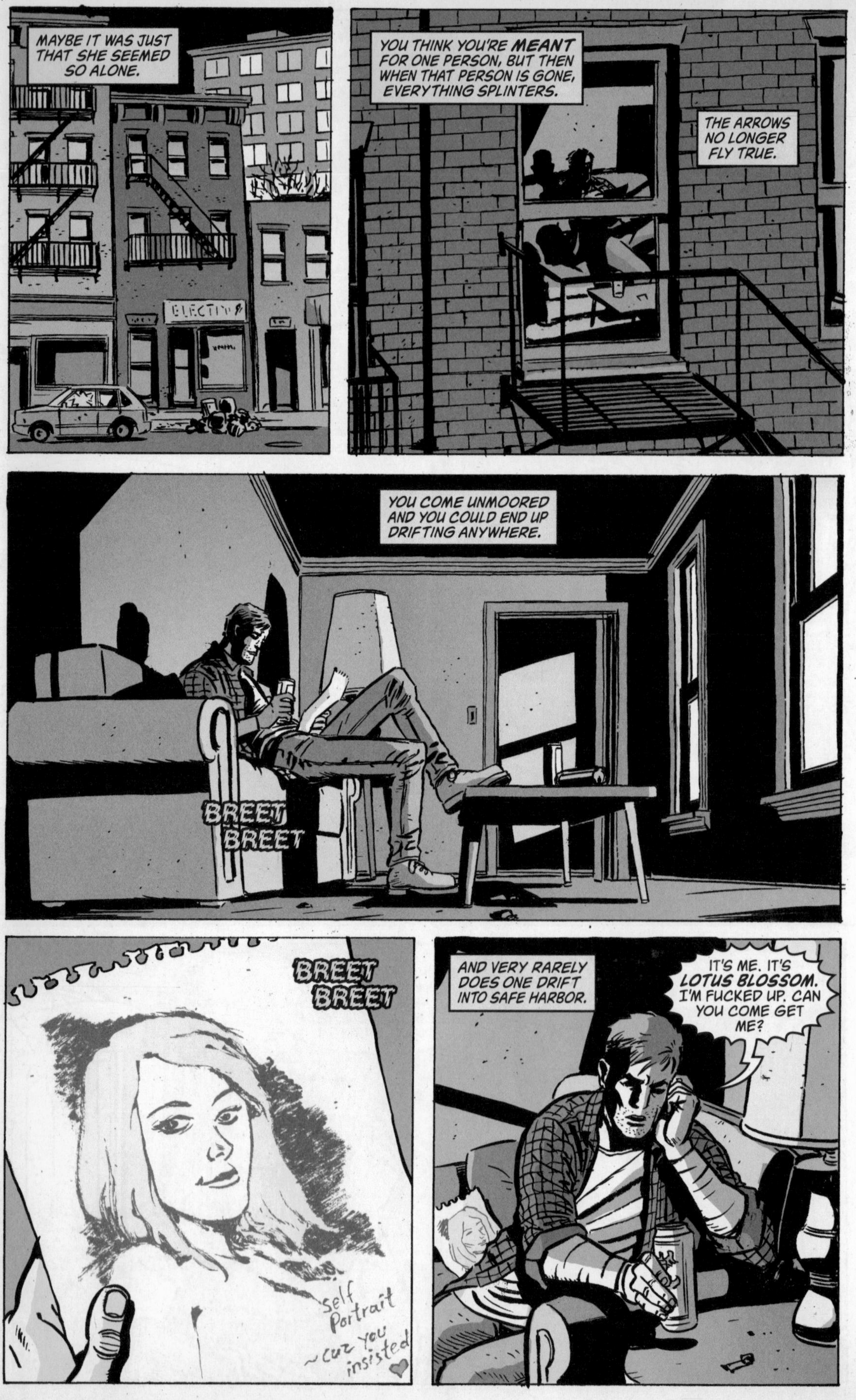
MAYBE IT WAS JUST THAT SHE SEEMED SO ALONE.
ELECTR
YOU THINK YOU'RE MEANT FOR ONE PERSON, BUT THEN WHEN THAT PERSON IS GONE, EVERYTHING SPLINTERS.
THE ARROWS NO LONGER FLY TRUE.
YOU COME UNMOORED AND YOU COULD END UP DRIFTING ANYWHERE.
BREET BREET
BREET BREET
Self Portrait ~cuz you insisted
AND VERY RARELY DOES ONE DRIFT INTO SAFE HARBOR.
IT'S ME. IT'S LOTUS BLOSSOM. I'M FUCKED UP. CAN YOU COME GET ME?

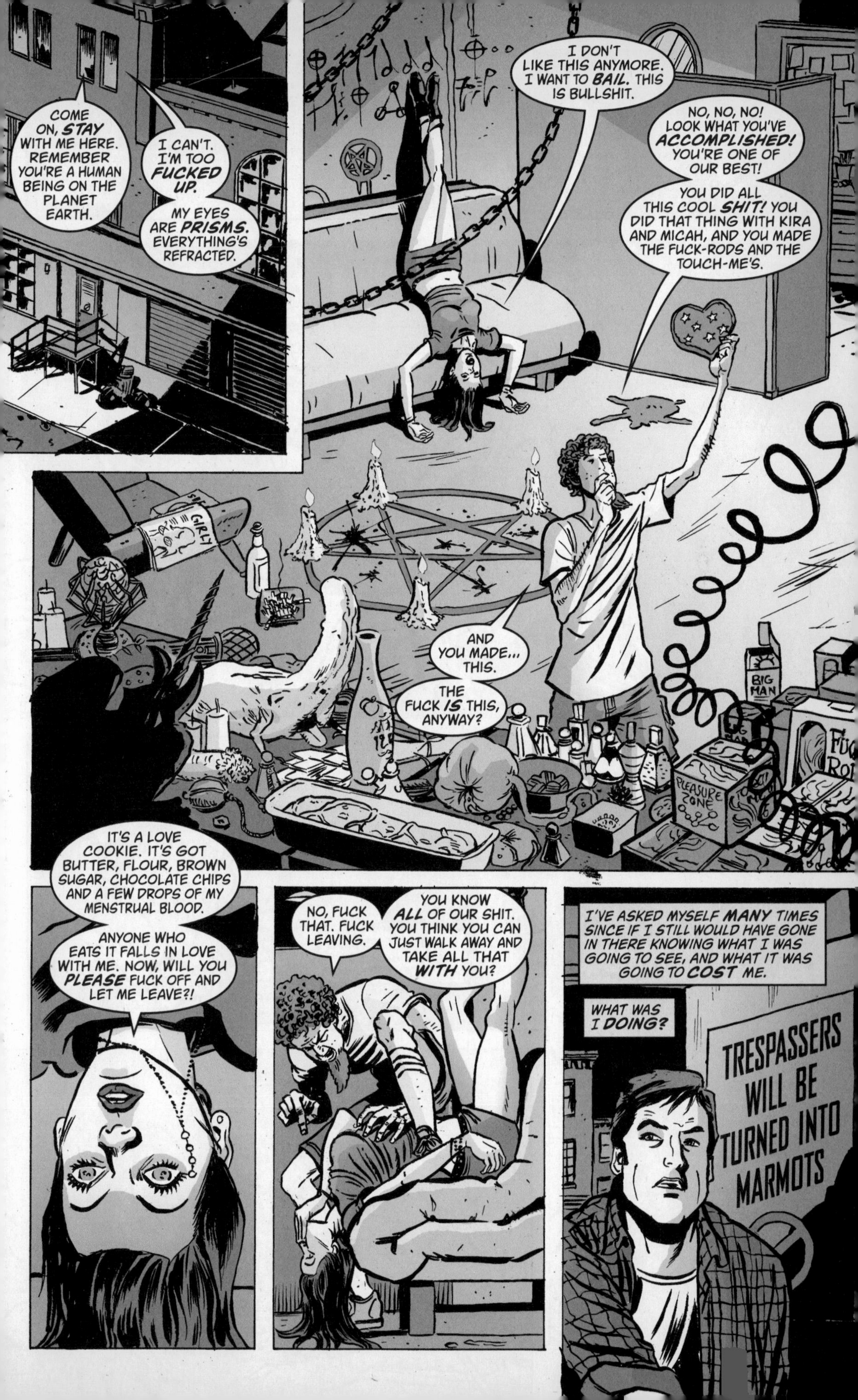
COME ON, STAY WITH ME HERE. REMEMBER YOU'RE A HUMAN BEING ON THE PLANET EARTH.
I CAN'T. I'M TOO FUCKED UP.
MY EYES ARE PRISMS. EVERYTHING'S REFRACTED.
I DON'T LIKE THIS ANYMORE. I WANT TO BAIL. THIS IS BULLSHIT.
NO, NO, NO! LOOK WHAT YOU'VE ACCOMPLISHED! YOU'RE ONE OF OUR BEST!
YOU DID ALL THIS COOL SHIT! YOU DID THAT THING WITH KIRA AND MICAH, AND YOU MADE THE FUCK-RODS AND THE TOUCH-ME'S.
GIRLY
AND YOU MADE... THIS.
THE FUCK IS THIS, ANYWAY?
BIG MAN
PLEASURE ZONE
IT'S A LOVE COOKIE. IT'S GOT BUTTER, FLOUR, BROWN SUGAR, CHOCOLATE CHIPS AND A FEW DROPS OF MY MENSTRUAL BLOOD.
ANYONE WHO EATS IT FALLS IN LOVE WITH ME. NOW, WILL YOU PLEASE FUCK OFF AND LET ME LEAVE?!
NO, FUCK THAT. FUCK LEAVING.
YOU KNOW ALL OF OUR SHIT. YOU THINK YOU CAN JUST WALK AWAY AND TAKE ALL THAT WITH YOU?
I'VE ASKED MYSELF MANY TIMES SINCE IF I STILL WOULD HAVE GONE IN THERE KNOWING WHAT I WAS GOING TO SEE, AND WHAT IT WAS GOING TO COST ME.
WHAT WAS I DOING?
TRESPASSERS WILL BE TURNED INTO MARMOTS

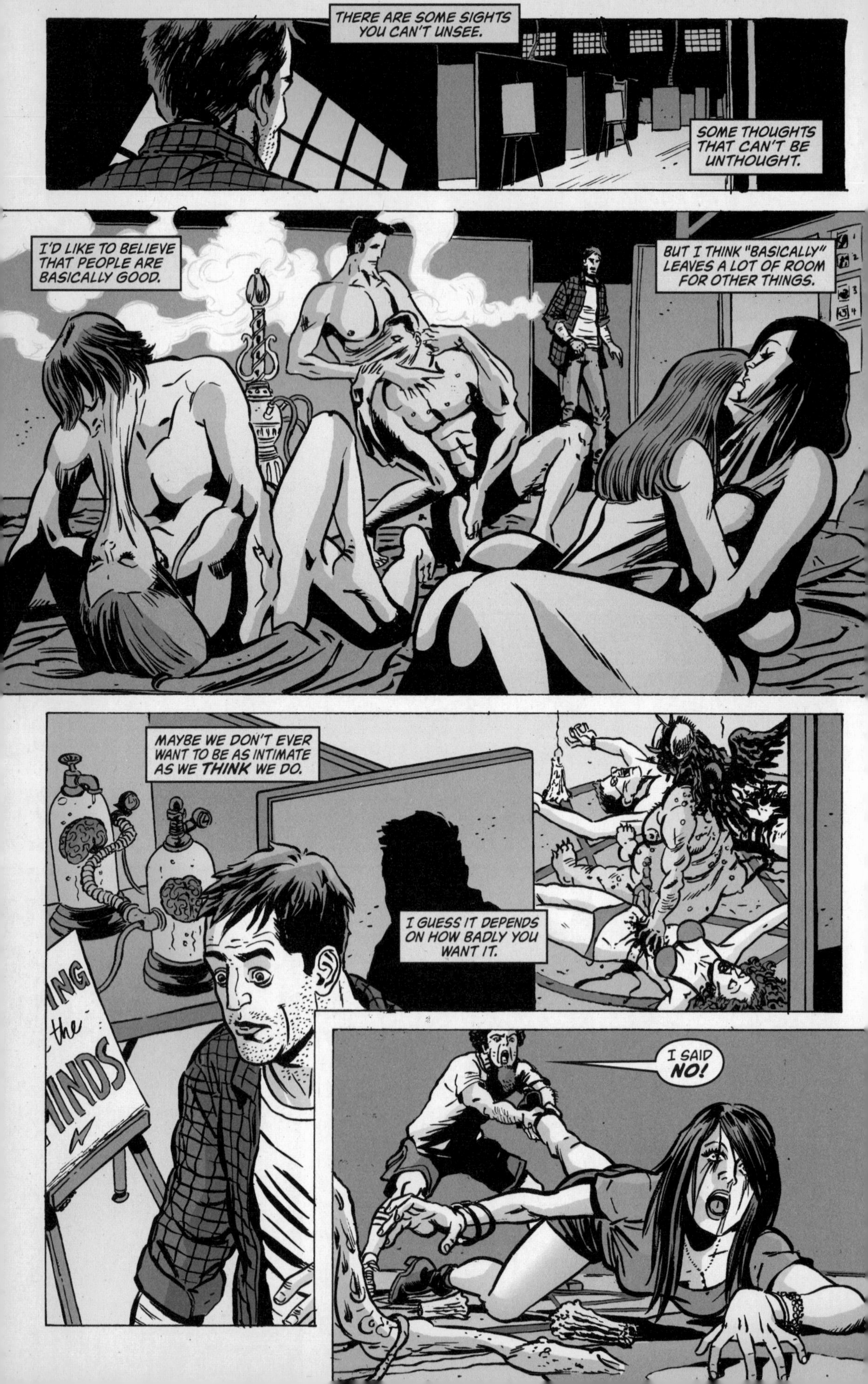
THERE ARE SOME SIGHTS YOU CAN'T UNSEE.
SOME THOUGHTS THAT CAN'T BE UNTHOUGHT.
I'D LIKE TO BELIEVE THAT PEOPLE ARE BASICALLY GOOD.
BUT I THINK "BASICALLY" LEAVES A LOT OF ROOM FOR OTHER THINGS.
MAYBE WE DON'T EVER WANT TO BE AS INTIMATE AS WE THINK WE DO.
I GUESS IT DEPENDS ON HOW BADLY YOU WANT IT.
I SAID NO!

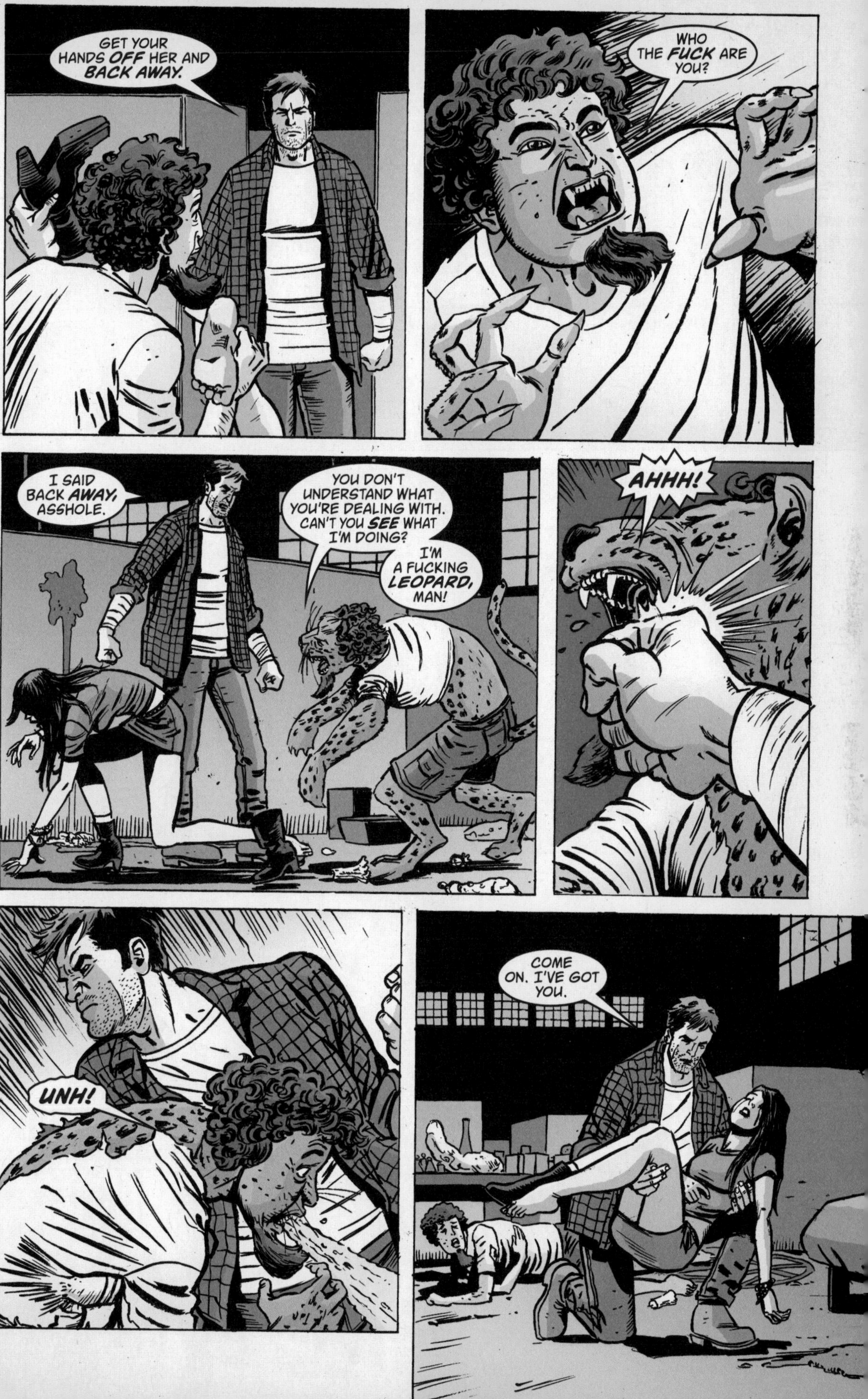
GET YOUR HANDS OFF HER AND BACK AWAY.
WHO THE FUCK ARE YOU?
I SAID BACK AWAY, ASSHOLE.
YOU DON'T UNDERSTAND WHAT YOU'RE DEALING WITH. CAN'T YOU SEE WHAT I'M DOING?
I'M A FUCKING LEOPARD, MAN!
AHHH!
UNH!
COME ON. I'VE GOT YOU.

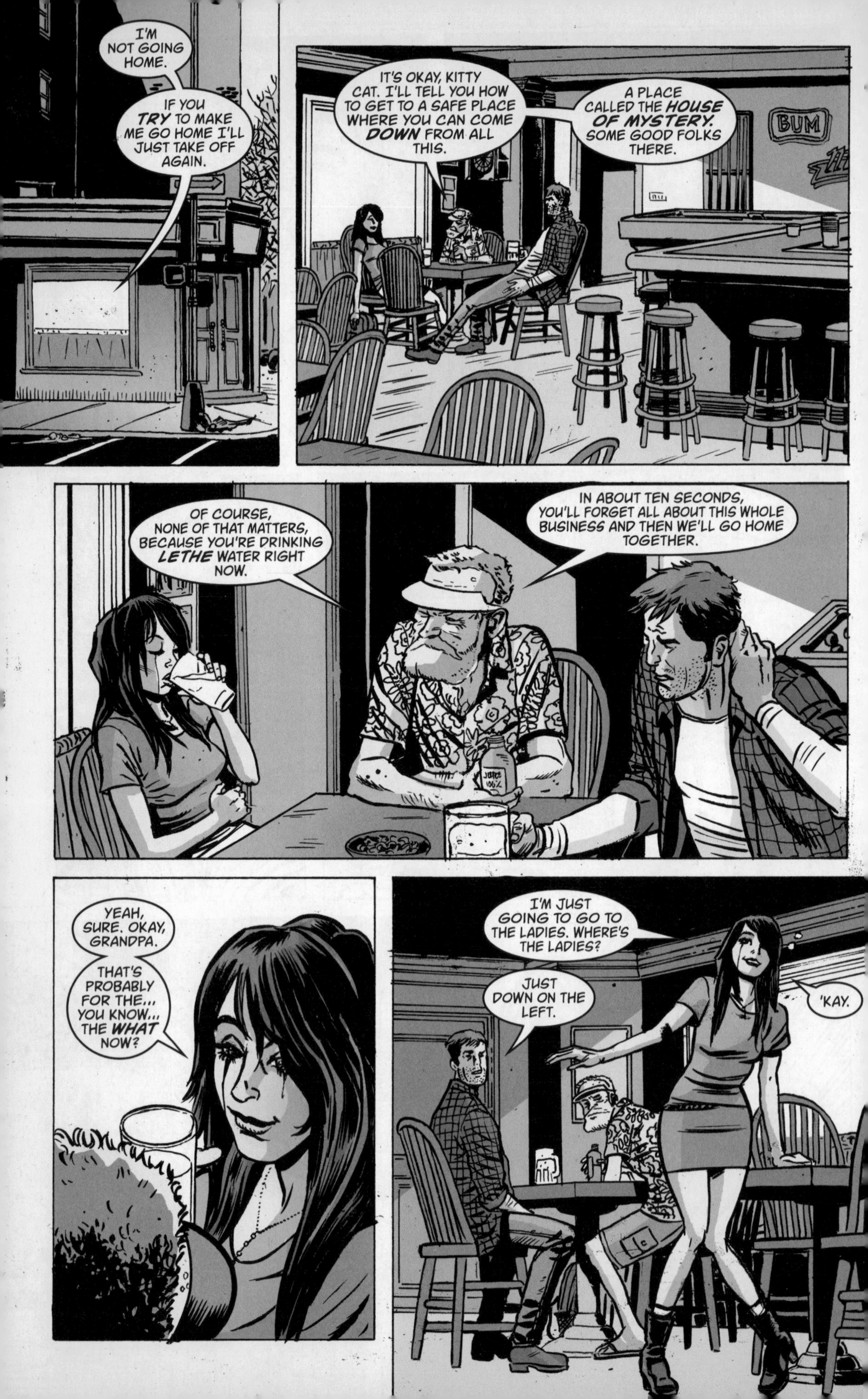
I'M NOT GOING HOME.
IF YOU TRY TO MAKE ME GO HOME I'LL JUST TAKE OFF AGAIN.
IT'S OKAY, KITTY CAT. I'LL TELL YOU HOW TO GET TO A SAFE PLACE WHERE YOU CAN COME DOWN FROM ALL THIS.
A PLACE CALLED THE HOUSE OF MYSTERY. SOME GOOD FOLKS THERE.
BUM
OF COURSE, NONE OF THAT MATTERS, BECAUSE YOU'RE DRINKING LETHE WATER RIGHT NOW.
IN ABOUT TEN SECONDS, YOU'LL FORGET ALL ABOUT THIS WHOLE BUSINESS AND THEN WE'LL GO HOME TOGETHER.
YEAH, SURE. OKAY, GRANDPA.
THAT'S PROBABLY FOR THE... YOU KNOW... THE WHAT NOW?
I'M JUST GOING TO GO TO THE LADIES. WHERE'S THE LADIES?
JUST DOWN ON THE LEFT.
'KAY.

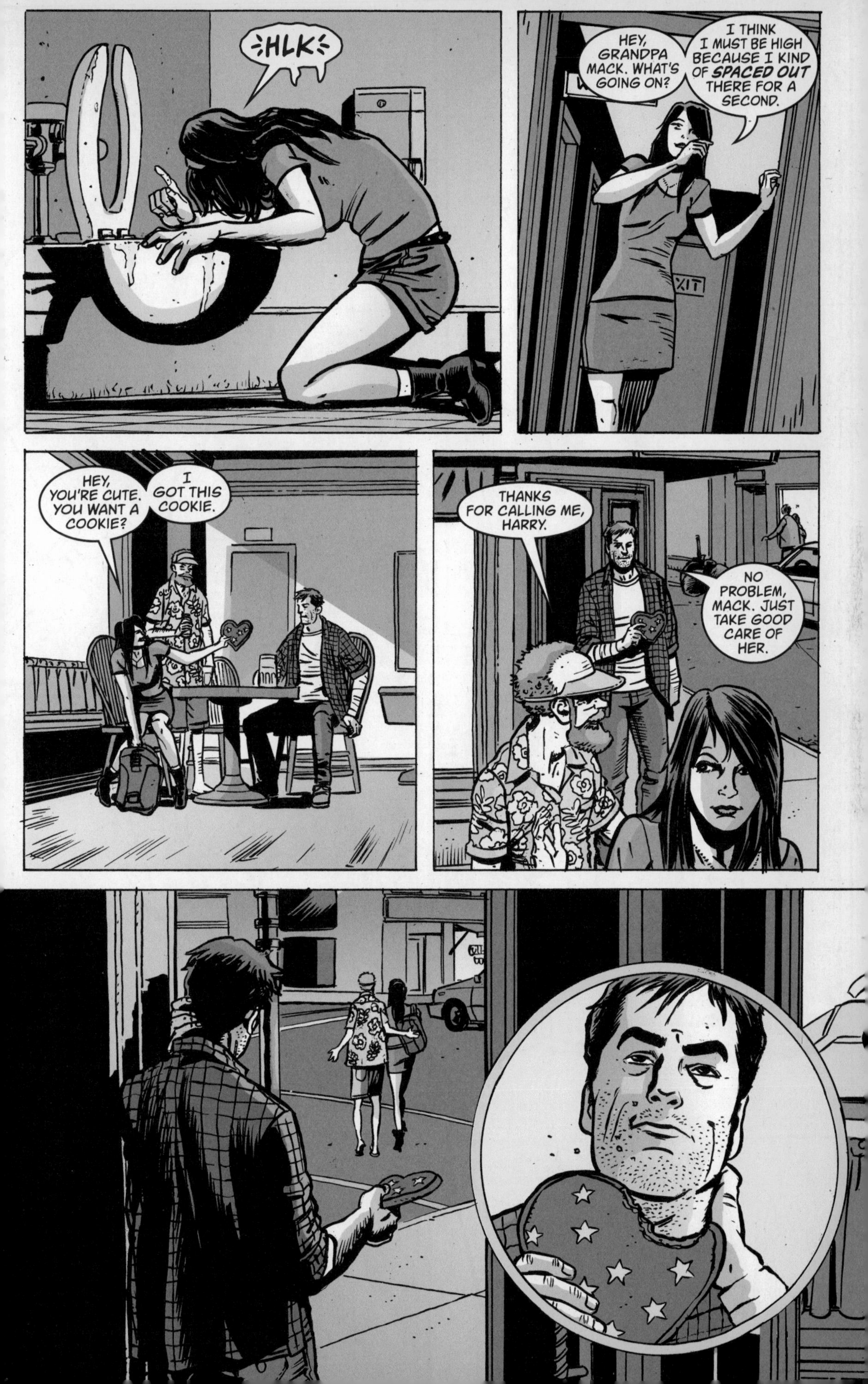
HLK
HEY, GRANDPA MACK. WHAT'S GOING ON?
I THINK I MUST BE HIGH BECAUSE I KIND OF SPACED OUT THERE FOR A SECOND.
HEY, YOU'RE CUTE. YOU WANT A COOKIE?
I GOT THIS COOKIE.
THANKS FOR CALLING ME, HARRY.
NO PROBLEM, MACK. JUST TAKE GOOD CARE OF HER.

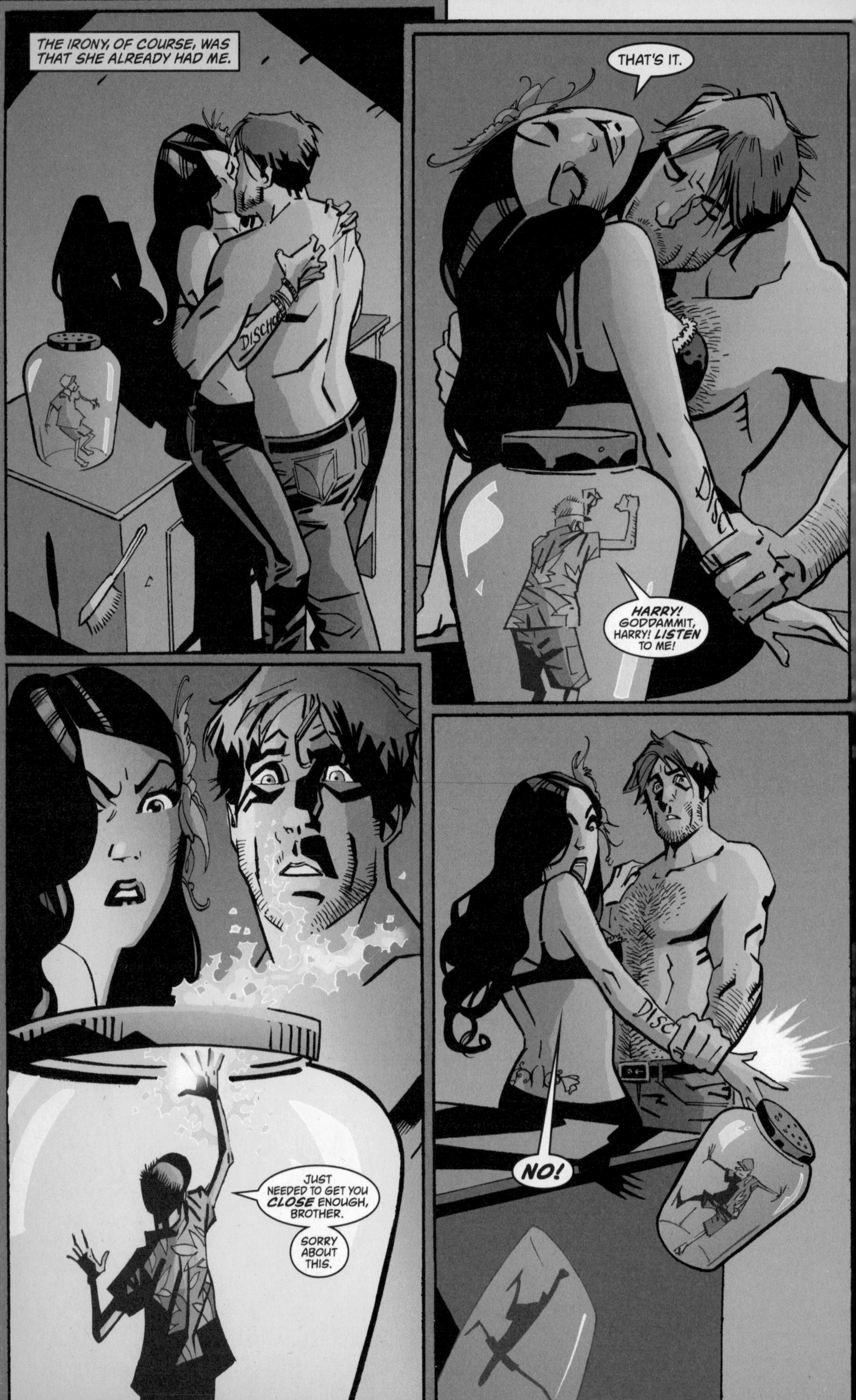
THE IRONY, OF COURSE, WAS THAT SHE ALREADY HAD ME.
DISCHO
THAT'S IT.
HARRY! GODDAMMIT, HARRY! LISTEN TO ME!
DISC
JUST NEEDED TO GET YOU CLOSE ENOUGH, BROTHER.
SORRY ABOUT THIS.
DISC
NO!

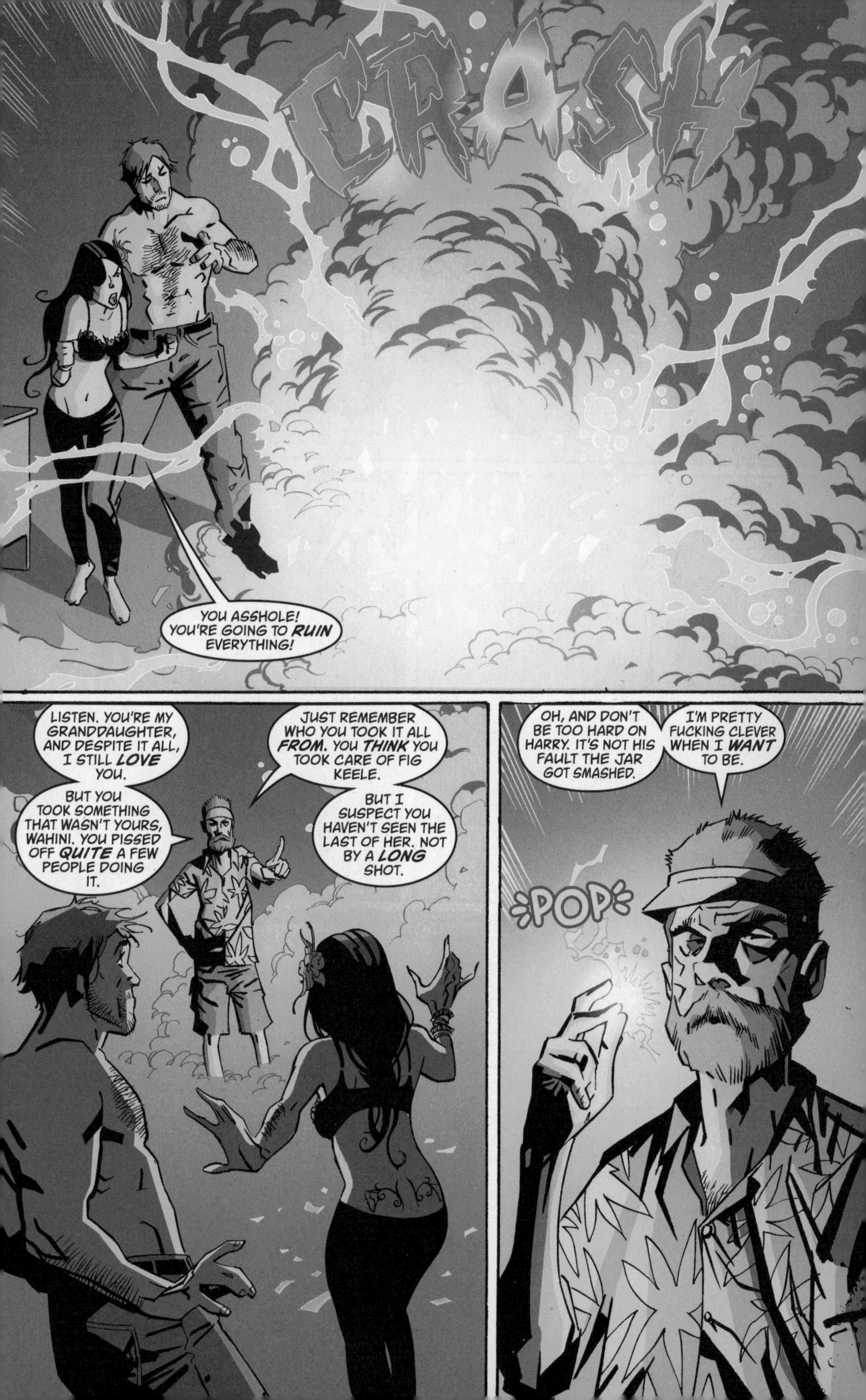
CRASH
YOU ASSHOLE! YOU'RE GOING TO RUIN EVERYTHING!
LISTEN. YOU'RE MY GRANDDAUGHTER, AND DESPITE IT ALL, I STILL LOVE YOU.
BUT YOU TOOK SOMETHING THAT WASN'T YOURS, WAHINI. YOU PISSED OFF QUITE A FEW PEOPLE DOING IT.
JUST REMEMBER WHO YOU TOOK IT ALL FROM. YOU THINK YOU TOOK CARE OF FIG KEELE.
BUT I SUSPECT YOU HAVEN'T SEEN THE LAST OF HER. NOT BY A LONG SHOT.
OH, AND DON'T BE TOO HARD ON HARRY. IT'S NOT HIS FAULT THE JAR GOT SMASHED.
I'M PRETTY FUCKING CLEVER WHEN I WANT TO BE.
POP

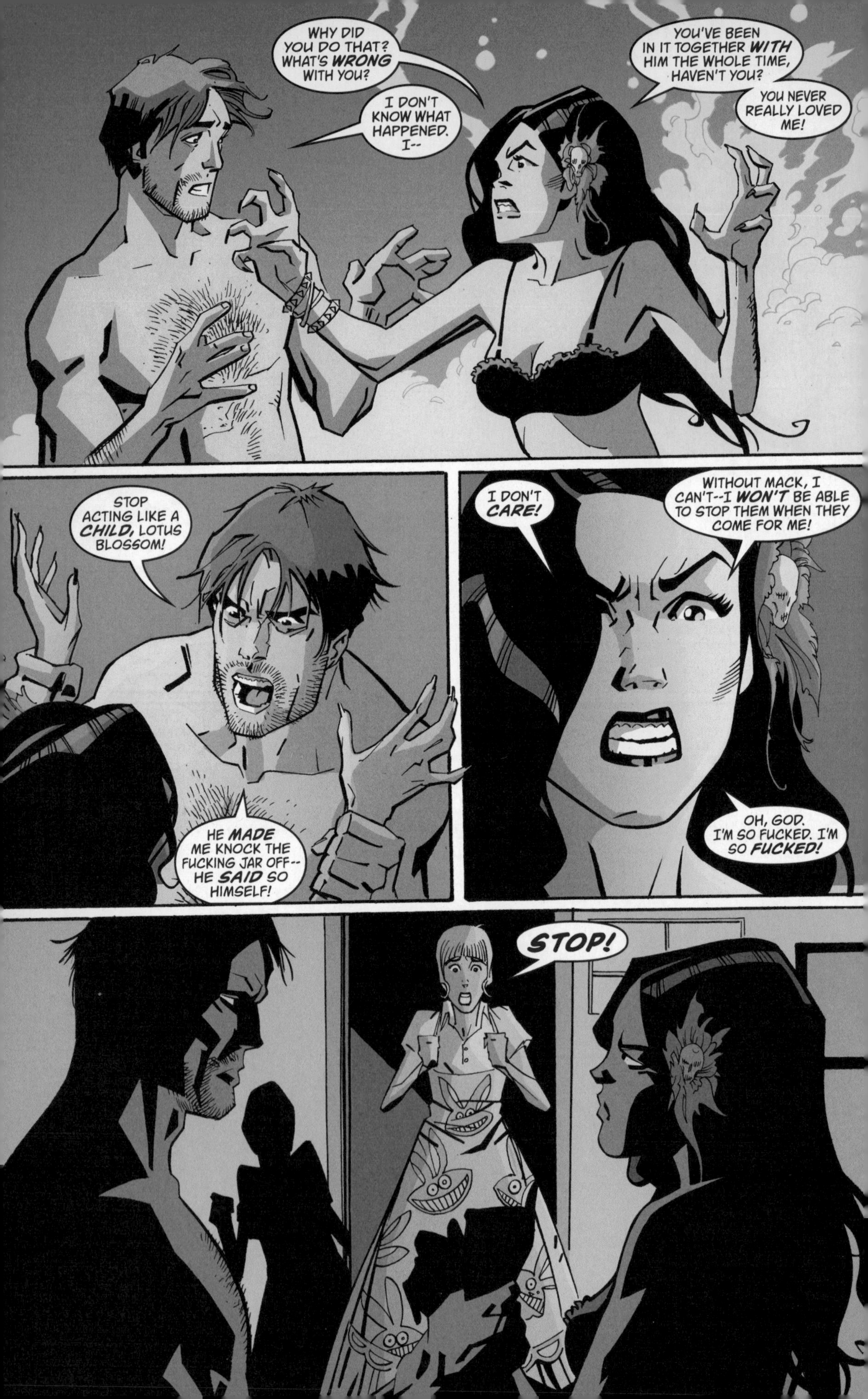
WHY DID YOU DO THAT? WHAT'S WRONG WITH YOU?
I DON'T KNOW WHAT HAPPENED. I--
YOU'VE BEEN IN IT TOGETHER WITH HIM THE WHOLE TIME, HAVEN'T YOU?
YOU NEVER REALLY LOVED ME!
STOP ACTING LIKE A CHILD, LOTUS BLOSSOM!
HE MADE ME KNOCK THE FUCKING JAR OFF-- HE SAID SO HIMSELF!
I DON'T CARE!
WITHOUT MACK, I CAN'T--I WON'T BE ABLE TO STOP THEM WHEN THEY COME FOR ME!
OH, GOD. I'M SO FUCKED. I'M SO FUCKED!
STOP!

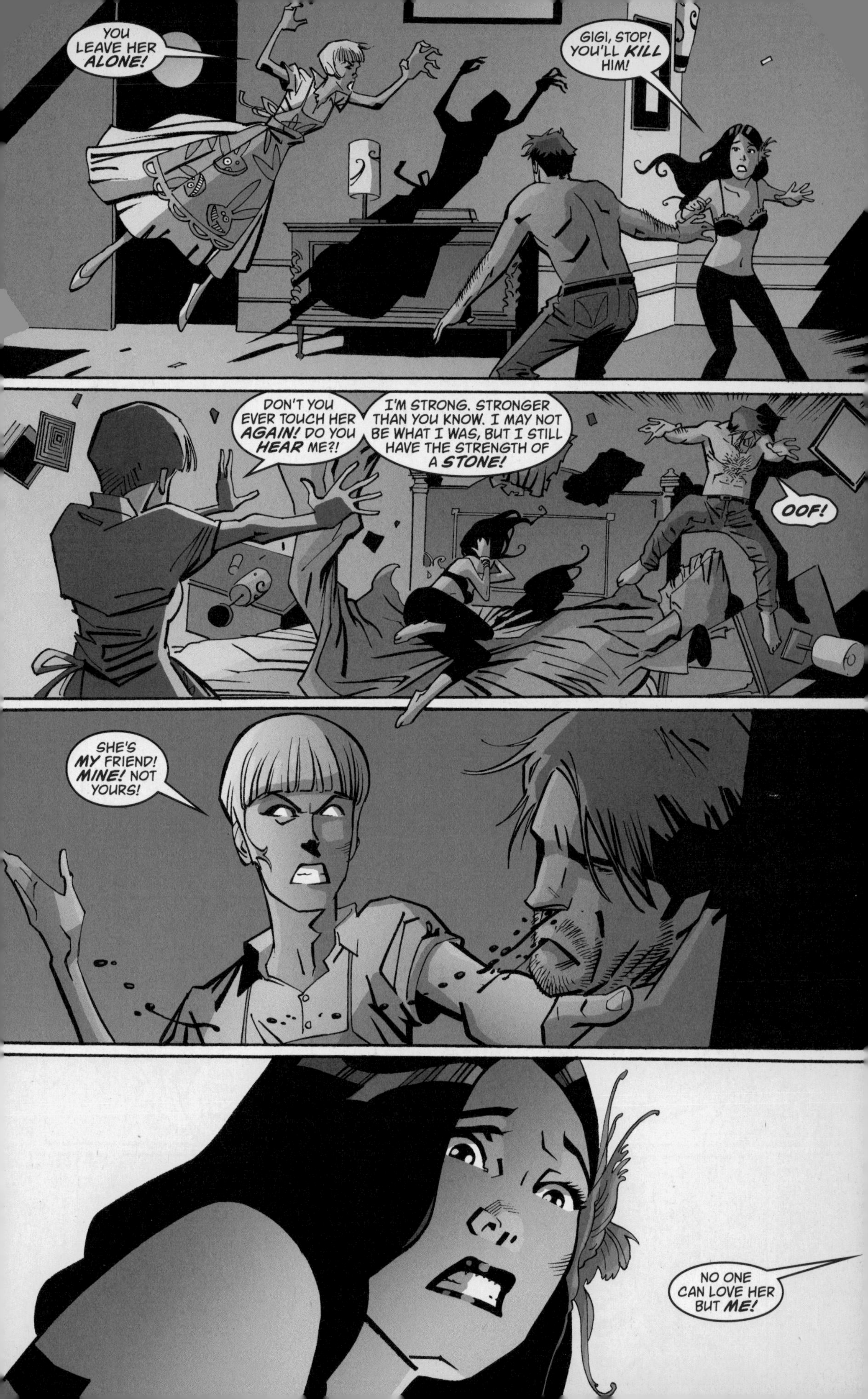
YOU LEAVE HER ALONE!
GIGI, STOP! YOU'LL KILL HIM!
DON'T YOU EVER TOUCH HER AGAIN! DO YOU HEAR ME?!
I'M STRONG. STRONGER THAN YOU KNOW. I MAY NOT BE WHAT I WAS, BUT I STILL HAVE THE STRENGTH OF A STONE!
OOF!
SHE'S MY FRIEND! MINE! NOT YOURS!
NO ONE CAN LOVE HER BUT ME!

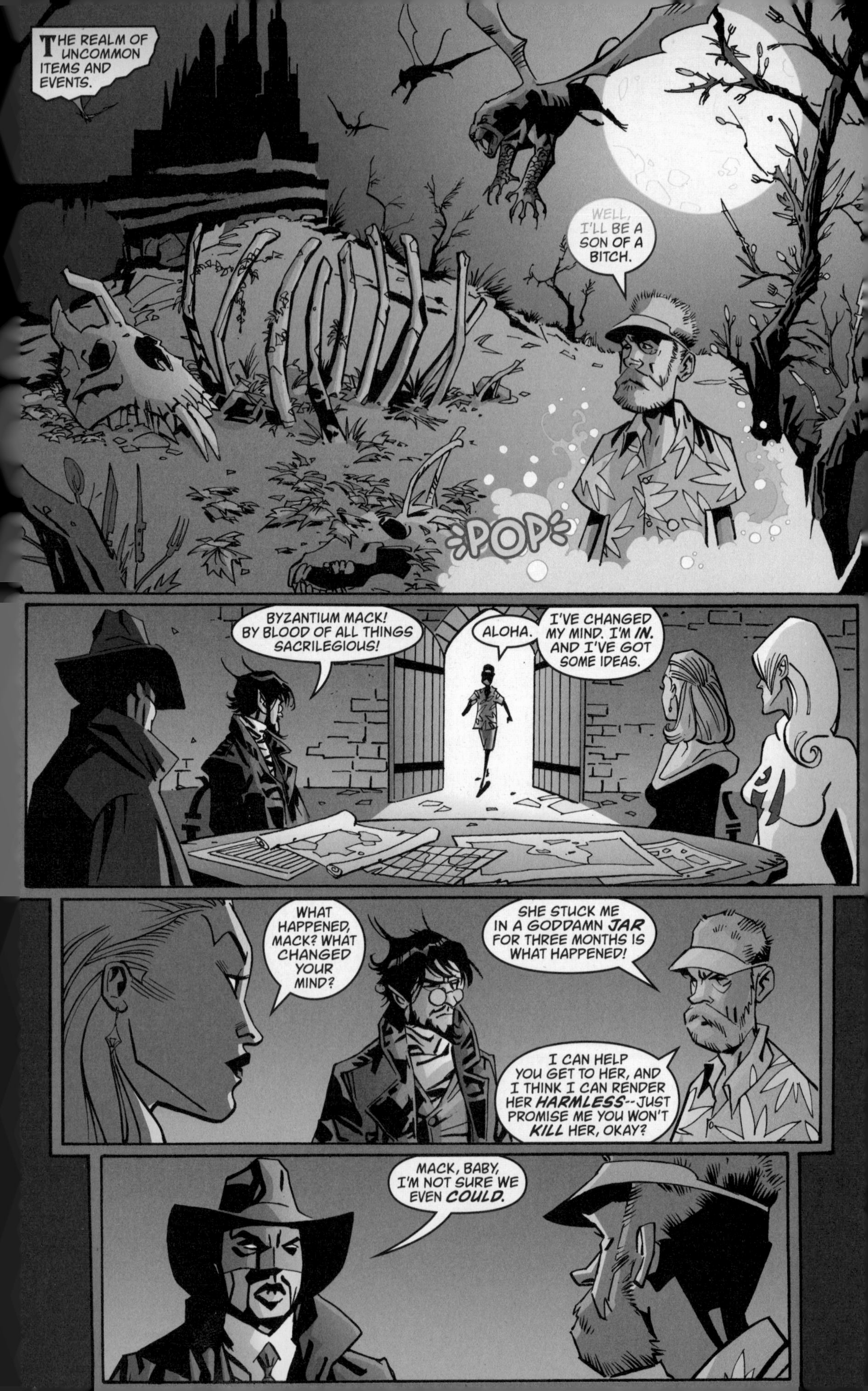
THE REALM OF UNCOMMON ITEMS AND EVENTS.
WELL, I'LL BE A SON OF A BITCH.
POP
BYZANTIUM MACK! BY BLOOD OF ALL THINGS SACRILEGIOUS!
ALOHA.
I'VE CHANGED MY MIND. I'M *IN.* AND I'VE GOT SOME IDEAS.
WHAT HAPPENED, MACK? WHAT CHANGED YOUR MIND?
SHE STUCK ME IN A GODDAMN *JAR* FOR THREE MONTHS IS WHAT HAPPENED!
I CAN HELP YOU GET TO HER, AND I THINK I CAN RENDER HER *HARMLESS*--JUST PROMISE ME YOU WON'T *KILL* HER, OKAY?
MACK, BABY, I'M NOT SURE WE EVEN *COULD.*

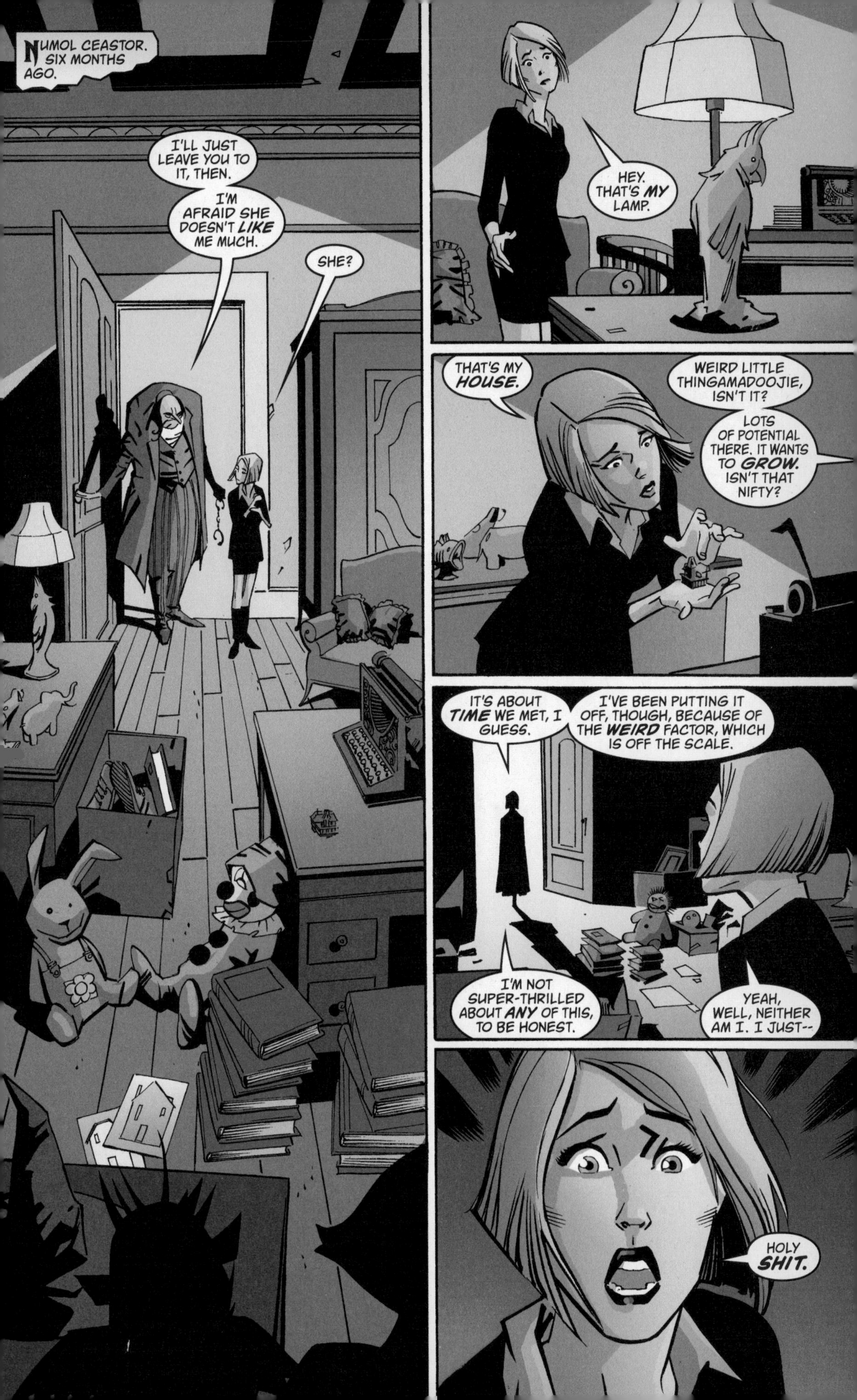
NUMOL CEASTOR. SIX MONTHS AGO.
I'LL JUST LEAVE YOU TO IT, THEN.
I'M AFRAID SHE DOESN'T LIKE ME MUCH.
SHE?
HEY. THAT'S MY LAMP.
THAT'S MY HOUSE.
WEIRD LITTLE THINGAMADOOJIE, ISN'T IT?
LOTS OF POTENTIAL THERE. IT WANTS TO GROW. ISN'T THAT NIFTY?
IT'S ABOUT TIME WE MET, I GUESS.
I'VE BEEN PUTTING IT OFF, THOUGH, BECAUSE OF THE WEIRD FACTOR, WHICH IS OFF THE SCALE.
I'M NOT SUPER-THRILLED ABOUT ANY OF THIS, TO BE HONEST.
YEAH, WELL, NEITHER AM I. I JUST--
HOLY SHIT.

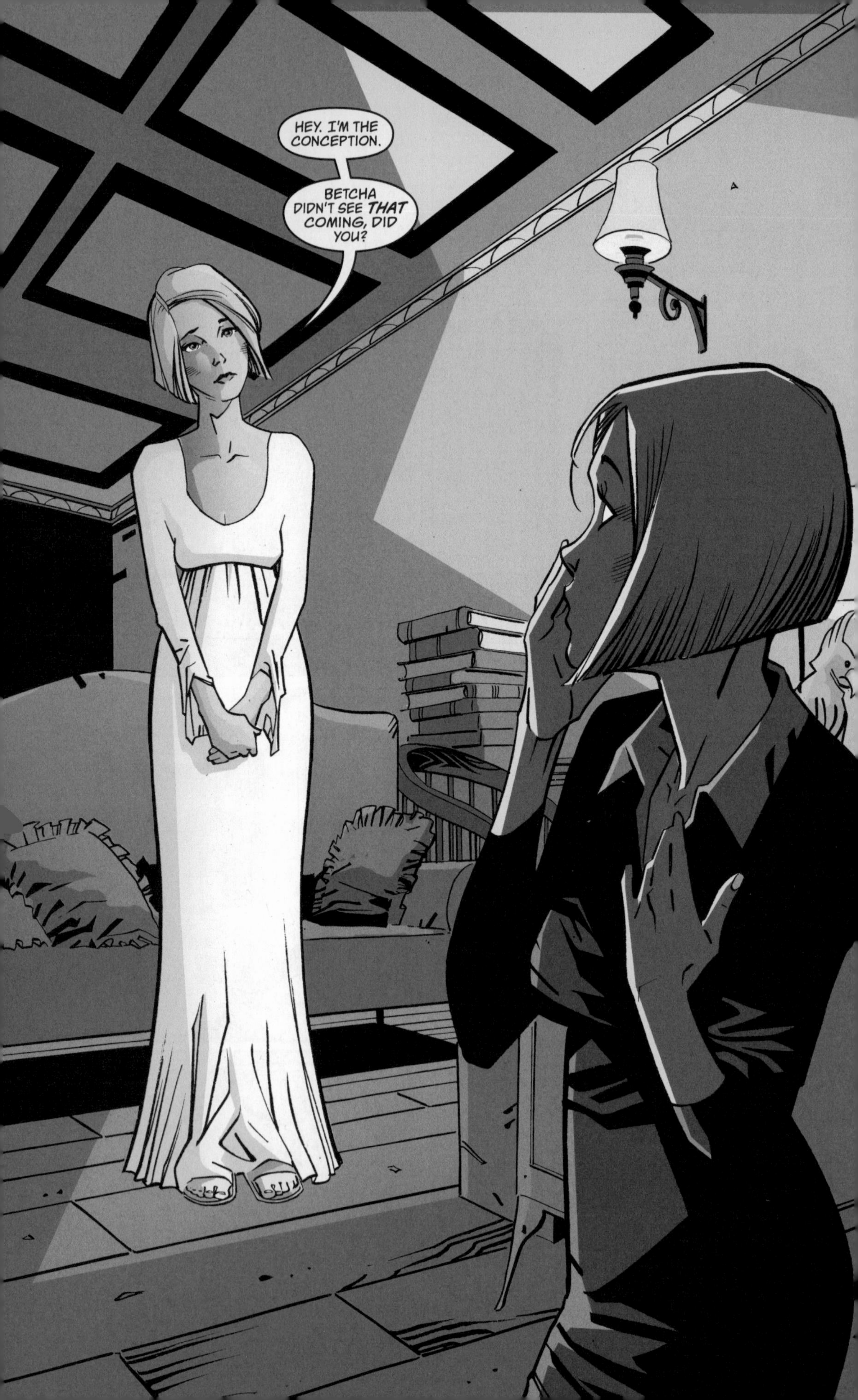
HEY. I'M THE CONCEPTION.
BETCHA DIDN'T SEE THAT COMING, DID YOU?

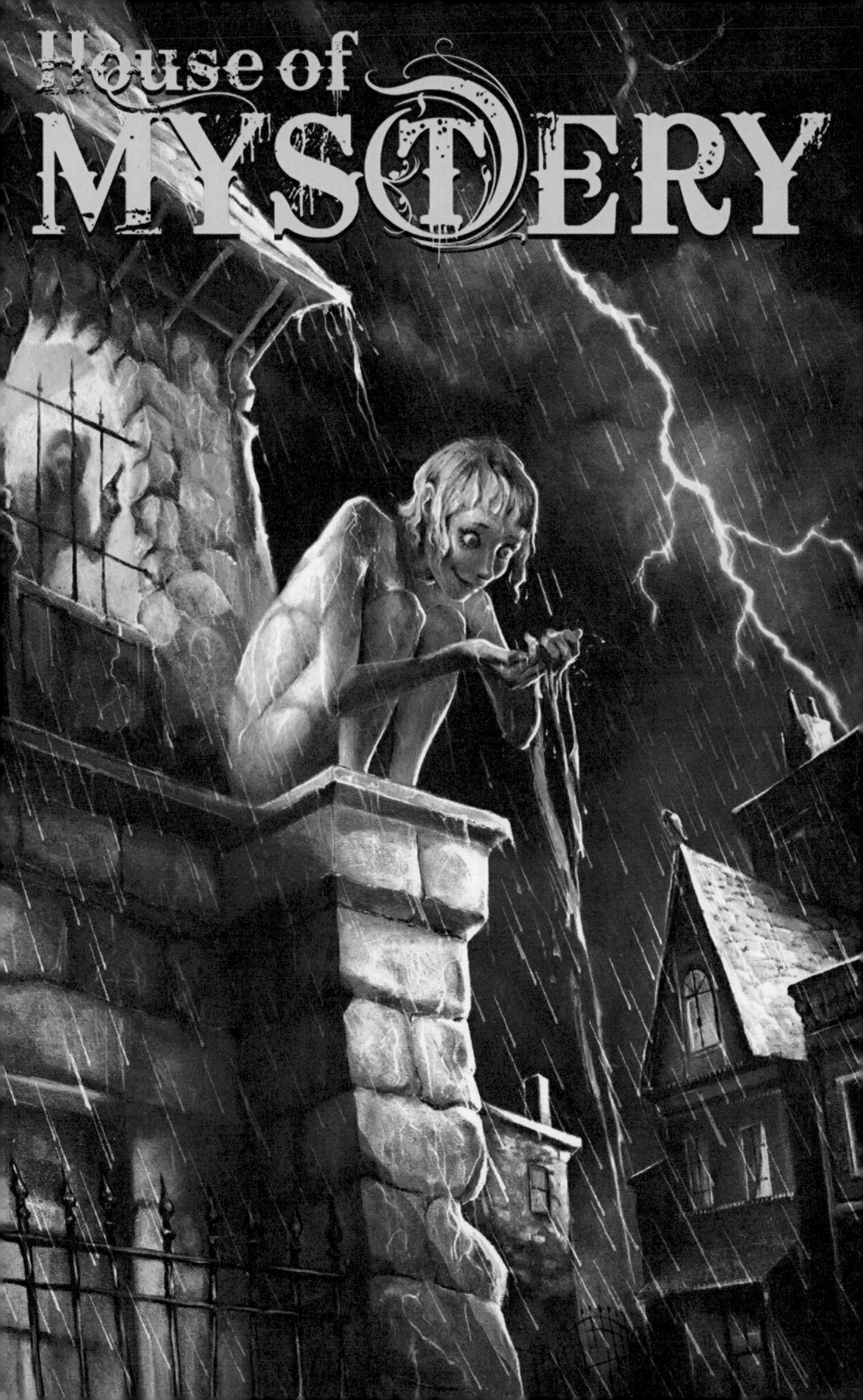
House of
MYSTERY

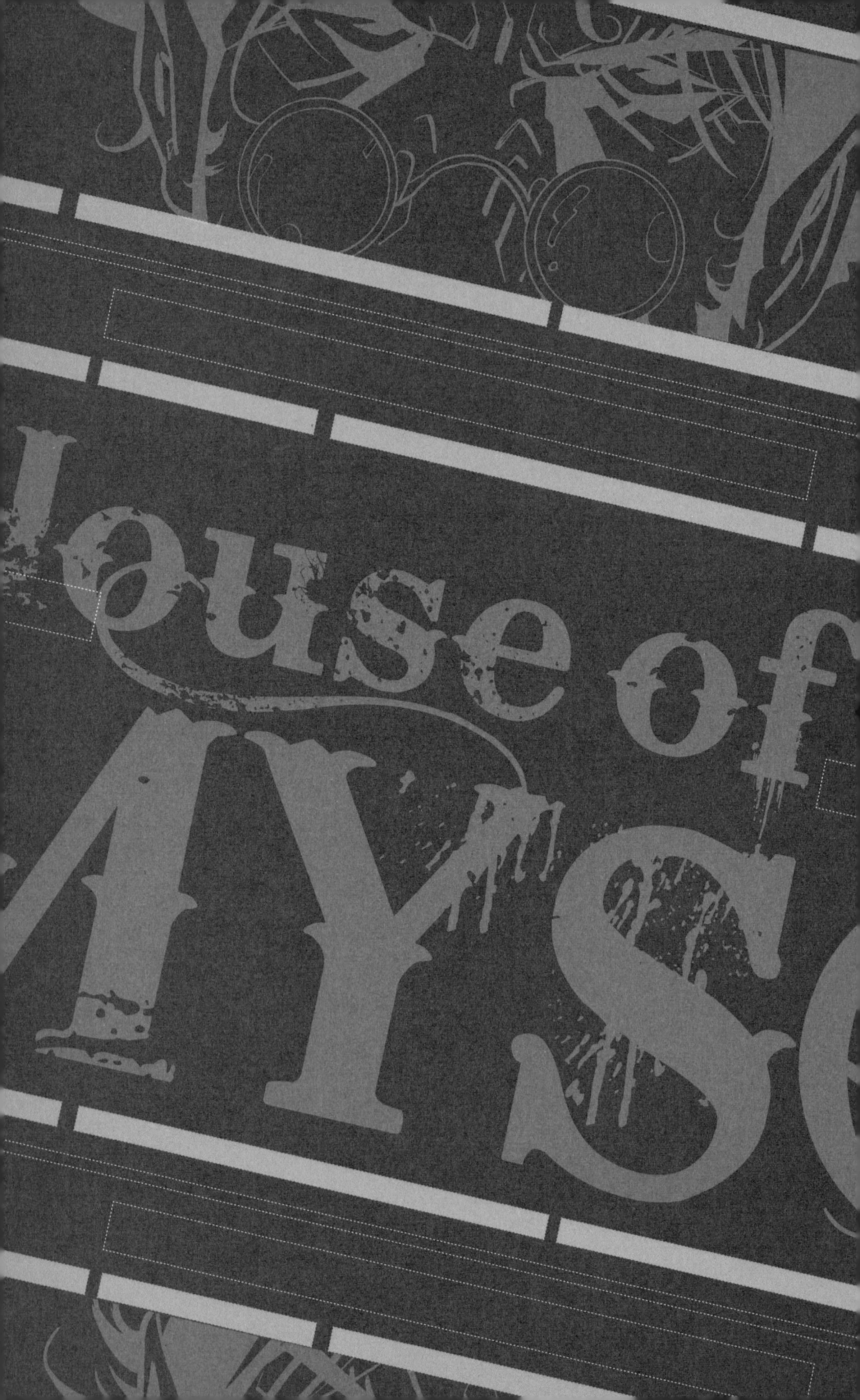
ouse of

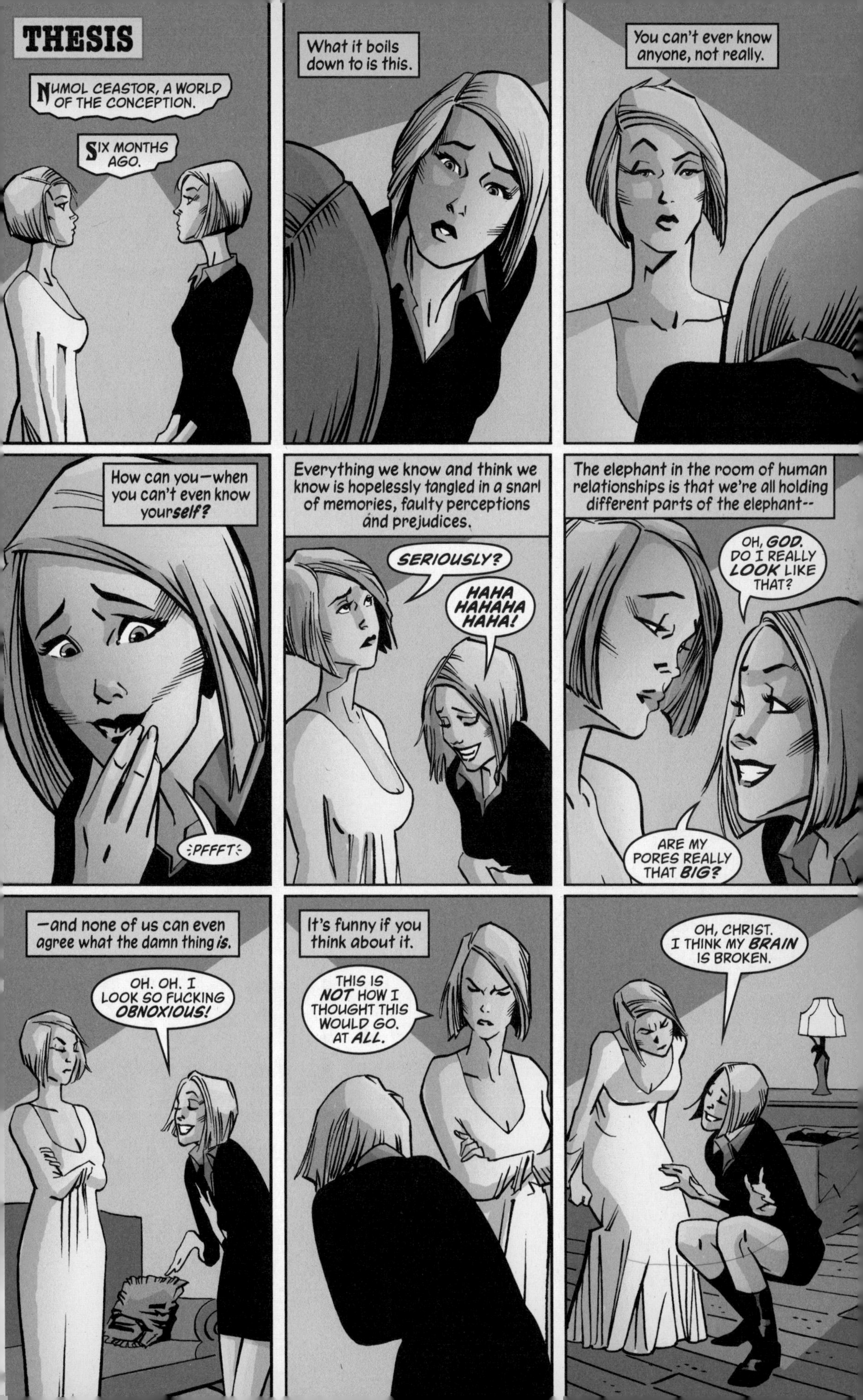
THESIS
NUMOL CEASTOR, A WORLD OF THE CONCEPTION.
SIX MONTHS AGO.
What it boils down to is this.
You can't ever know anyone, not really.
How can you—when you can't even know yourself?
PFFFT
Everything we know and think we know is hopelessly tangled in a snarl of memories, faulty perceptions and prejudices.
SERIOUSLY?
HAHA HAHAHA HAHA!
The elephant in the room of human relationships is that we're all holding different parts of the elephant--
OH, GOD. DO I REALLY LOOK LIKE THAT?
ARE MY PORES REALLY THAT BIG?
—and none of us can even agree what the damn thing is.
OH. OH. I LOOK SO FUCKING OBNOXIOUS!
It's funny if you think about it.
THIS IS NOT HOW I THOUGHT THIS WOULD GO. AT ALL.
OH, CHRIST. I THINK MY BRAIN IS BROKEN.

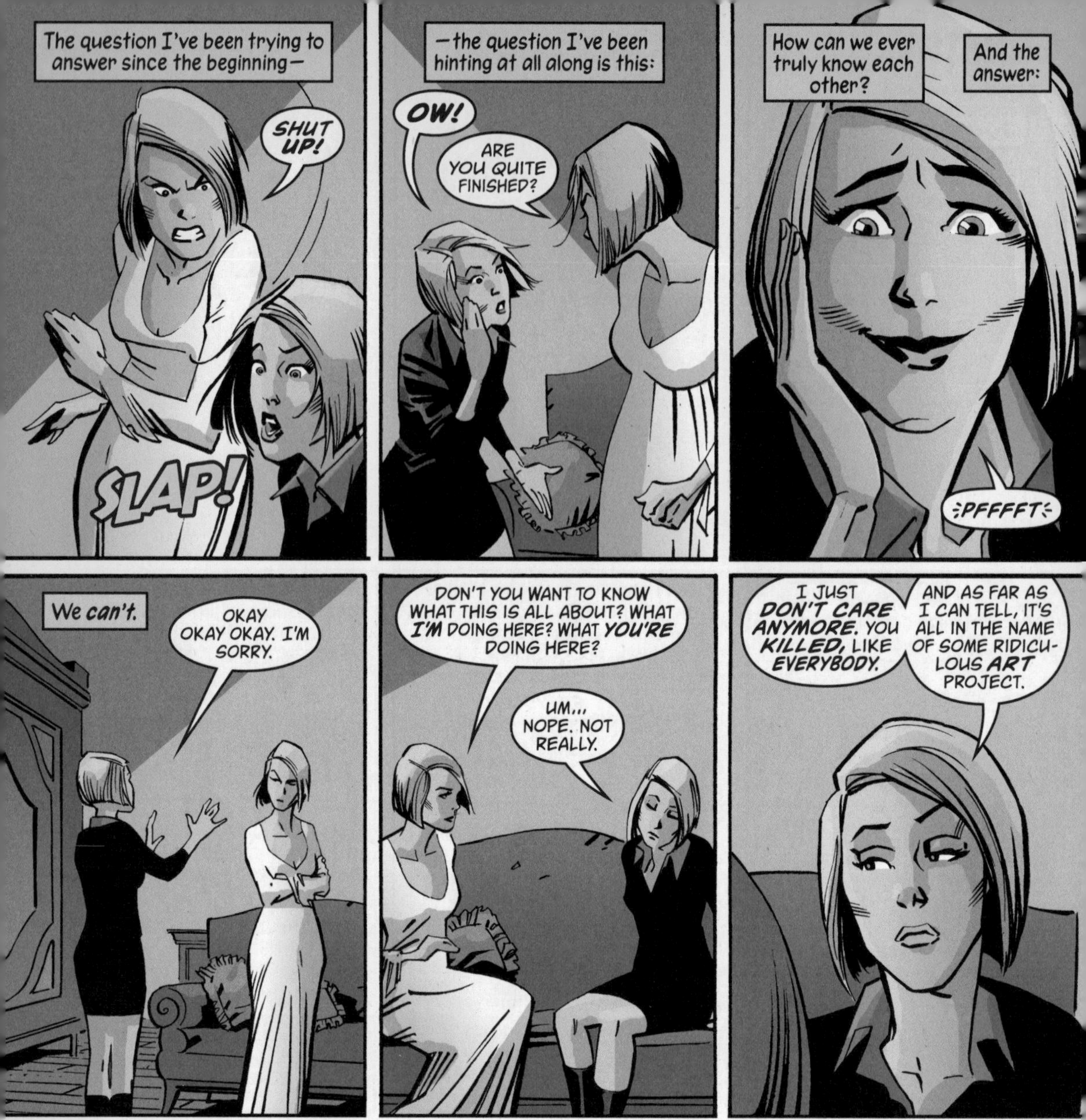
The question I've been trying to answer since the beginning—
SHUT UP!
SLAP!
—the question I've been hinting at all along is this:
OW!
ARE YOU QUITE FINISHED?
How can we ever truly know each other?
And the answer:
PFFFFT
We can't.
OKAY OKAY OKAY. I'M SORRY.
DON'T YOU WANT TO KNOW WHAT THIS IS ALL ABOUT? WHAT I'M DOING HERE? WHAT YOU'RE DOING HERE?
UM... NOPE. NOT REALLY.
I JUST DON'T CARE ANYMORE. YOU KILLED, LIKE EVERYBODY.
AND AS FAR AS I CAN TELL, IT'S ALL IN THE NAME OF SOME RIDICULOUS ART PROJECT.

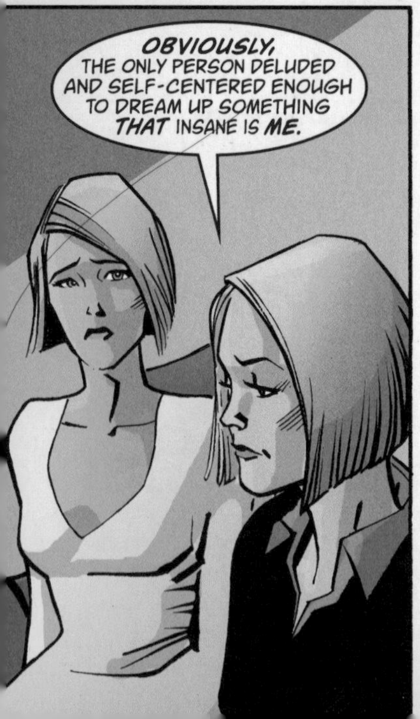
OBVIOUSLY, THE ONLY PERSON DELUDED AND SELF-CENTERED ENOUGH TO DREAM UP SOMETHING THAT INSANE IS ME.

TEETERING INFINITIES

Desolation Part 4 of 5

MATTHEW STURGES: writer
LUCA ROSSI: pencils
JOSÉ MARZÁN, JR: inks

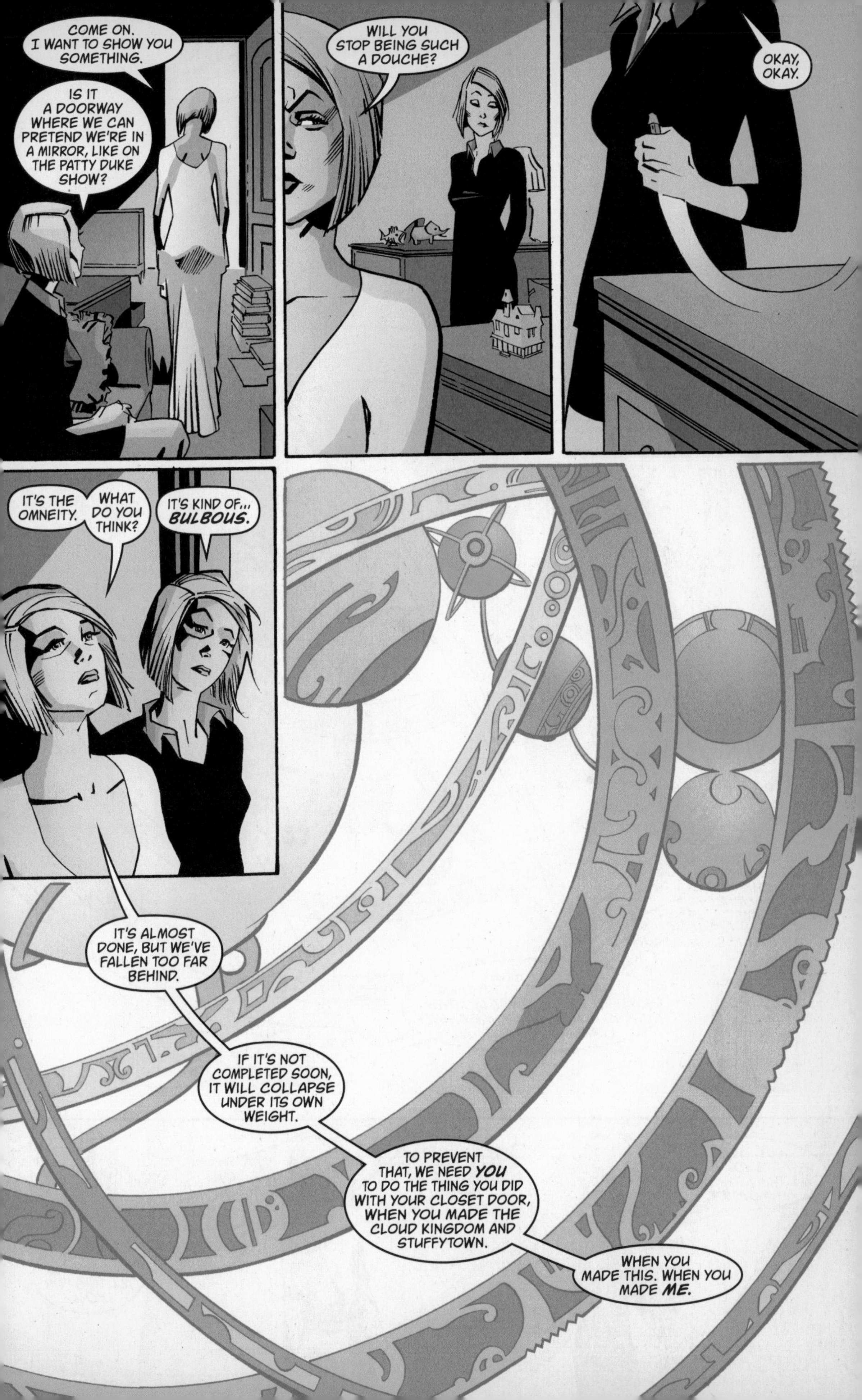
COME ON. I WANT TO SHOW YOU SOMETHING.
IS IT A DOORWAY WHERE WE CAN PRETEND WE'RE IN A MIRROR, LIKE ON THE PATTY DUKE SHOW?
WILL YOU STOP BEING SUCH A DOUCHE?
OKAY, OKAY.
IT'S THE OMNEITY.
WHAT DO YOU THINK?
IT'S KIND OF... *BULBOUS.*
IT'S ALMOST DONE, BUT WE'VE FALLEN TOO FAR BEHIND.
IF IT'S NOT COMPLETED SOON, IT WILL COLLAPSE UNDER ITS OWN WEIGHT.
TO PREVENT THAT, WE NEED *YOU* TO DO THE THING YOU DID WITH YOUR CLOSET DOOR, WHEN YOU MADE THE CLOUD KINGDOM AND STUFFYTOWN.
WHEN YOU MADE THIS. WHEN YOU MADE *ME.*

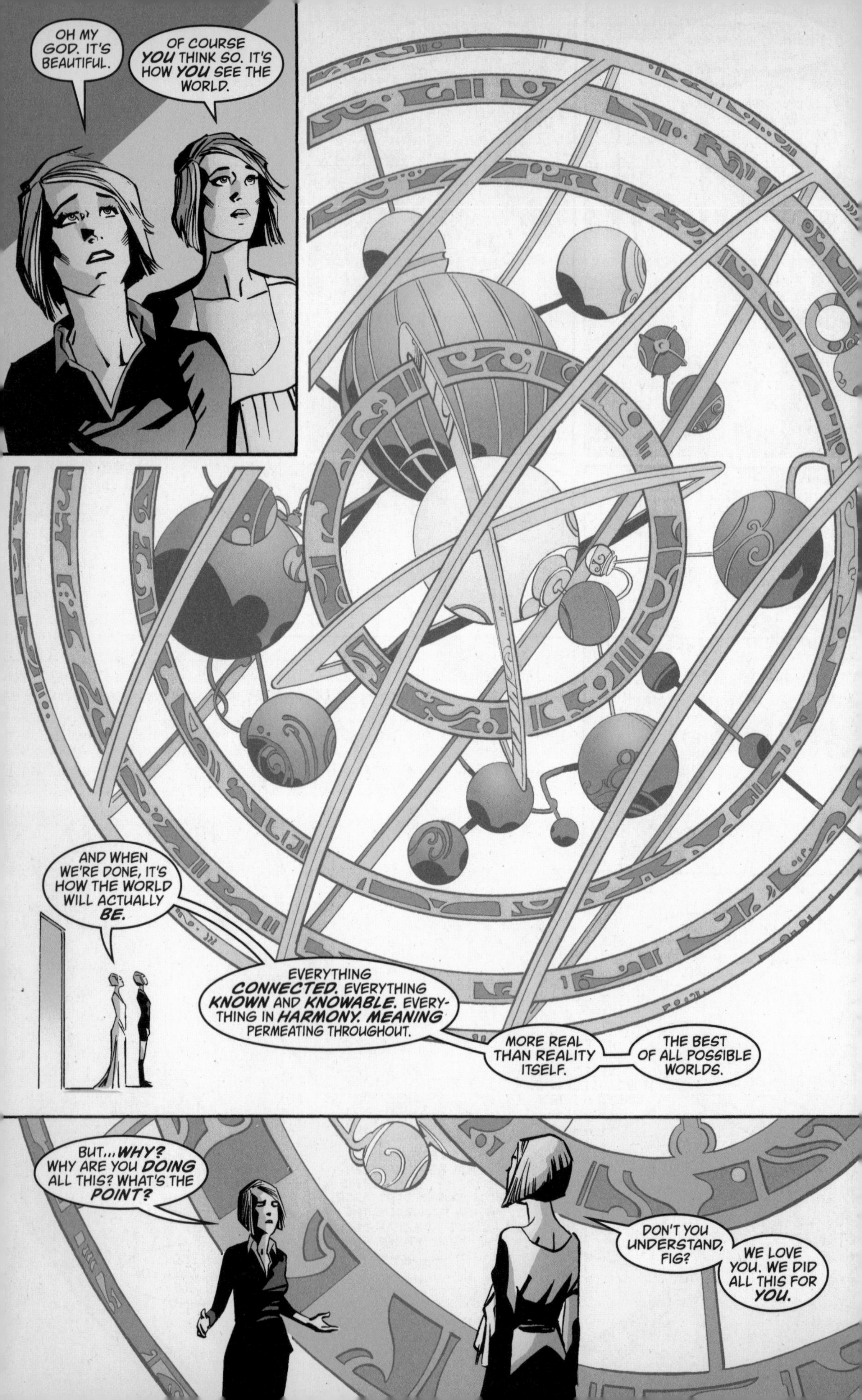
OH MY GOD. IT'S BEAUTIFUL.
OF COURSE YOU THINK SO. IT'S HOW YOU SEE THE WORLD.
AND WHEN WE'RE DONE, IT'S HOW THE WORLD WILL ACTUALLY BE.
EVERYTHING CONNECTED. EVERYTHING KNOWN AND KNOWABLE. EVERYTHING IN HARMONY. MEANING PERMEATING THROUGHOUT.
MORE REAL THAN REALITY ITSELF.
THE BEST OF ALL POSSIBLE WORLDS.
BUT... WHY? WHY ARE YOU DOING ALL THIS? WHAT'S THE POINT?
DON'T YOU UNDERSTAND, FIG?
WE LOVE YOU. WE DID ALL THIS FOR YOU.

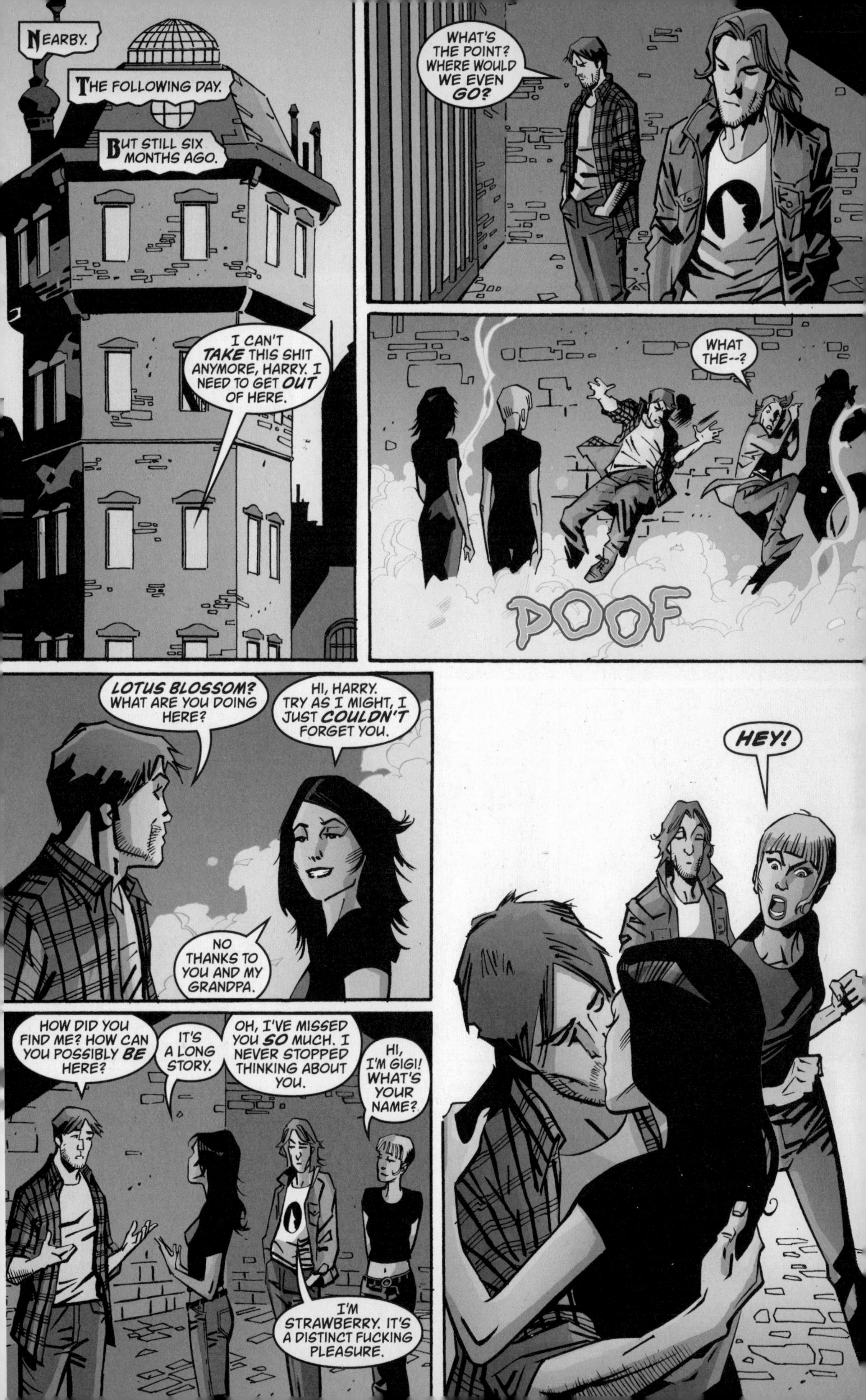

NEARBY.
THE FOLLOWING DAY.
BUT STILL SIX MONTHS AGO.
I CAN'T TAKE THIS SHIT ANYMORE, HARRY. I NEED TO GET OUT OF HERE.
WHAT'S THE POINT? WHERE WOULD WE EVEN GO?
WHAT THE--?
POOF
LOTUS BLOSSOM? WHAT ARE YOU DOING HERE?
HI, HARRY. TRY AS I MIGHT, I JUST COULDN'T FORGET YOU.
NO THANKS TO YOU AND MY GRANDPA.
HOW DID YOU FIND ME? HOW CAN YOU POSSIBLY BE HERE?
IT'S A LONG STORY.
OH, I'VE MISSED YOU SO MUCH. I NEVER STOPPED THINKING ABOUT YOU.
HI, I'M GIGI! WHAT'S YOUR NAME?
I'M STRAWBERRY. IT'S A DISTINCT FUCKING PLEASURE.
HEY!

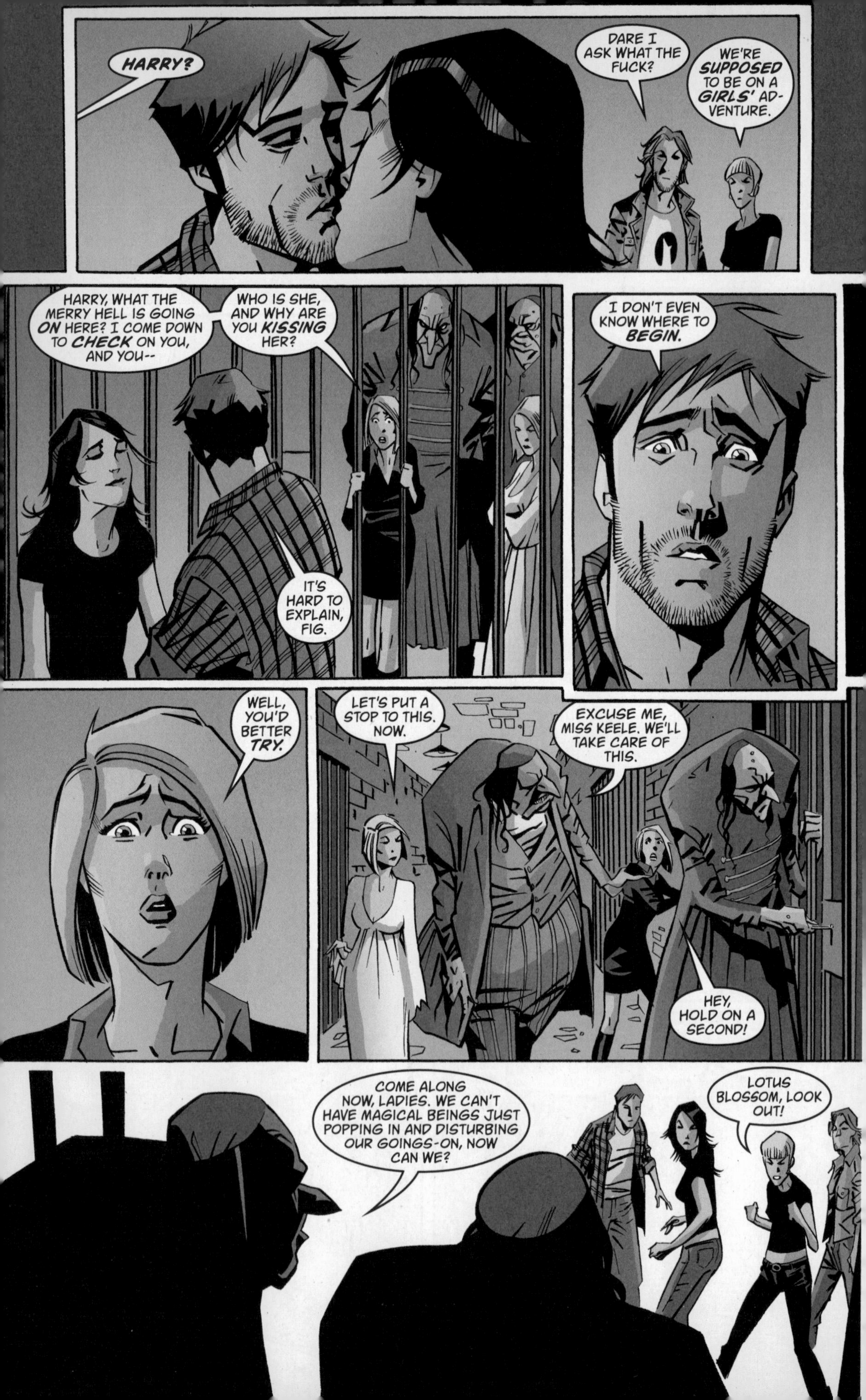
HARRY?
DARE I ASK WHAT THE FUCK?
WE'RE SUPPOSED TO BE ON A GIRLS' ADVENTURE.
HARRY, WHAT THE MERRY HELL IS GOING ON HERE? I COME DOWN TO CHECK ON YOU, AND YOU--
WHO IS SHE, AND WHY ARE YOU KISSING HER?
IT'S HARD TO EXPLAIN, FIG.
I DON'T EVEN KNOW WHERE TO BEGIN.
WELL, YOU'D BETTER TRY.
LET'S PUT A STOP TO THIS. NOW.
EXCUSE ME, MISS KEELE. WE'LL TAKE CARE OF THIS.
HEY, HOLD ON A SECOND!
COME ALONG NOW, LADIES. WE CAN'T HAVE MAGICAL BEINGS JUST POPPING IN AND DISTURBING OUR GOINGS-ON, NOW CAN WE?
LOTUS BLOSSOM, LOOK OUT!

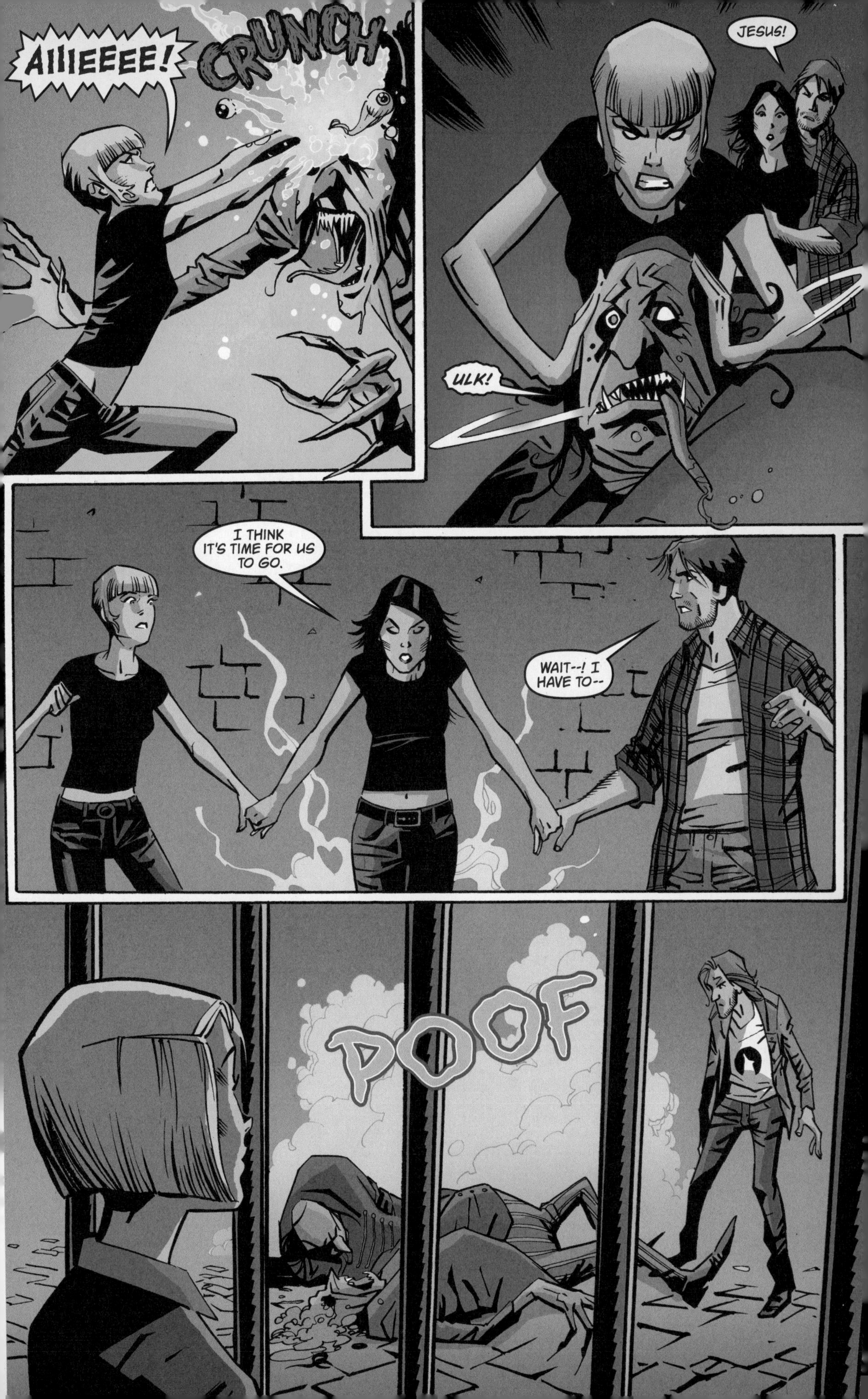
AIIIEEEE!
CRUNCH
JESUS!
ULK!
I THINK IT'S TIME FOR US TO GO.
WAIT--! I HAVE TO--
POOF

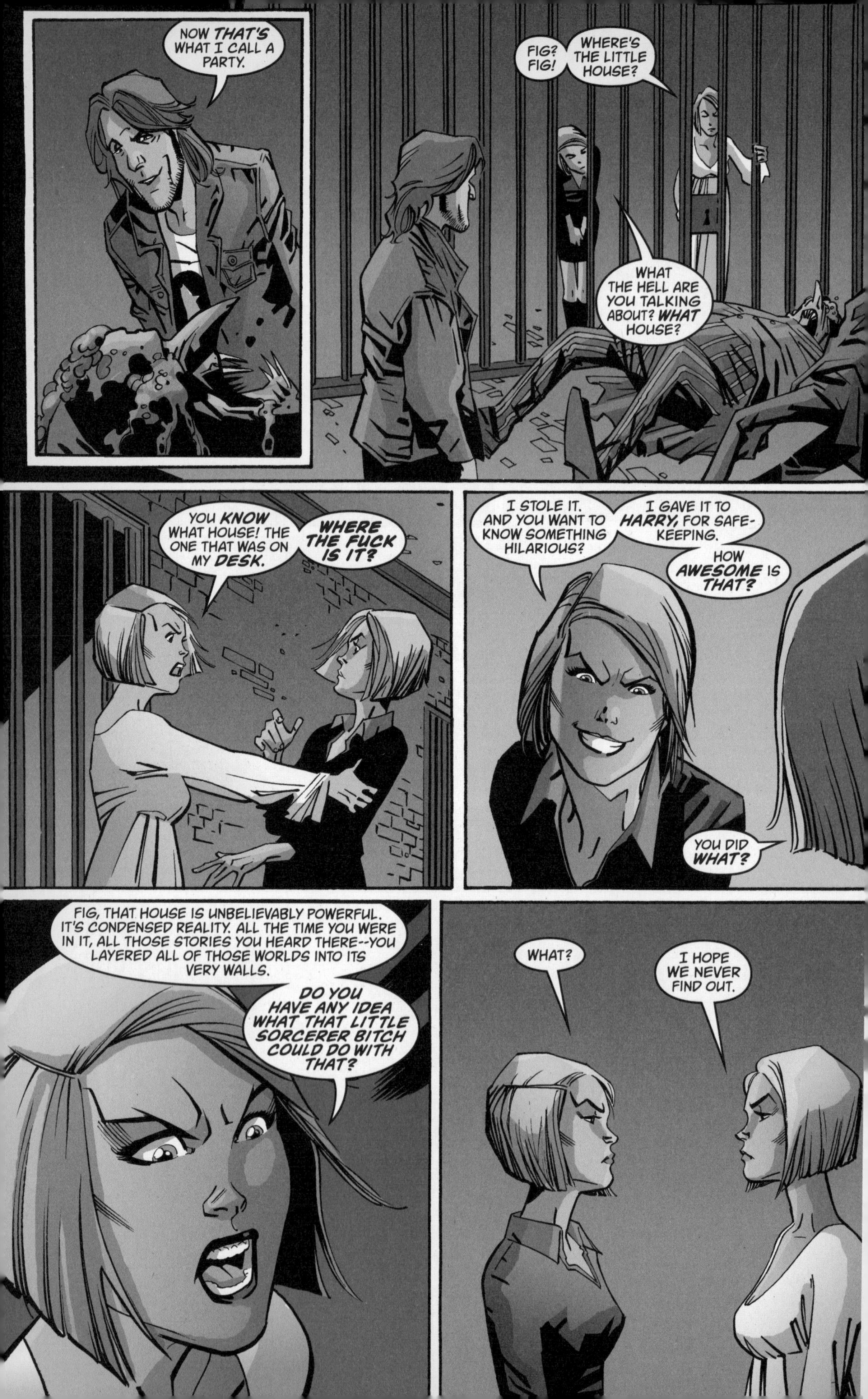
NOW THAT'S WHAT I CALL A PARTY.
FIG? FIG!
WHERE'S THE LITTLE HOUSE?
WHAT THE HELL ARE YOU TALKING ABOUT? WHAT HOUSE?
YOU KNOW WHAT HOUSE! THE ONE THAT WAS ON MY DESK.
WHERE THE FUCK IS IT?
I STOLE IT. AND YOU WANT TO KNOW SOMETHING HILARIOUS?
I GAVE IT TO HARRY, FOR SAFE-KEEPING.
HOW AWESOME IS THAT?
YOU DID WHAT?
FIG, THAT HOUSE IS UNBELIEVABLY POWERFUL. IT'S CONDENSED REALITY. ALL THE TIME YOU WERE IN IT, ALL THOSE STORIES YOU HEARD THERE--YOU LAYERED ALL OF THOSE WORLDS INTO ITS VERY WALLS.
DO YOU HAVE ANY IDEA WHAT THAT LITTLE SORCERER BITCH COULD DO WITH THAT?
WHAT?
I HOPE WE NEVER FIND OUT.

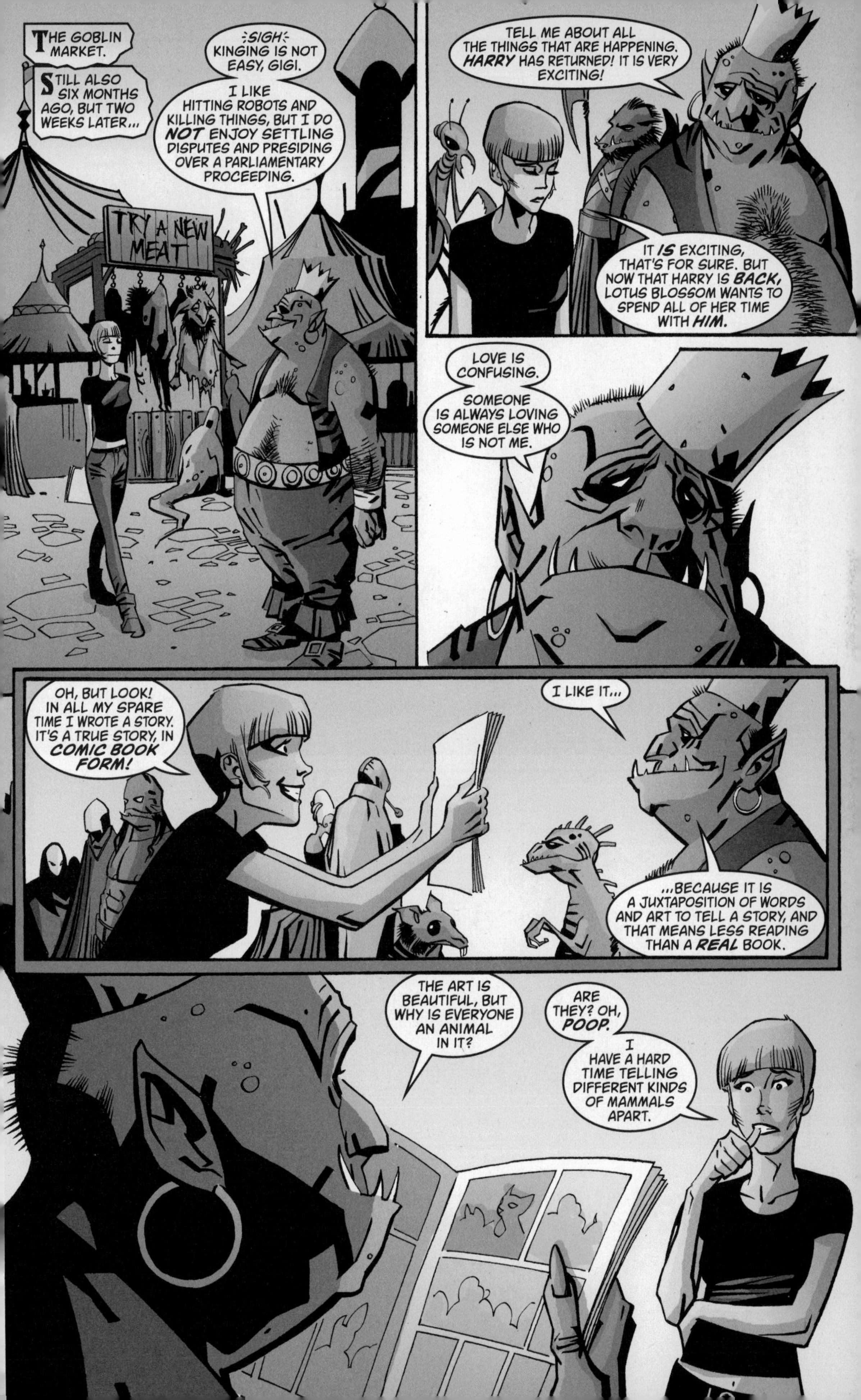
THE GOBLIN MARKET.
STILL ALSO SIX MONTHS AGO, BUT TWO WEEKS LATER...
:SIGH: KINGING IS NOT EASY, GIGI.
I LIKE HITTING ROBOTS AND KILLING THINGS, BUT I DO NOT ENJOY SETTLING DISPUTES AND PRESIDING OVER A PARLIAMENTARY PROCEEDING.
TRY A NEW MEAT
TELL ME ABOUT ALL THE THINGS THAT ARE HAPPENING. HARRY HAS RETURNED! IT IS VERY EXCITING!
IT IS EXCITING, THAT'S FOR SURE. BUT NOW THAT HARRY IS BACK, LOTUS BLOSSOM WANTS TO SPEND ALL OF HER TIME WITH HIM.
LOVE IS CONFUSING.
SOMEONE IS ALWAYS LOVING SOMEONE ELSE WHO IS NOT ME.
OH, BUT LOOK! IN ALL MY SPARE TIME I WROTE A STORY. IT'S A TRUE STORY, IN COMIC BOOK FORM!
I LIKE IT...
...BECAUSE IT IS A JUXTAPOSITION OF WORDS AND ART TO TELL A STORY, AND THAT MEANS LESS READING THAN A REAL BOOK.
THE ART IS BEAUTIFUL, BUT WHY IS EVERYONE AN ANIMAL IN IT?
ARE THEY? OH, POOP.
I HAVE A HARD TIME TELLING DIFFERENT KINDS OF MAMMALS APART.

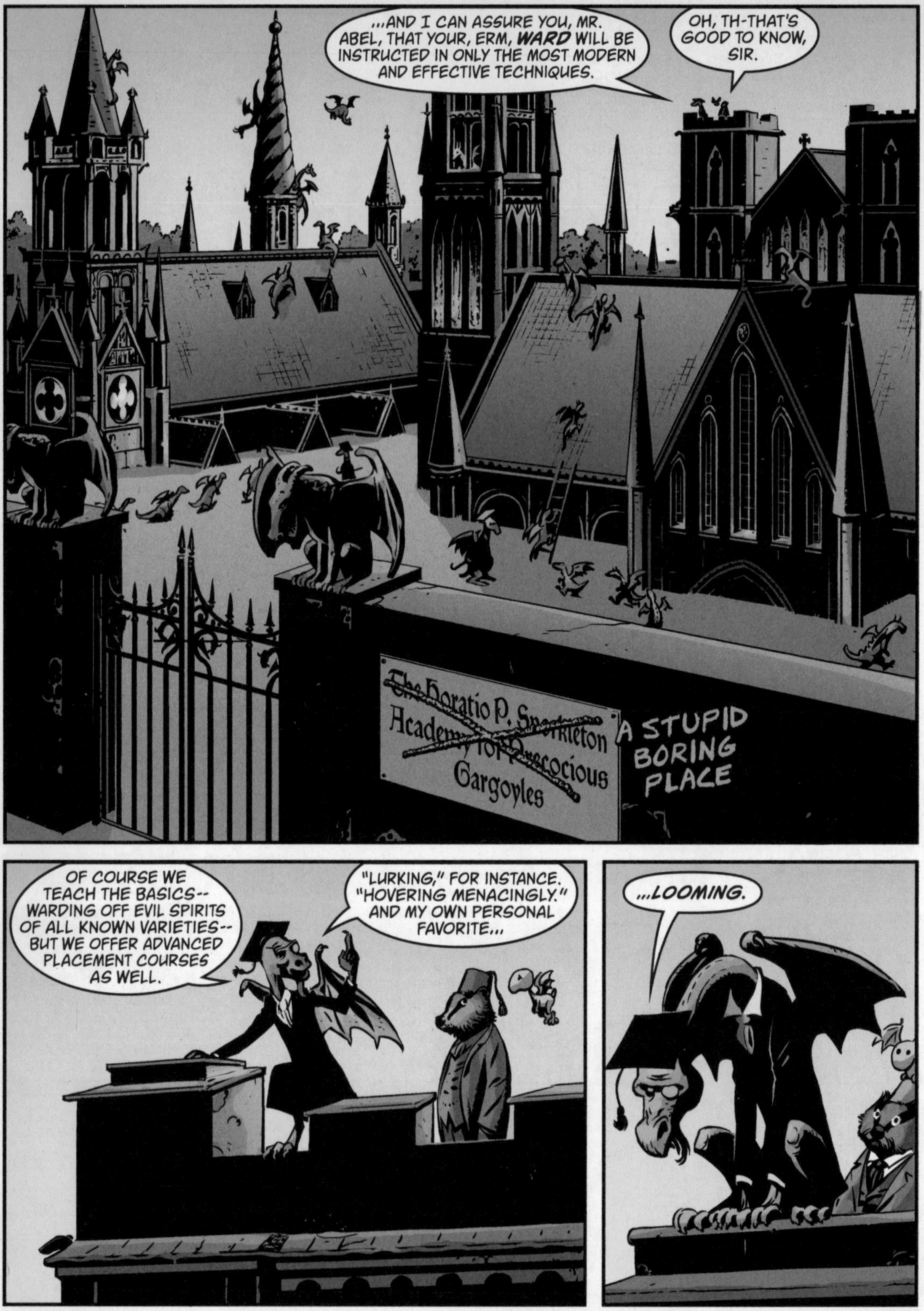
...AND I CAN ASSURE YOU, MR. ABEL, THAT YOUR, ERM, *WARD* WILL BE INSTRUCTED IN ONLY THE MOST MODERN AND EFFECTIVE TECHNIQUES.
OH, TH-THAT'S GOOD TO KNOW, SIR.
Gargoyles
A STUPID BORING PLACE
OF COURSE WE TEACH THE BASICS--WARDING OFF EVIL SPIRITS OF ALL KNOWN VARIETIES--BUT WE OFFER ADVANCED PLACEMENT COURSES AS WELL.
"LURKING," FOR INSTANCE. "HOVERING MENACINGLY." AND MY OWN PERSONAL FAVORITE...
...LOOMING.

Title: A Story About a Gargoyle and a Girl

Nice words written by: Matthew Sturges (that's my pen name! All the best writers have them!)

Pretty Pictures Drawn by: Peter Snejbjerg

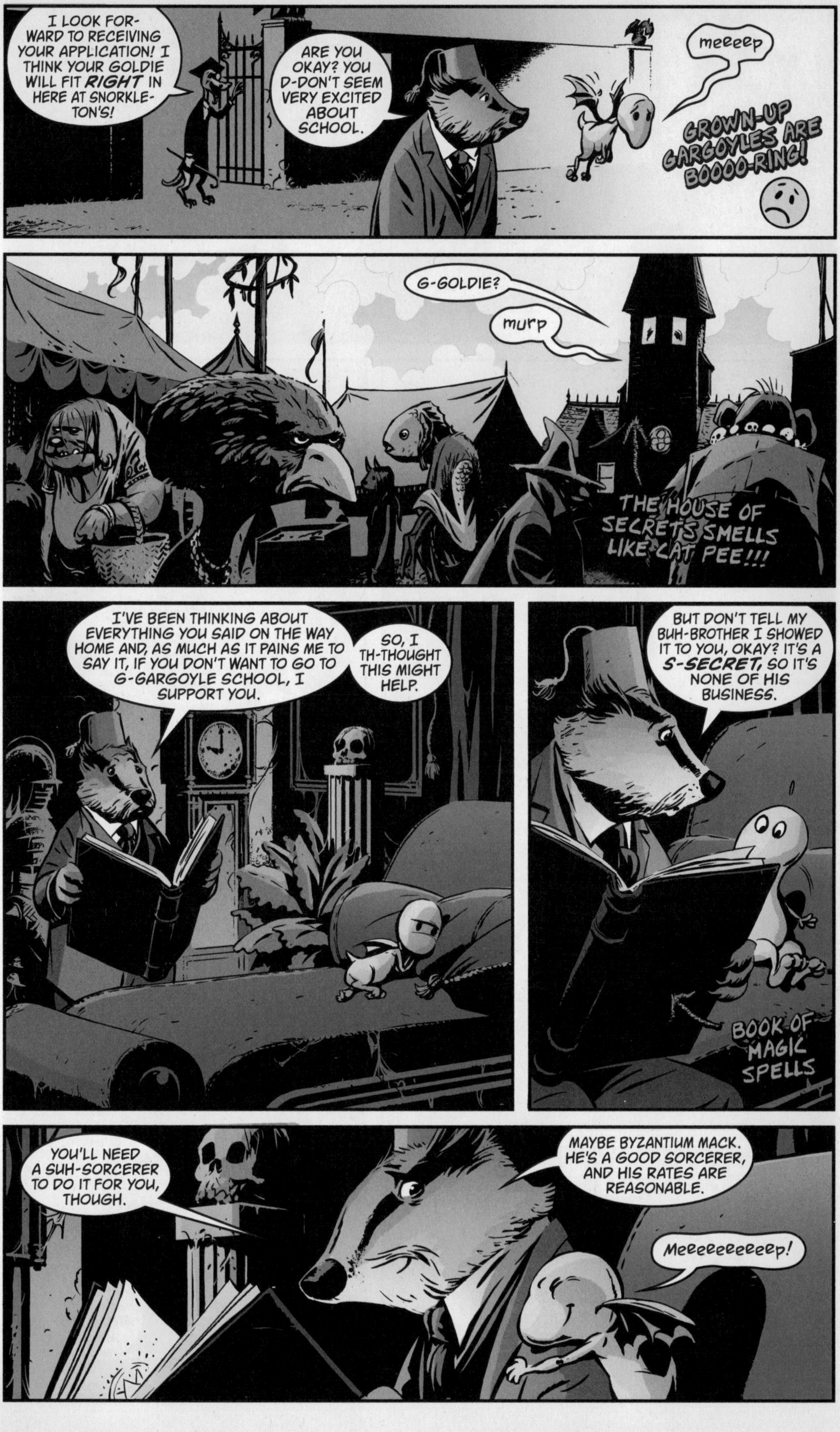
I LOOK FORWARD TO RECEIVING YOUR APPLICATION! I THINK YOUR GOLDIE WILL FIT RIGHT IN HERE AT SNORKLETON'S!
ARE YOU OKAY? YOU D-DON'T SEEM VERY EXCITED ABOUT SCHOOL.
meeeep
GROWN-UP GARGOYLES ARE BOOOO-RING!
G-GOLDIE?
murp
THE HOUSE OF SECRETS SMELLS LIKE CAT PEE!!!
I'VE BEEN THINKING ABOUT EVERYTHING YOU SAID ON THE WAY HOME AND, AS MUCH AS IT PAINS ME TO SAY IT, IF YOU DON'T WANT TO GO TO G-GARGOYLE SCHOOL, I SUPPORT YOU.
SO, I TH-THOUGHT THIS MIGHT HELP.
BUT DON'T TELL MY BUH-BROTHER I SHOWED IT TO YOU, OKAY? IT'S A S-SECRET, SO IT'S NONE OF HIS BUSINESS.
BOOK OF MAGIC SPELLS
YOU'LL NEED A SUH-SORCERER TO DO IT FOR YOU, THOUGH.
MAYBE BYZANTIUM MACK. HE'S A GOOD SORCERER, AND HIS RATES ARE REASONABLE.
Meeeeeeeeeep!

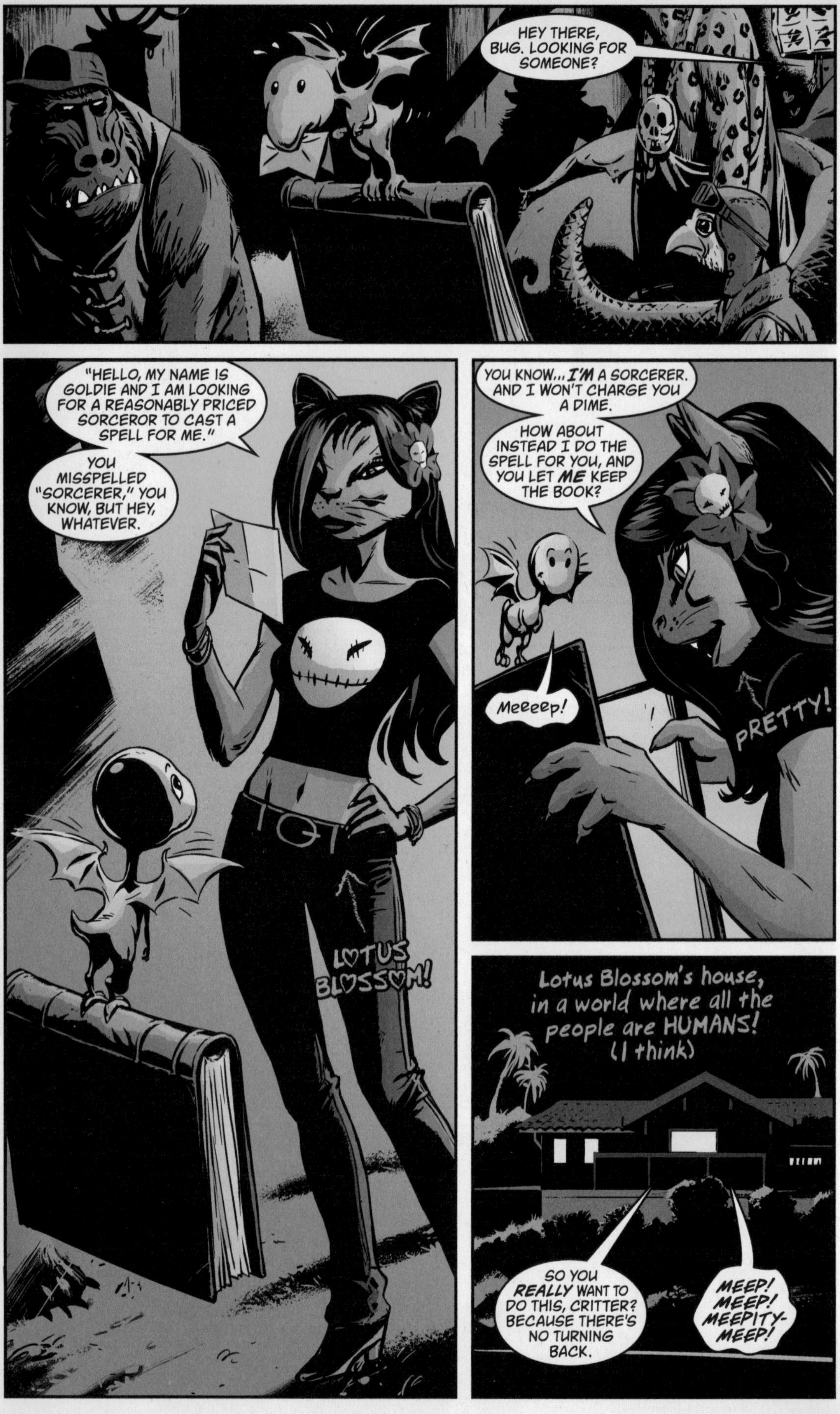
HEY THERE, BUG. LOOKING FOR SOMEONE?
"HELLO, MY NAME IS GOLDIE AND I AM LOOKING FOR A REASONABLY PRICED SORCEROR TO CAST A SPELL FOR ME."
YOU MISSPELLED "SORCERER," YOU KNOW, BUT HEY, WHATEVER.
LOTUS BLOSSOM!
YOU KNOW... I'M A SORCERER. AND I WON'T CHARGE YOU A DIME.
HOW ABOUT INSTEAD I DO THE SPELL FOR YOU, AND YOU LET ME KEEP THE BOOK?
Meeeep!
PRETTY!
Lotus Blossom's house, in a world where all the people are HUMANS! (I think)
SO YOU REALLY WANT TO DO THIS, CRITTER? BECAUSE THERE'S NO TURNING BACK.
MEEP! MEEP! MEEPITY-MEEP!

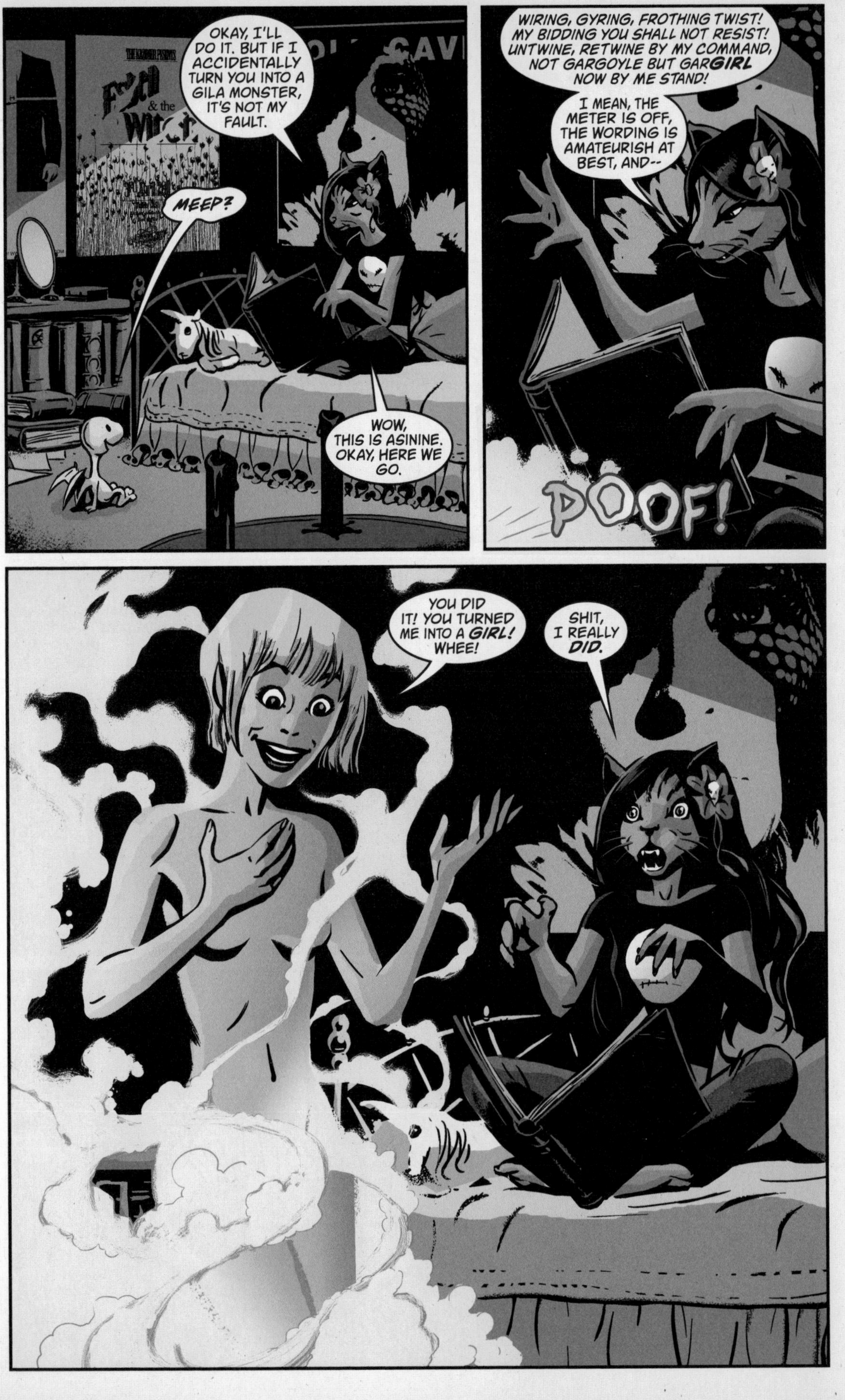
OKAY, I'LL DO IT. BUT IF I ACCIDENTALLY TURN YOU INTO A GILA MONSTER, IT'S NOT MY FAULT.
MEEP?
WOW, THIS IS ASININE. OKAY, HERE WE GO.
WIRING, GYRING, FROTHING TWIST! MY BIDDING YOU SHALL NOT RESIST! UNTWINE, RETWINE BY MY COMMAND, NOT GARGOYLE BUT GARGIRL NOW BY ME STAND!
I MEAN, THE METER IS OFF, THE WORDING IS AMATEURISH AT BEST, AND--
POOF!
YOU DID IT! YOU TURNED ME INTO A GIRL! WHEE!
SHIT, I REALLY DID.

THEN WE HAD ADVENTURES!

(It all happened very fast and I might be remembering some of it wrong.)

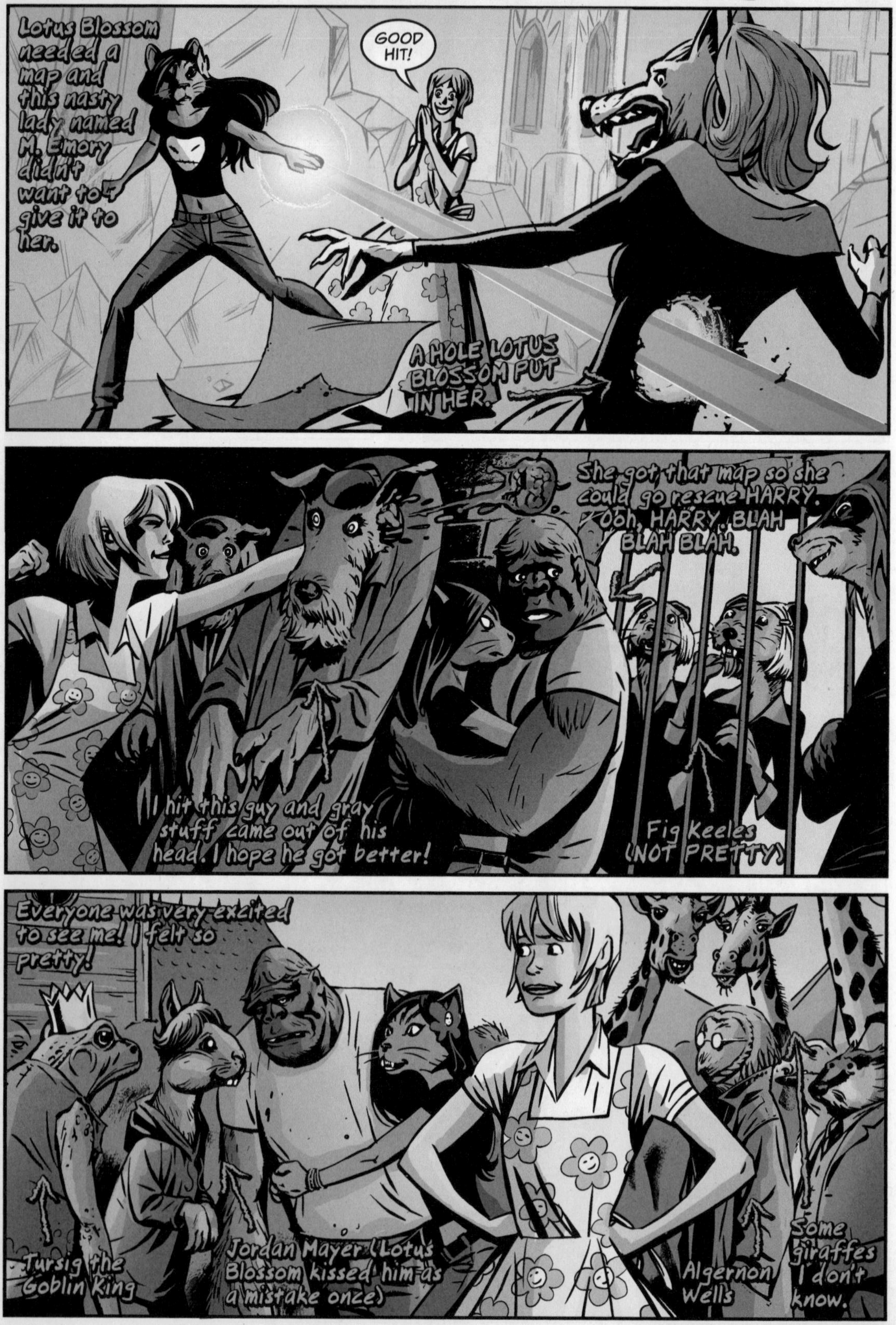
Lotus Blossom needed a map and this nasty lady named M. Emory didn't want to give it to her.
GOOD HIT!
A HOLE LOTUS BLOSSOM PUT IN HER.
She got that map so she could go rescue HARRY. Ooh, HARRY, BLAH BLAH BLAH.
I hit this guy and gray stuff came out of his head. I hope he got better!
Fig Keeles (NOT PRETTY)
Everyone was very excited to see me! I felt so pretty!
Tursig the Goblin King
Jordan Mayer (Lotus Blossom kissed him as a mistake once)
Algernon Wells
Some giraffes I don't know.

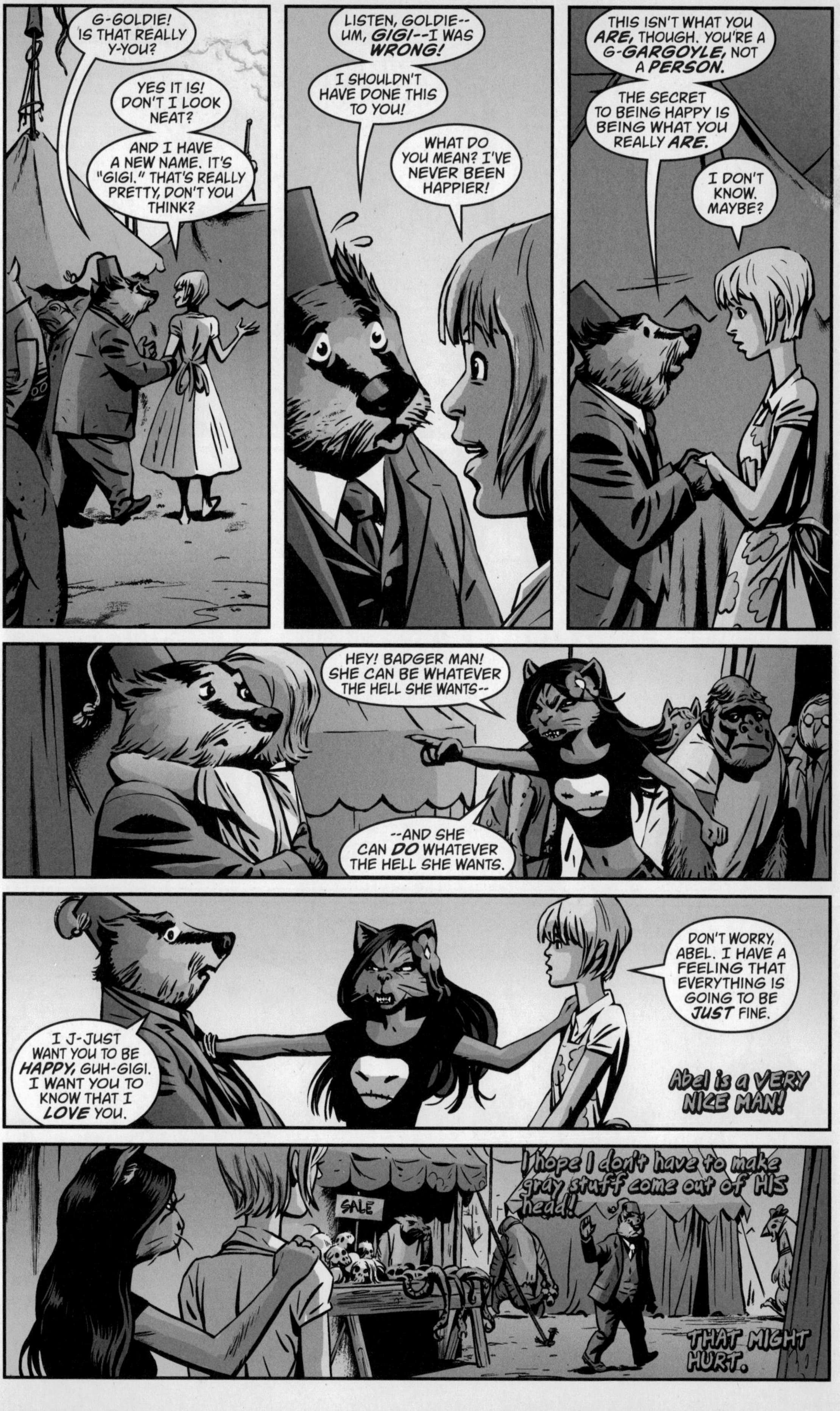
G-GOLDIE! IS THAT REALLY Y-YOU?
YES IT IS! DON'T I LOOK NEAT?
AND I HAVE A NEW NAME. IT'S "GIGI." THAT'S REALLY PRETTY, DON'T YOU THINK?
LISTEN, GOLDIE-- UM, GIGI--I WAS WRONG!
I SHOULDN'T HAVE DONE THIS TO YOU!
WHAT DO YOU MEAN? I'VE NEVER BEEN HAPPIER!
THIS ISN'T WHAT YOU ARE, THOUGH. YOU'RE A G-GARGOYLE, NOT A PERSON.
THE SECRET TO BEING HAPPY IS BEING WHAT YOU REALLY ARE.
I DON'T KNOW. MAYBE?
HEY! BADGER MAN! SHE CAN BE WHATEVER THE HELL SHE WANTS--
--AND SHE CAN DO WHATEVER THE HELL SHE WANTS.
I J-JUST WANT YOU TO BE HAPPY, GUH-GIGI. I WANT YOU TO KNOW THAT I LOVE YOU.
DON'T WORRY, ABEL. I HAVE A FEELING THAT EVERYTHING IS GOING TO BE JUST FINE.
Abel is a VERY NICE MAN!
SALE
I hope I don't have to make gray stuff come out of HIS head!
THAT MIGHT HURT.

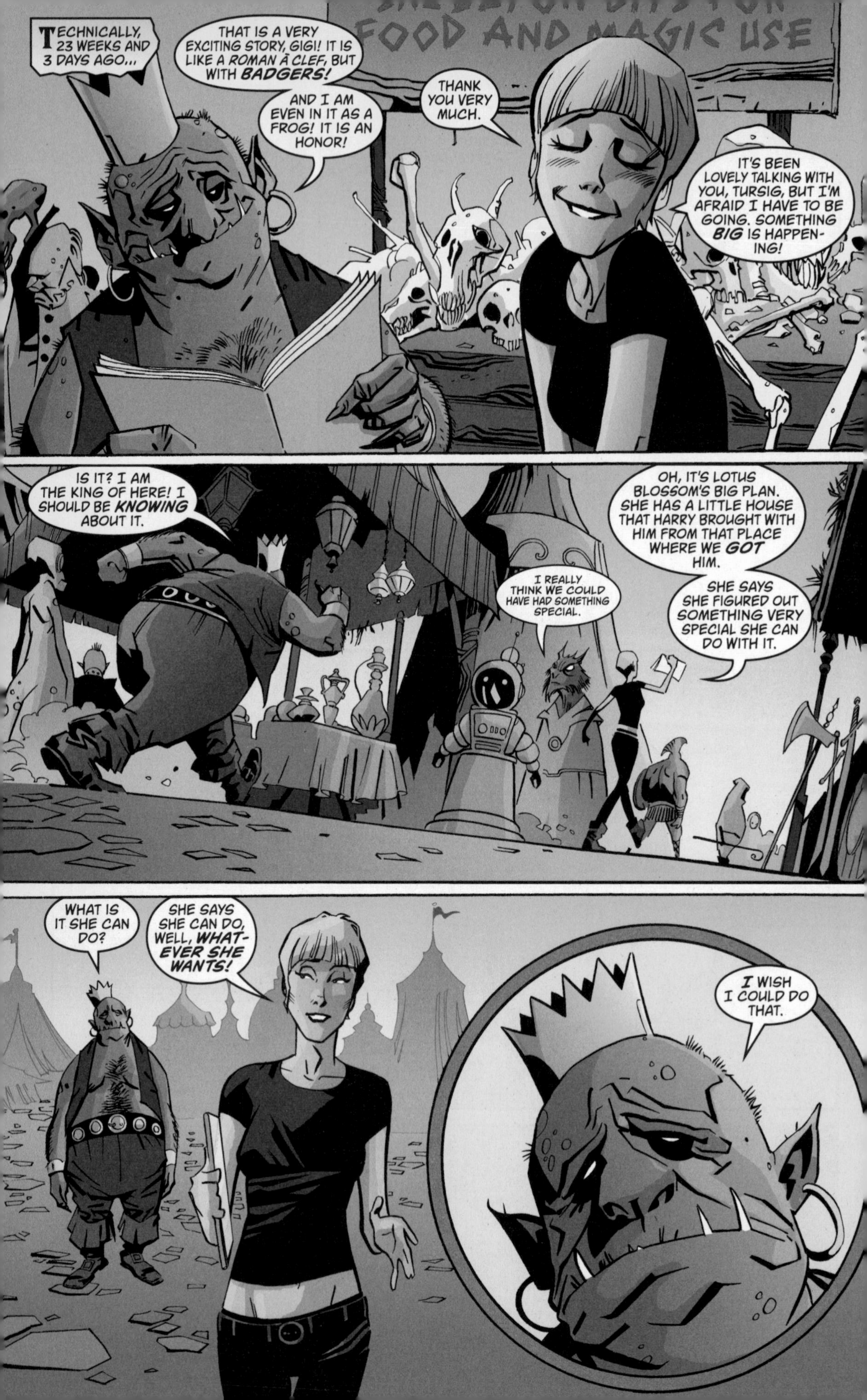
TECHNICALLY, 23 WEEKS AND 3 DAYS AGO...
FOOD AND MAGIC USE
THAT IS A VERY EXCITING STORY, GIGI! IT IS LIKE A ROMAN À CLEF, BUT WITH BADGERS!
AND I AM EVEN IN IT AS A FROG! IT IS AN HONOR!
THANK YOU VERY MUCH.
IT'S BEEN LOVELY TALKING WITH YOU, TURSIG, BUT I'M AFRAID I HAVE TO BE GOING. SOMETHING BIG IS HAPPENING!
IS IT? I AM THE KING OF HERE! I SHOULD BE KNOWING ABOUT IT.
OH, IT'S LOTUS BLOSSOM'S BIG PLAN. SHE HAS A LITTLE HOUSE THAT HARRY BROUGHT WITH HIM FROM THAT PLACE WHERE WE GOT HIM.
I REALLY THINK WE COULD HAVE HAD SOMETHING SPECIAL.
SHE SAYS SHE FIGURED OUT SOMETHING VERY SPECIAL SHE CAN DO WITH IT.
WHAT IS IT SHE CAN DO?
SHE SAYS SHE CAN DO, WELL, WHATEVER SHE WANTS!
I WISH I COULD DO THAT.

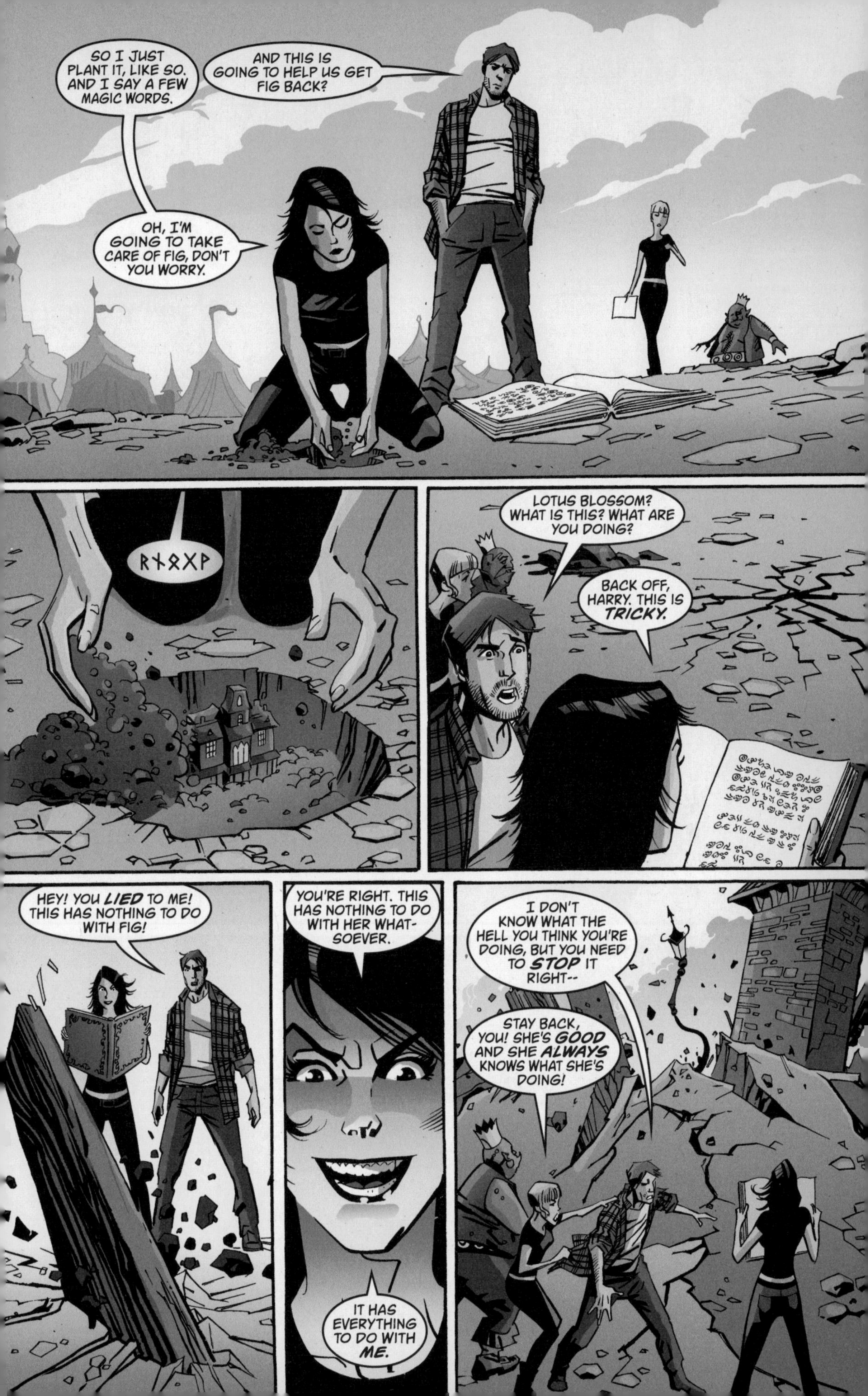

SO I JUST PLANT IT, LIKE SO. AND I SAY A FEW MAGIC WORDS.
AND THIS IS GOING TO HELP US GET FIG BACK?
OH, I'M GOING TO TAKE CARE OF FIG, DON'T YOU WORRY.
LOTUS BLOSSOM? WHAT IS THIS? WHAT ARE YOU DOING?
BACK OFF, HARRY. THIS IS TRICKY.
HEY! YOU LIED TO ME! THIS HAS NOTHING TO DO WITH FIG!
YOU'RE RIGHT. THIS HAS NOTHING TO DO WITH HER WHAT-SOEVER.
IT HAS EVERYTHING TO DO WITH ME.
I DON'T KNOW WHAT THE HELL YOU THINK YOU'RE DOING, BUT YOU NEED TO STOP IT RIGHT--
STAY BACK, YOU! SHE'S GOOD AND SHE ALWAYS KNOWS WHAT SHE'S DOING!

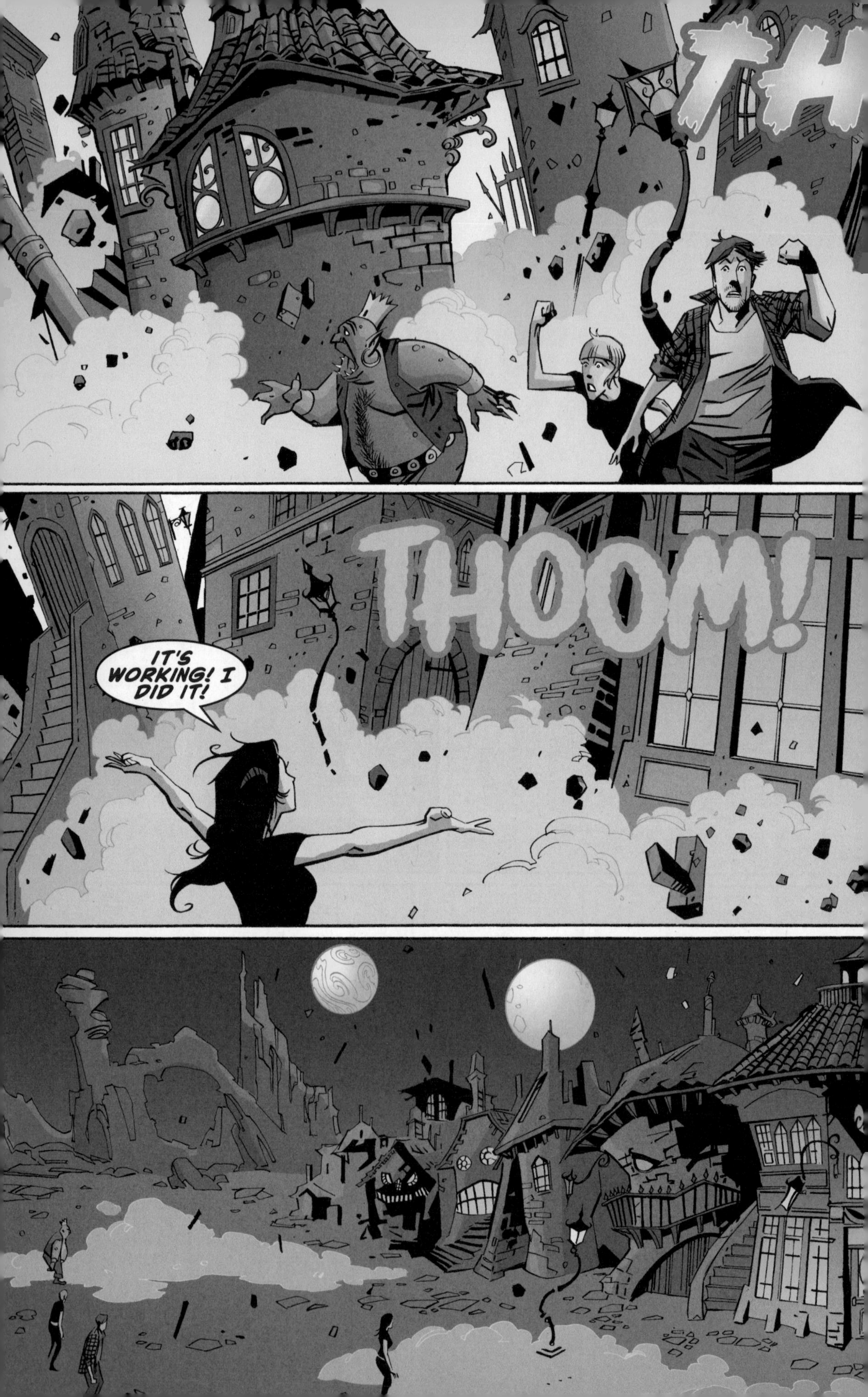
TH
THOOM!
IT'S WORKING! I DID IT!

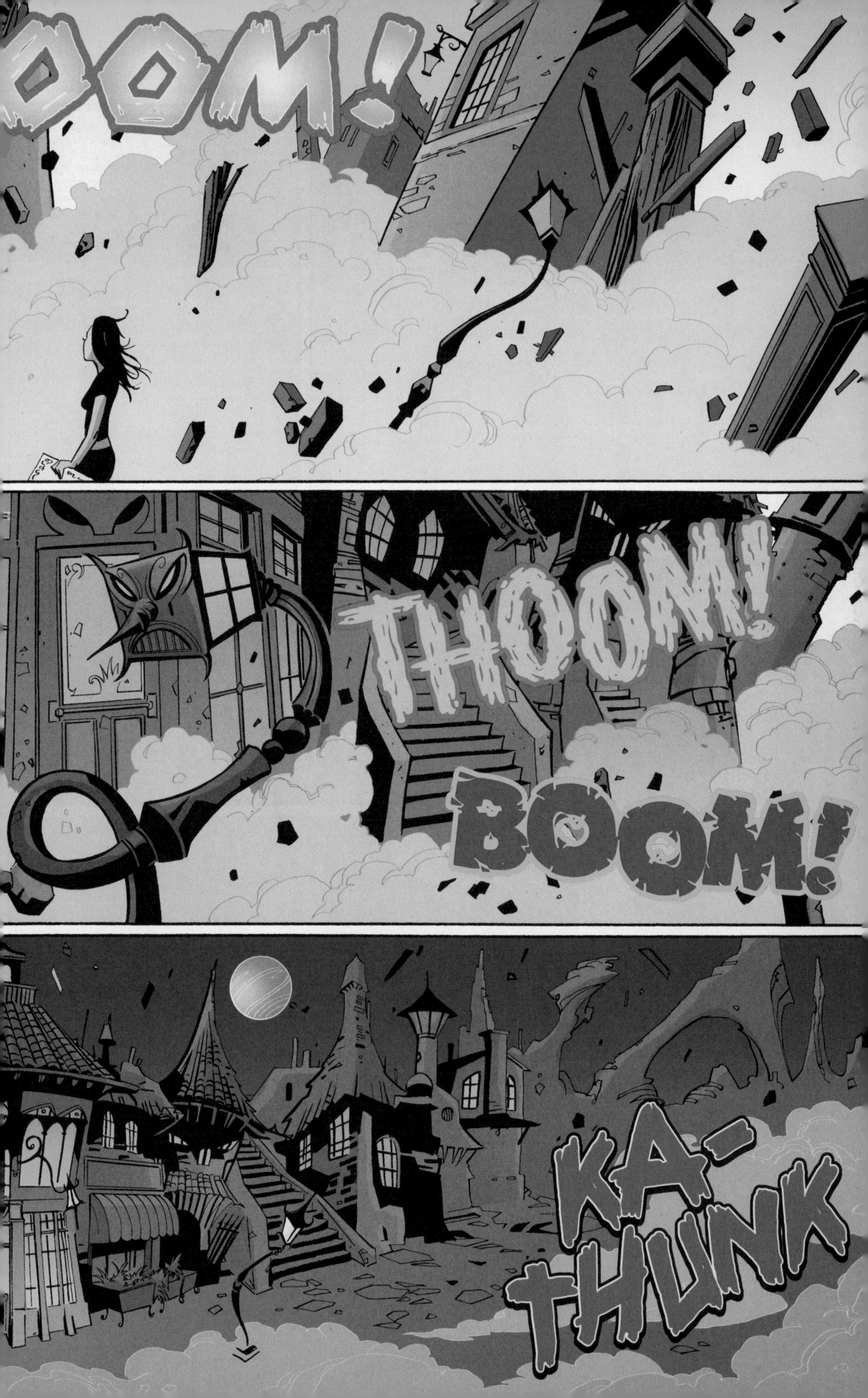
OOM!
THOOM!
BOOM!
KA-THUNK

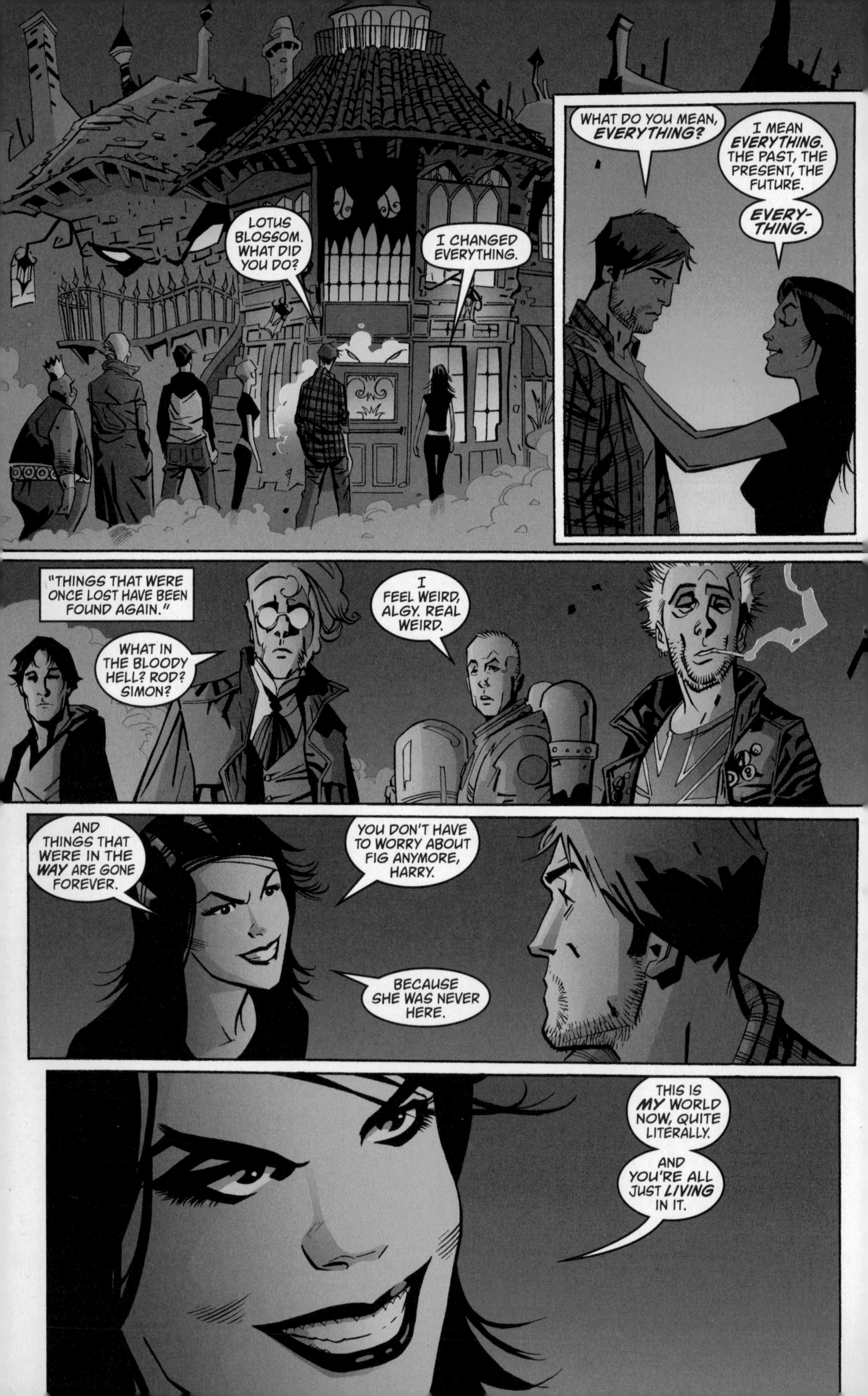
LOTUS BLOSSOM. WHAT DID YOU DO?
I CHANGED EVERYTHING.
WHAT DO YOU MEAN, EVERYTHING?
I MEAN EVERYTHING. THE PAST, THE PRESENT, THE FUTURE.
EVERY-THING.
"THINGS THAT WERE ONCE LOST HAVE BEEN FOUND AGAIN."
WHAT IN THE BLOODY HELL? ROD? SIMON?
I FEEL WEIRD, ALGY. REAL WEIRD.
AND THINGS THAT WERE IN THE WAY ARE GONE FOREVER.
YOU DON'T HAVE TO WORRY ABOUT FIG ANYMORE, HARRY.
BECAUSE SHE WAS NEVER HERE.
THIS IS MY WORLD NOW, QUITE LITERALLY.
AND YOU'RE ALL JUST LIVING IN IT.

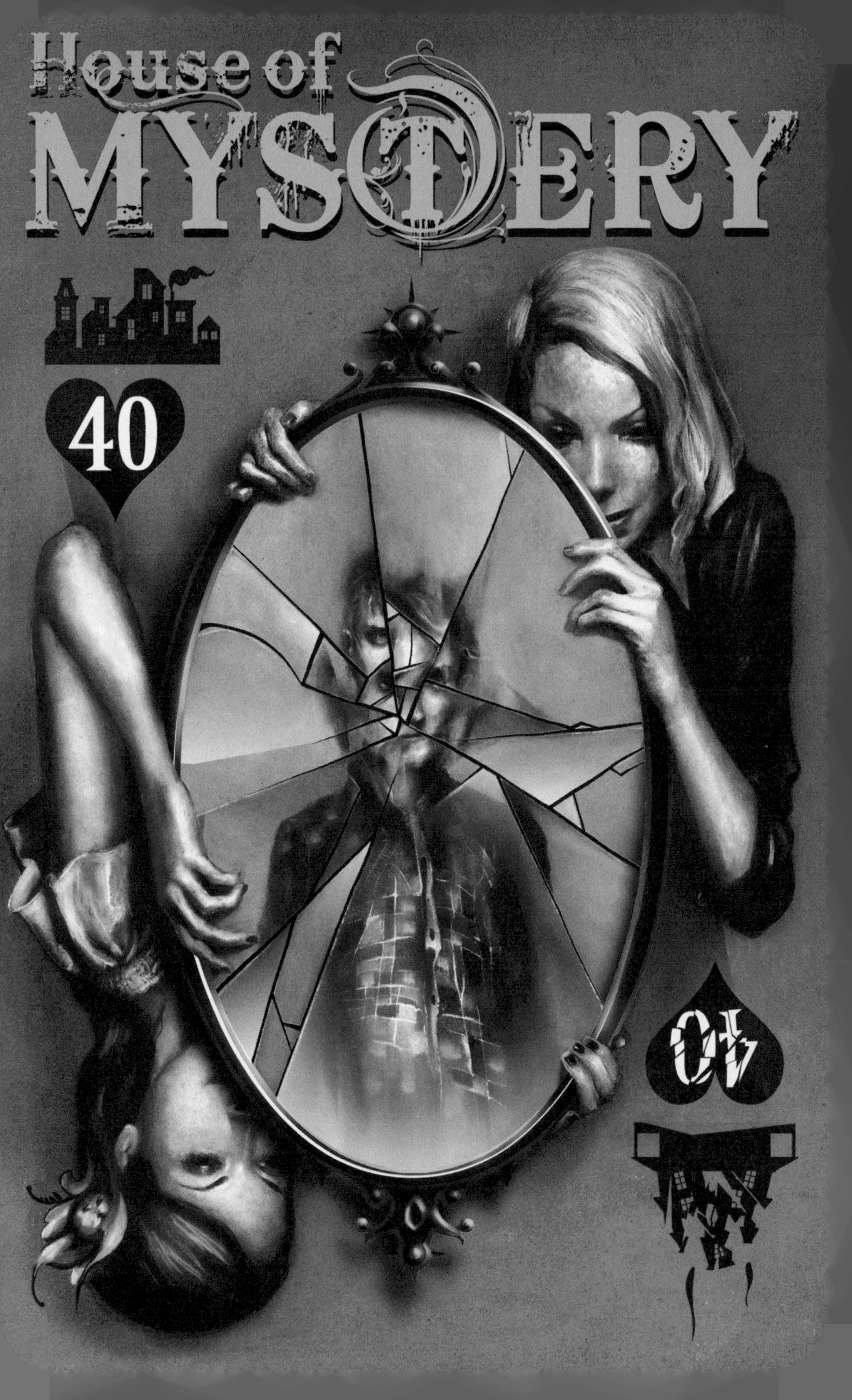
House of MYSTERY
40

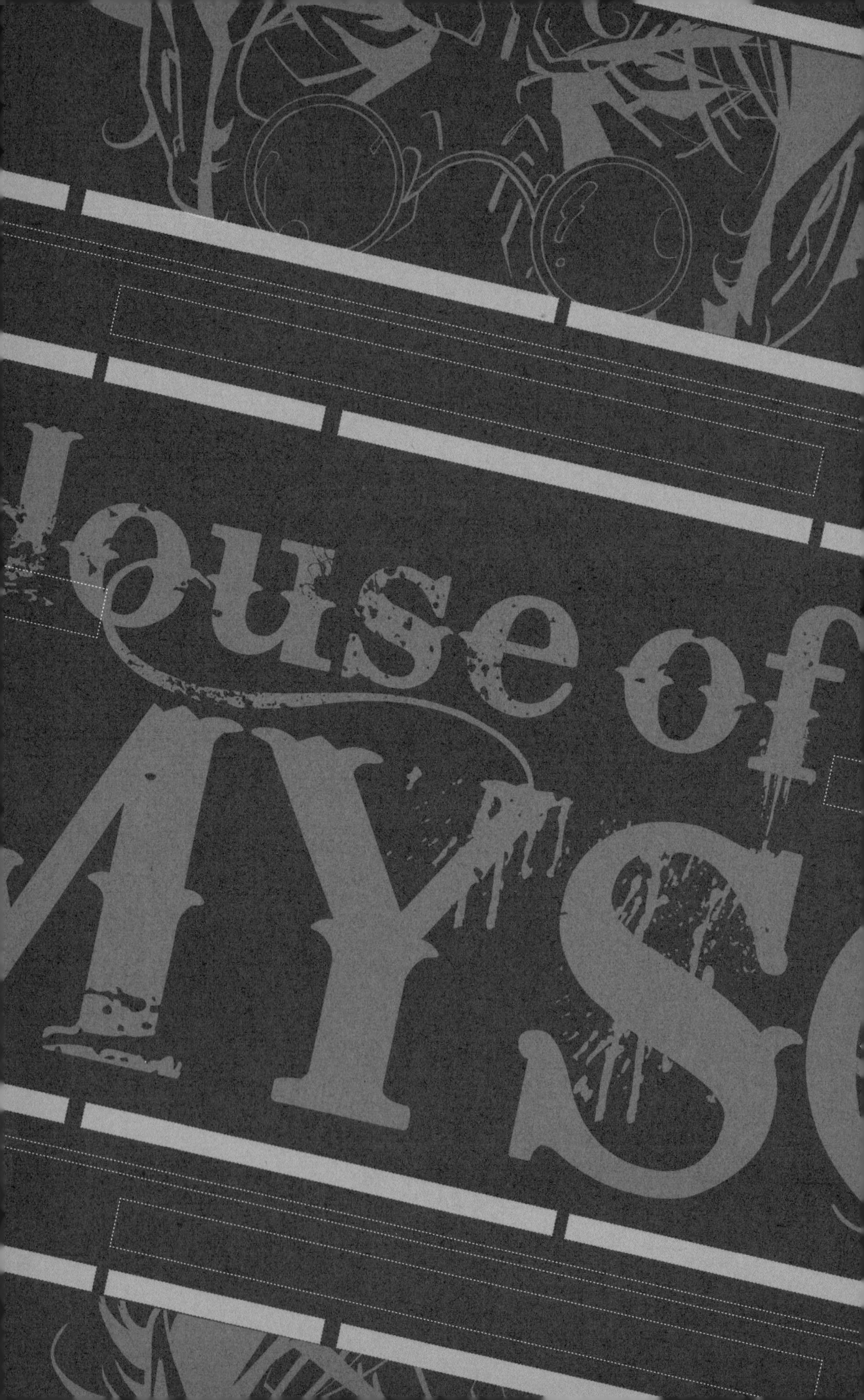
ouse of

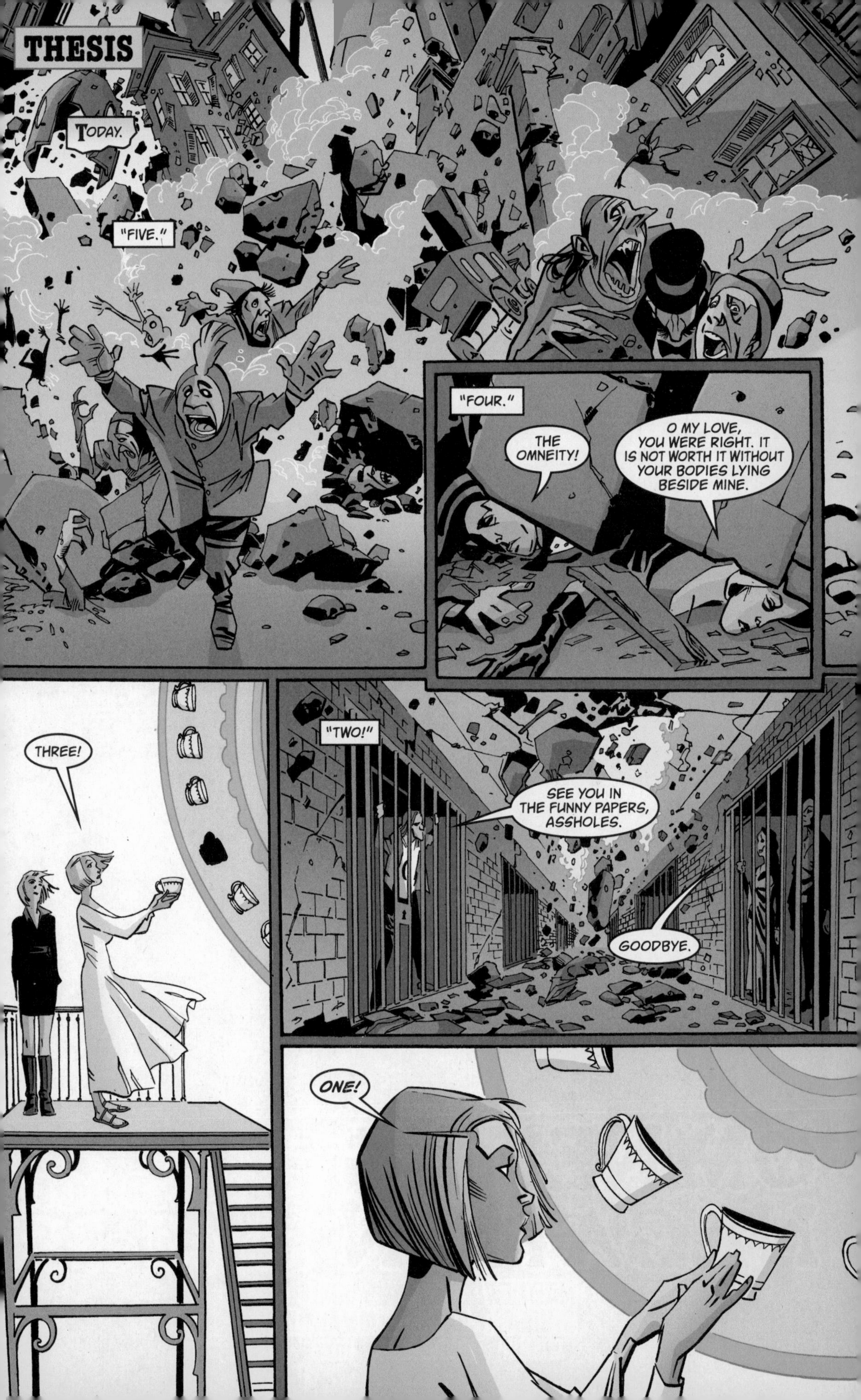
THESIS
TODAY.
"FIVE."
"FOUR."
THE OMNEITY!
O MY LOVE, YOU WERE RIGHT. IT IS NOT WORTH IT WITHOUT YOUR BODIES LYING BESIDE MINE.
THREE!
"TWO!"
SEE YOU IN THE FUNNY PAPERS, ASSHOLES.
GOODBYE.
ONE!

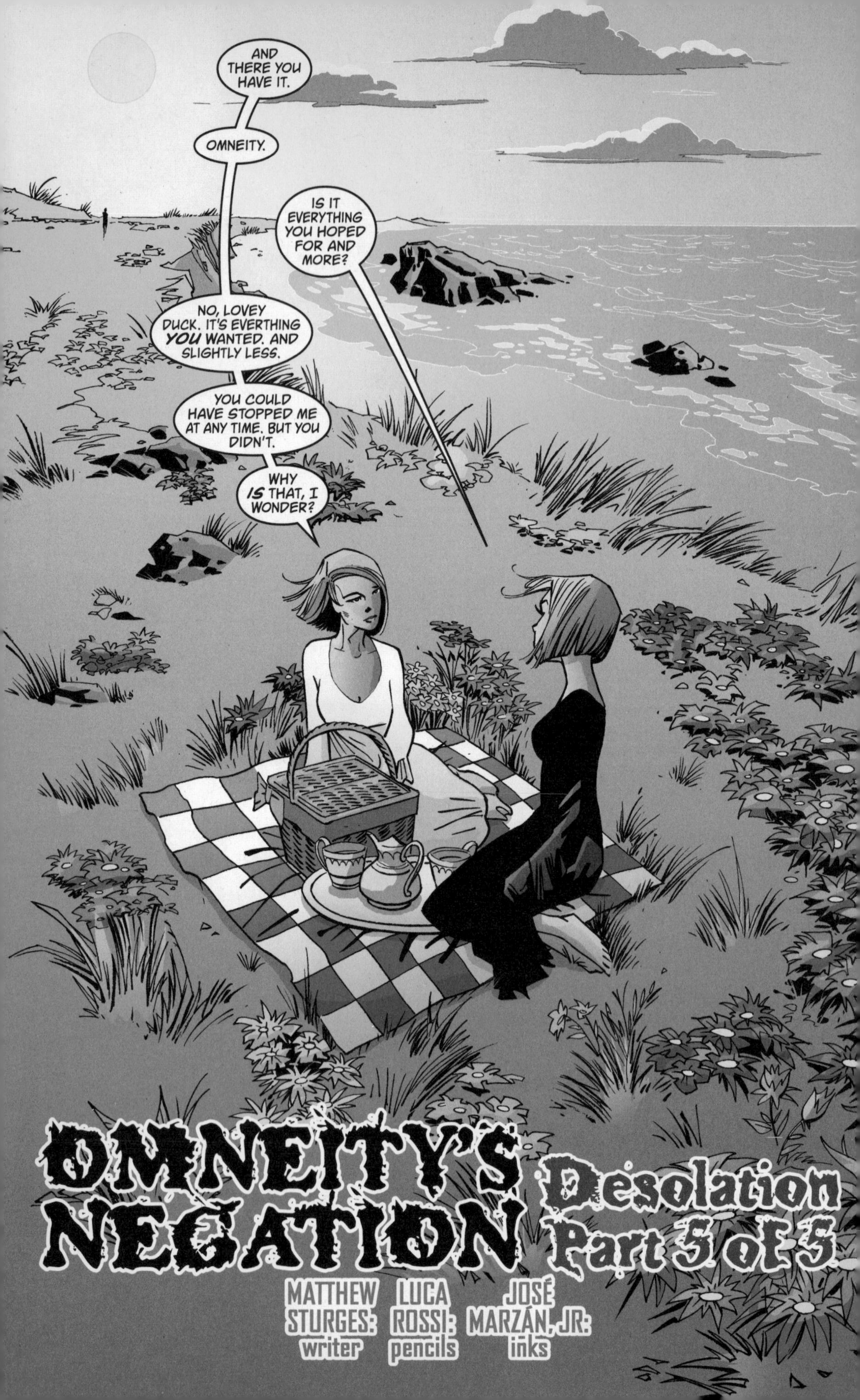
AND THERE YOU HAVE IT.
OMNEITY.
IS IT EVERYTHING YOU HOPED FOR AND MORE?
NO, LOVEY DUCK. IT'S EVERTHING YOU WANTED. AND SLIGHTLY LESS.
YOU COULD HAVE STOPPED ME AT ANY TIME. BUT YOU DIDN'T.
WHY IS THAT, I WONDER?
OMNEITY'S NEGATION
Desolation Part 5 of 5
MATTHEW STURGES: writer
LUCA ROSSI: pencils
JOSÉ MARZÁN, JR: inks

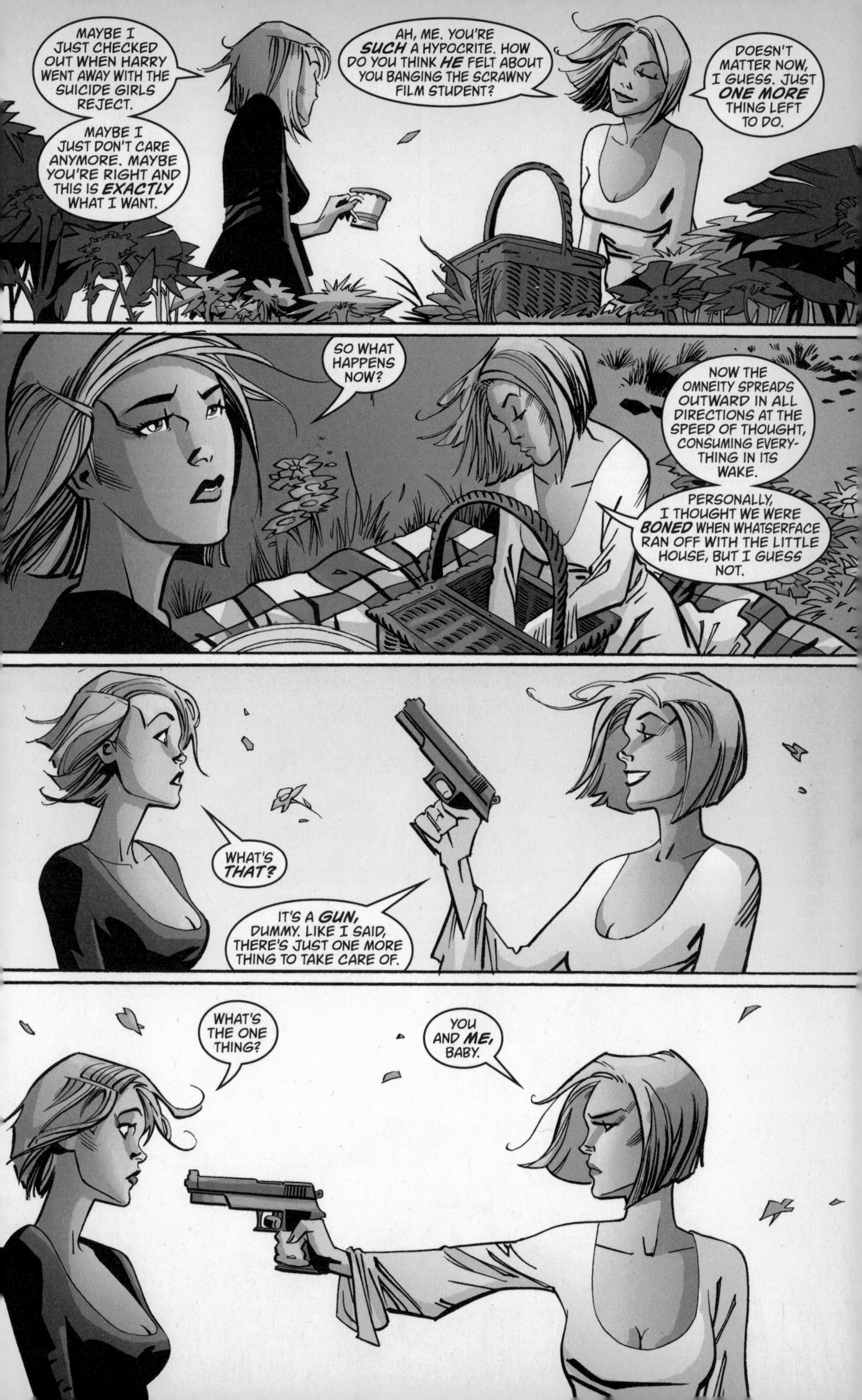
MAYBE I JUST CHECKED OUT WHEN HARRY WENT AWAY WITH THE SUICIDE GIRLS REJECT.
MAYBE I JUST DON'T CARE ANYMORE. MAYBE YOU'RE RIGHT AND THIS IS EXACTLY WHAT I WANT.
AH, ME. YOU'RE SUCH A HYPOCRITE. HOW DO YOU THINK HE FELT ABOUT YOU BANGING THE SCRAWNY FILM STUDENT?
DOESN'T MATTER NOW, I GUESS. JUST ONE MORE THING LEFT TO DO.
SO WHAT HAPPENS NOW?
NOW THE OMNEITY SPREADS OUTWARD IN ALL DIRECTIONS AT THE SPEED OF THOUGHT, CONSUMING EVERY-THING IN ITS WAKE.
PERSONALLY, I THOUGHT WE WERE BONED WHEN WHATSERFACE RAN OFF WITH THE LITTLE HOUSE, BUT I GUESS NOT.
WHAT'S THAT?
IT'S A GUN, DUMMY. LIKE I SAID, THERE'S JUST ONE MORE THING TO TAKE CARE OF.
WHAT'S THE ONE THING?
YOU AND ME, BABY.

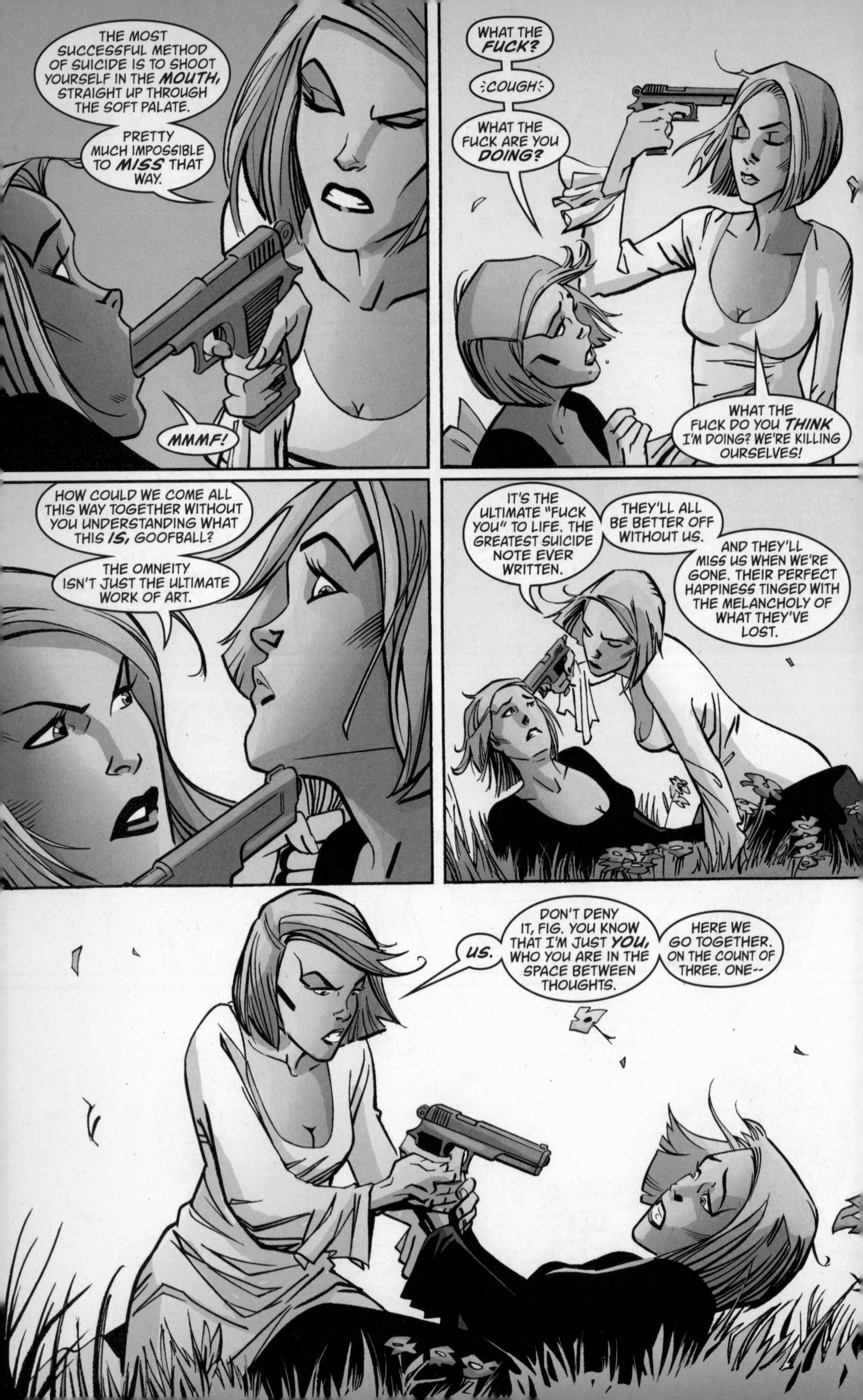

THE MOST SUCCESSFUL METHOD OF SUICIDE IS TO SHOOT YOURSELF IN THE MOUTH, STRAIGHT UP THROUGH THE SOFT PALATE.
PRETTY MUCH IMPOSSIBLE TO MISS THAT WAY.
MMMF!
WHAT THE FUCK?
COUGH
WHAT THE FUCK ARE YOU DOING?
WHAT THE FUCK DO YOU THINK I'M DOING? WE'RE KILLING OURSELVES!
HOW COULD WE COME ALL THIS WAY TOGETHER WITHOUT YOU UNDERSTANDING WHAT THIS IS, GOOFBALL?
THE OMNEITY ISN'T JUST THE ULTIMATE WORK OF ART.
IT'S THE ULTIMATE "FUCK YOU" TO LIFE. THE GREATEST SUICIDE NOTE EVER WRITTEN.
THEY'LL ALL BE BETTER OFF WITHOUT US.
AND THEY'LL MISS US WHEN WE'RE GONE. THEIR PERFECT HAPPINESS TINGED WITH THE MELANCHOLY OF WHAT THEY'VE LOST.
US.
DON'T DENY IT, FIG. YOU KNOW THAT I'M JUST YOU, WHO YOU ARE IN THE SPACE BETWEEN THOUGHTS.
HERE WE GO TOGETHER. ON THE COUNT OF THREE. ONE--

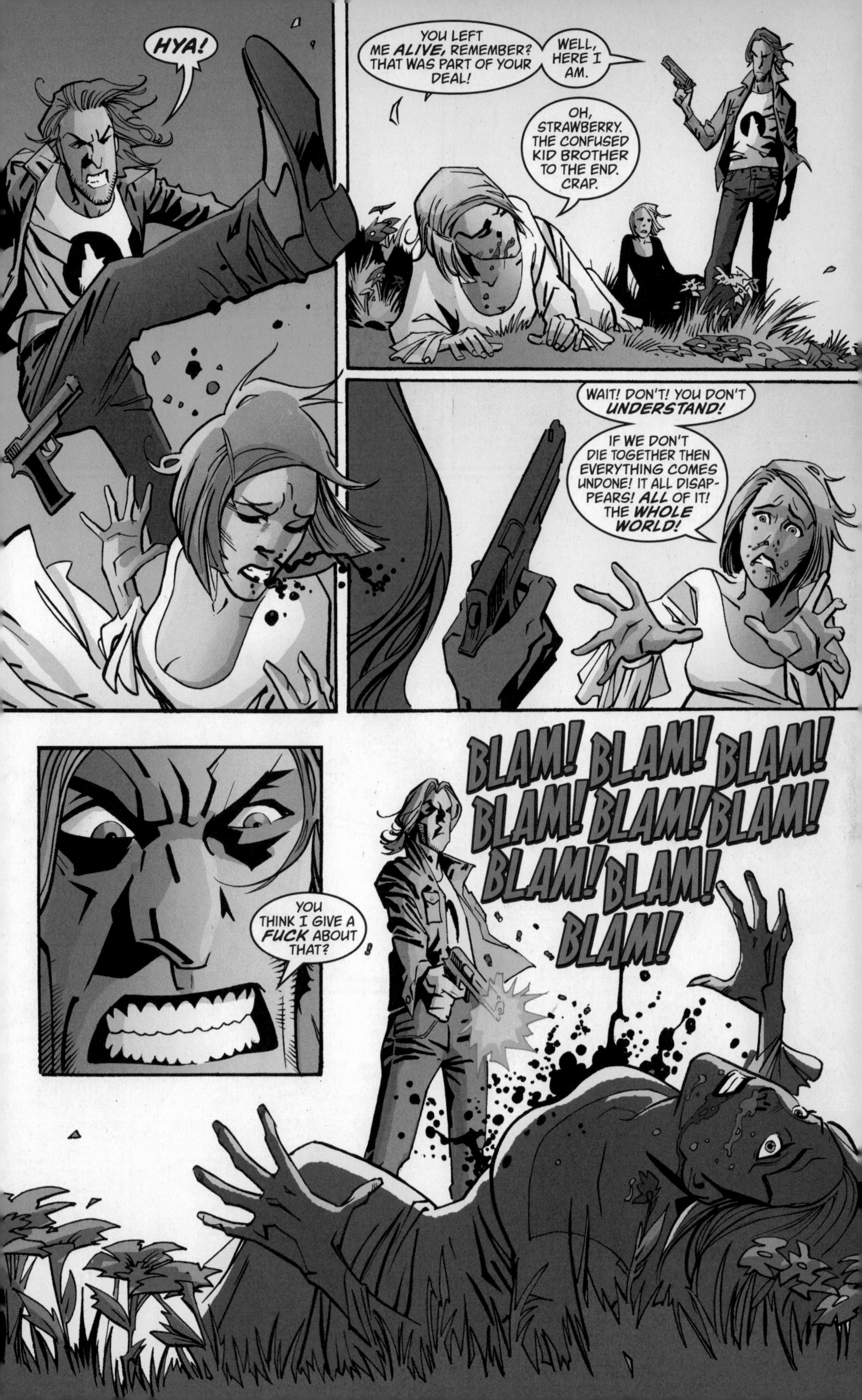

HYA!
YOU LEFT ME ALIVE, REMEMBER? THAT WAS PART OF YOUR DEAL!
WELL, HERE I AM.
OH, STRAWBERRY. THE CONFUSED KID BROTHER TO THE END. CRAP.
WAIT! DON'T! YOU DON'T UNDERSTAND!
IF WE DON'T DIE TOGETHER THEN EVERYTHING COMES UNDONE! IT ALL DISAP-PEARS! ALL OF IT! THE WHOLE WORLD!
YOU THINK I GIVE A FUCK ABOUT THAT?
BLAM! BLAM! BLAM! BLAM! BLAM! BLAM! BLAM! BLAM! BLAM!

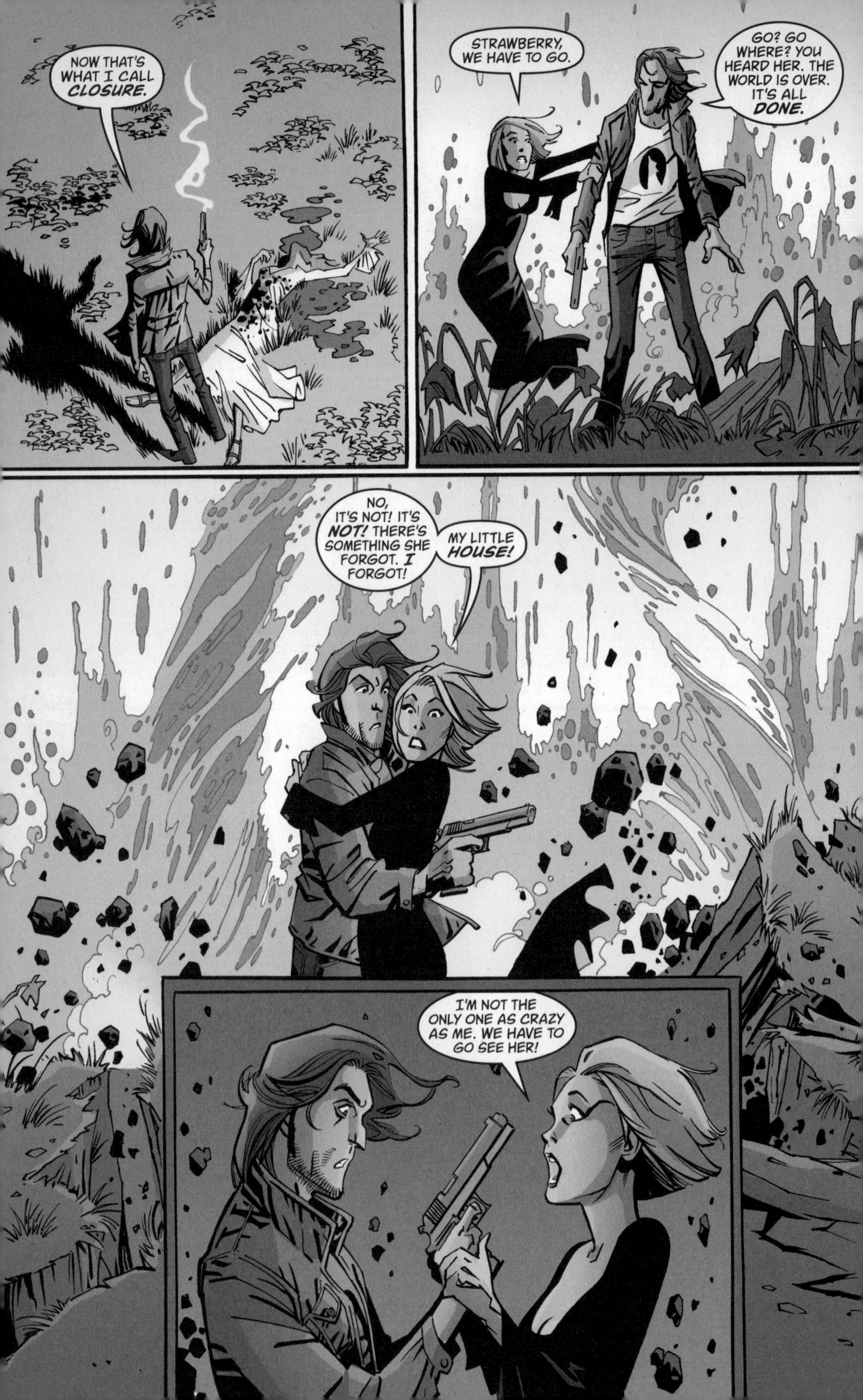
NOW THAT'S WHAT I CALL CLOSURE.
STRAWBERRY, WE HAVE TO GO.
GO? GO WHERE? YOU HEARD HER. THE WORLD IS OVER. IT'S ALL DONE.
NO, IT'S NOT! IT'S NOT! THERE'S SOMETHING SHE FORGOT. I FORGOT!
MY LITTLE HOUSE!
I'M NOT THE ONLY ONE AS CRAZY AS ME. WE HAVE TO GO SEE HER!

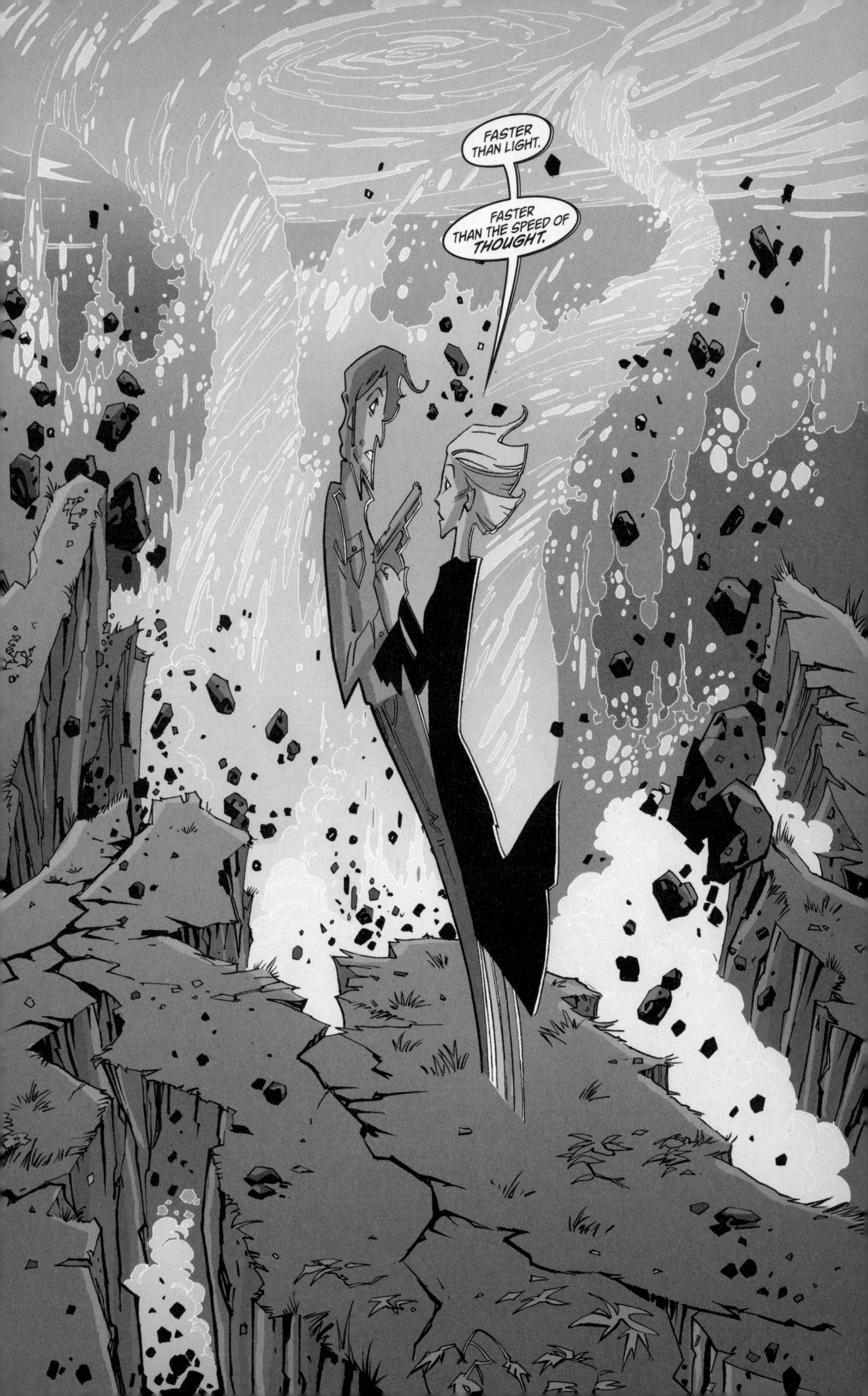
FASTER THAN LIGHT.
FASTER THAN THE SPEED OF THOUGHT.

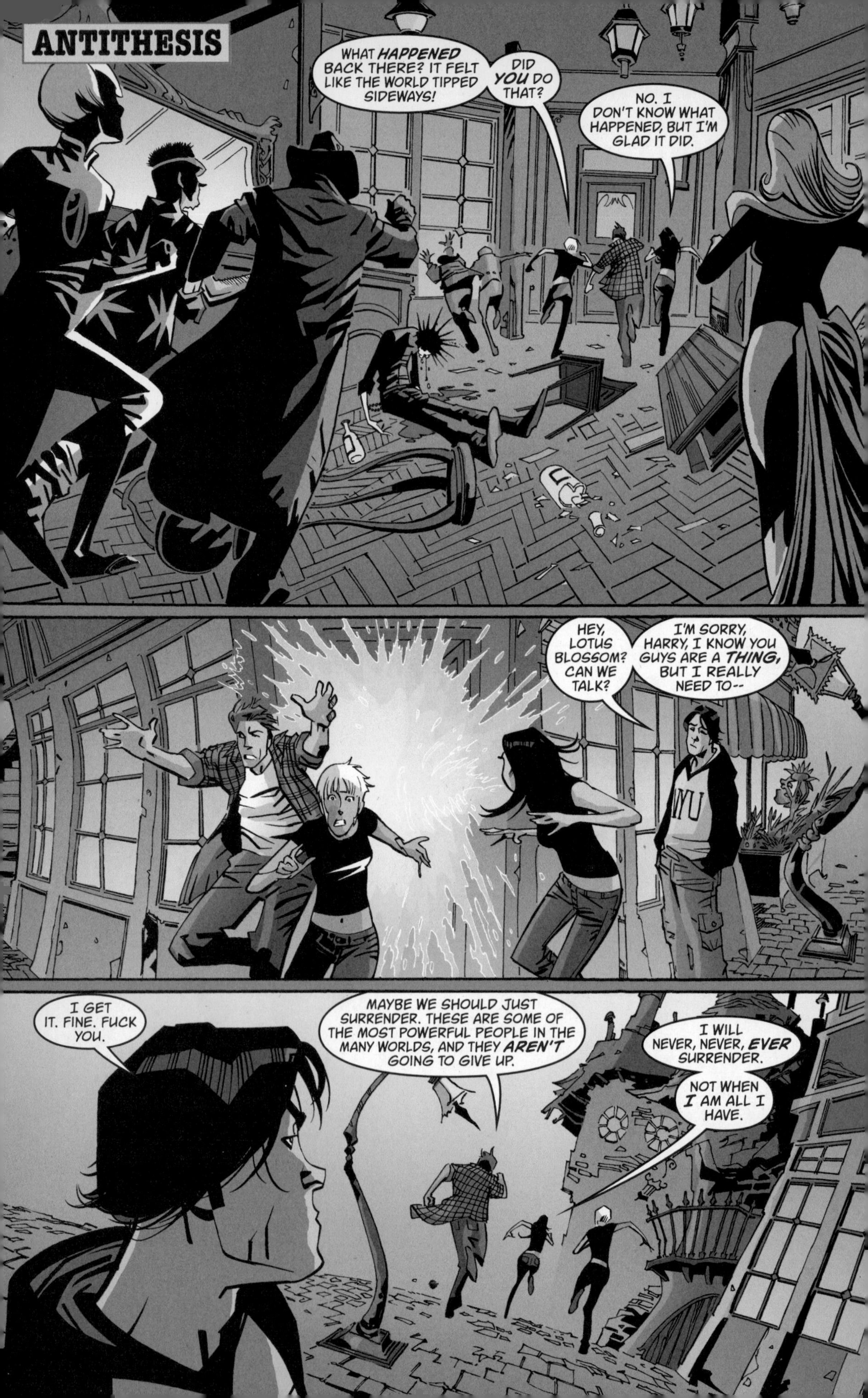
ANTITHESIS
WHAT HAPPENED BACK THERE? IT FELT LIKE THE WORLD TIPPED SIDEWAYS!
DID YOU DO THAT?
NO. I DON'T KNOW WHAT HAPPENED, BUT I'M GLAD IT DID.
HEY, LOTUS BLOSSOM? CAN WE TALK?
I'M SORRY, HARRY, I KNOW YOU GUYS ARE A THING, BUT I REALLY NEED TO--
I GET IT. FINE. FUCK YOU.
MAYBE WE SHOULD JUST SURRENDER. THESE ARE SOME OF THE MOST POWERFUL PEOPLE IN THE MANY WORLDS, AND THEY AREN'T GOING TO GIVE UP.
I WILL NEVER, NEVER, EVER SURRENDER.
NOT WHEN I AM ALL I HAVE.
NYU

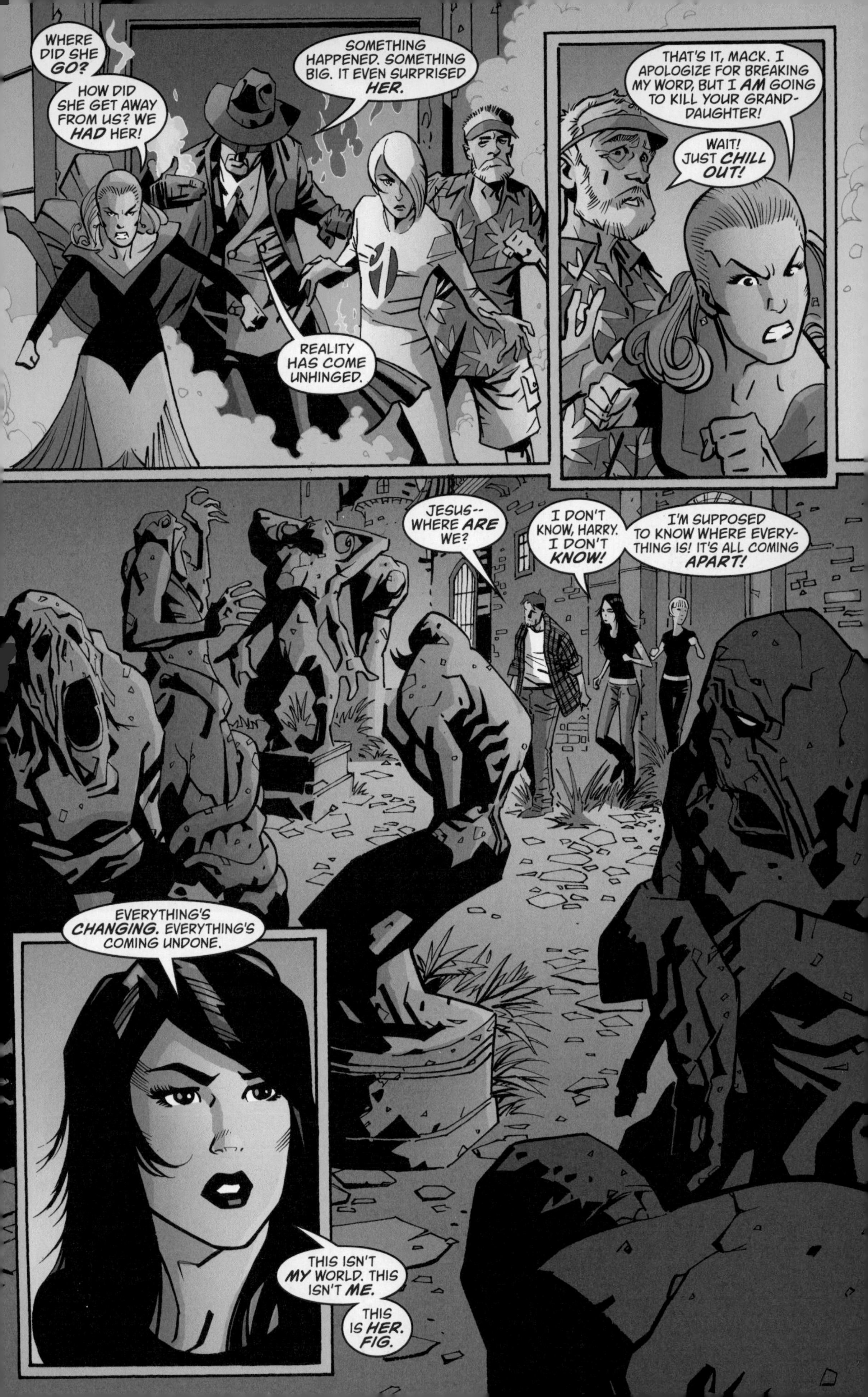
WHERE DID SHE GO?
HOW DID SHE GET AWAY FROM US? WE HAD HER!
SOMETHING HAPPENED. SOMETHING BIG. IT EVEN SURPRISED HER.
REALITY HAS COME UNHINGED.
THAT'S IT, MACK. I APOLOGIZE FOR BREAKING MY WORD, BUT I AM GOING TO KILL YOUR GRAND-DAUGHTER!
WAIT! JUST CHILL OUT!
JESUS-- WHERE ARE WE?
I DON'T KNOW, HARRY. I DON'T KNOW!
I'M SUPPOSED TO KNOW WHERE EVERY-THING IS! IT'S ALL COMING APART!
EVERYTHING'S CHANGING. EVERYTHING'S COMING UNDONE.
THIS ISN'T MY WORLD. THIS ISN'T ME.
THIS IS HER. FIG.

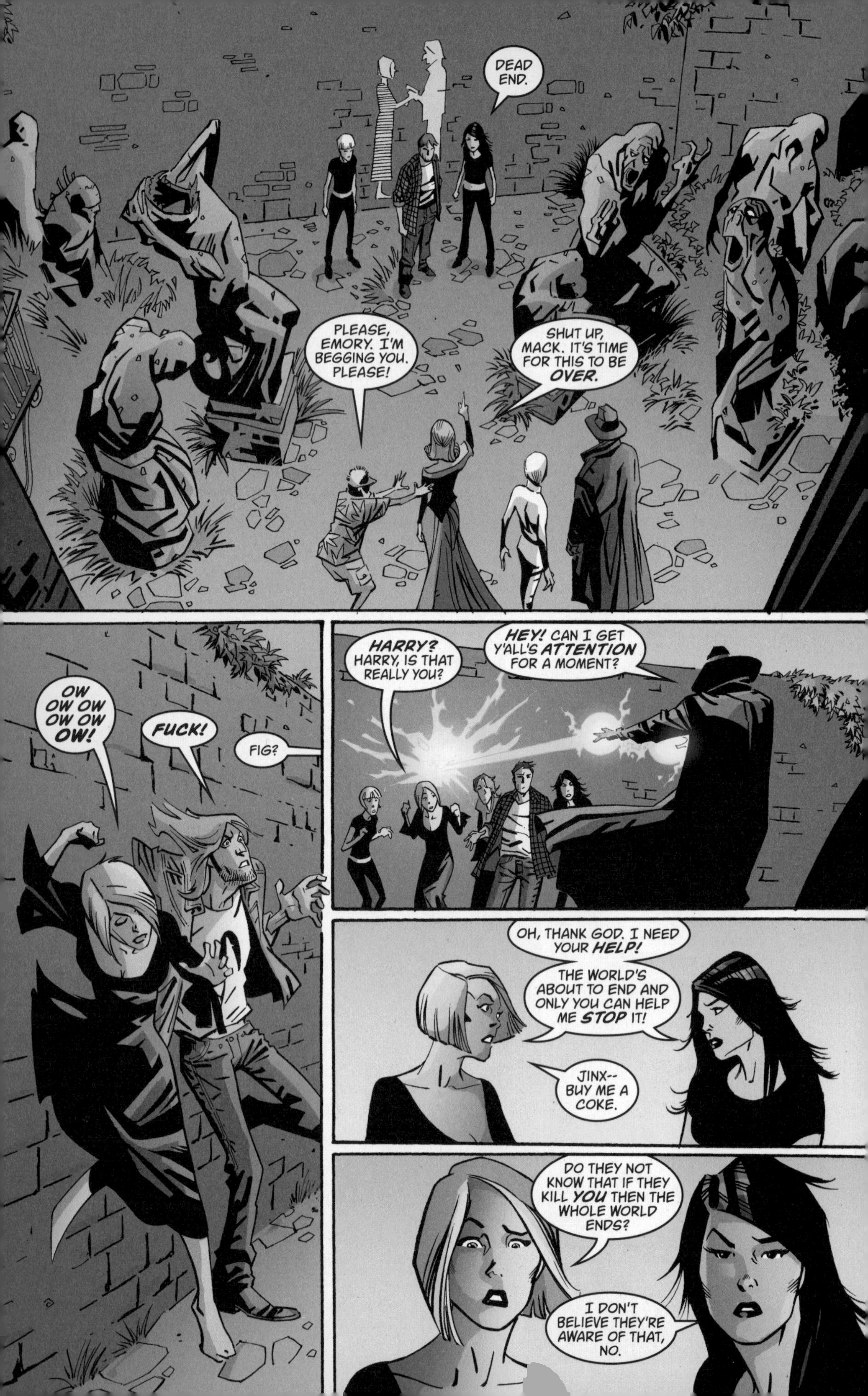
DEAD END.
PLEASE, EMORY. I'M BEGGING YOU. PLEASE!
SHUT UP, MACK. IT'S TIME FOR THIS TO BE OVER.
OW OW OW OW OW OW!
FUCK!
FIG?
HARRY? HARRY, IS THAT REALLY YOU?
HEY! CAN I GET Y'ALL'S ATTENTION FOR A MOMENT?
OH, THANK GOD. I NEED YOUR HELP!
THE WORLD'S ABOUT TO END AND ONLY YOU CAN HELP ME STOP IT!
JINX-- BUY ME A COKE.
DO THEY NOT KNOW THAT IF THEY KILL YOU THEN THE WHOLE WORLD ENDS?
I DON'T BELIEVE THEY'RE AWARE OF THAT, NO.

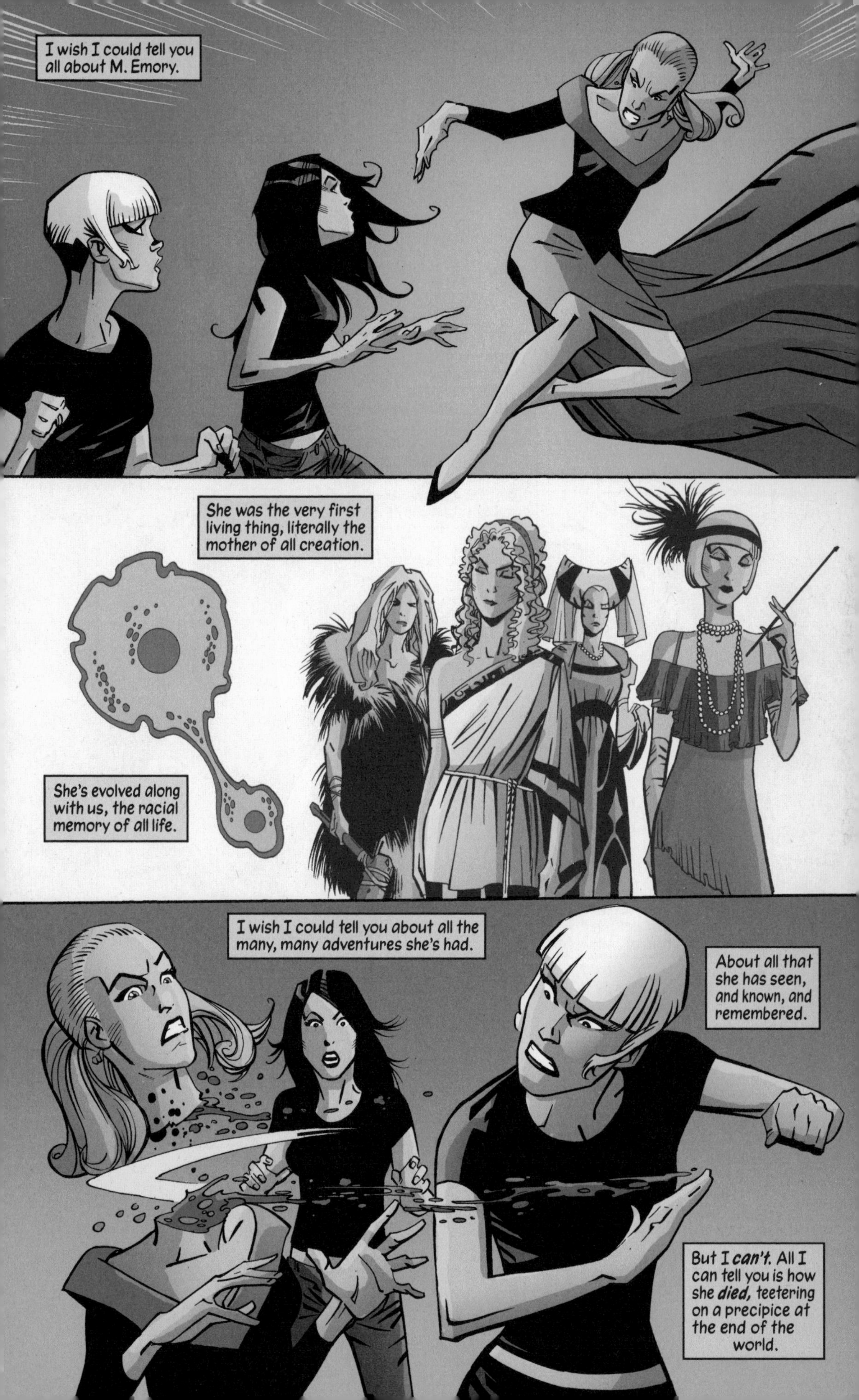
I wish I could tell you all about M. Emory.
She was the very first living thing, literally the mother of all creation.
She's evolved along with us, the racial memory of all life.
I wish I could tell you about all the many, many adventures she's had.
About all that she has seen, and known, and remembered.
But I *can't.* All I can tell you is how she *died,* teetering on a precipice at the end of the world.

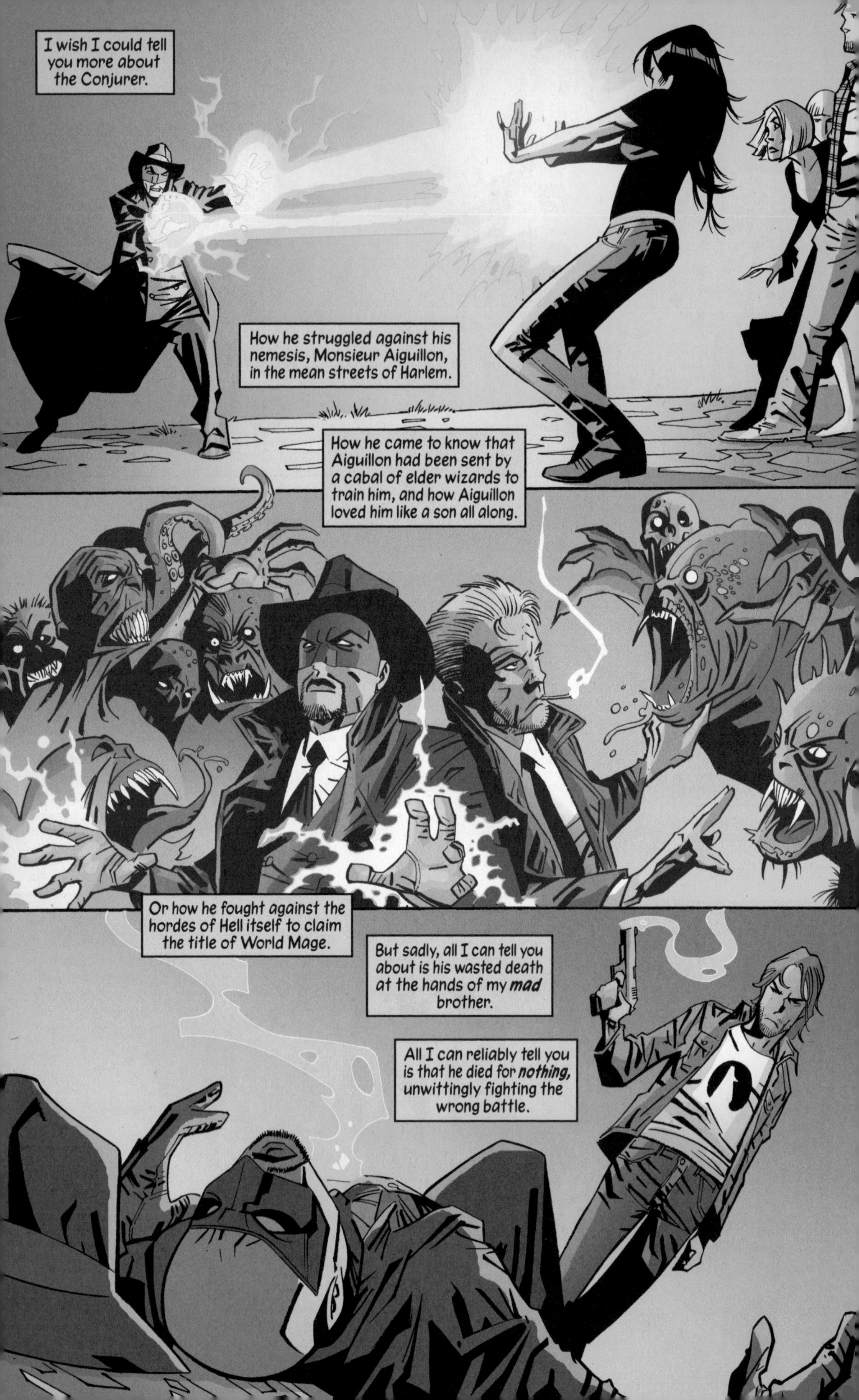

I wish I could tell you more about the Conjurer.
How he struggled against his nemesis, Monsieur Aiguillon, in the mean streets of Harlem.
How he came to know that Aiguillon had been sent by a cabal of elder wizards to train him, and how Aiguillon loved him like a son all along.
Or how he fought against the hordes of Hell itself to claim the title of World Mage.
But sadly, all I can tell you about is his wasted death at the hands of my *mad* brother.
All I can reliably tell you is that he died for ***nothing,*** unwittingly fighting the wrong battle.

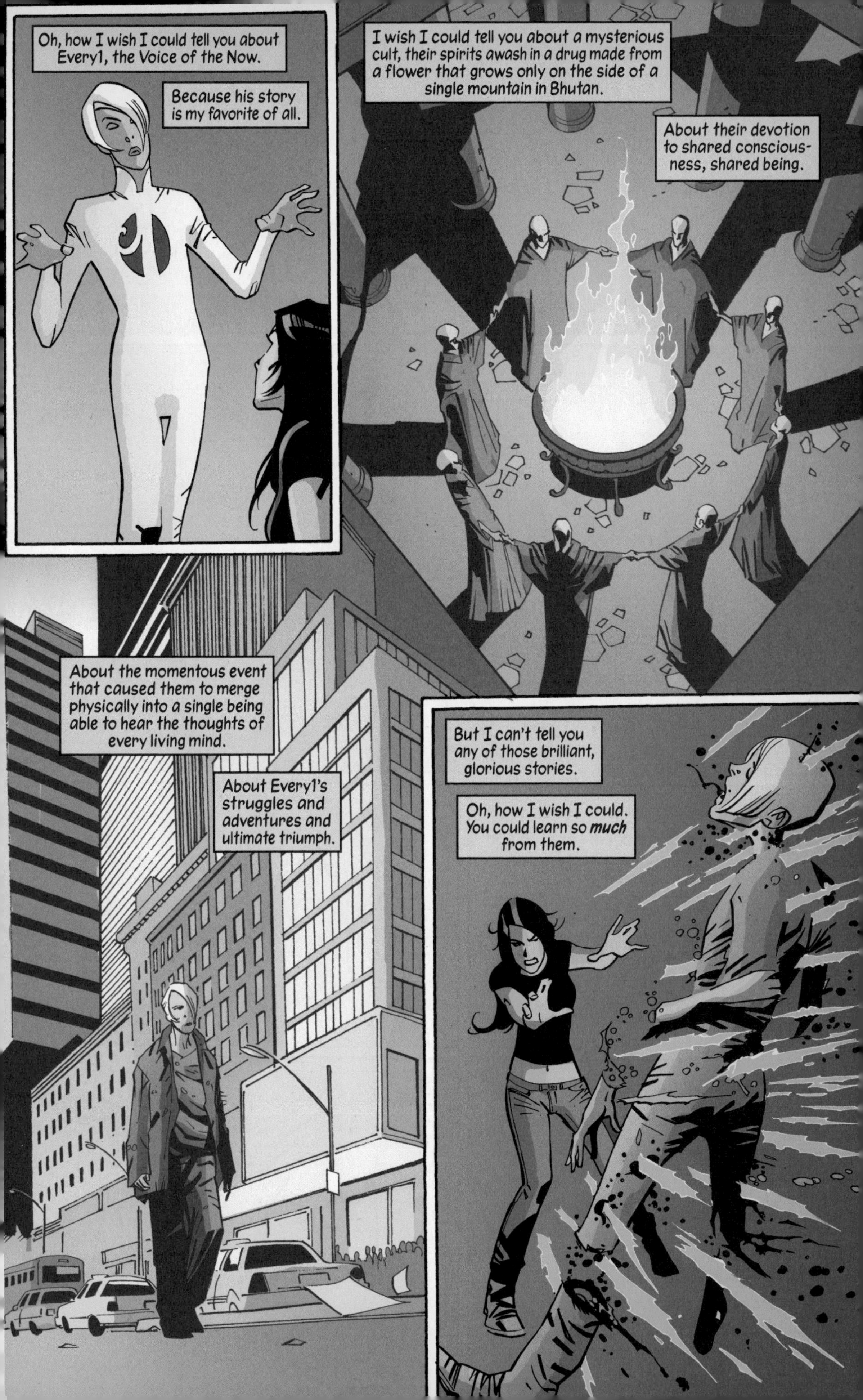

Oh, how I wish I could tell you about Every1, the Voice of the Now.
Because his story is my favorite of all.
I wish I could tell you about a mysterious cult, their spirits awash in a drug made from a flower that grows only on the side of a single mountain in Bhutan.
About their devotion to shared consciousness, shared being.
About the momentous event that caused them to merge physically into a single being able to hear the thoughts of every living mind.
About Every1's struggles and adventures and ultimate triumph.
But I can't tell you any of those brilliant, glorious stories.
Oh, how I wish I could. You could learn so *much* from them.

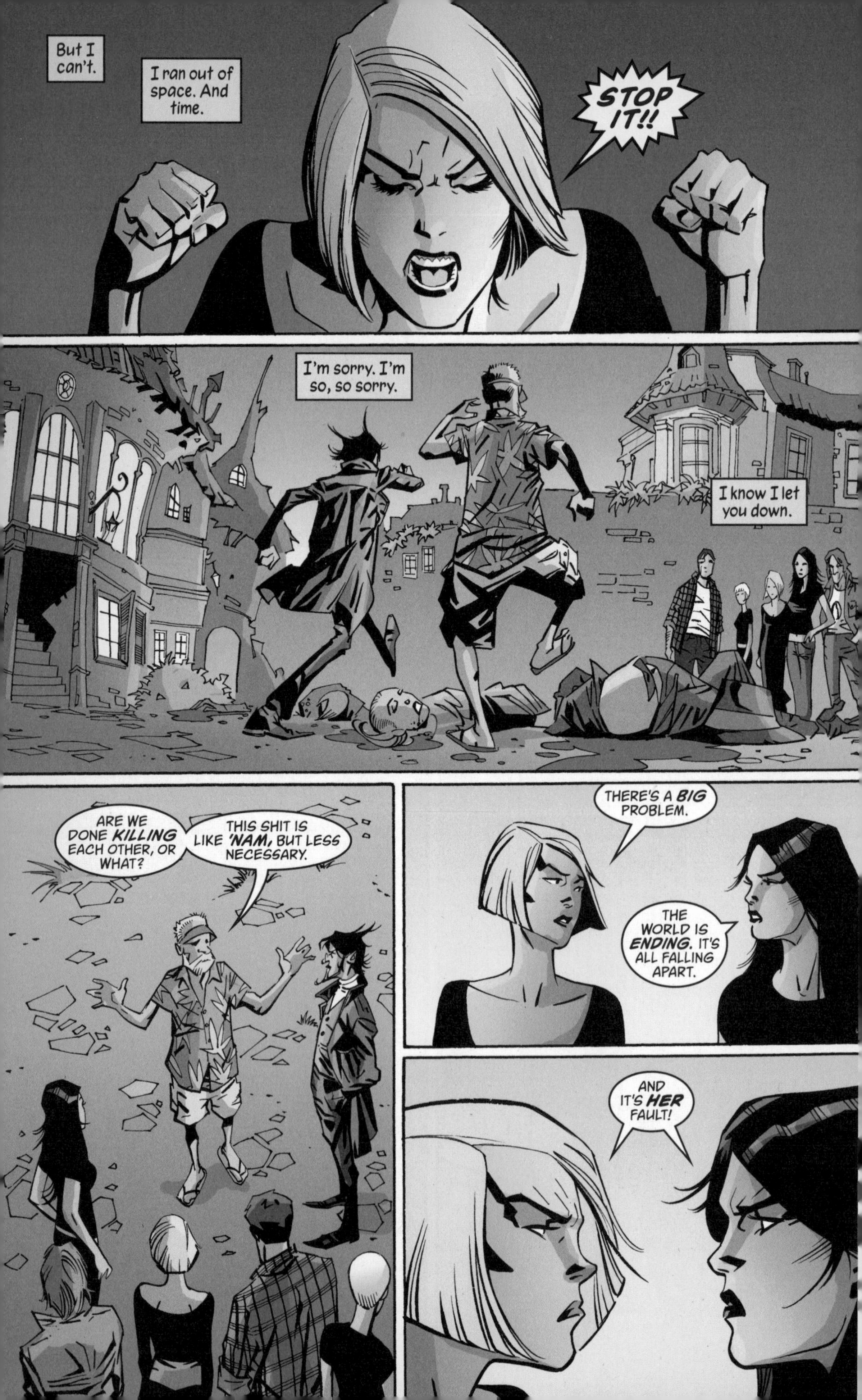
But I can't.
I ran out of space. And time.
STOP IT!!
I'm sorry. I'm so, so sorry.
I know I let you down.
ARE WE DONE KILLING EACH OTHER, OR WHAT?
THIS SHIT IS LIKE 'NAM, BUT LESS NECESSARY.
THERE'S A BIG PROBLEM.
THE WORLD IS ENDING. IT'S ALL FALLING APART.
AND IT'S HER FAULT!

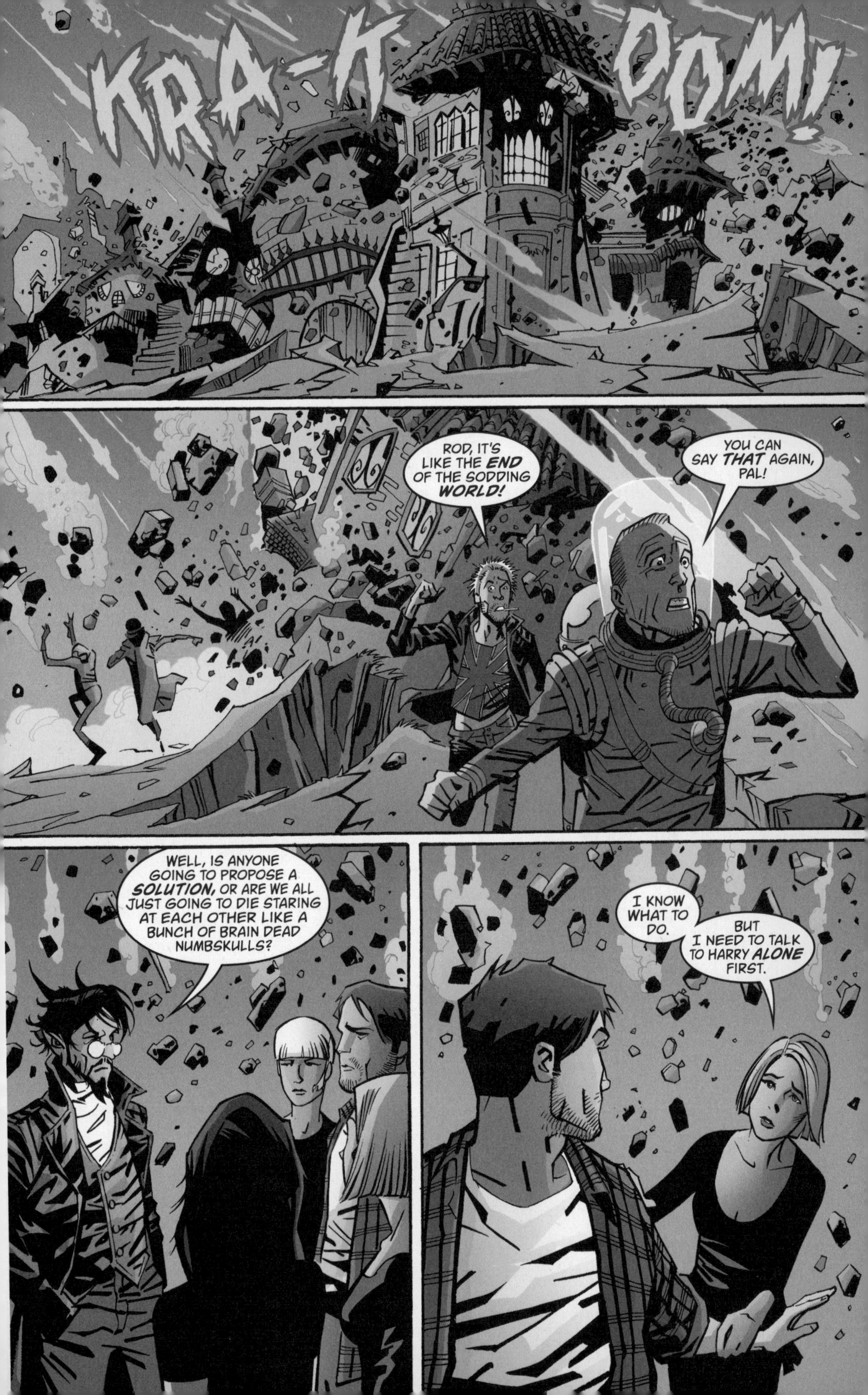
KRA-KOOM!
ROD, IT'S LIKE THE END OF THE SODDING WORLD!
YOU CAN SAY THAT AGAIN, PAL!
WELL, IS ANYONE GOING TO PROPOSE A SOLUTION, OR ARE WE ALL JUST GOING TO DIE STARING AT EACH OTHER LIKE A BUNCH OF BRAIN DEAD NUMBSKULLS?
I KNOW WHAT TO DO.
BUT I NEED TO TALK TO HARRY ALONE FIRST.

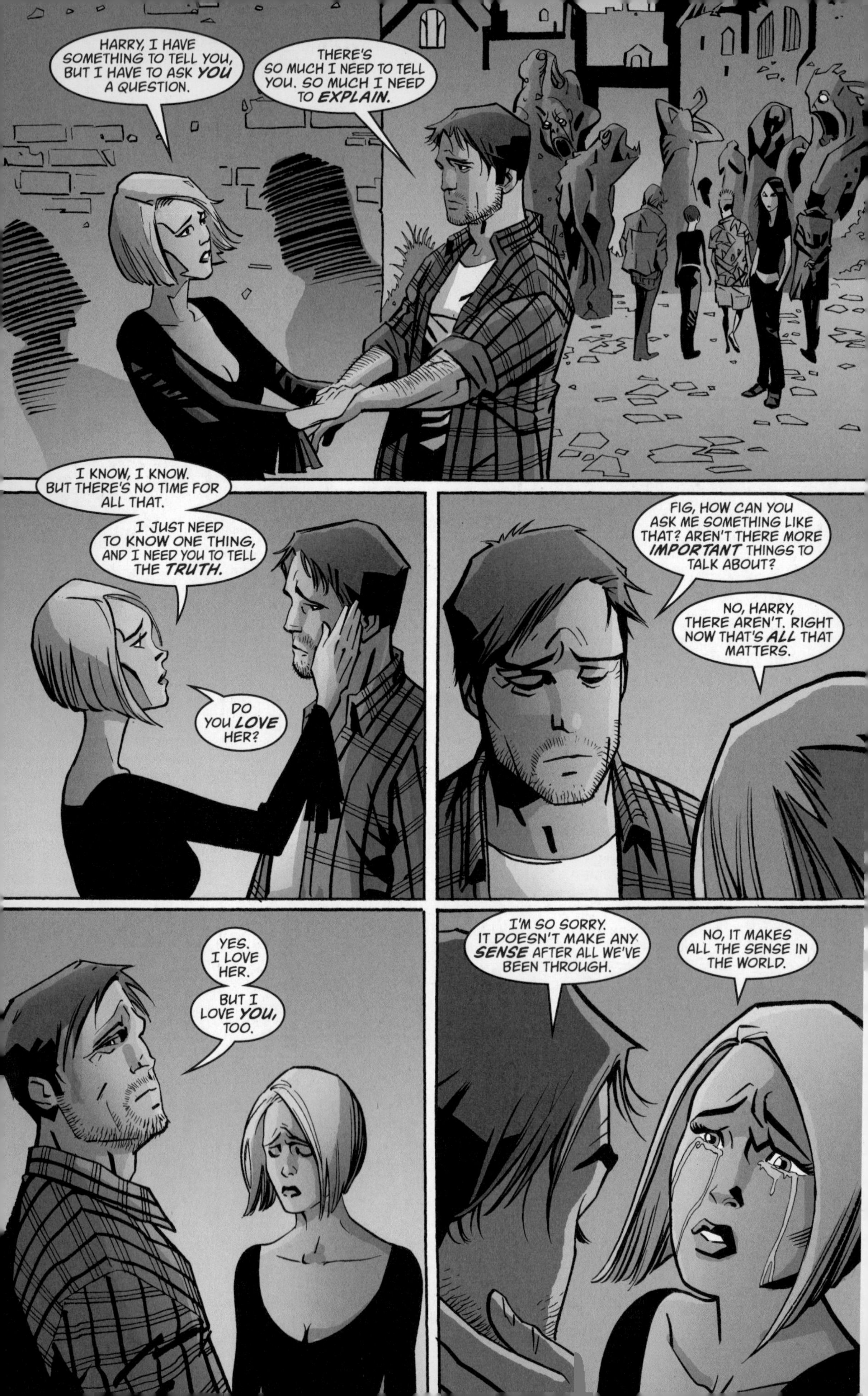
HARRY, I HAVE SOMETHING TO TELL YOU, BUT I HAVE TO ASK YOU A QUESTION.
THERE'S SO MUCH I NEED TO TELL YOU. SO MUCH I NEED TO EXPLAIN.
I KNOW, I KNOW. BUT THERE'S NO TIME FOR ALL THAT.
I JUST NEED TO KNOW ONE THING, AND I NEED YOU TO TELL THE TRUTH.
DO YOU LOVE HER?
FIG, HOW CAN YOU ASK ME SOMETHING LIKE THAT? AREN'T THERE MORE IMPORTANT THINGS TO TALK ABOUT?
NO, HARRY, THERE AREN'T. RIGHT NOW THAT'S ALL THAT MATTERS.
YES. I LOVE HER.
BUT I LOVE YOU, TOO.
I'M SO SORRY. IT DOESN'T MAKE ANY SENSE AFTER ALL WE'VE BEEN THROUGH.
NO, IT MAKES ALL THE SENSE IN THE WORLD.

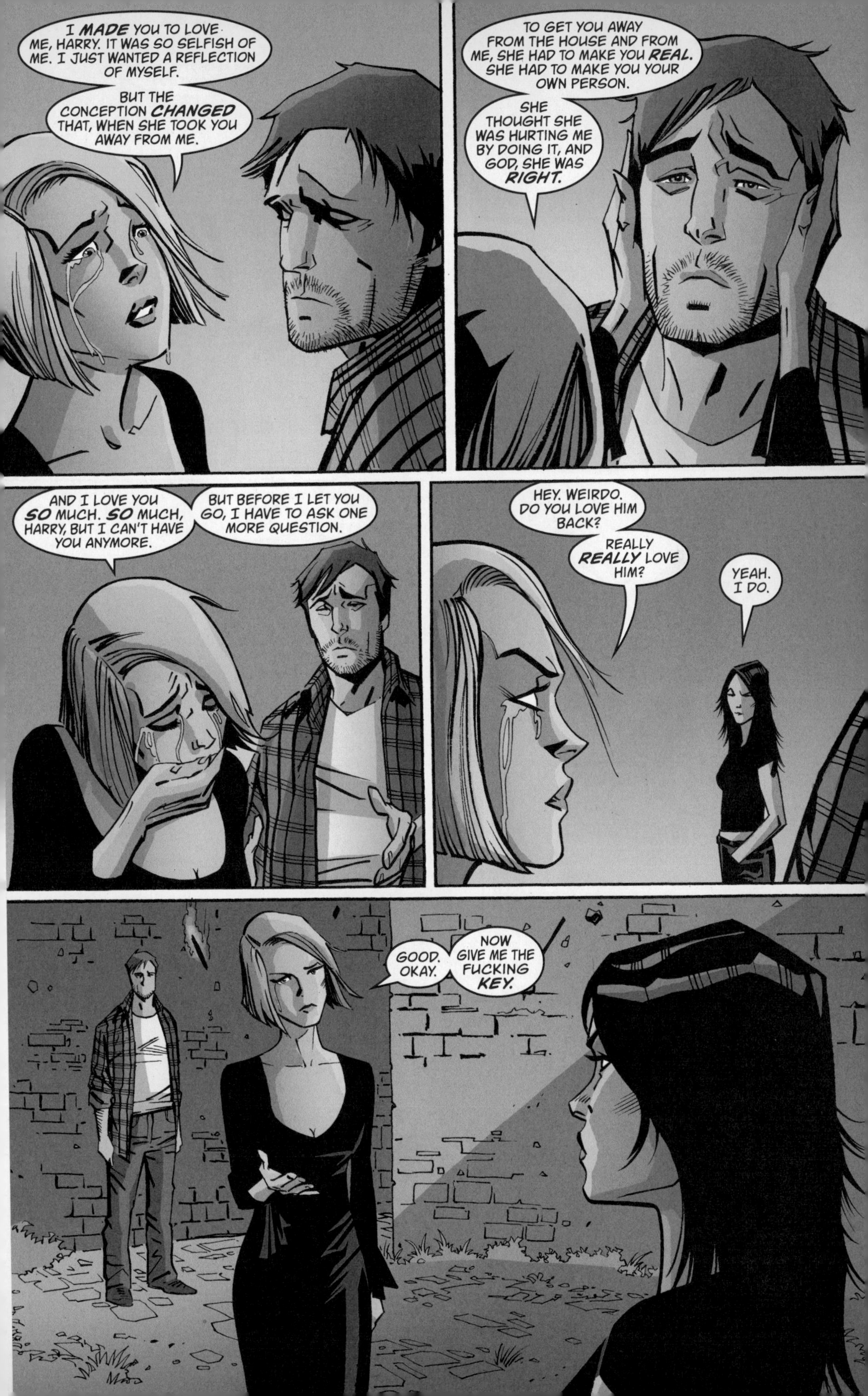
I MADE YOU TO LOVE ME, HARRY. IT WAS SO SELFISH OF ME. I JUST WANTED A REFLECTION OF MYSELF.
BUT THE CONCEPTION CHANGED THAT, WHEN SHE TOOK YOU AWAY FROM ME.
TO GET YOU AWAY FROM THE HOUSE AND FROM ME, SHE HAD TO MAKE YOU REAL. SHE HAD TO MAKE YOU YOUR OWN PERSON.
SHE THOUGHT SHE WAS HURTING ME BY DOING IT, AND GOD, SHE WAS RIGHT.
AND I LOVE YOU SO MUCH. SO MUCH, HARRY, BUT I CAN'T HAVE YOU ANYMORE.
BUT BEFORE I LET YOU GO, I HAVE TO ASK ONE MORE QUESTION.
HEY. WEIRDO. DO YOU LOVE HIM BACK?
REALLY REALLY LOVE HIM?
YEAH. I DO.
GOOD. OKAY.
NOW GIVE ME THE FUCKING KEY.

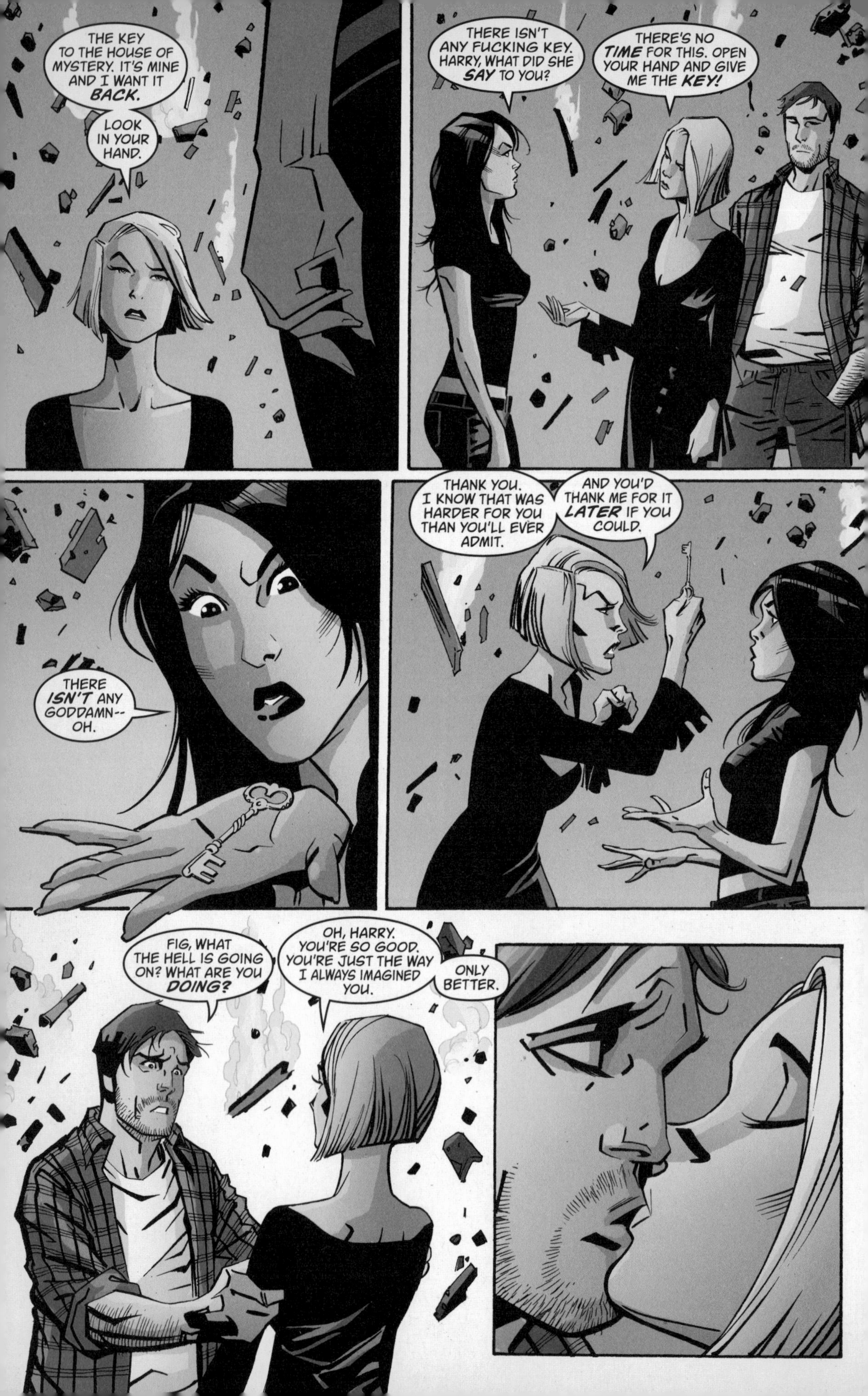
THE KEY TO THE HOUSE OF MYSTERY. IT'S MINE AND I WANT IT BACK.
LOOK IN YOUR HAND.
THERE ISN'T ANY FUCKING KEY. HARRY, WHAT DID SHE SAY TO YOU?
THERE'S NO TIME FOR THIS. OPEN YOUR HAND AND GIVE ME THE KEY!
THERE ISN'T ANY GODDAMN-- OH.
THANK YOU. I KNOW THAT WAS HARDER FOR YOU THAN YOU'LL EVER ADMIT.
AND YOU'D THANK ME FOR IT LATER IF YOU COULD.
FIG, WHAT THE HELL IS GOING ON? WHAT ARE YOU DOING?
OH, HARRY. YOU'RE SO GOOD. YOU'RE JUST THE WAY I ALWAYS IMAGINED YOU.
ONLY BETTER.

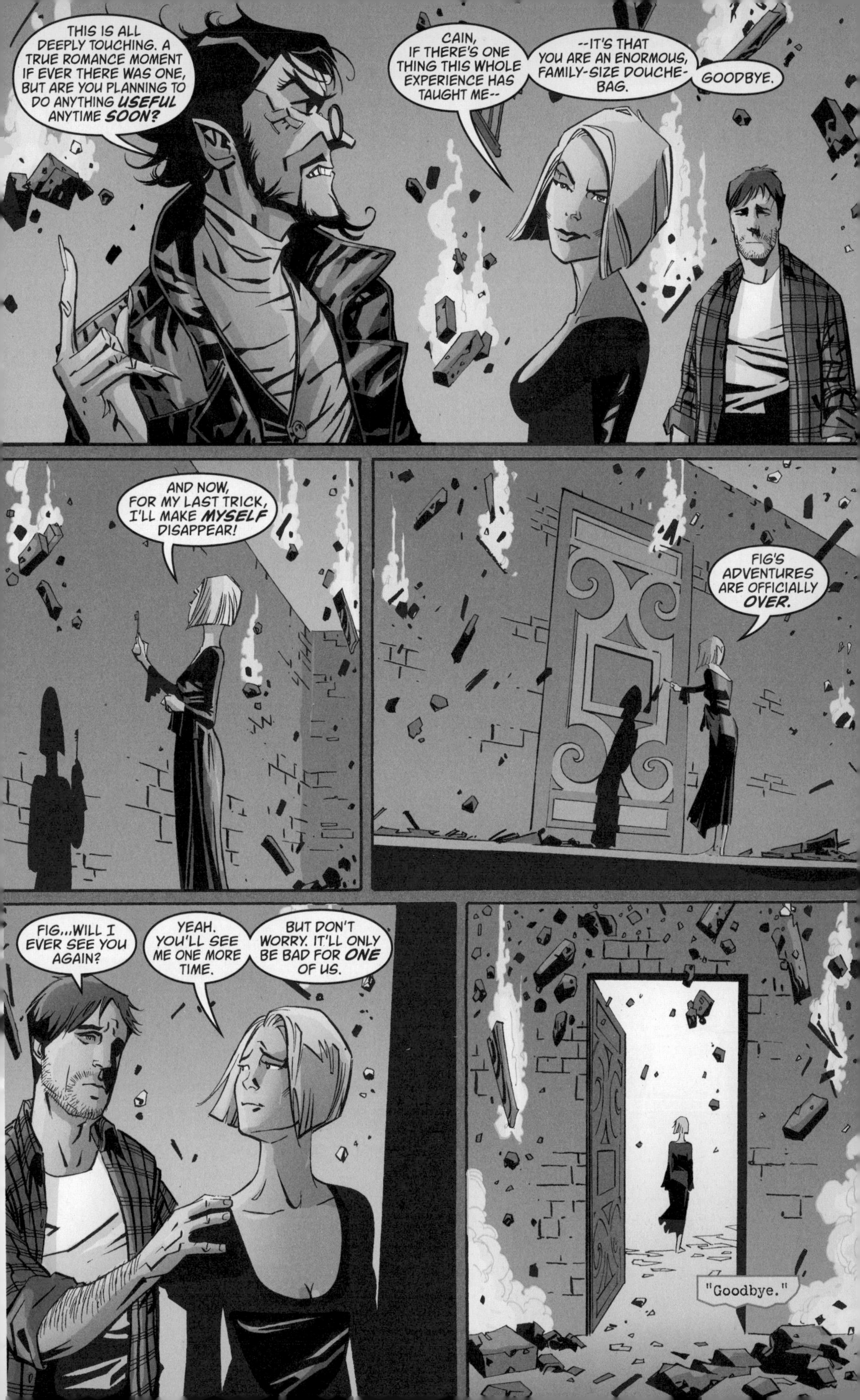
THIS IS ALL DEEPLY TOUCHING. A TRUE ROMANCE MOMENT IF EVER THERE WAS ONE, BUT ARE YOU PLANNING TO DO ANYTHING USEFUL ANYTIME SOON?
CAIN, IF THERE'S ONE THING THIS WHOLE EXPERIENCE HAS TAUGHT ME--
--IT'S THAT YOU ARE AN ENORMOUS, FAMILY-SIZE DOUCHE-BAG.
GOODBYE.
AND NOW, FOR MY LAST TRICK, I'LL MAKE MYSELF DISAPPEAR!
FIG'S ADVENTURES ARE OFFICIALLY OVER.
FIG...WILL I EVER SEE YOU AGAIN?
YEAH. YOU'LL SEE ME ONE MORE TIME.
BUT DON'T WORRY. IT'LL ONLY BE BAD FOR ONE OF US.
"Goodbye."

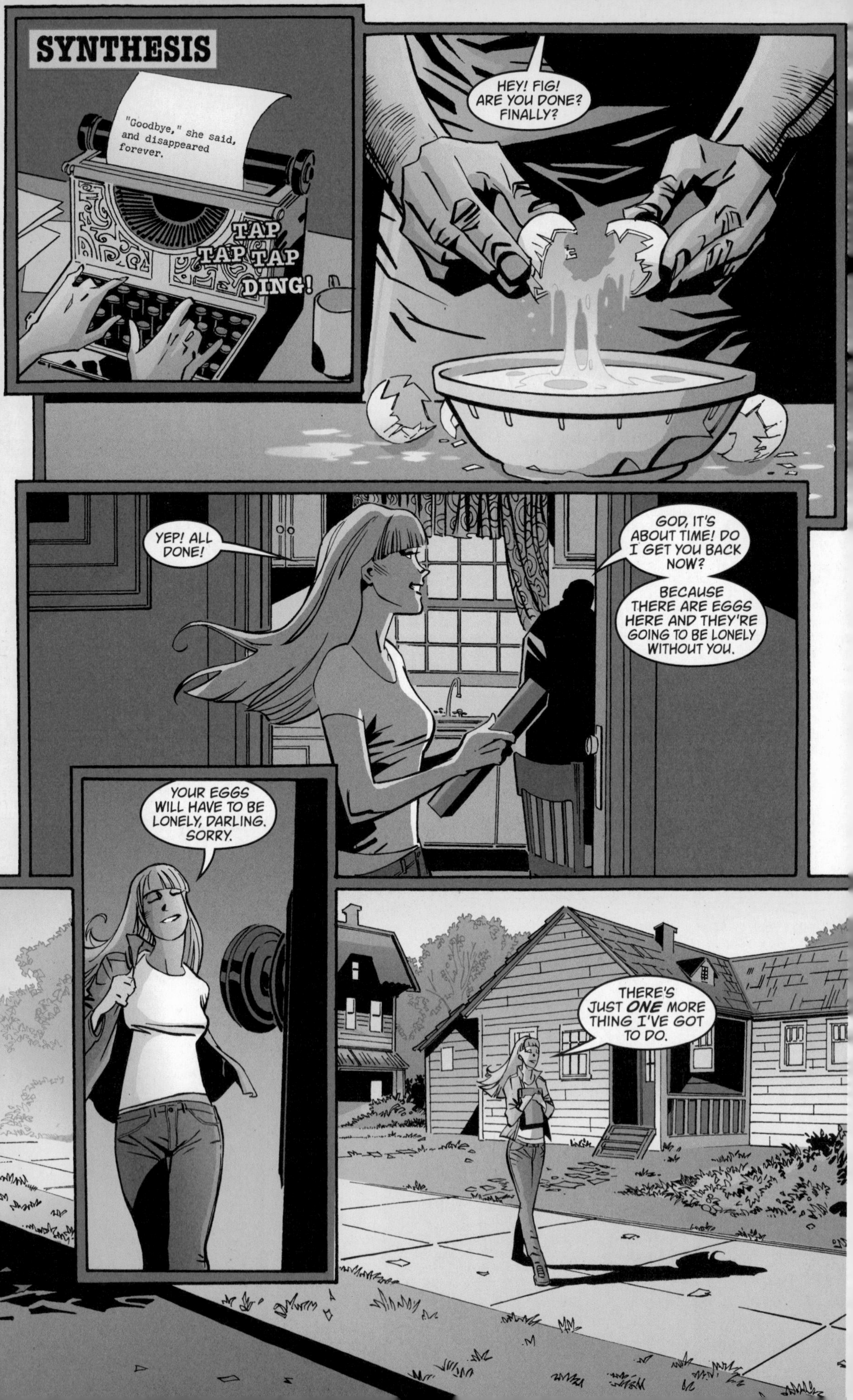
SYNTHESIS
"Goodbye," she said, and disappeared forever.
TAP TAP TAP DING!
HEY! FIG! ARE YOU DONE? FINALLY?
YEP! ALL DONE!
GOD, IT'S ABOUT TIME! DO I GET YOU BACK NOW?
BECAUSE THERE ARE EGGS HERE AND THEY'RE GOING TO BE LONELY WITHOUT YOU.
YOUR EGGS WILL HAVE TO BE LONELY, DARLING. SORRY.
THERE'S JUST ONE MORE THING I'VE GOT TO DO.

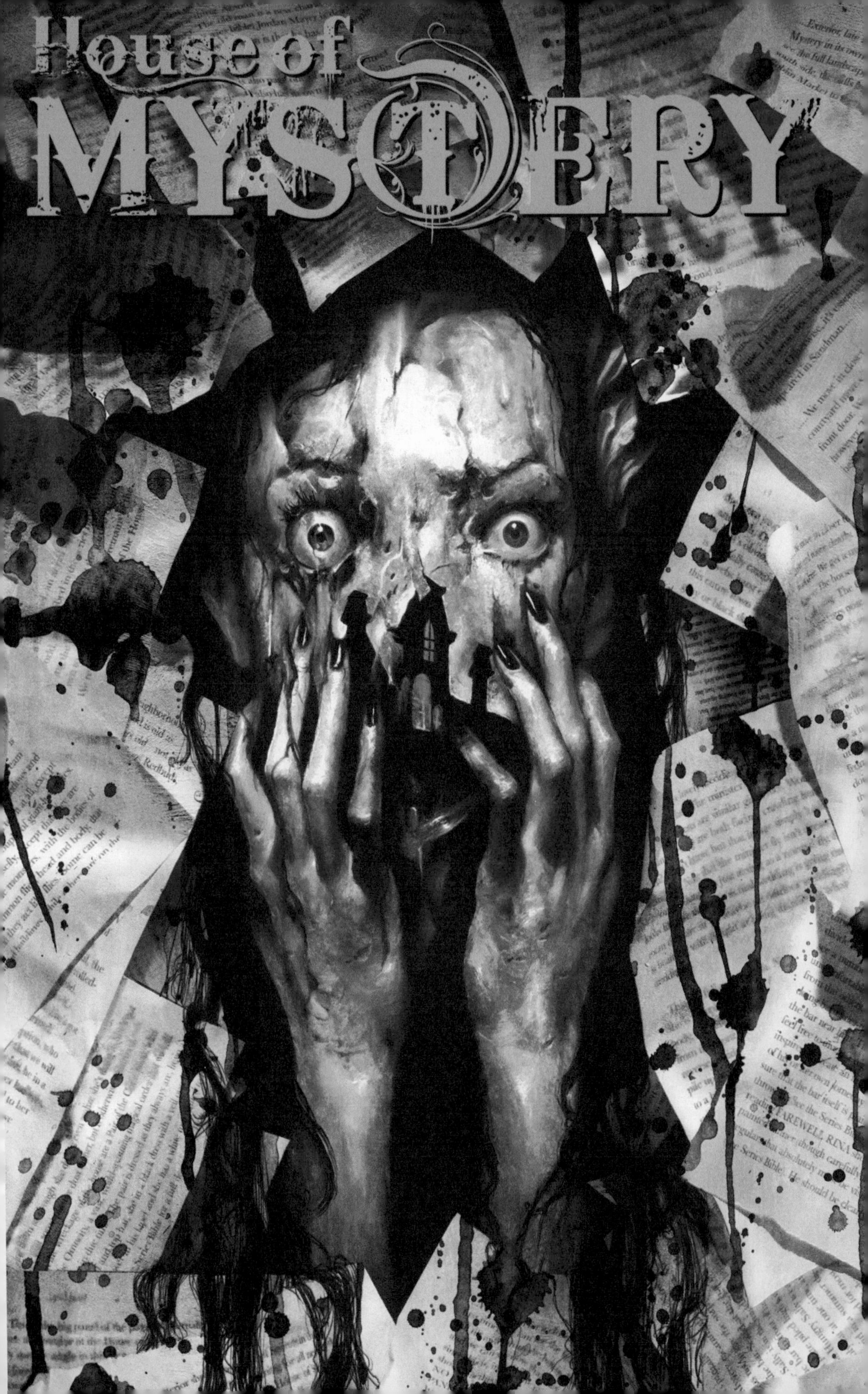
House of
MYSTERY

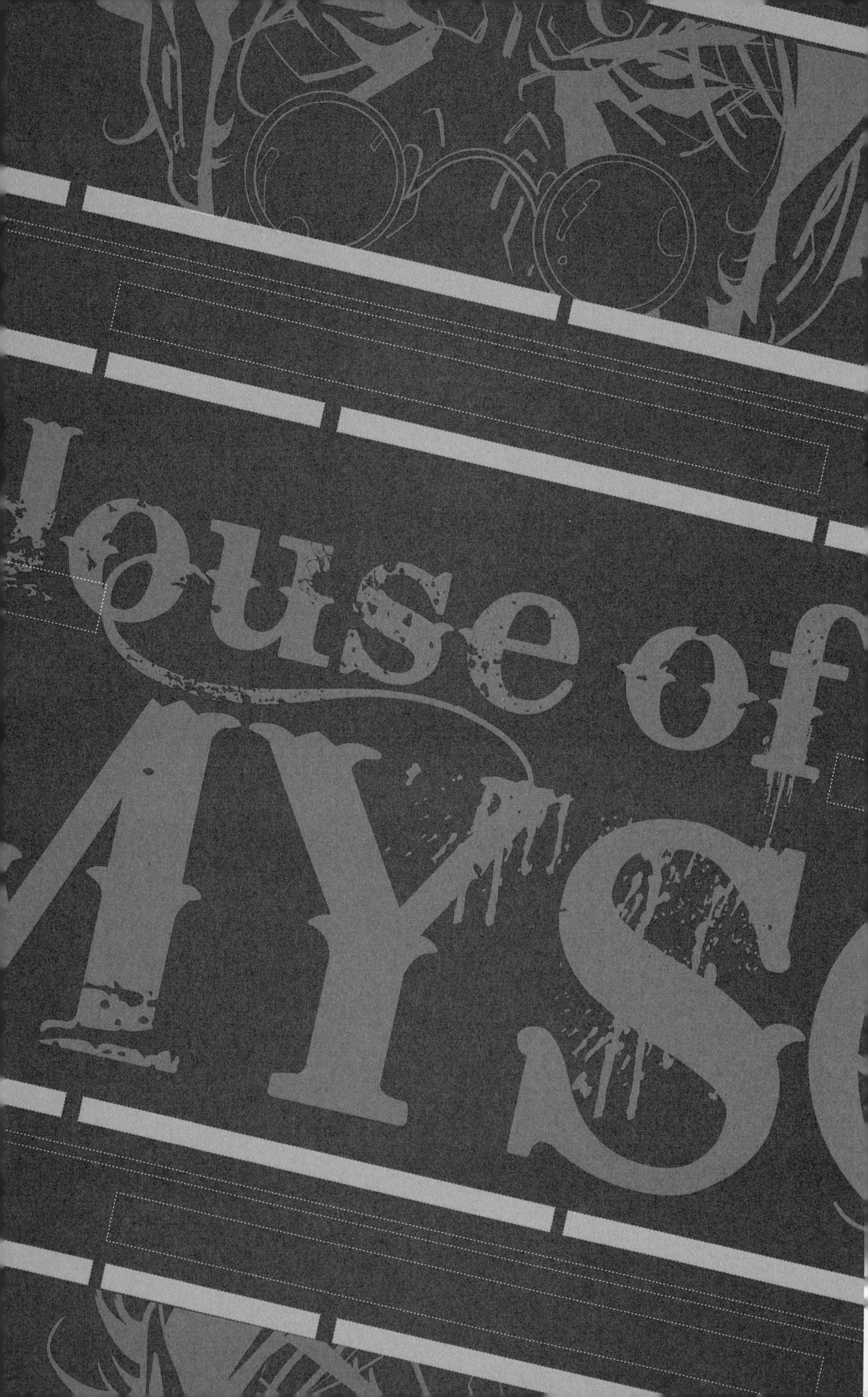
ouse of

SYNTHESIS

The next time you're in a bar, take a look at everyone around you.

Really *look*.

If you try hard, you can sense that within every one of those people is an entire *world* of stories--

--beginning with their earliest memories and continuing right up to the present moment and beyond into the imagined future.

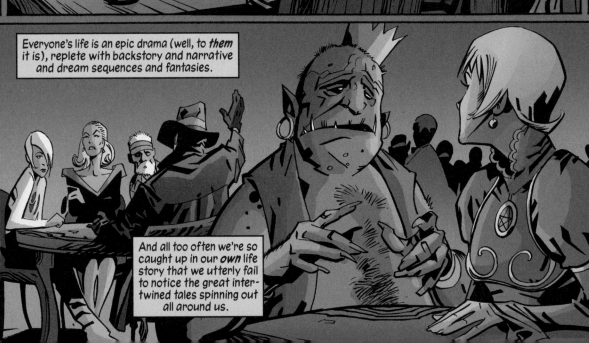

Everyone's life is an epic drama (well, to *them* it is), replete with backstory and narrative and dream sequences and fantasies.

And all too often we're so caught up in our *own* life story that we utterly fail to notice the great intertwined tales spinning out all around us.

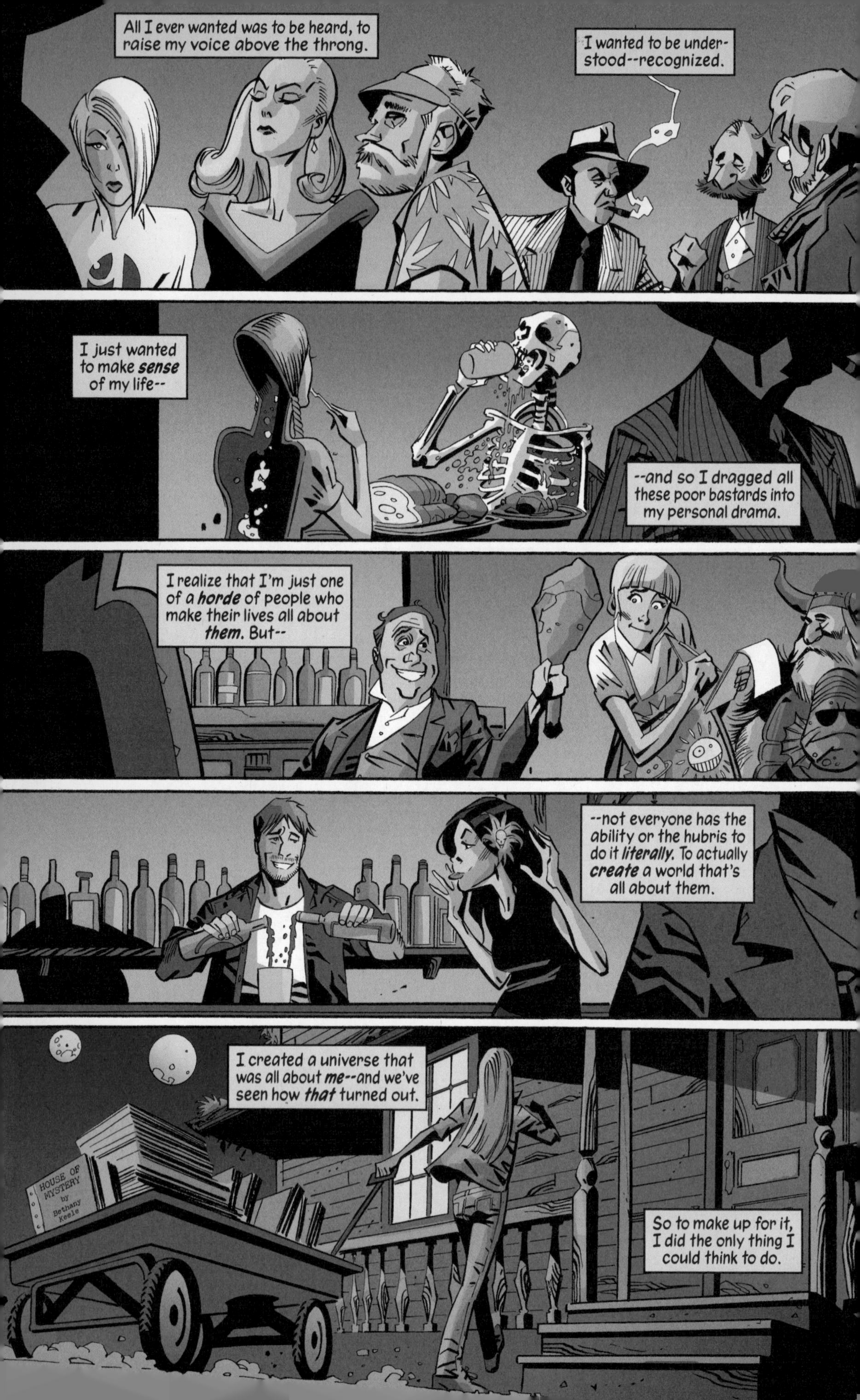
All I ever wanted was to be heard, to raise my voice above the throng.
I wanted to be under-stood--recognized.
I just wanted to make *sense* of my life--
--and so I dragged all these poor bastards into my personal drama.
I realize that I'm just one of a *horde* of people who make their lives all about *them*. But--
--not everyone has the ability or the hubris to do it *literally*. To actually *create* a world that's all about them.
I created a universe that was all about *me*--and we've seen how *that* turned out.
HOUSE OF MYSTERY by Bethany Keele
So to make up for it, I did the only thing I could think to do.

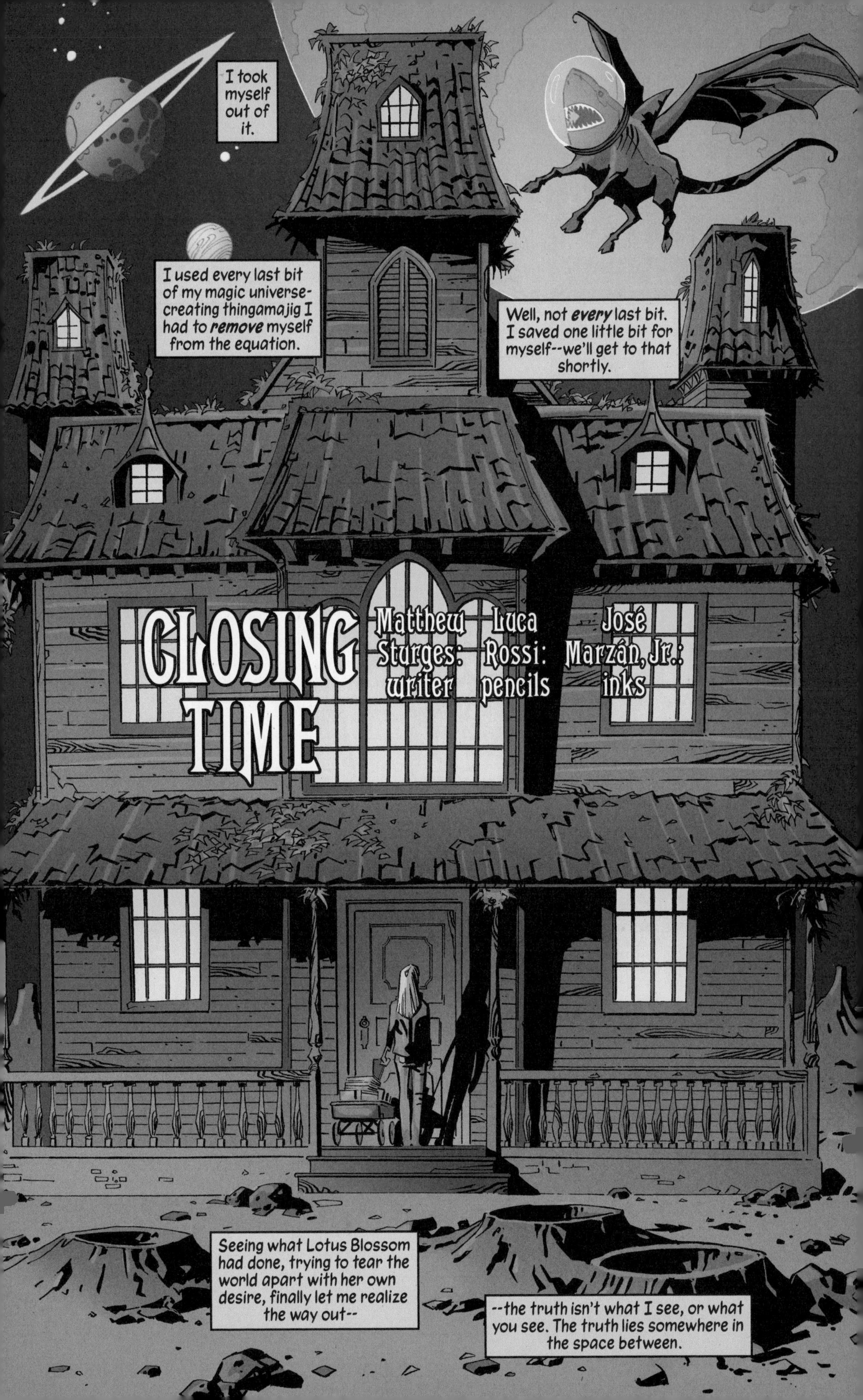
I took myself out of it.
I used every last bit of my magic universe-creating thingamajig I had to *remove* myself from the equation.
Well, not *every* last bit. I saved one little bit for myself--we'll get to that shortly.
CLOSING TIME
Matthew Sturges: writer
Luca Rossi: pencils
José Marzán, Jr.: inks
Seeing what Lotus Blossom had done, trying to tear the world apart with her own desire, finally let me realize the way out--
--the truth isn't what I see, or what you see. The truth lies somewhere in the space between.

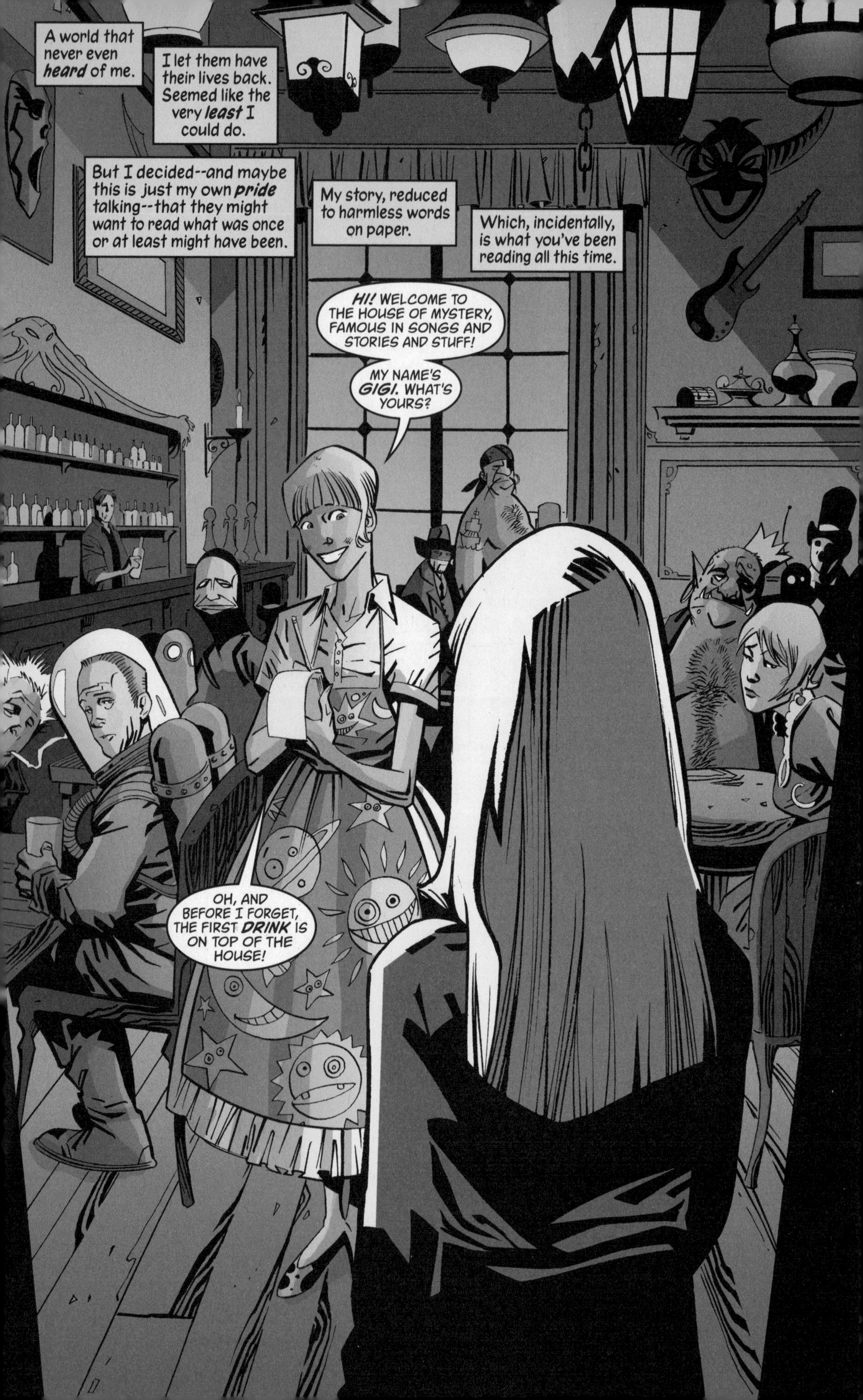

A world that never even *heard* of me.
I let them have their lives back. Seemed like the very *least* I could do.
But I decided--and maybe this is just my own *pride* talking--that they might want to read what was once or at least might have been.
My story, reduced to harmless words on paper.
Which, incidentally, is what you've been reading all this time.
HI! WELCOME TO THE HOUSE OF MYSTERY, FAMOUS IN SONGS AND STORIES AND STUFF!
MY NAME'S *GIGI*. WHAT'S YOURS?
OH, AND BEFORE I FORGET, THE FIRST *DRINK* IS ON TOP OF THE HOUSE!

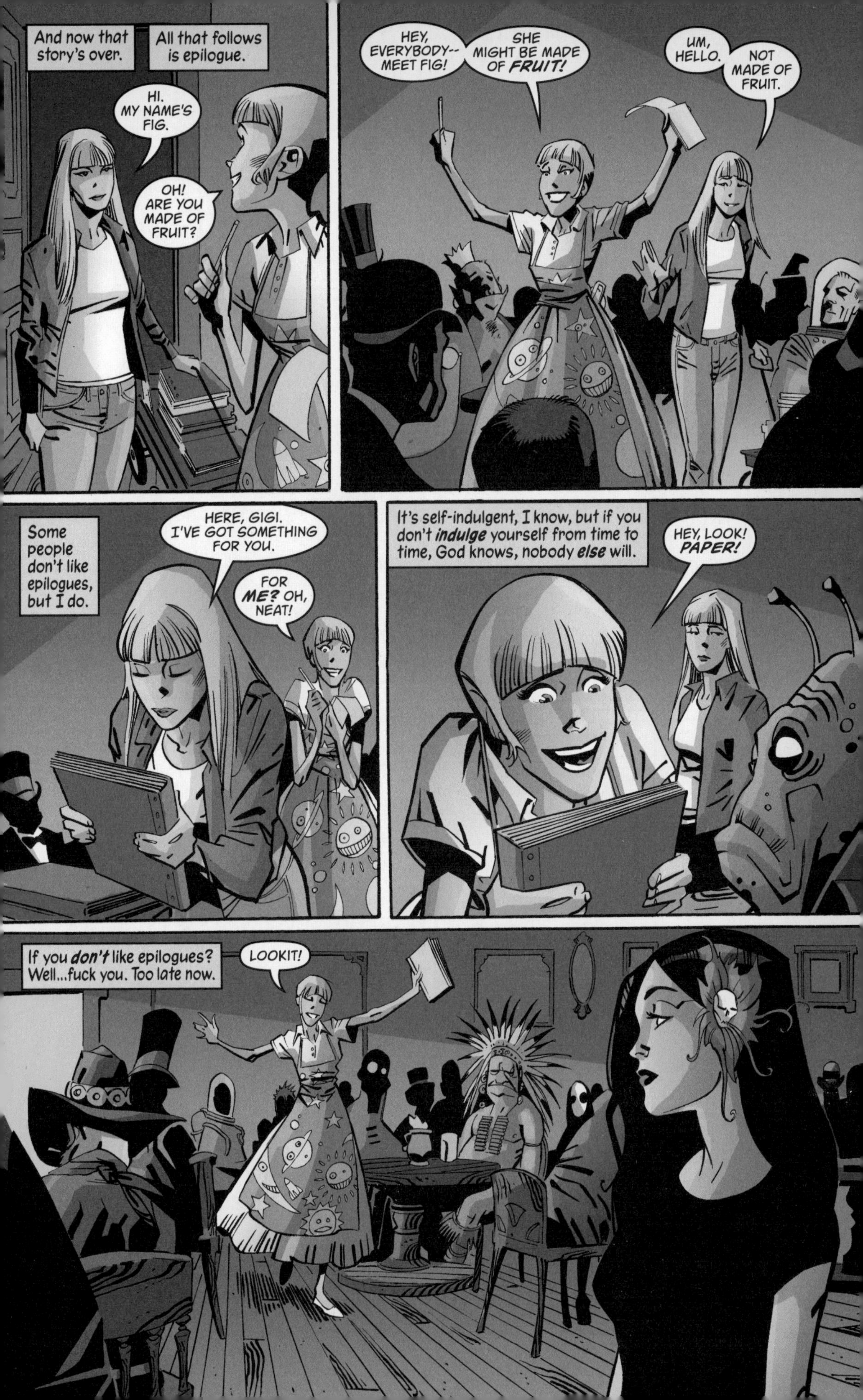

And now that story's over.
All that follows is epilogue.
HI. MY NAME'S FIG.
OH! ARE YOU MADE OF FRUIT?
HEY, EVERYBODY-- MEET FIG!
SHE MIGHT BE MADE OF ***FRUIT!***
UM, HELLO.
NOT MADE OF FRUIT.
Some people don't like epilogues, but I do.
HERE, GIGI. I'VE GOT SOMETHING FOR YOU.
FOR ***ME?*** OH, NEAT!
It's self-indulgent, I know, but if you don't ***indulge*** yourself from time to time, God knows, nobody ***else*** will.
HEY, LOOK! ***PAPER!***
If you ***don't*** like epilogues? Well...fuck you. Too late now.
LOOKIT!

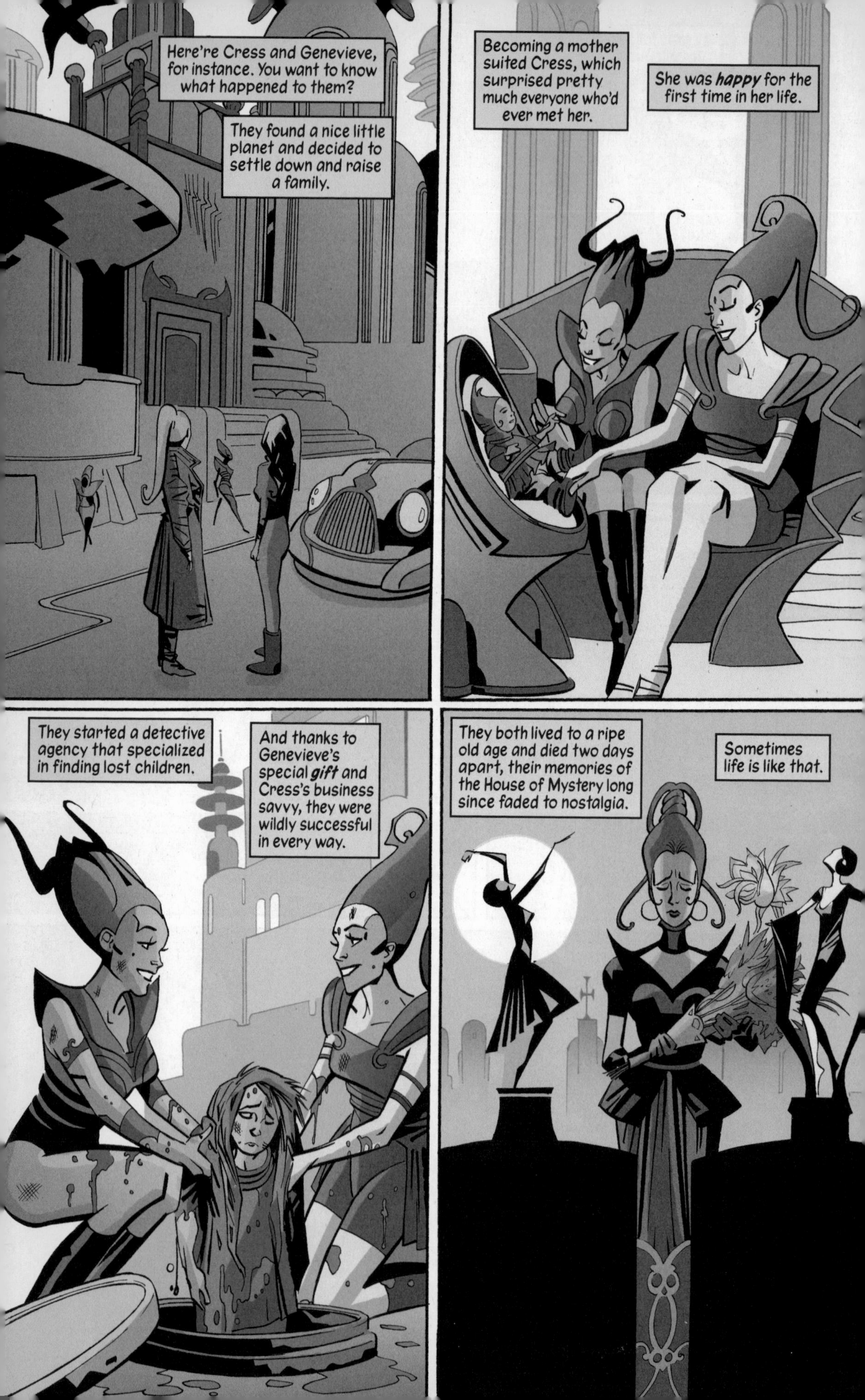
Here're Cress and Genevieve, for instance. You want to know what happened to them?
They found a nice little planet and decided to settle down and raise a family.
Becoming a mother suited Cress, which surprised pretty much everyone who'd ever met her.
She was *happy* for the first time in her life.
They started a detective agency that specialized in finding lost children.
And thanks to Genevieve's special *gift* and Cress's business savvy, they were wildly successful in every way.
They both lived to a ripe old age and died two days apart, their memories of the House of Mystery long since faded to nostalgia.
Sometimes life is like that.

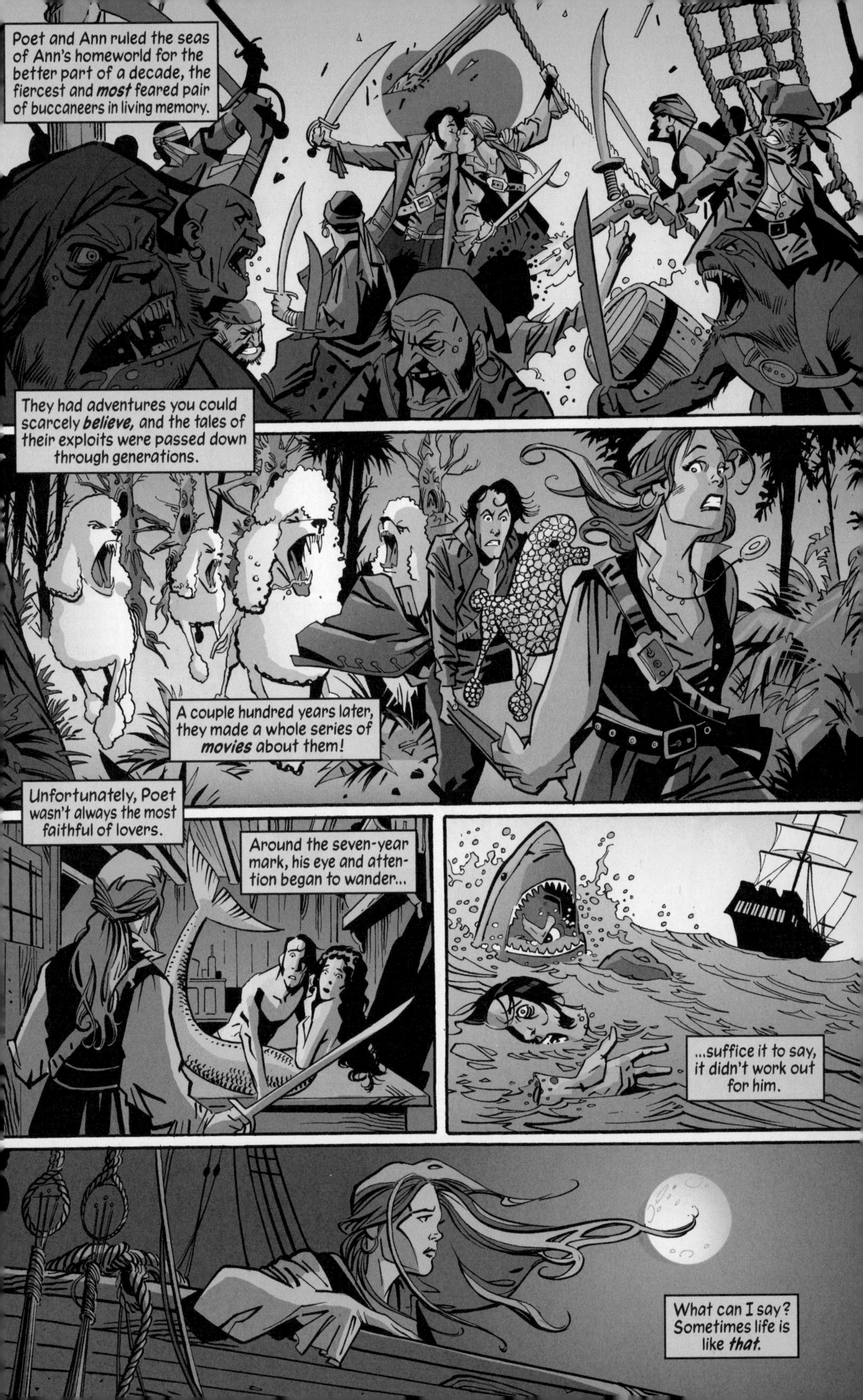
Poet and Ann ruled the seas of Ann's homeworld for the better part of a decade, the fiercest and *most* feared pair of buccaneers in living memory.
They had adventures you could scarcely ***believe,*** and the tales of their exploits were passed down through generations.
A couple hundred years later, they made a whole series of ***movies*** about them!
Unfortunately, Poet wasn't always the most faithful of lovers.
Around the seven-year mark, his eye and attention began to wander...
...suffice it to say, it didn't work out for him.
What can I say? Sometimes life is like ***that.***

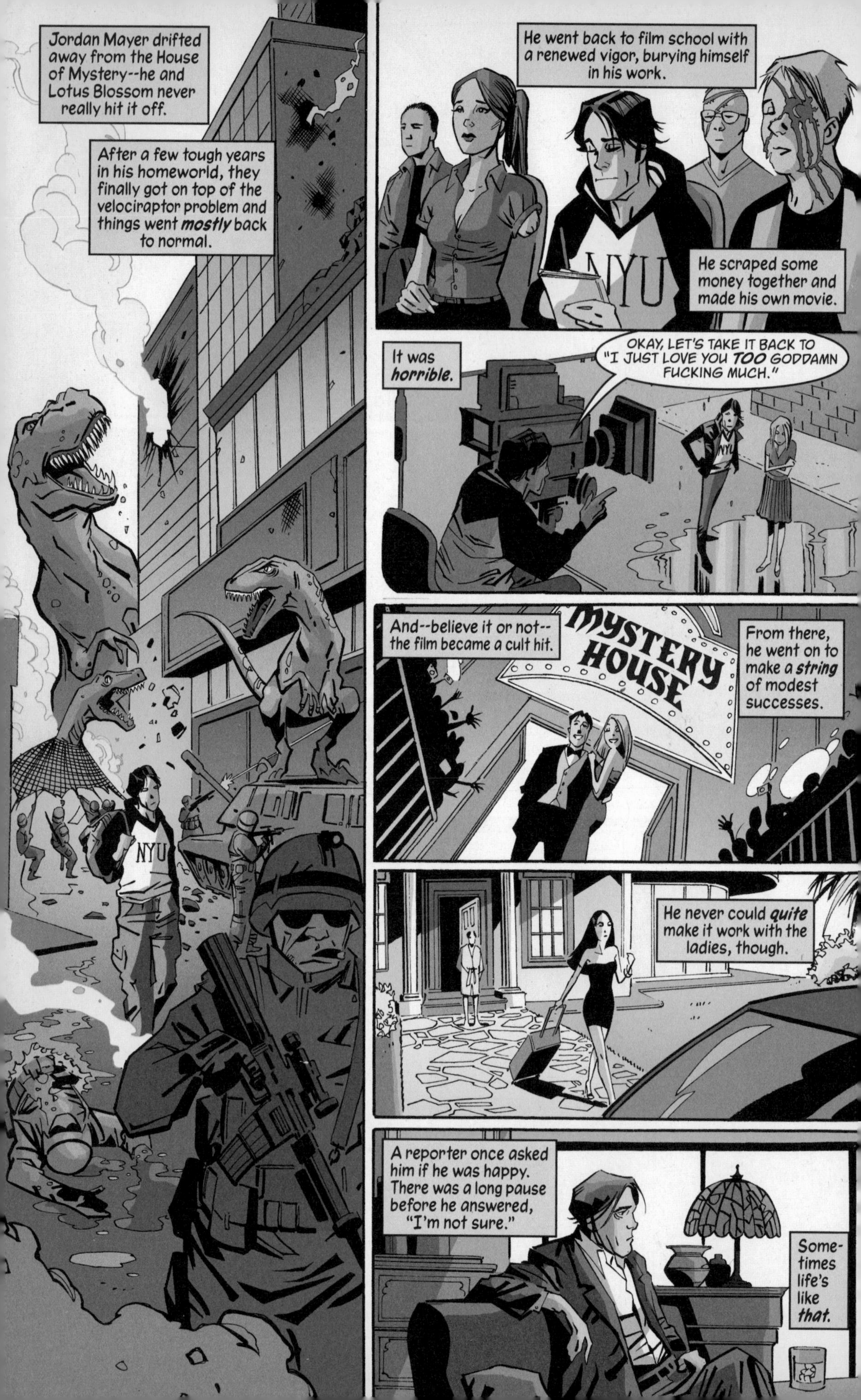
Jordan Mayer drifted away from the House of Mystery--he and Lotus Blossom never really hit it off.
After a few tough years in his homeworld, they finally got on top of the velociraptor problem and things went *mostly* back to normal.
NYU
He went back to film school with a renewed vigor, burying himself in his work.
NYU
He scraped some money together and made his own movie.
It was *horrible*.
OKAY, LET'S TAKE IT BACK TO "I JUST LOVE YOU ***TOO*** GODDAMN FUCKING MUCH."
NYU
And--believe it or not--the film became a cult hit.
MYSTERY HOUSE
From there, he went on to make a *string* of modest successes.
He never could *quite* make it work with the ladies, though.
A reporter once asked him if he was happy. There was a long pause before he answered, "I'm not sure."
Some-times life's like *that*.

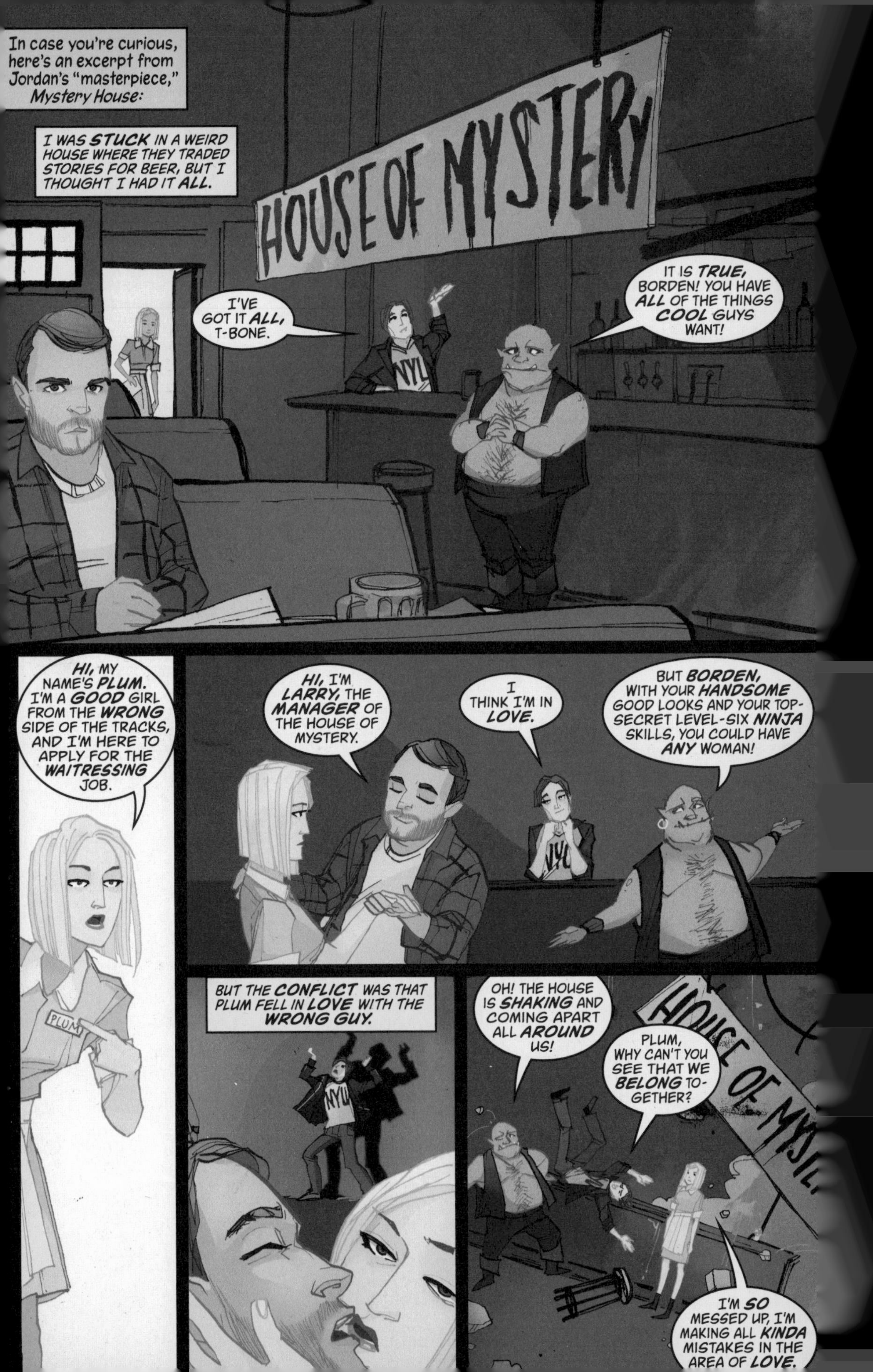
In case you're curious, here's an excerpt from Jordan's "masterpiece," Mystery House:
I WAS STUCK IN A WEIRD HOUSE WHERE THEY TRADED STORIES FOR BEER, BUT I THOUGHT I HAD IT ALL.
HOUSE OF MYSTERY
I'VE GOT IT ALL, T-BONE.
IT IS TRUE, BORDEN! YOU HAVE ALL OF THE THINGS COOL GUYS WANT!
NYU
HI, MY NAME'S PLUM. I'M A GOOD GIRL FROM THE WRONG SIDE OF THE TRACKS, AND I'M HERE TO APPLY FOR THE WAITRESSING JOB.
PLUM
HI, I'M LARRY, THE MANAGER OF THE HOUSE OF MYSTERY.
I THINK I'M IN LOVE.
BUT BORDEN, WITH YOUR HANDSOME GOOD LOOKS AND YOUR TOP-SECRET LEVEL-SIX NINJA SKILLS, YOU COULD HAVE ANY WOMAN!
BUT THE CONFLICT WAS THAT PLUM FELL IN LOVE WITH THE WRONG GUY.
NYU
OH! THE HOUSE IS SHAKING AND COMING APART ALL AROUND US!
PLUM, WHY CAN'T YOU SEE THAT WE BELONG TO-GETHER?
I'M SO MESSED UP, I'M MAKING ALL KINDA MISTAKES IN THE AREA OF LOVE.

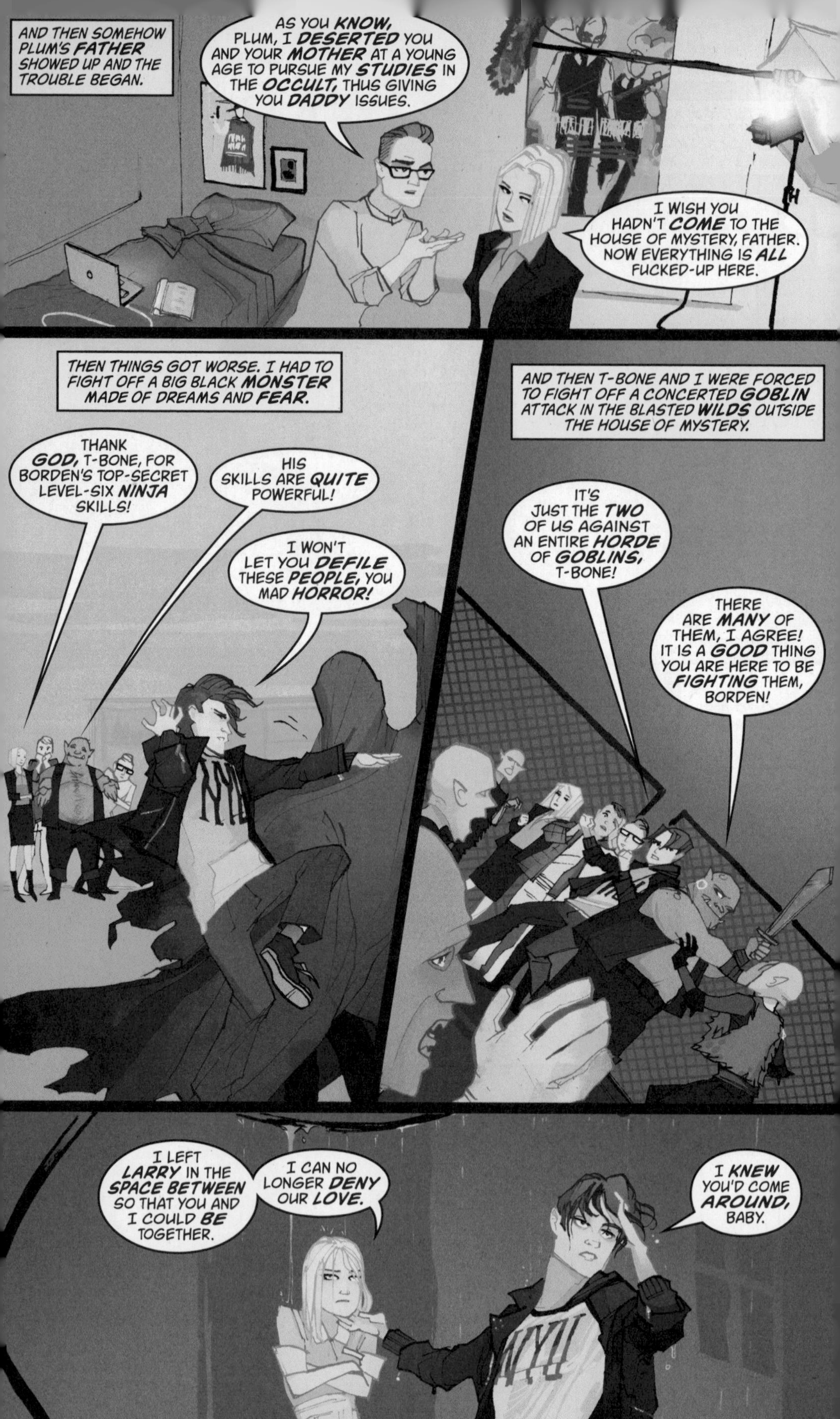
AND THEN SOMEHOW PLUM'S FATHER SHOWED UP AND THE TROUBLE BEGAN.
AS YOU KNOW, PLUM, I DESERTED YOU AND YOUR MOTHER AT A YOUNG AGE TO PURSUE MY STUDIES IN THE OCCULT, THUS GIVING YOU DADDY ISSUES.
I WISH YOU HADN'T COME TO THE HOUSE OF MYSTERY, FATHER. NOW EVERYTHING IS ALL FUCKED-UP HERE.
THEN THINGS GOT WORSE. I HAD TO FIGHT OFF A BIG BLACK MONSTER MADE OF DREAMS AND FEAR.
THANK GOD, T-BONE, FOR BORDEN'S TOP-SECRET LEVEL-SIX NINJA SKILLS!
HIS SKILLS ARE QUITE POWERFUL!
I WON'T LET YOU DEFILE THESE PEOPLE, YOU MAD HORROR!
AND THEN T-BONE AND I WERE FORCED TO FIGHT OFF A CONCERTED GOBLIN ATTACK IN THE BLASTED WILDS OUTSIDE THE HOUSE OF MYSTERY.
IT'S JUST THE TWO OF US AGAINST AN ENTIRE HORDE OF GOBLINS, T-BONE!
THERE ARE MANY OF THEM, I AGREE! IT IS A GOOD THING YOU ARE HERE TO BE FIGHTING THEM, BORDEN!
I LEFT LARRY IN THE SPACE BETWEEN SO THAT YOU AND I COULD BE TOGETHER.
I CAN NO LONGER DENY OUR LOVE.
I KNEW YOU'D COME AROUND, BABY.

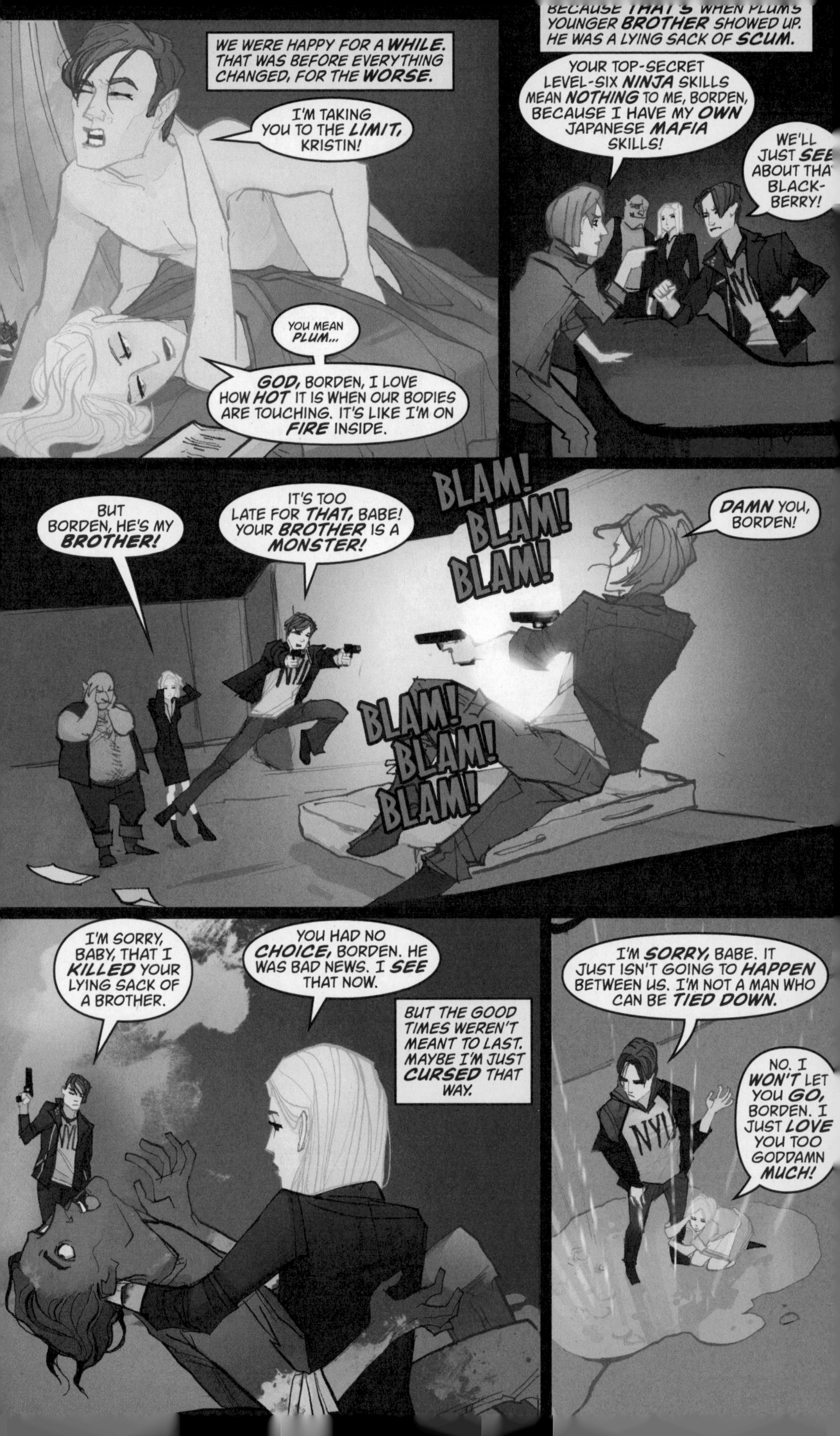
WE WERE HAPPY FOR A WHILE. THAT WAS BEFORE EVERYTHING CHANGED, FOR THE WORSE.
I'M TAKING YOU TO THE LIMIT, KRISTIN!
YOU MEAN PLUM...
GOD, BORDEN, I LOVE HOW HOT IT IS WHEN OUR BODIES ARE TOUCHING. IT'S LIKE I'M ON FIRE INSIDE.
BECAUSE THAT'S WHEN PLUM'S YOUNGER BROTHER SHOWED UP. HE WAS A LYING SACK OF SCUM.
YOUR TOP-SECRET LEVEL-SIX NINJA SKILLS MEAN NOTHING TO ME, BORDEN, BECAUSE I HAVE MY OWN JAPANESE MAFIA SKILLS!
WE'LL JUST SEE ABOUT THAT BLACK-BERRY!
BUT BORDEN, HE'S MY BROTHER!
IT'S TOO LATE FOR THAT, BABE! YOUR BROTHER IS A MONSTER!
BLAM! BLAM! BLAM!
DAMN YOU, BORDEN!
BLAM! BLAM! BLAM!
I'M SORRY, BABY, THAT I KILLED YOUR LYING SACK OF A BROTHER.
YOU HAD NO CHOICE, BORDEN. HE WAS BAD NEWS. I SEE THAT NOW.
BUT THE GOOD TIMES WEREN'T MEANT TO LAST. MAYBE I'M JUST CURSED THAT WAY.
I'M SORRY, BABE. IT JUST ISN'T GOING TO HAPPEN BETWEEN US. I'M NOT A MAN WHO CAN BE TIED DOWN.
NO. I WON'T LET YOU GO, BORDEN. I JUST LOVE YOU TOO GODDAMN MUCH!

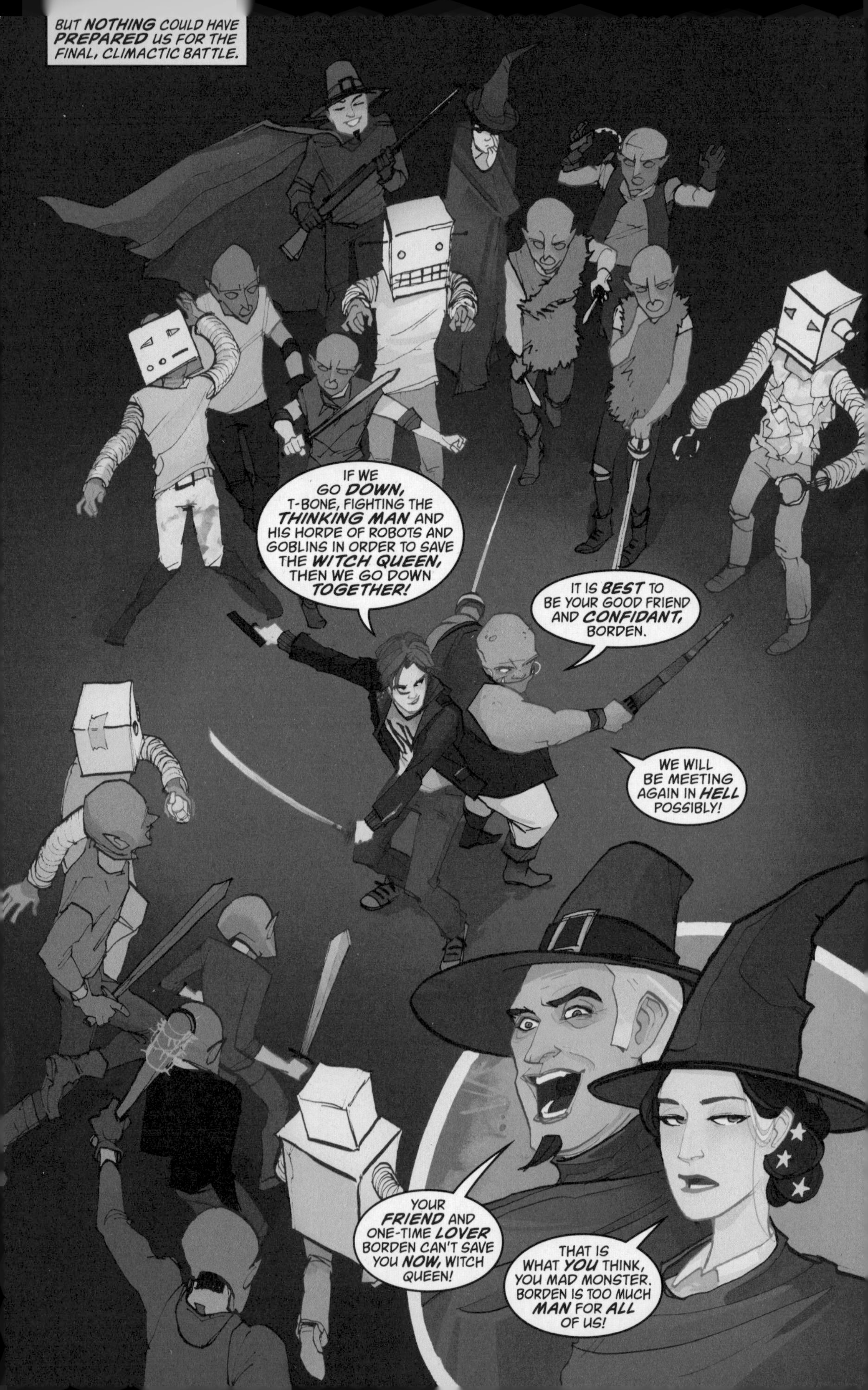
BUT NOTHING COULD HAVE PREPARED US FOR THE FINAL, CLIMACTIC BATTLE.
IF WE GO DOWN, T-BONE, FIGHTING THE THINKING MAN AND HIS HORDE OF ROBOTS AND GOBLINS IN ORDER TO SAVE THE WITCH QUEEN, THEN WE GO DOWN TOGETHER!
IT IS BEST TO BE YOUR GOOD FRIEND AND CONFIDANT, BORDEN.
WE WILL BE MEETING AGAIN IN HELL POSSIBLY!
YOUR FRIEND AND ONE-TIME LOVER BORDEN CAN'T SAVE YOU NOW, WITCH QUEEN!
THAT IS WHAT YOU THINK, YOU MAD MONSTER. BORDEN IS TOO MUCH MAN FOR ALL OF US!

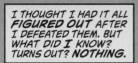

I THOUGHT I HAD IT ALL *FIGURED OUT* AFTER I DEFEATED THEM. BUT WHAT DID *I* KNOW? TURNS OUT? *NOTHING.*

YOU SHOULD HAVE HELD ON TO *PLUM,* WHO WAS THE LOVE OF YOUR *LIFE,* MAYBE!

NO, T-BONE. I CAN'T *AFFORD* TO *LOVE.* IT'S TOO DANGEROUS FOR THE *WOMEN* IN MY LIFE.

THIS IS VERY *WISE.* BUT YOU WILL LOVE *AGAIN,* I THINK.

AND, *JUST* WHEN I THOUGHT MY LIFE WAS BASICALLY *OVER,* THAT'S WHEN EVERY-THING *CHANGED.*

HI, I'M LOTUS BLOSSOM, THE *NEW* KID IN TOWN. WHO ARE YOU?

YOU DON'T WANT *ME,* BABE. I'M DAMAGED GOODS.

AND *I'M* THE KIND OF GIRL YOUR MOTHER *WARNED* YOU ABOUT, OR *WOULD* HAVE IF SHE HADN'T *DIED* TRAGICALLY, LEAVING YOU AN ORPHAN AT THE AGE OF *SIX.*

IT *IS* A *HAPPY ENDING* AFTER ALL!

FIN.

MYSTERY HOUSE

illustrated by
ANNIE WU

written, directed and produced by and starring
JORDAN MAYER   (special thanks to DAVE JUSTUS)

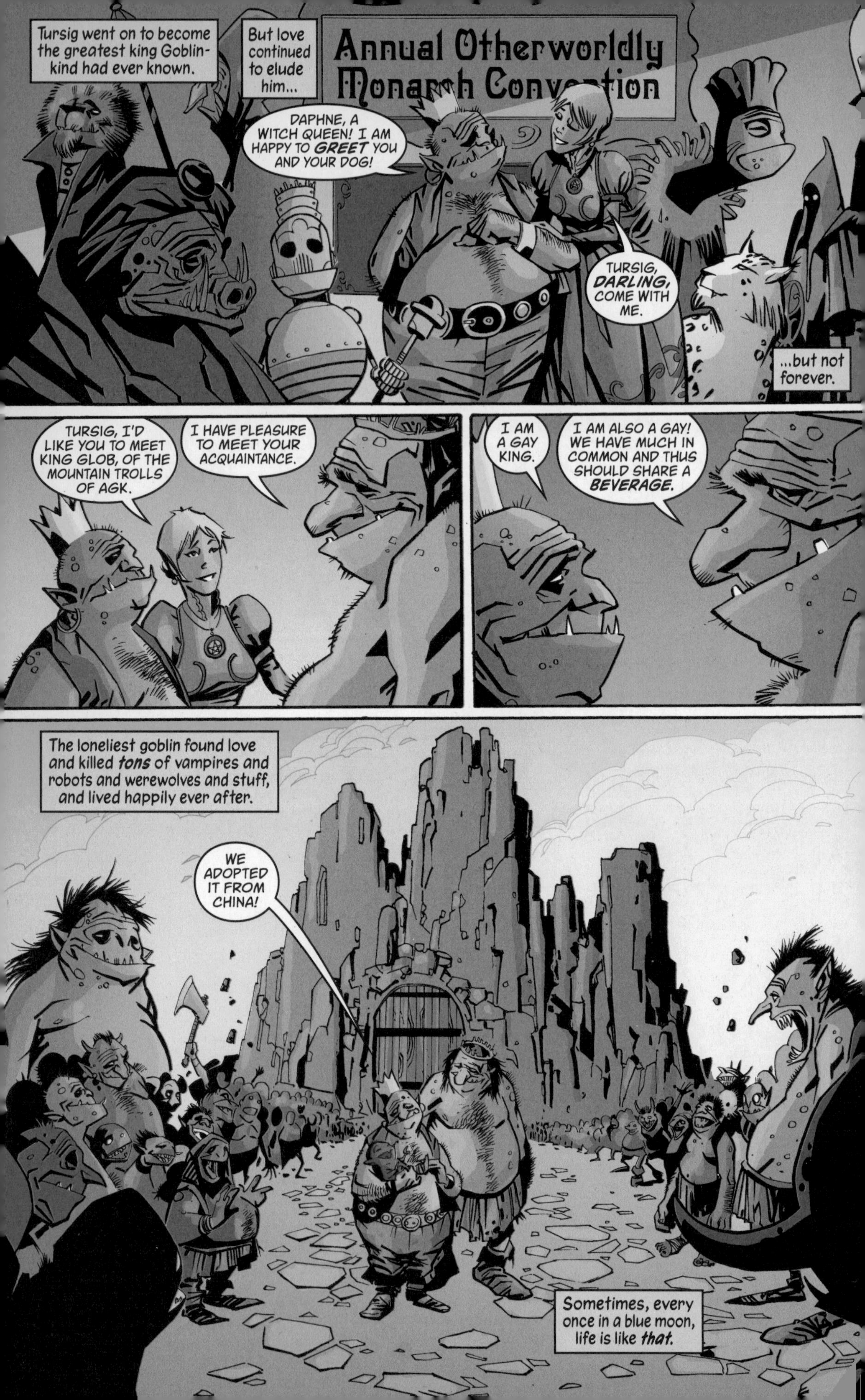
Tursig went on to become the greatest king Goblin-kind had ever known.
But love continued to elude him...
Annual Otherworldly Monarch Convention
DAPHNE, A WITCH QUEEN! I AM HAPPY TO GREET YOU AND YOUR DOG!
TURSIG, DARLING, COME WITH ME.
...but not forever.
TURSIG, I'D LIKE YOU TO MEET KING GLOB, OF THE MOUNTAIN TROLLS OF AGK.
I HAVE PLEASURE TO MEET YOUR ACQUAINTANCE.
I AM A GAY KING.
I AM ALSO A GAY! WE HAVE MUCH IN COMMON AND THUS SHOULD SHARE A BEVERAGE.
The loneliest goblin found love and killed tons of vampires and robots and werewolves and stuff, and lived happily ever after.
WE ADOPTED IT FROM CHINA!
Sometimes, every once in a blue moon, life is like that.

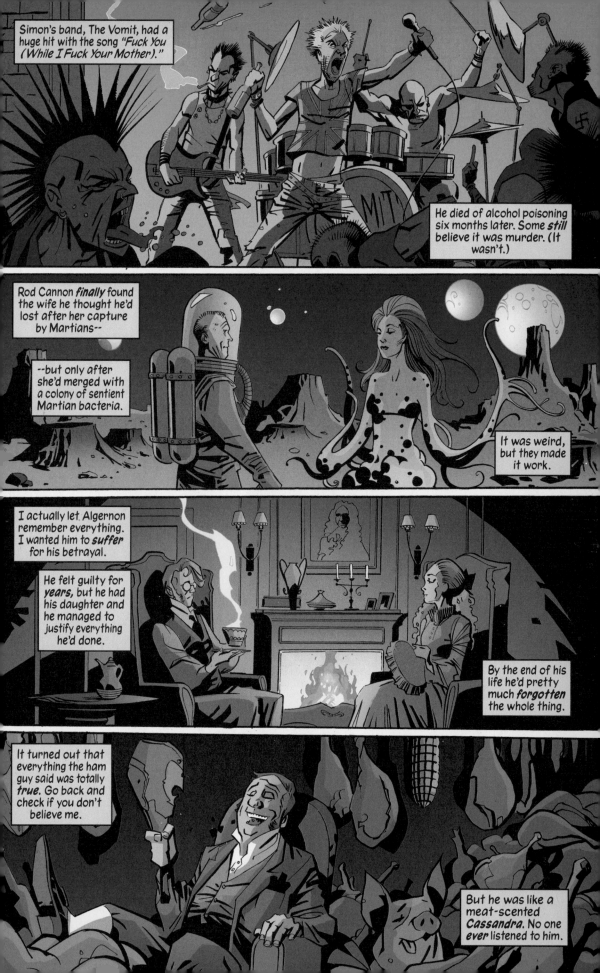

Simon's band, The Vomit, had a huge hit with the song *"Fuck You (While I Fuck Your Mother)."*

He died of alcohol poisoning six months later. Some *still* believe it was murder. (It wasn't.)

Rod Cannon *finally* found the wife he thought he'd lost after her capture by Martians--

--but only after she'd merged with a colony of sentient Martian bacteria.

It was weird, but they made it work.

I actually let Algernon remember everything. I wanted him to *suffer* for his betrayal.

He felt guilty for *years*, but he had his daughter and he managed to justify everything he'd done.

By the end of his life he'd pretty much *forgotten* the whole thing.

It turned out that everything the ham guy said was totally *true.* Go back and check if you don't believe me.

But he was like a meat-scented *Cassandra.* No one *ever* listened to him.

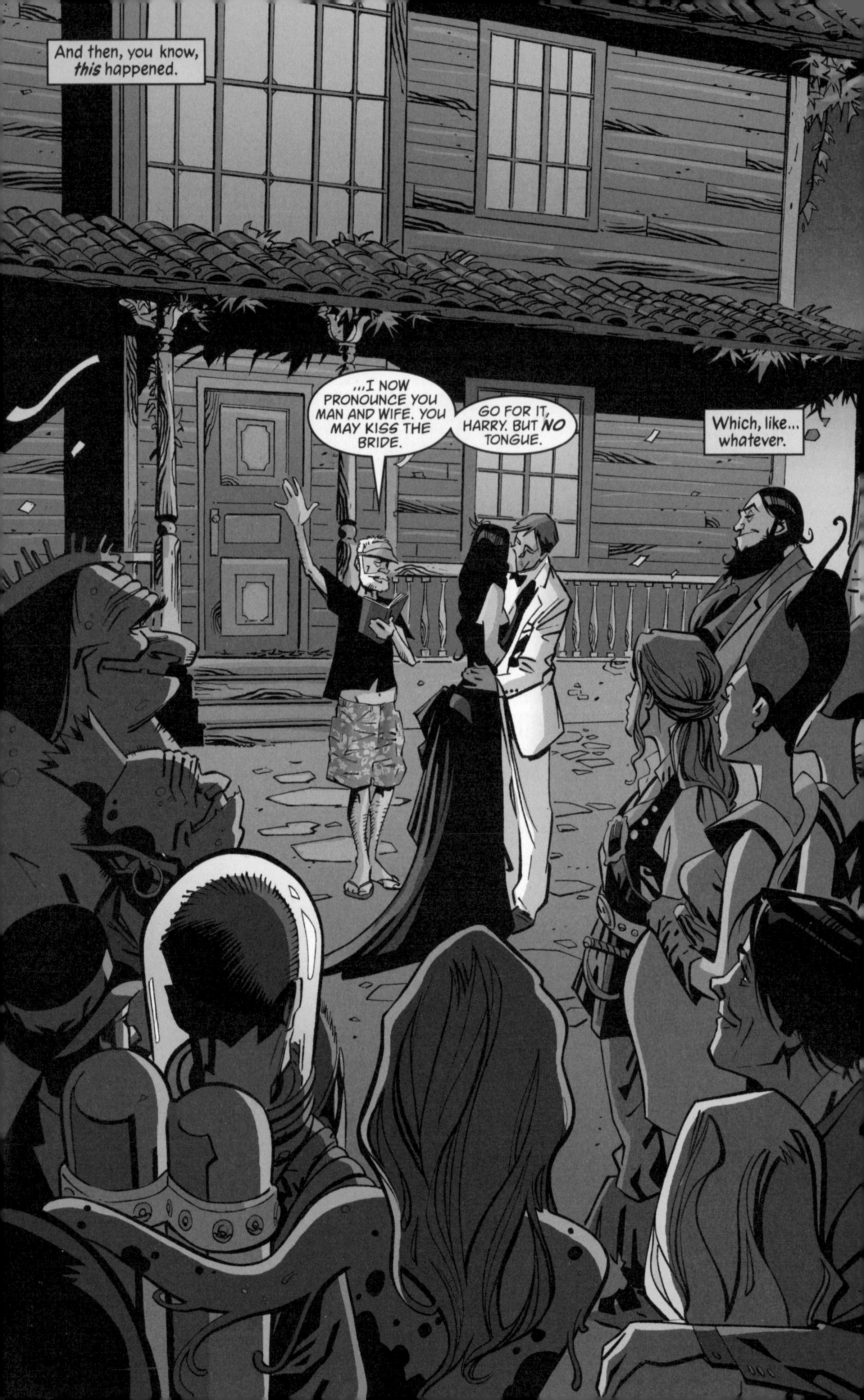
And then, you know, *this* happened.
...I NOW PRONOUNCE YOU MAN AND WIFE. YOU MAY KISS THE BRIDE.
GO FOR IT, HARRY. BUT **NO** TONGUE.
Which, like... whatever.

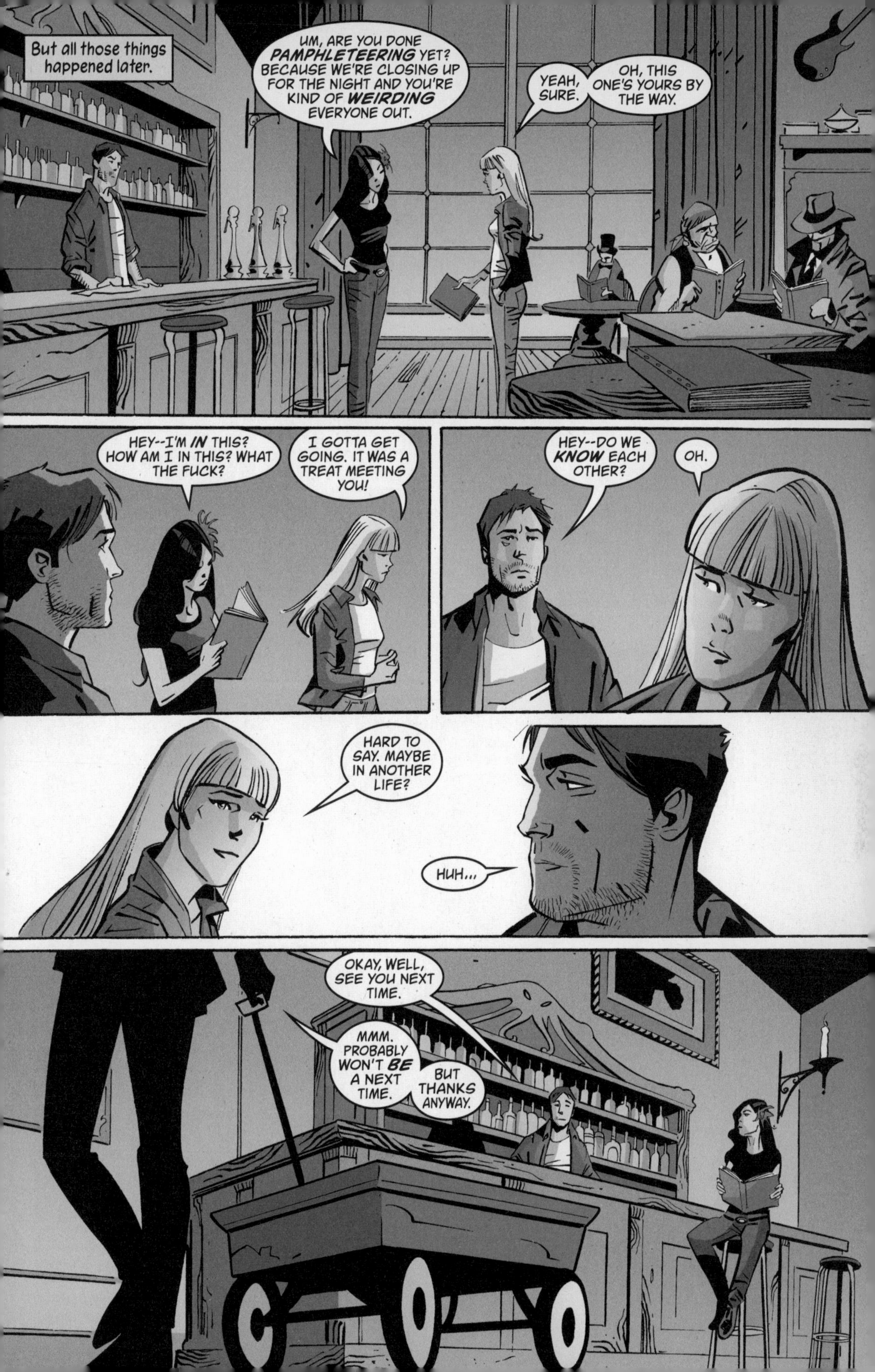
But all those things happened later.
UM, ARE YOU DONE PAMPHLETEERING YET? BECAUSE WE'RE CLOSING UP FOR THE NIGHT AND YOU'RE KIND OF WEIRDING EVERYONE OUT.
YEAH, SURE.
OH, THIS ONE'S YOURS BY THE WAY.
HEY--I'M IN THIS? HOW AM I IN THIS? WHAT THE FUCK?
I GOTTA GET GOING. IT WAS A TREAT MEETING YOU!
HEY--DO WE KNOW EACH OTHER?
OH.
HARD TO SAY. MAYBE IN ANOTHER LIFE?
HUH...
OKAY, WELL, SEE YOU NEXT TIME.
MMM. PROBABLY WON'T BE A NEXT TIME.
BUT THANKS ANYWAY.

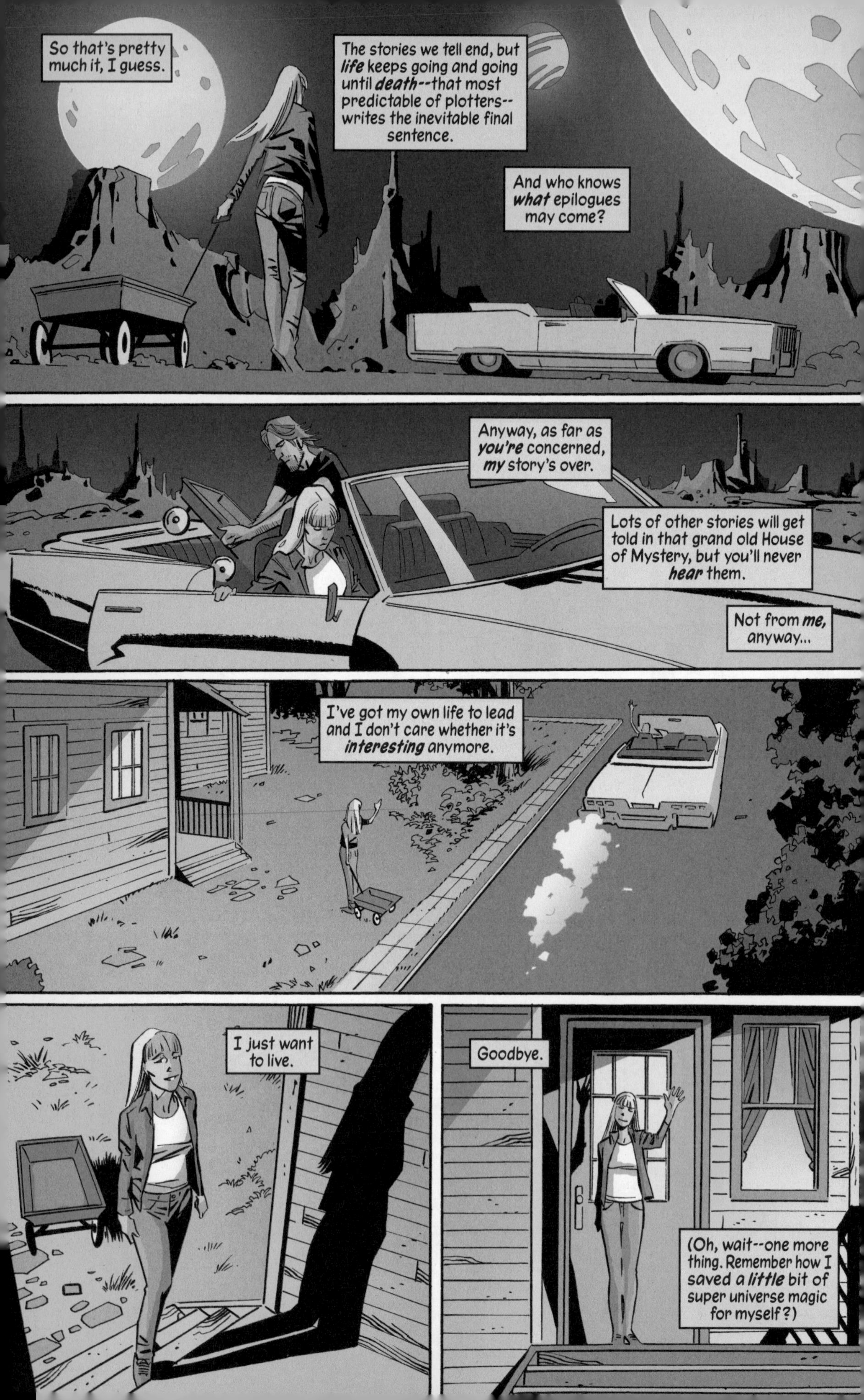
So that's pretty much it, I guess.
The stories we tell end, but life keeps going and going until death--that most predictable of plotters--writes the inevitable final sentence.
And who knows what epilogues may come?
Anyway, as far as you're concerned, my story's over.
Lots of other stories will get told in that grand old House of Mystery, but you'll never hear them.
Not from me, anyway...
I've got my own life to lead and I don't care whether it's interesting anymore.
I just want to live.
Goodbye.
(Oh, wait--one more thing. Remember how I saved a little bit of super universe magic for myself?)

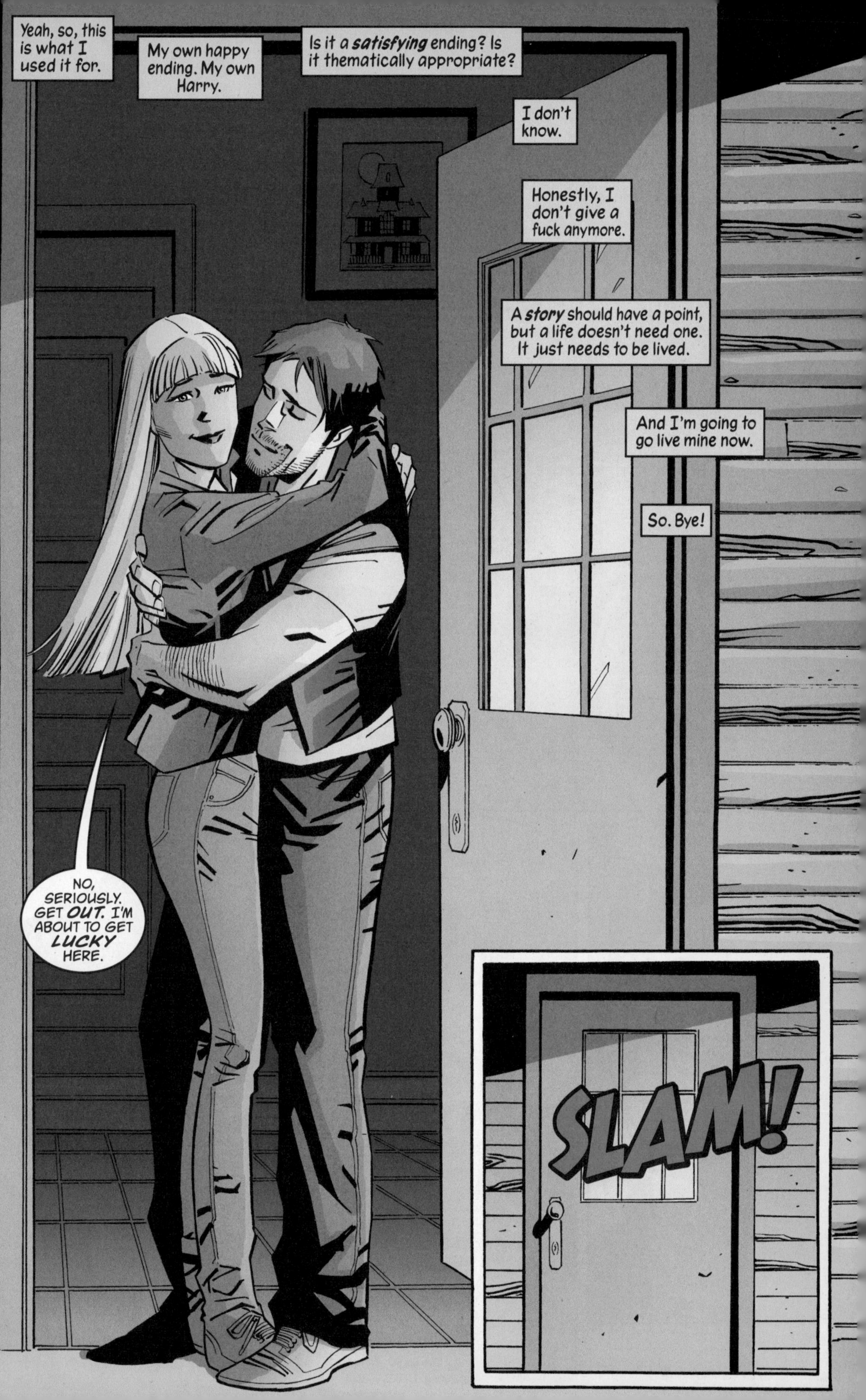
Yeah, so, this is what I used it for.
My own happy ending. My own Harry.
Is it a *satisfying* ending? Is it thematically appropriate?
I don't know.
Honestly, I don't give a fuck anymore.
A *story* should have a point, but a life doesn't need one. It just needs to be lived.
And I'm going to go live mine now.
So. Bye!
NO, SERIOUSLY. GET *OUT.* I'M ABOUT TO GET *LUCKY* HERE.
SLAM!

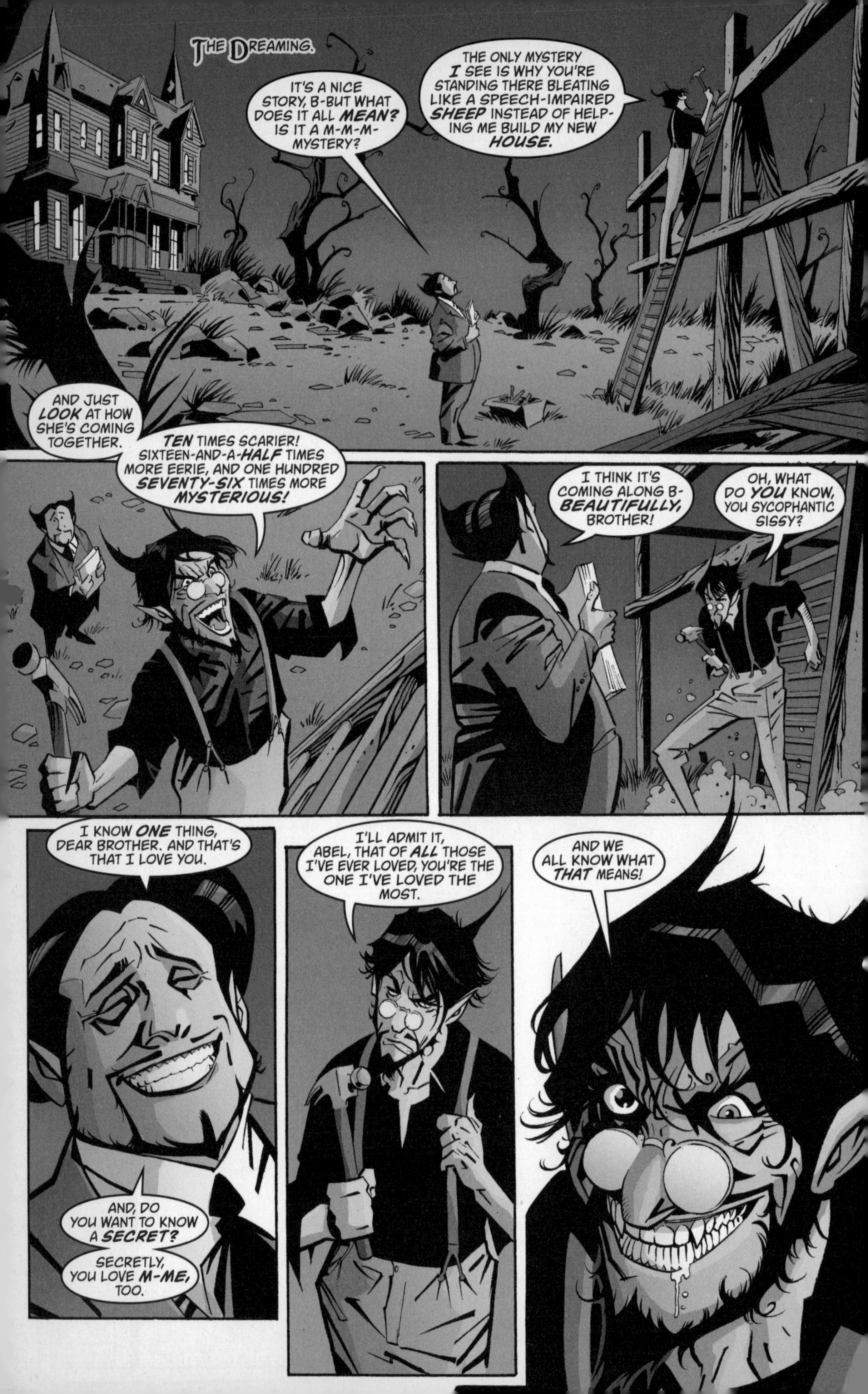
THE DREAMING.
IT'S A NICE STORY, B-BUT WHAT DOES IT ALL MEAN? IS IT A M-M-M-MYSTERY?
THE ONLY MYSTERY I SEE IS WHY YOU'RE STANDING THERE BLEATING LIKE A SPEECH-IMPAIRED SHEEP INSTEAD OF HELPING ME BUILD MY NEW HOUSE.
AND JUST LOOK AT HOW SHE'S COMING TOGETHER.
TEN TIMES SCARIER! SIXTEEN-AND-A-HALF TIMES MORE EERIE, AND ONE HUNDRED SEVENTY-SIX TIMES MORE MYSTERIOUS!
I THINK IT'S COMING ALONG B-BEAUTIFULLY, BROTHER!
OH, WHAT DO YOU KNOW, YOU SYCOPHANTIC SISSY?
I KNOW ONE THING, DEAR BROTHER. AND THAT'S THAT I LOVE YOU.
AND, DO YOU WANT TO KNOW A SECRET?
SECRETLY, YOU LOVE M-ME, TOO.
I'LL ADMIT IT, ABEL, THAT OF ALL THOSE I'VE EVER LOVED, YOU'RE THE ONE I'VE LOVED THE MOST.
AND WE ALL KNOW WHAT THAT MEANS!

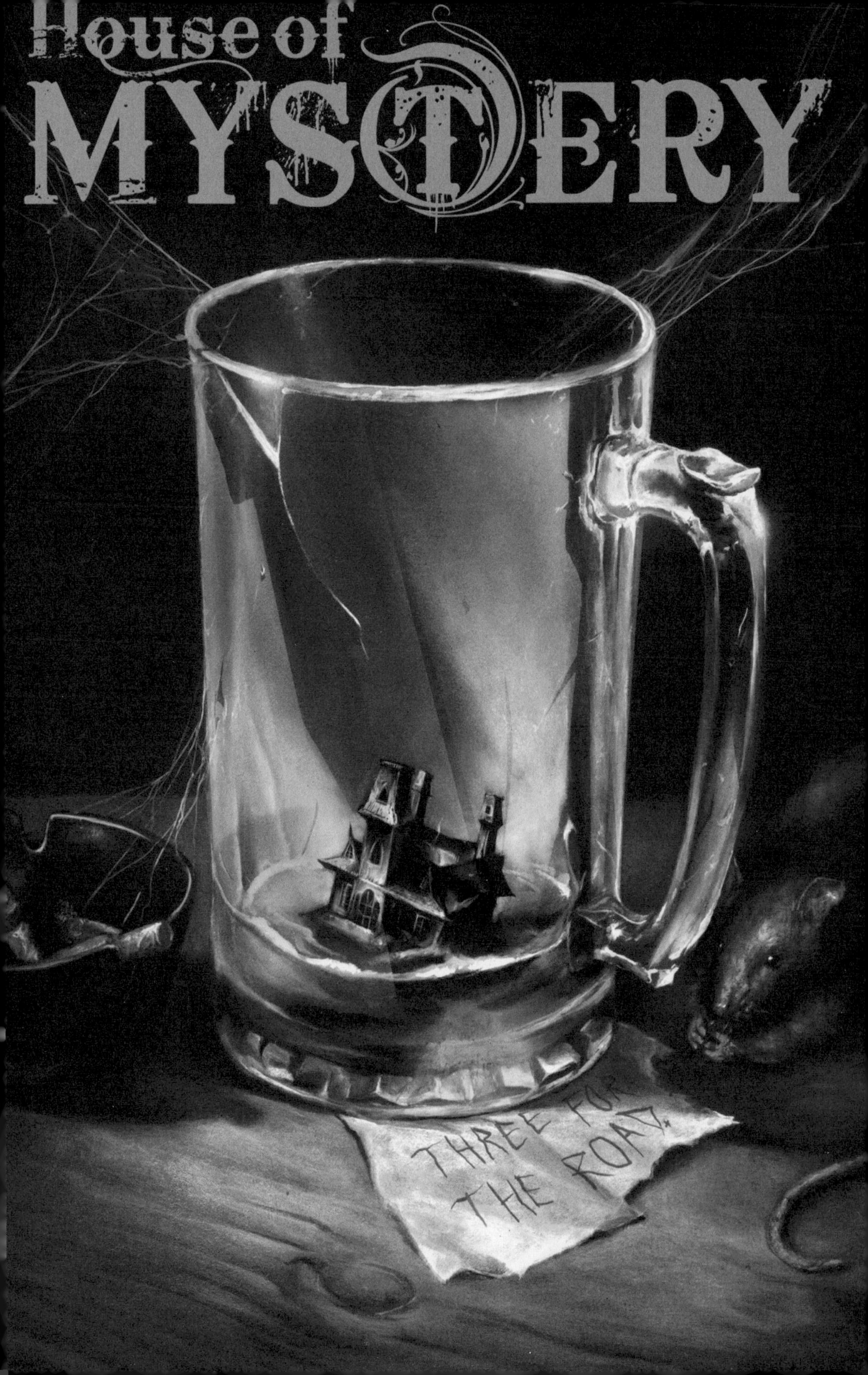
House of
MYSTERY
THREE FOR
THE ROAD.

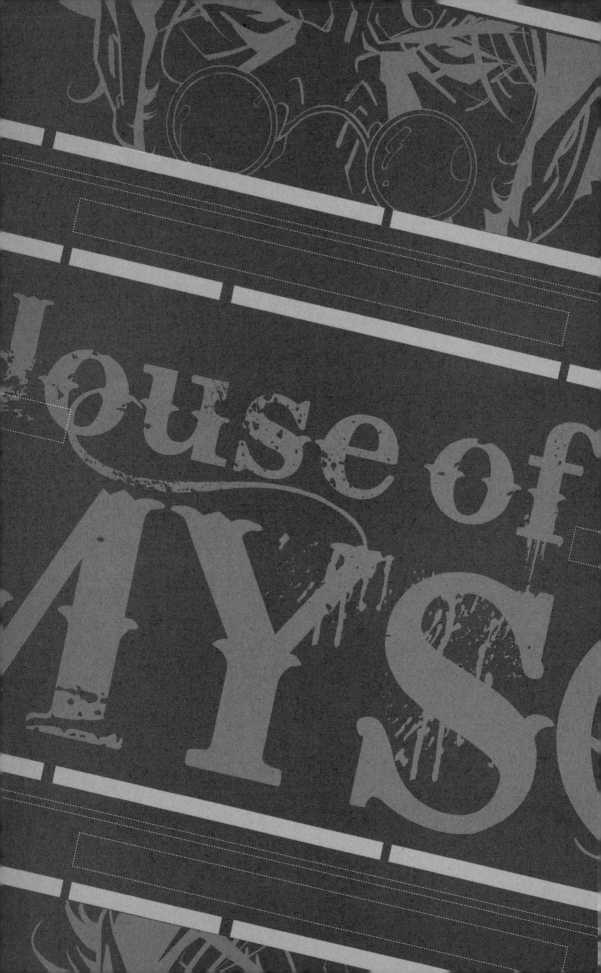

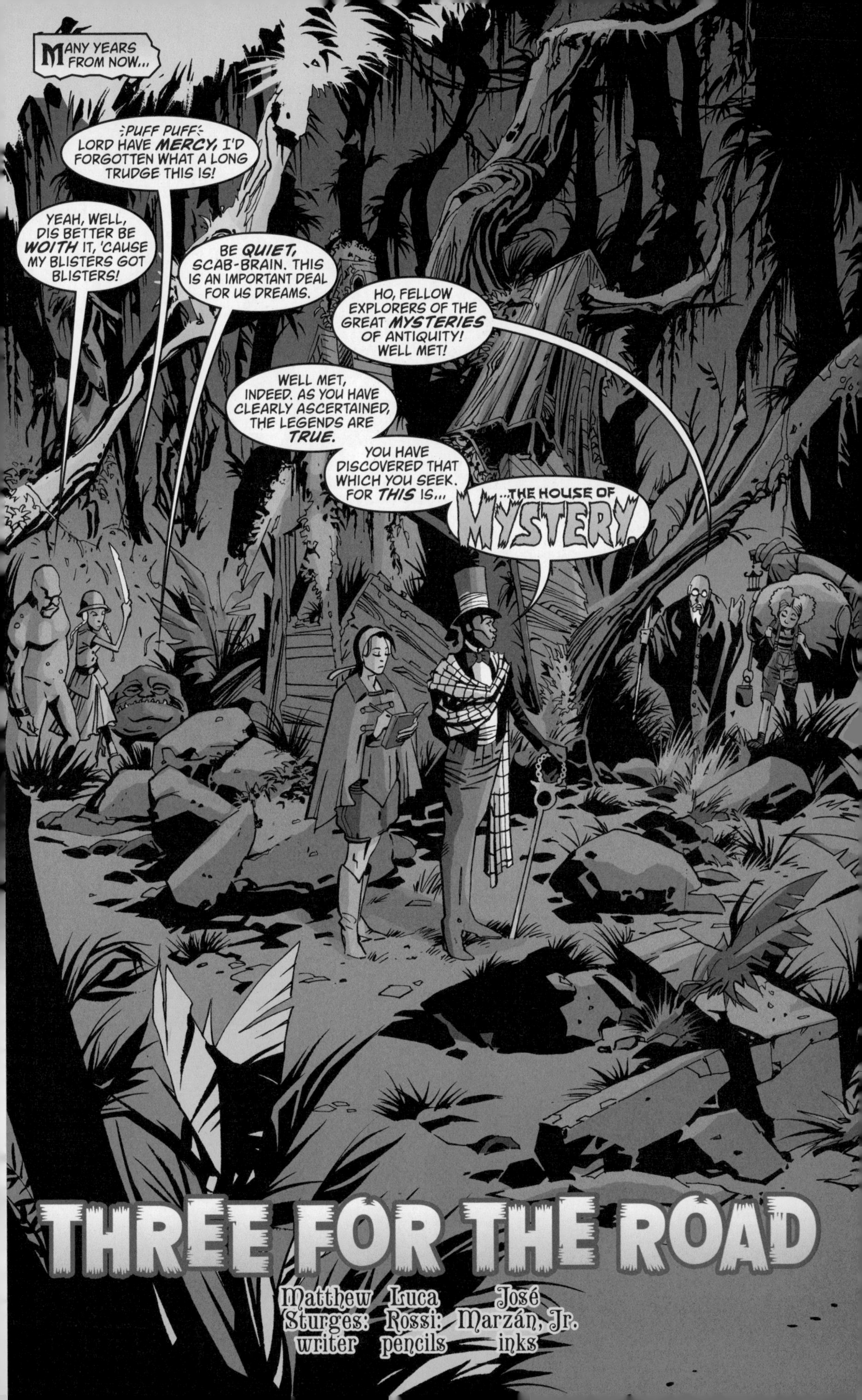
MANY YEARS FROM NOW...
PUFF PUFF
LORD HAVE MERCY, I'D FORGOTTEN WHAT A LONG TRUDGE THIS IS!
YEAH, WELL, DIS BETTER BE WOITH IT, 'CAUSE MY BLISTERS GOT BLISTERS!
BE QUIET, SCAB-BRAIN. THIS IS AN IMPORTANT DEAL FOR US DREAMS.
HO, FELLOW EXPLORERS OF THE GREAT MYSTERIES OF ANTIQUITY! WELL MET!
WELL MET, INDEED. AS YOU HAVE CLEARLY ASCERTAINED, THE LEGENDS ARE TRUE.
YOU HAVE DISCOVERED THAT WHICH YOU SEEK. FOR THIS IS...
...THE HOUSE OF MYSTERY.
THREE FOR THE ROAD
Matthew Sturges: writer
Luca Rossi: pencils
José Marzán, Jr. inks

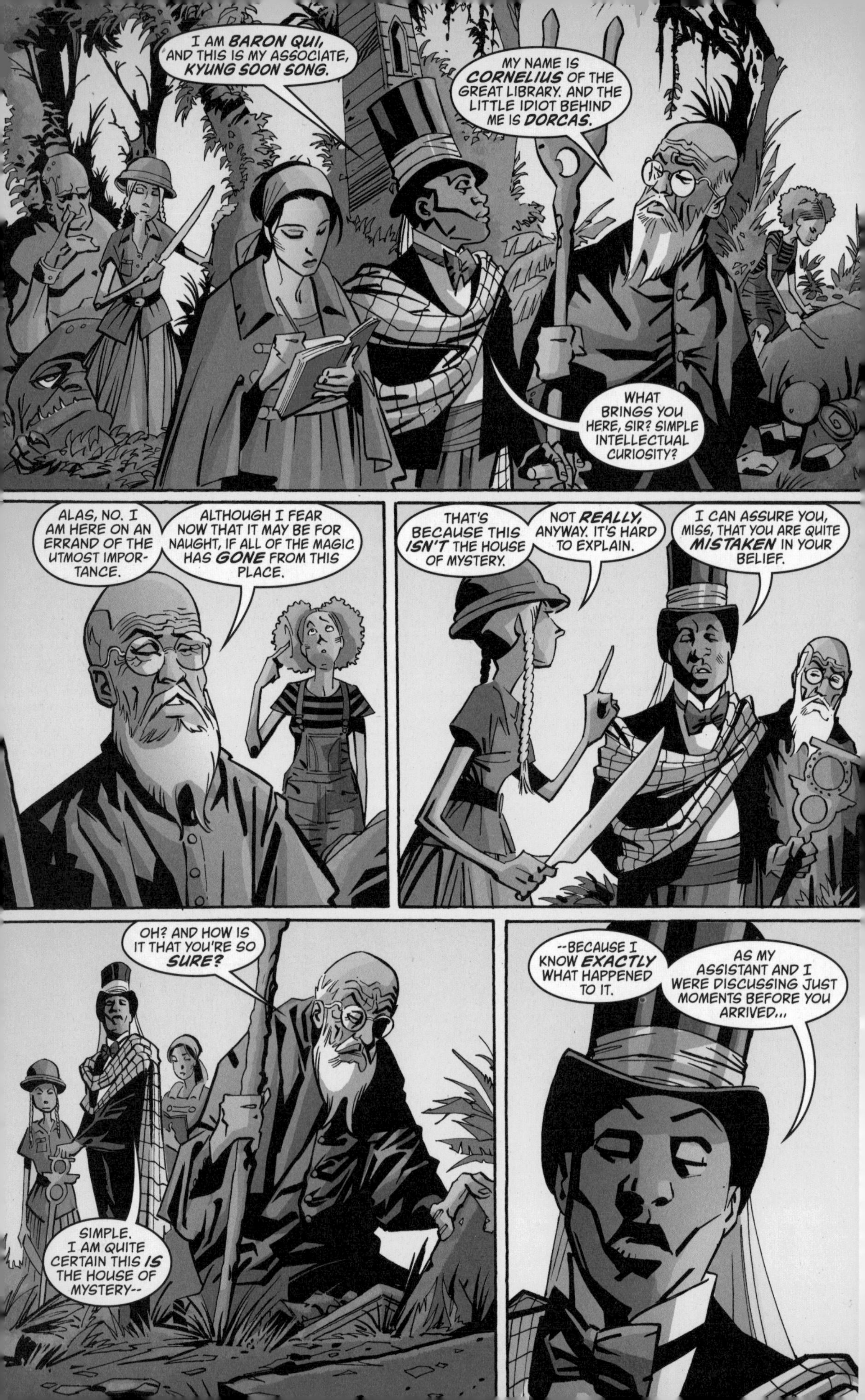
I AM BARON QUI, AND THIS IS MY ASSOCIATE, KYUNG SOON SONG.
MY NAME IS CORNELIUS OF THE GREAT LIBRARY. AND THE LITTLE IDIOT BEHIND ME IS DORCAS.
WHAT BRINGS YOU HERE, SIR? SIMPLE INTELLECTUAL CURIOSITY?
ALAS, NO. I AM HERE ON AN ERRAND OF THE UTMOST IMPORTANCE.
ALTHOUGH I FEAR NOW THAT IT MAY BE FOR NAUGHT, IF ALL OF THE MAGIC HAS GONE FROM THIS PLACE.
THAT'S BECAUSE THIS ISN'T THE HOUSE OF MYSTERY.
NOT REALLY, ANYWAY. IT'S HARD TO EXPLAIN.
I CAN ASSURE YOU, MISS, THAT YOU ARE QUITE MISTAKEN IN YOUR BELIEF.
OH? AND HOW IS IT THAT YOU'RE SO SURE?
SIMPLE. I AM QUITE CERTAIN THIS IS THE HOUSE OF MYSTERY--
--BECAUSE I KNOW EXACTLY WHAT HAPPENED TO IT.
AS MY ASSISTANT AND I WERE DISCUSSING JUST MOMENTS BEFORE YOU ARRIVED...

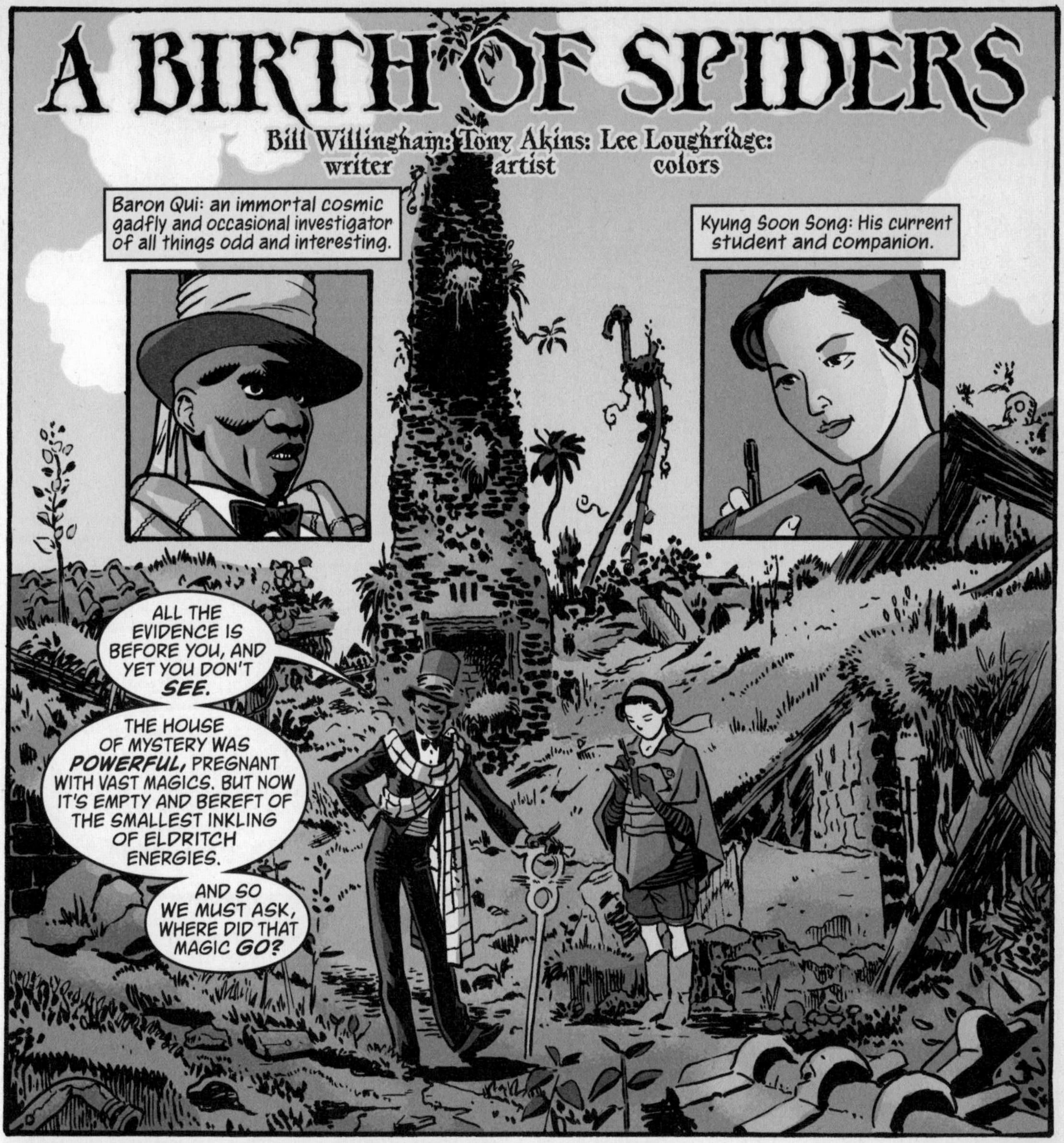
A BIRTH OF SPIDERS
Bill Willingham: writer
Tony Akins: artist
Lee Loughridge: colors
Baron Qui: an immortal cosmic gadfly and occasional investigator of all things odd and interesting.
Kyung Soon Song: His current student and companion.
ALL THE EVIDENCE IS BEFORE YOU, AND YET YOU DON'T SEE.
THE HOUSE OF MYSTERY WAS POWERFUL, PREGNANT WITH VAST MAGICS. BUT NOW IT'S EMPTY AND BEREFT OF THE SMALLEST INKLING OF ELDRITCH ENERGIES.
AND SO WE MUST ASK, WHERE DID THAT MAGIC GO?

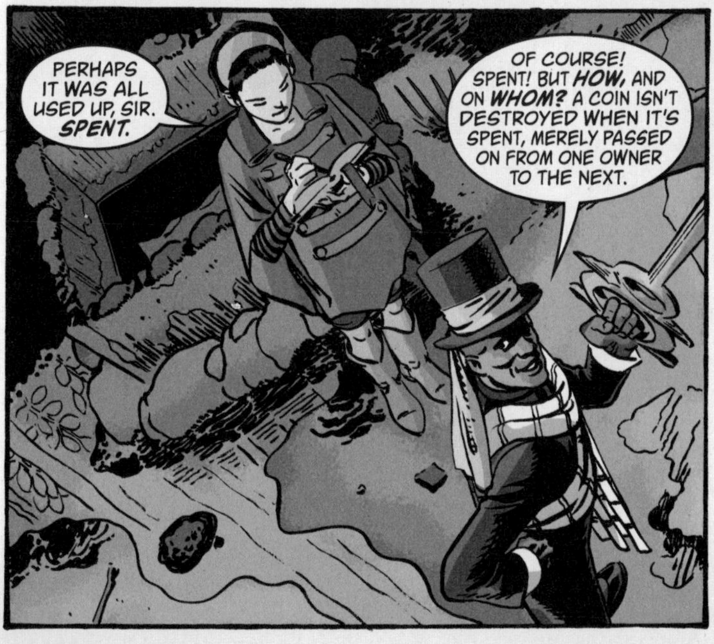
PERHAPS IT WAS ALL USED UP, SIR. SPENT.
OF COURSE! SPENT! BUT HOW, AND ON WHOM? A COIN ISN'T DESTROYED WHEN IT'S SPENT, MERELY PASSED ON FROM ONE OWNER TO THE NEXT.

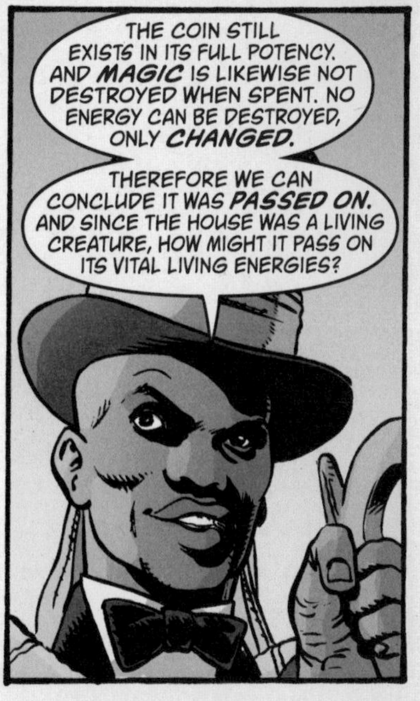
THE COIN STILL EXISTS IN ITS FULL POTENCY. AND MAGIC IS LIKEWISE NOT DESTROYED WHEN SPENT. NO ENERGY CAN BE DESTROYED, ONLY CHANGED.
THEREFORE WE CAN CONCLUDE IT WAS PASSED ON. AND SINCE THE HOUSE WAS A LIVING CREATURE, HOW MIGHT IT PASS ON ITS VITAL LIVING ENERGIES?

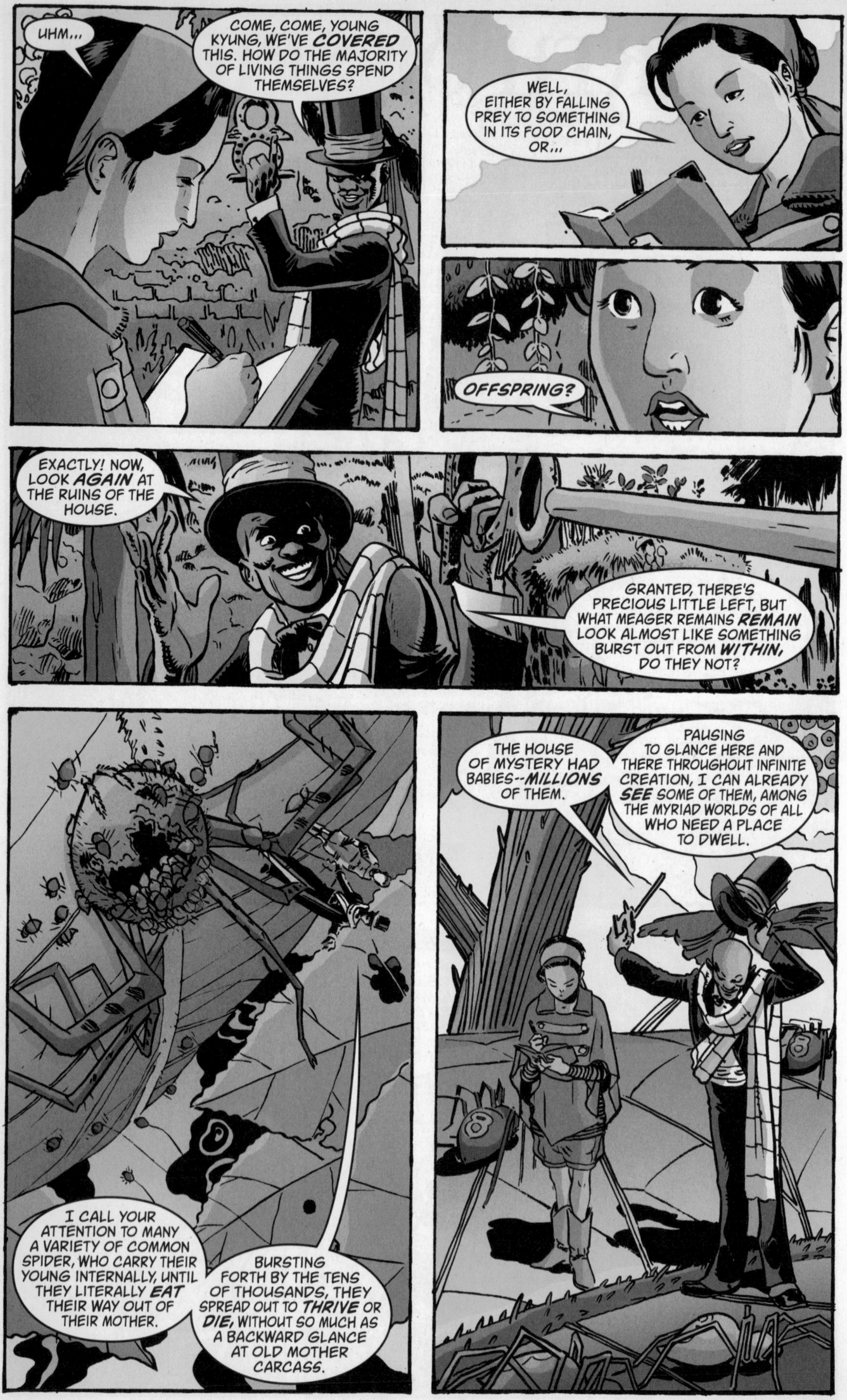
UHM...
COME, COME, YOUNG KYUNG, WE'VE *COVERED* THIS. HOW DO THE MAJORITY OF LIVING THINGS SPEND THEMSELVES?
WELL, EITHER BY FALLING PREY TO SOMETHING IN ITS FOOD CHAIN, OR...
OFFSPRING?
EXACTLY! NOW, LOOK *AGAIN* AT THE RUINS OF THE HOUSE.
GRANTED, THERE'S PRECIOUS LITTLE LEFT, BUT WHAT MEAGER REMAINS *REMAIN* LOOK ALMOST LIKE SOMETHING BURST OUT FROM *WITHIN,* DO THEY NOT?
I CALL YOUR ATTENTION TO MANY A VARIETY OF COMMON SPIDER, WHO CARRY THEIR YOUNG INTERNALLY, UNTIL THEY LITERALLY *EAT* THEIR WAY OUT OF THEIR MOTHER.
BURSTING FORTH BY THE TENS OF THOUSANDS, THEY SPREAD OUT TO *THRIVE* OR *DIE,* WITHOUT SO MUCH AS A BACKWARD GLANCE AT OLD MOTHER CARCASS.
THE HOUSE OF MYSTERY HAD BABIES--*MILLIONS* OF THEM.
PAUSING TO GLANCE HERE AND THERE THROUGHOUT INFINITE CREATION, I CAN ALREADY *SEE* SOME OF THEM, AMONG THE MYRIAD WORLDS OF ALL WHO NEED A PLACE TO DWELL.

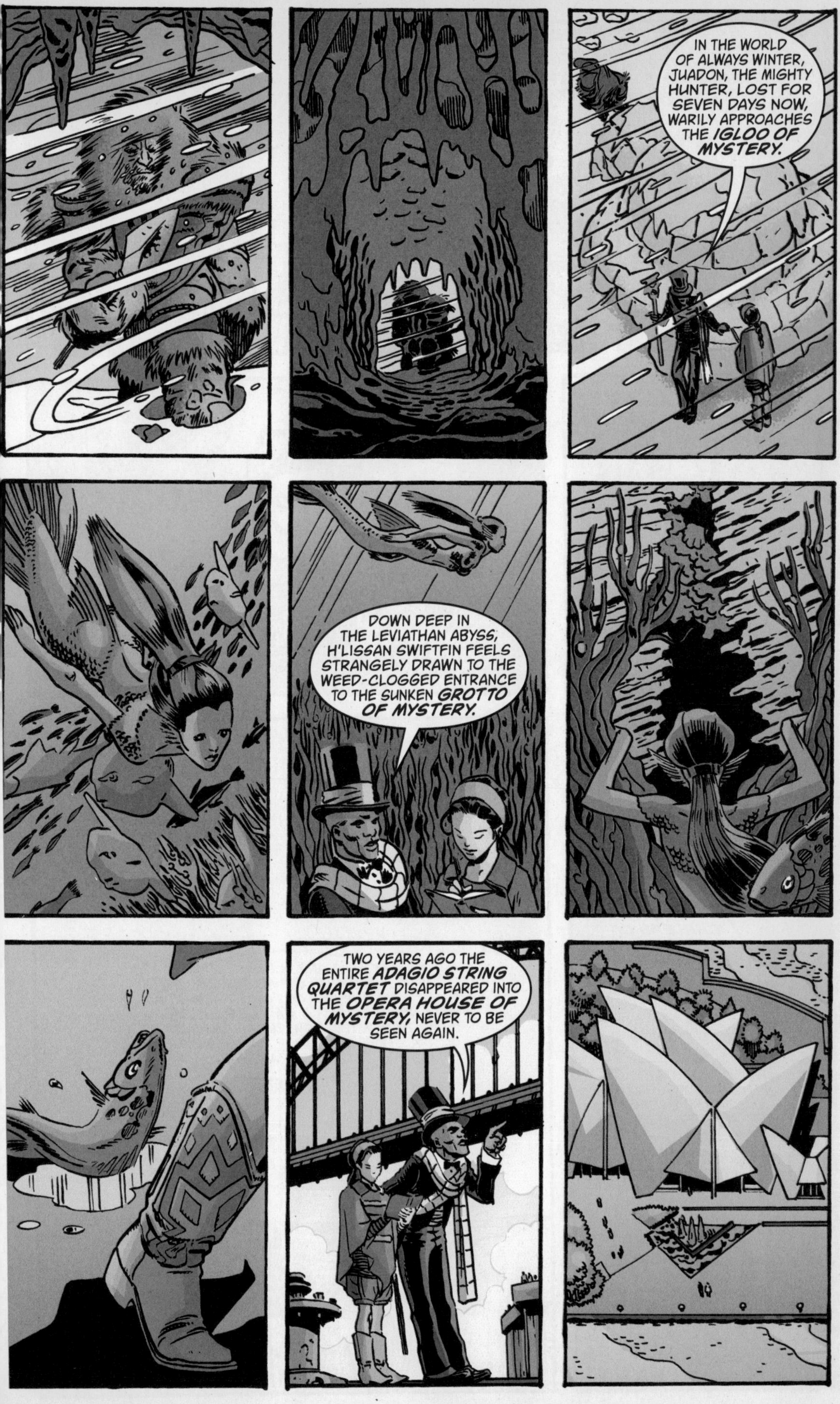
IN THE WORLD OF ALWAYS WINTER, JUADON, THE MIGHTY HUNTER, LOST FOR SEVEN DAYS NOW, WARILY APPROACHES THE IGLOO OF MYSTERY.
DOWN DEEP IN THE LEVIATHAN ABYSS, H'LISSAN SWIFTFIN FEELS STRANGELY DRAWN TO THE WEED-CLOGGED ENTRANCE TO THE SUNKEN GROTTO OF MYSTERY.
TWO YEARS AGO THE ENTIRE ADAGIO STRING QUARTET DISAPPEARED INTO THE OPERA HOUSE OF MYSTERY, NEVER TO BE SEEN AGAIN.

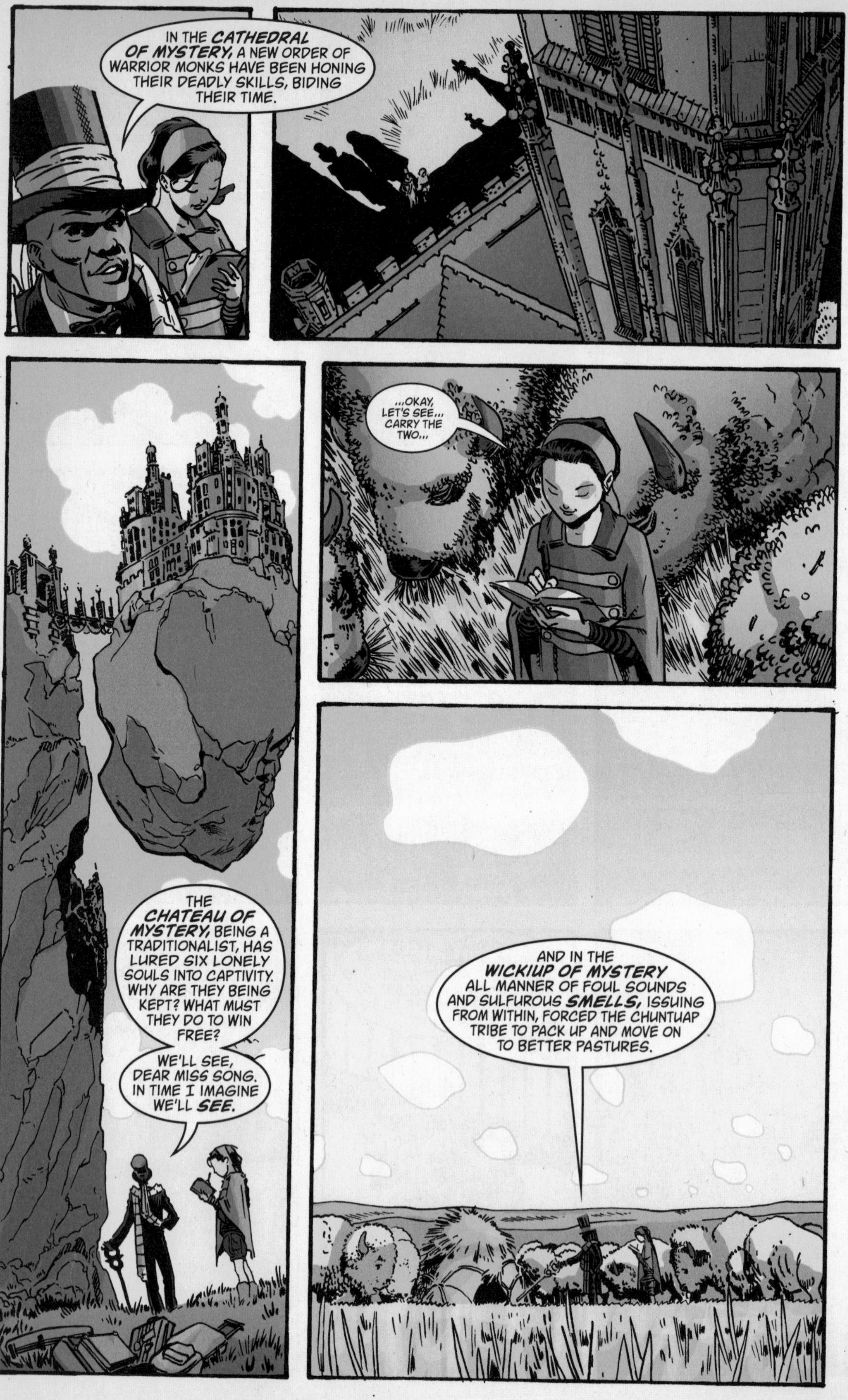
IN THE CATHEDRAL OF MYSTERY, A NEW ORDER OF WARRIOR MONKS HAVE BEEN HONING THEIR DEADLY SKILLS, BIDING THEIR TIME.
...OKAY, LET'S SEE... CARRY THE TWO...
THE CHATEAU OF MYSTERY, BEING A TRADITIONALIST, HAS LURED SIX LONELY SOULS INTO CAPTIVITY. WHY ARE THEY BEING KEPT? WHAT MUST THEY DO TO WIN FREE?
WE'LL SEE, DEAR MISS SONG. IN TIME I IMAGINE WE'LL SEE.
AND IN THE WICKIUP OF MYSTERY ALL MANNER OF FOUL SOUNDS AND SULFUROUS SMELLS, ISSUING FROM WITHIN, FORCED THE CHUNTUAP TRIBE TO PACK UP AND MOVE ON TO BETTER PASTURES.

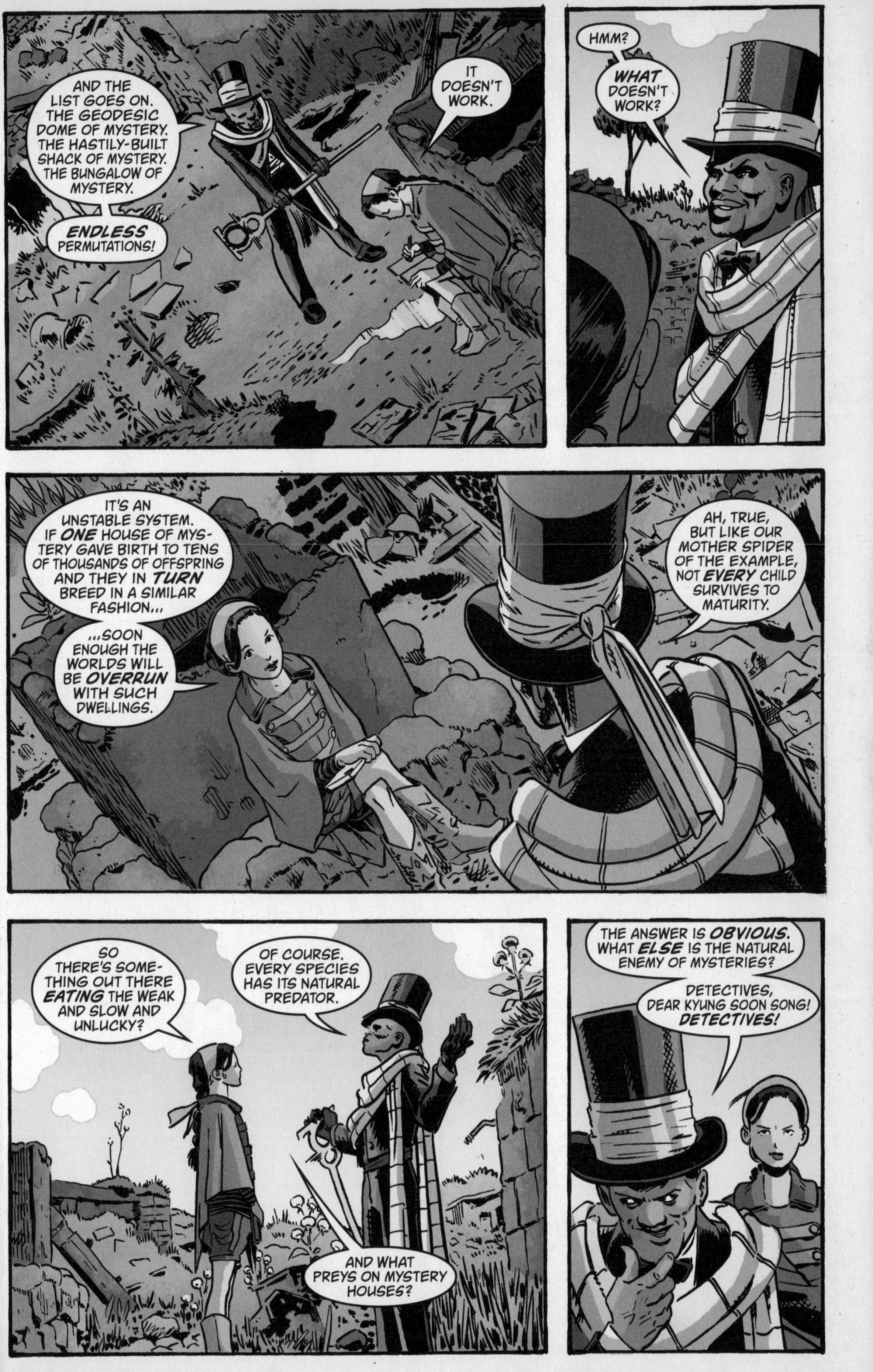
AND THE LIST GOES ON. THE GEODESIC DOME OF MYSTERY. THE HASTILY-BUILT SHACK OF MYSTERY. THE BUNGALOW OF MYSTERY.
ENDLESS PERMUTATIONS!
IT DOESN'T WORK.
HMM?
WHAT DOESN'T WORK?
IT'S AN UNSTABLE SYSTEM. IF ONE HOUSE OF MYSTERY GAVE BIRTH TO TENS OF THOUSANDS OF OFFSPRING AND THEY IN TURN BREED IN A SIMILAR FASHION...
...SOON ENOUGH THE WORLDS WILL BE OVERRUN WITH SUCH DWELLINGS.
AH, TRUE, BUT LIKE OUR MOTHER SPIDER OF THE EXAMPLE, NOT EVERY CHILD SURVIVES TO MATURITY.
SO THERE'S SOMETHING OUT THERE EATING THE WEAK AND SLOW AND UNLUCKY?
OF COURSE. EVERY SPECIES HAS ITS NATURAL PREDATOR.
AND WHAT PREYS ON MYSTERY HOUSES?
THE ANSWER IS OBVIOUS. WHAT ELSE IS THE NATURAL ENEMY OF MYSTERIES?
DETECTIVES, DEAR KYUNG SOON SONG! DETECTIVES!

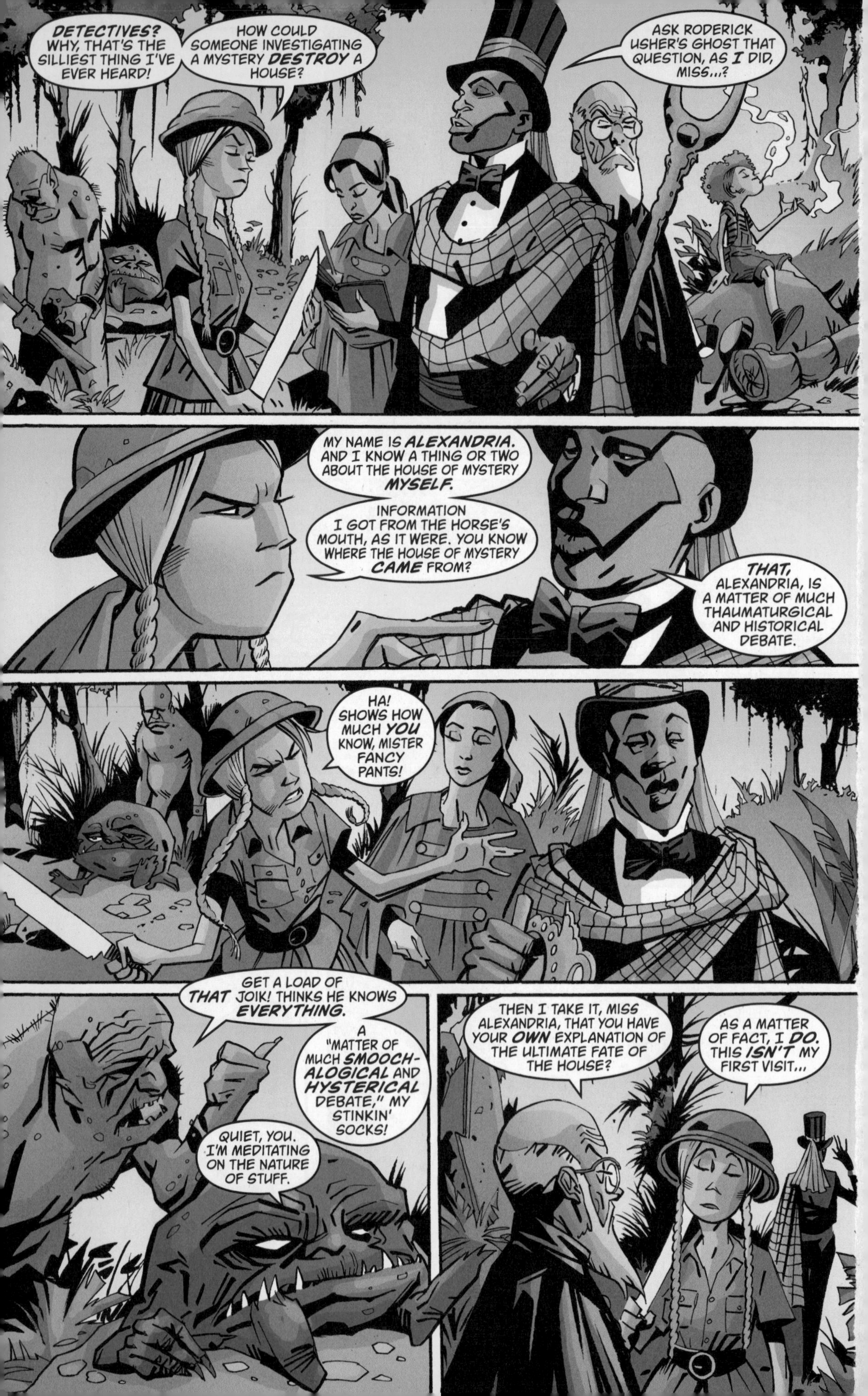
DETECTIVES? WHY, THAT'S THE SILLIEST THING I'VE EVER HEARD!
HOW COULD SOMEONE INVESTIGATING A MYSTERY DESTROY A HOUSE?
ASK RODERICK USHER'S GHOST THAT QUESTION, AS I DID, MISS...?
MY NAME IS ALEXANDRIA. AND I KNOW A THING OR TWO ABOUT THE HOUSE OF MYSTERY MYSELF.
INFORMATION I GOT FROM THE HORSE'S MOUTH, AS IT WERE. YOU KNOW WHERE THE HOUSE OF MYSTERY CAME FROM?
THAT, ALEXANDRIA, IS A MATTER OF MUCH THAUMATURGICAL AND HISTORICAL DEBATE.
HA! SHOWS HOW MUCH YOU KNOW, MISTER FANCY PANTS!
GET A LOAD OF THAT JOIK! THINKS HE KNOWS EVERYTHING.
A "MATTER OF MUCH SMOOCH-ALOGICAL AND HYSTERICAL DEBATE," MY STINKIN' SOCKS!
QUIET, YOU. I'M MEDITATING ON THE NATURE OF STUFF.
THEN I TAKE IT, MISS ALEXANDRIA, THAT YOU HAVE YOUR OWN EXPLANATION OF THE ULTIMATE FATE OF THE HOUSE?
AS A MATTER OF FACT, I DO. THIS ISN'T MY FIRST VISIT...

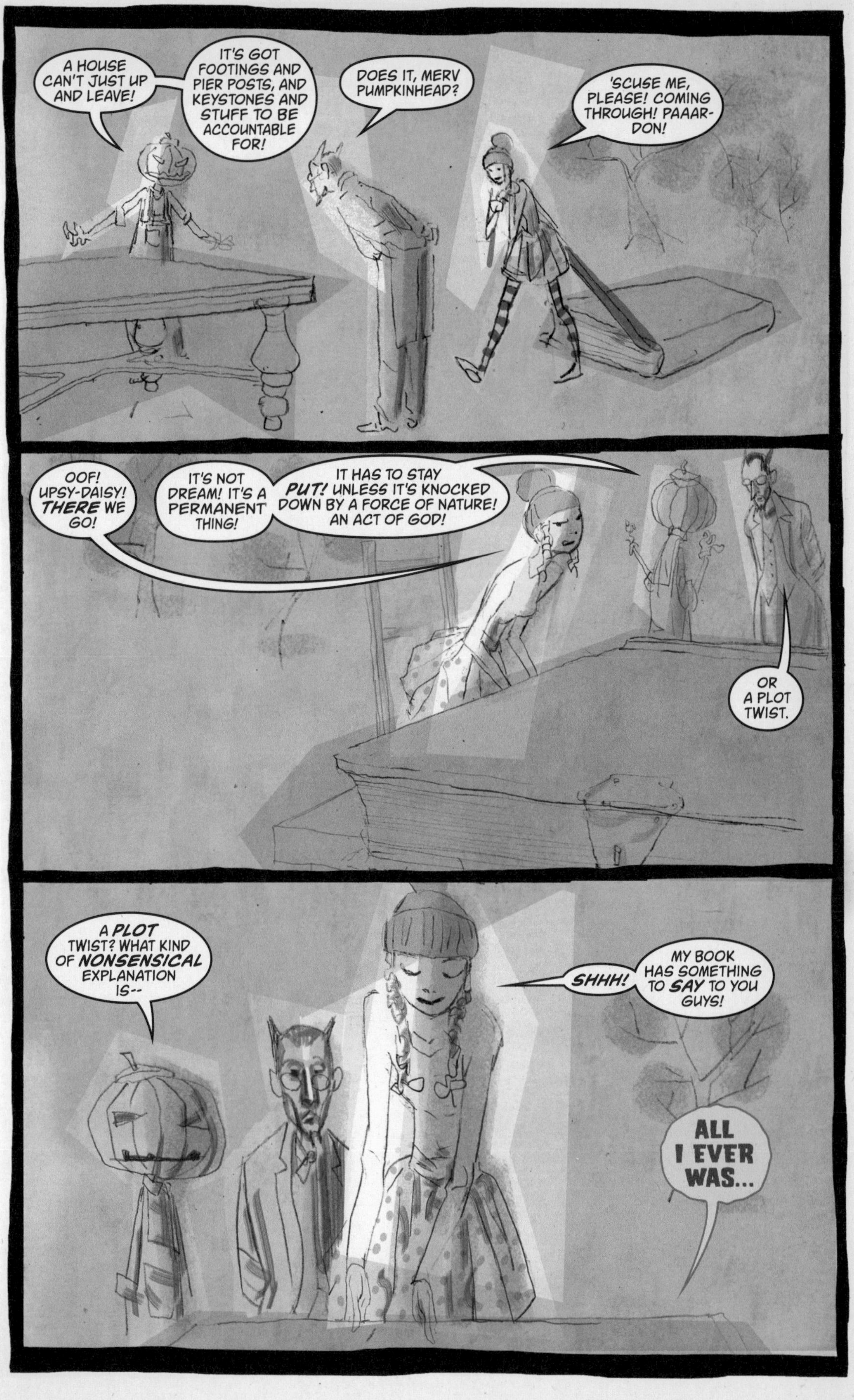

A HOUSE CAN'T JUST UP AND LEAVE!
IT'S GOT FOOTINGS AND PIER POSTS, AND KEYSTONES AND STUFF TO BE ACCOUNTABLE FOR!
DOES IT, MERV PUMPKINHEAD?
'SCUSE ME, PLEASE! COMING THROUGH! PAAAR-DON!
OOF! UPSY-DAISY! *THERE* WE GO!
IT'S NOT DREAM! IT'S A PERMANENT THING!
IT HAS TO STAY *PUT!* UNLESS IT'S KNOCKED DOWN BY A FORCE OF NATURE! AN ACT OF GOD!
OR A PLOT TWIST.
A *PLOT* TWIST? WHAT KIND OF *NONSENSICAL* EXPLANATION IS--
SHHH!
MY BOOK HAS SOMETHING TO *SAY* TO YOU GUYS!
ALL I EVER WAS...

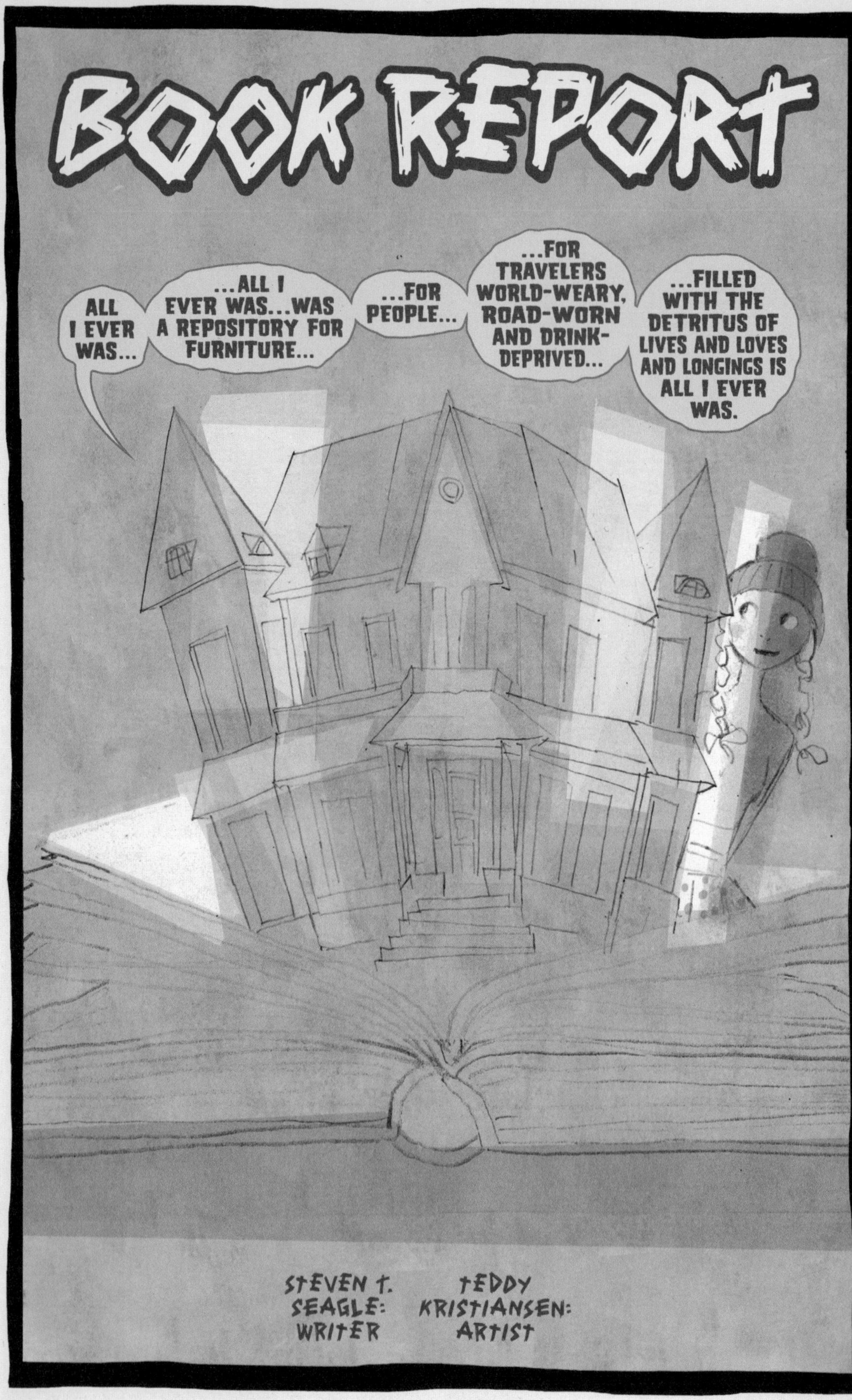
BOOK REPORT
ALL I EVER WAS...
...ALL I EVER WAS...WAS A REPOSITORY FOR FURNITURE...
...FOR PEOPLE...
...FOR TRAVELERS WORLD-WEARY, ROAD-WORN AND DRINK-DEPRIVED...
...FILLED WITH THE DETRITUS OF LIVES AND LOVES AND LONGINGS IS ALL I EVER WAS.
STEVEN T. SEAGLE: WRITER
TEDDY KRISTIANSEN: ARTIST

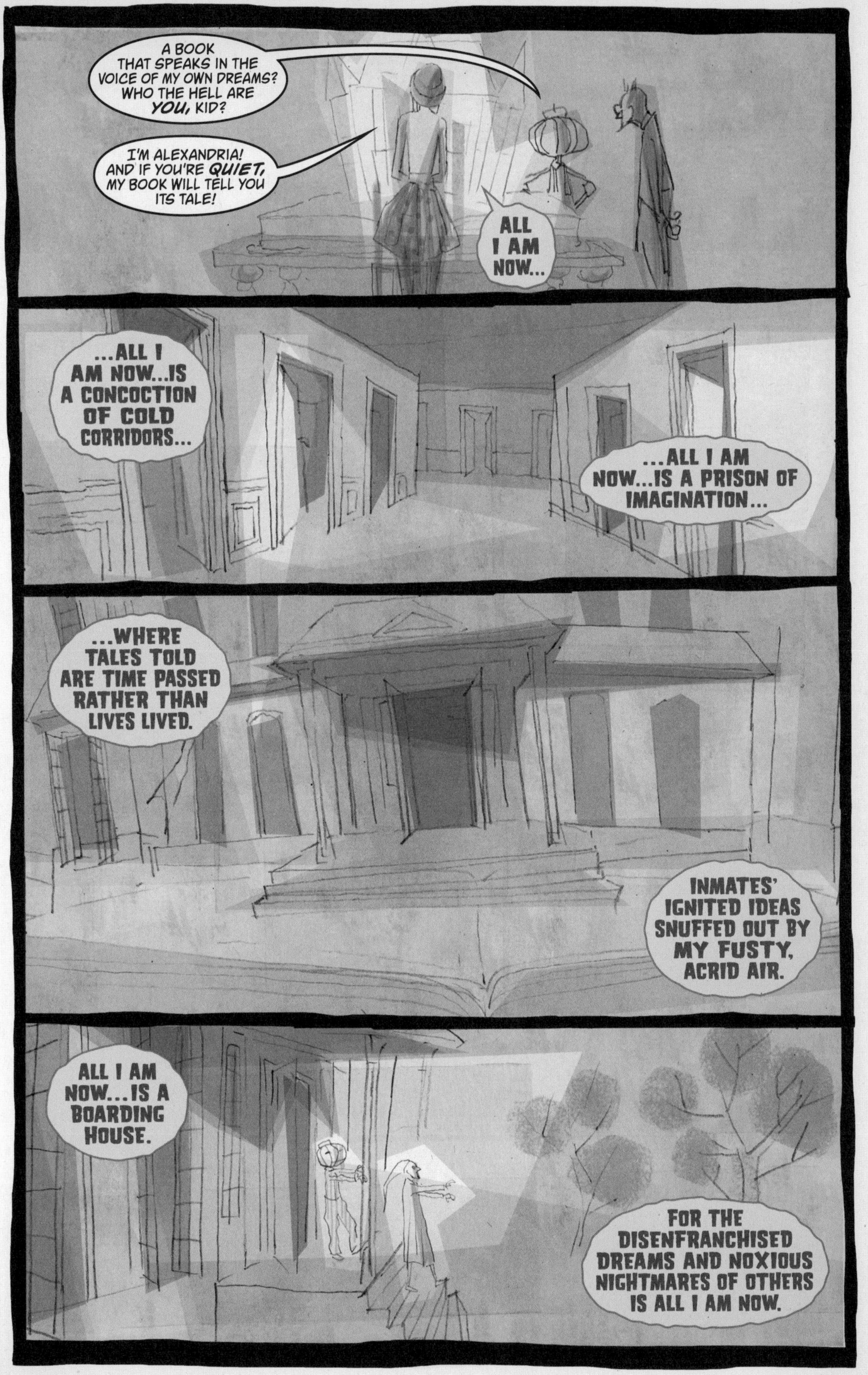
A BOOK THAT SPEAKS IN THE VOICE OF MY OWN DREAMS? WHO THE HELL ARE YOU, KID?
I'M ALEXANDRIA! AND IF YOU'RE QUIET, MY BOOK WILL TELL YOU ITS TALE!
ALL I AM NOW...
...ALL I AM NOW...IS A CONCOCTION OF COLD CORRIDORS...
...ALL I AM NOW...IS A PRISON OF IMAGINATION...
...WHERE TALES TOLD ARE TIME PASSED RATHER THAN LIVES LIVED.
INMATES' IGNITED IDEAS SNUFFED OUT BY MY FUSTY, ACRID AIR.
ALL I AM NOW...IS A BOARDING HOUSE.
FOR THE DISENFRANCHISED DREAMS AND NOXIOUS NIGHTMARES OF OTHERS IS ALL I AM NOW.

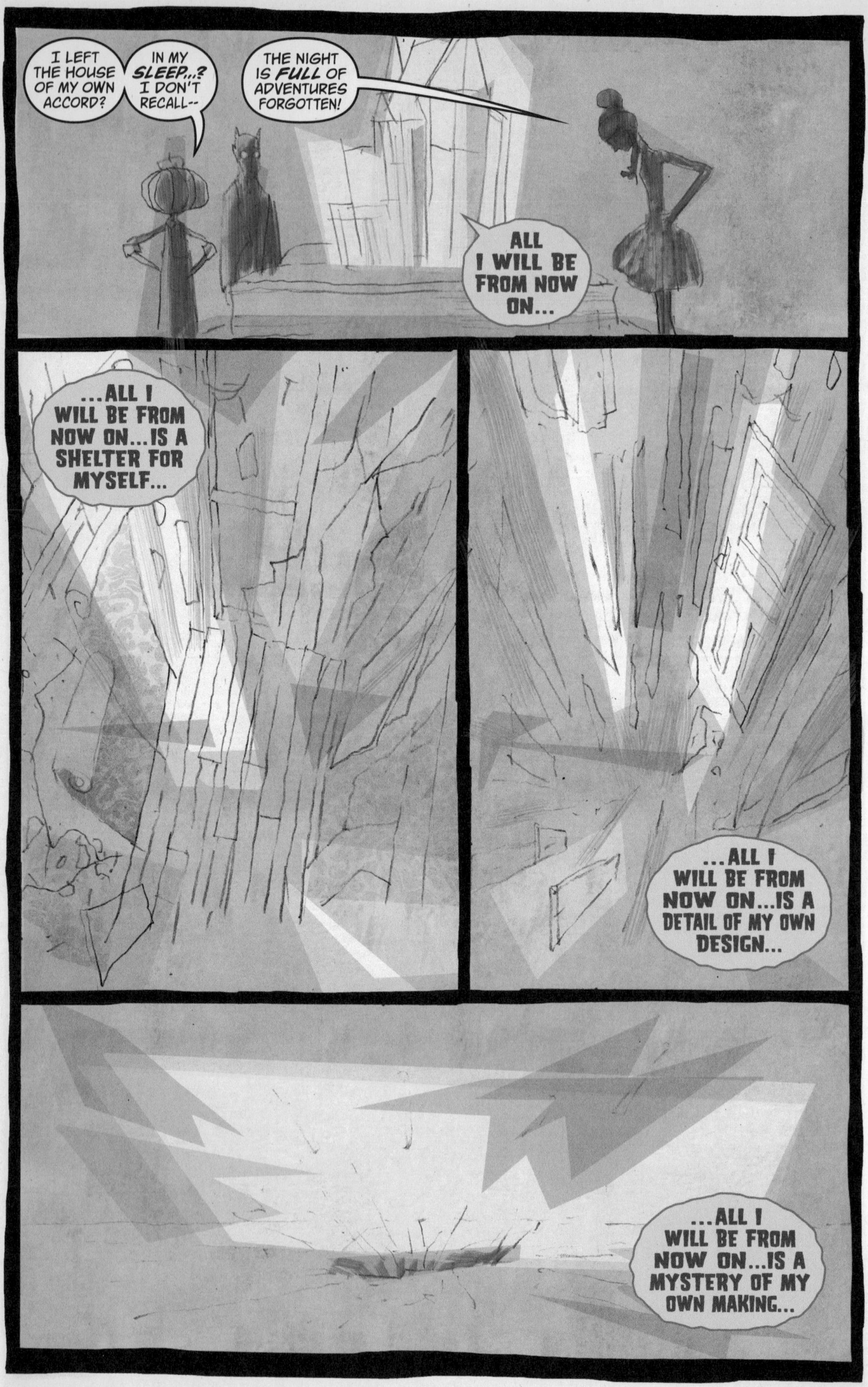
I LEFT THE HOUSE OF MY OWN ACCORD?
IN MY *SLEEP...?* I DON'T RECALL--
THE NIGHT IS *FULL* OF ADVENTURES FORGOTTEN!
ALL I WILL BE FROM NOW ON...
...ALL I WILL BE FROM NOW ON...IS A SHELTER FOR MYSELF...
...ALL I WILL BE FROM NOW ON...IS A DETAIL OF MY OWN DESIGN...
...ALL I WILL BE FROM NOW ON...IS A MYSTERY OF MY OWN MAKING...

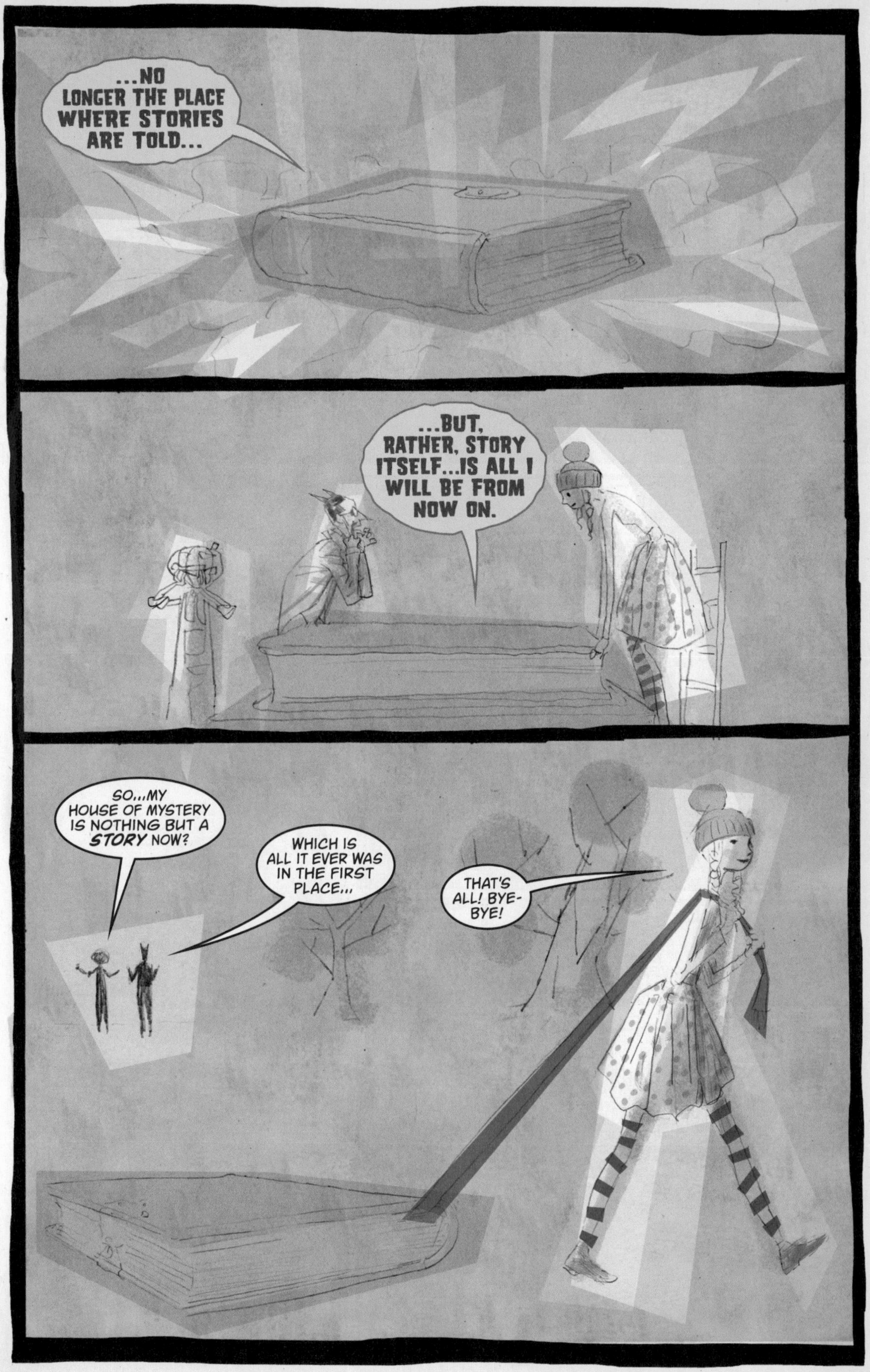
...NO LONGER THE PLACE WHERE STORIES ARE TOLD...
...BUT, RATHER, STORY ITSELF...IS ALL I WILL BE FROM NOW ON.
SO...MY HOUSE OF MYSTERY IS NOTHING BUT A *STORY* NOW?
WHICH IS ALL IT EVER WAS IN THE FIRST PLACE...
THAT'S ALL! BYE-BYE!

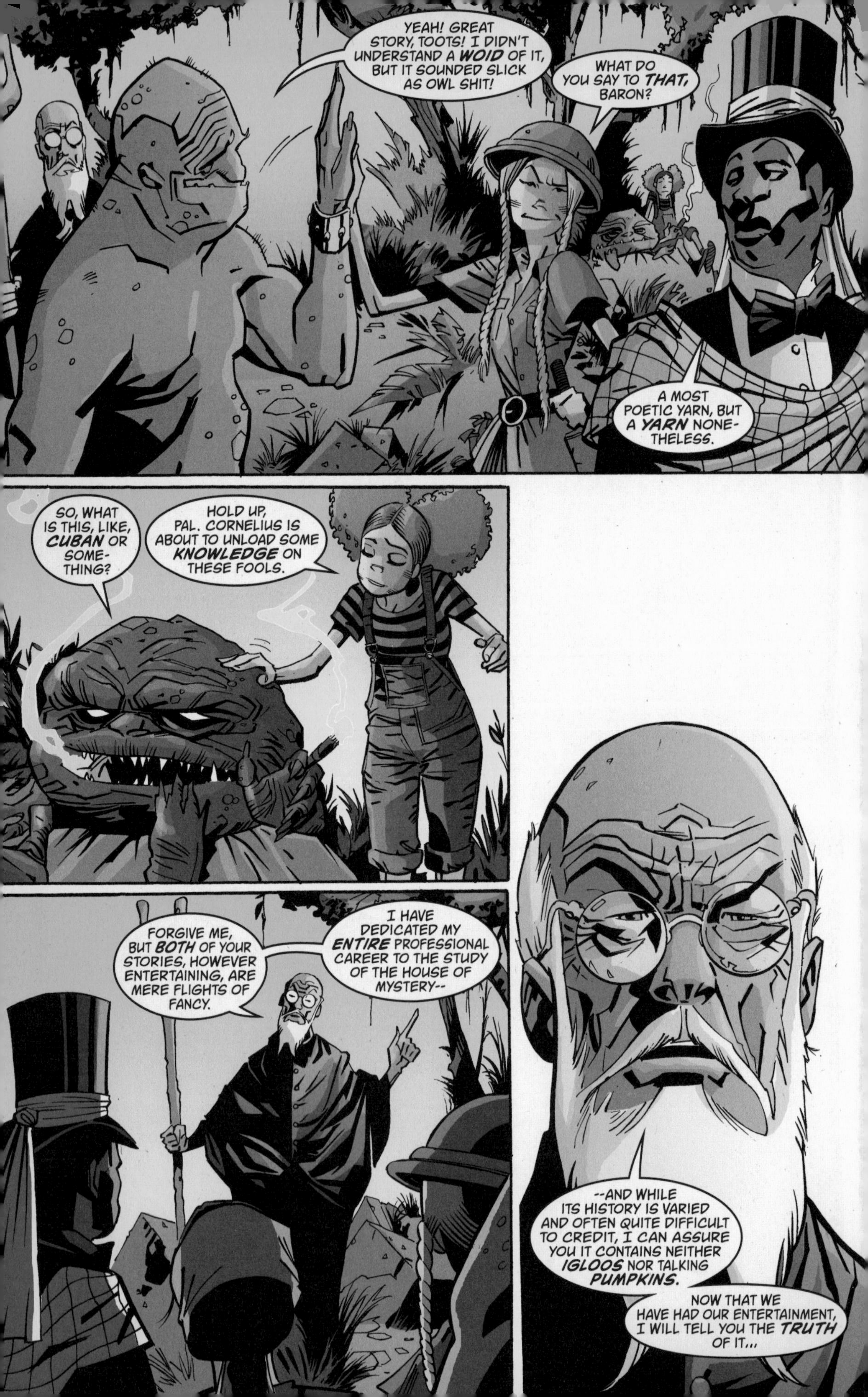
YEAH! GREAT STORY, TOOTS! I DIDN'T UNDERSTAND A WOID OF IT, BUT IT SOUNDED SLICK AS OWL SHIT!
WHAT DO YOU SAY TO THAT, BARON?
A MOST POETIC YARN, BUT A YARN NONE-THELESS.
SO, WHAT IS THIS, LIKE, CUBAN OR SOME-THING?
HOLD UP, PAL. CORNELIUS IS ABOUT TO UNLOAD SOME KNOWLEDGE ON THESE FOOLS.
FORGIVE ME, BUT BOTH OF YOUR STORIES, HOWEVER ENTERTAINING, ARE MERE FLIGHTS OF FANCY.
I HAVE DEDICATED MY ENTIRE PROFESSIONAL CAREER TO THE STUDY OF THE HOUSE OF MYSTERY--
--AND WHILE ITS HISTORY IS VARIED AND OFTEN QUITE DIFFICULT TO CREDIT, I CAN ASSURE YOU IT CONTAINS NEITHER IGLOOS NOR TALKING PUMPKINS.
NOW THAT WE HAVE HAD OUR ENTERTAINMENT, I WILL TELL YOU THE TRUTH OF IT...

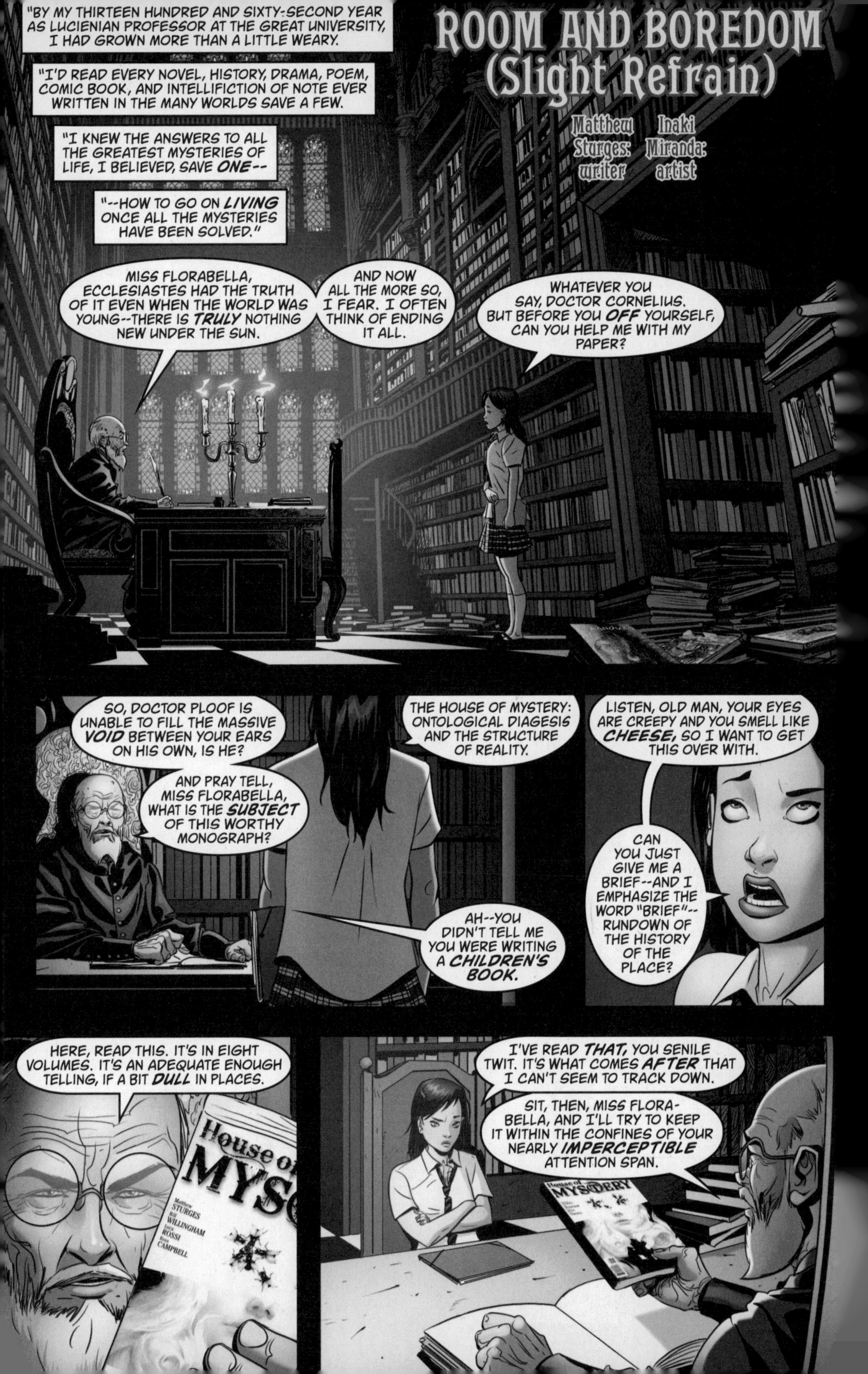

"BY MY THIRTEEN HUNDRED AND SIXTY-SECOND YEAR AS LUCIENIAN PROFESSOR AT THE GREAT UNIVERSITY, I HAD GROWN MORE THAN A LITTLE WEARY.
ROOM AND BOREDOM (Slight Refrain)
Matthew Sturges: writer
Inaki Miranda: artist
"I'D READ EVERY NOVEL, HISTORY, DRAMA, POEM, COMIC BOOK, AND INTELLIFICTION OF NOTE EVER WRITTEN IN THE MANY WORLDS SAVE A FEW.
"I KNEW THE ANSWERS TO ALL THE GREATEST MYSTERIES OF LIFE, I BELIEVED, SAVE ONE--
"--HOW TO GO ON LIVING ONCE ALL THE MYSTERIES HAVE BEEN SOLVED."
MISS FLORABELLA, ECCLESIASTES HAD THE TRUTH OF IT EVEN WHEN THE WORLD WAS YOUNG--THERE IS TRULY NOTHING NEW UNDER THE SUN.
AND NOW ALL THE MORE SO, I FEAR. I OFTEN THINK OF ENDING IT ALL.
WHATEVER YOU SAY, DOCTOR CORNELIUS. BUT BEFORE YOU OFF YOURSELF, CAN YOU HELP ME WITH MY PAPER?
SO, DOCTOR PLOOF IS UNABLE TO FILL THE MASSIVE VOID BETWEEN YOUR EARS ON HIS OWN, IS HE?
AND PRAY TELL, MISS FLORABELLA, WHAT IS THE SUBJECT OF THIS WORTHY MONOGRAPH?
THE HOUSE OF MYSTERY: ONTOLOGICAL DIAGESIS AND THE STRUCTURE OF REALITY.
AH--YOU DIDN'T TELL ME YOU WERE WRITING A CHILDREN'S BOOK.
LISTEN, OLD MAN, YOUR EYES ARE CREEPY AND YOU SMELL LIKE CHEESE, SO I WANT TO GET THIS OVER WITH.
CAN YOU JUST GIVE ME A BRIEF--AND I EMPHASIZE THE WORD "BRIEF"--RUNDOWN OF THE HISTORY OF THE PLACE?
HERE, READ THIS. IT'S IN EIGHT VOLUMES. IT'S AN ADEQUATE ENOUGH TELLING, IF A BIT DULL IN PLACES.
I'VE READ THAT, YOU SENILE TWIT. IT'S WHAT COMES AFTER THAT I CAN'T SEEM TO TRACK DOWN.
SIT, THEN, MISS FLORA-BELLA, AND I'LL TRY TO KEEP IT WITHIN THE CONFINES OF YOUR NEARLY IMPERCEPTIBLE ATTENTION SPAN.

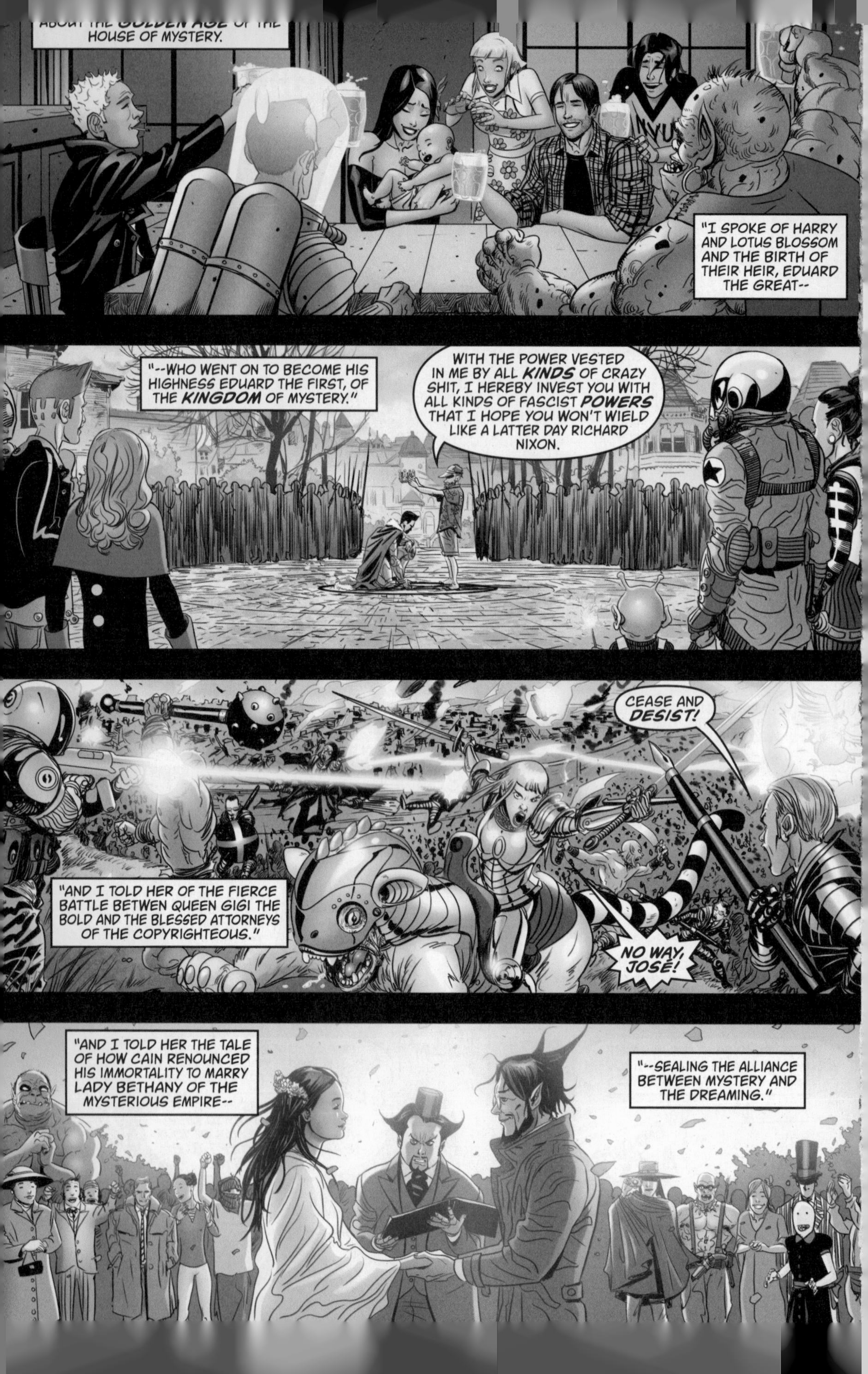
ABOUT THE GOLDEN AGE OF THE HOUSE OF MYSTERY.
"I SPOKE OF HARRY AND LOTUS BLOSSOM AND THE BIRTH OF THEIR HEIR, EDUARD THE GREAT--
"--WHO WENT ON TO BECOME HIS HIGHNESS EDUARD THE FIRST, OF THE KINGDOM OF MYSTERY."
WITH THE POWER VESTED IN ME BY ALL KINDS OF CRAZY SHIT, I HEREBY INVEST YOU WITH ALL KINDS OF FASCIST POWERS THAT I HOPE YOU WON'T WIELD LIKE A LATTER DAY RICHARD NIXON.
CEASE AND DESIST!
"AND I TOLD HER OF THE FIERCE BATTLE BETWEN QUEEN GIGI THE BOLD AND THE BLESSED ATTORNEYS OF THE COPYRIGHTEOUS."
NO WAY, JOSÉ!
"AND I TOLD HER THE TALE OF HOW CAIN RENOUNCED HIS IMMORTALITY TO MARRY LADY BETHANY OF THE MYSTERIOUS EMPIRE--
"--SEALING THE ALLIANCE BETWEEN MYSTERY AND THE DREAMING."

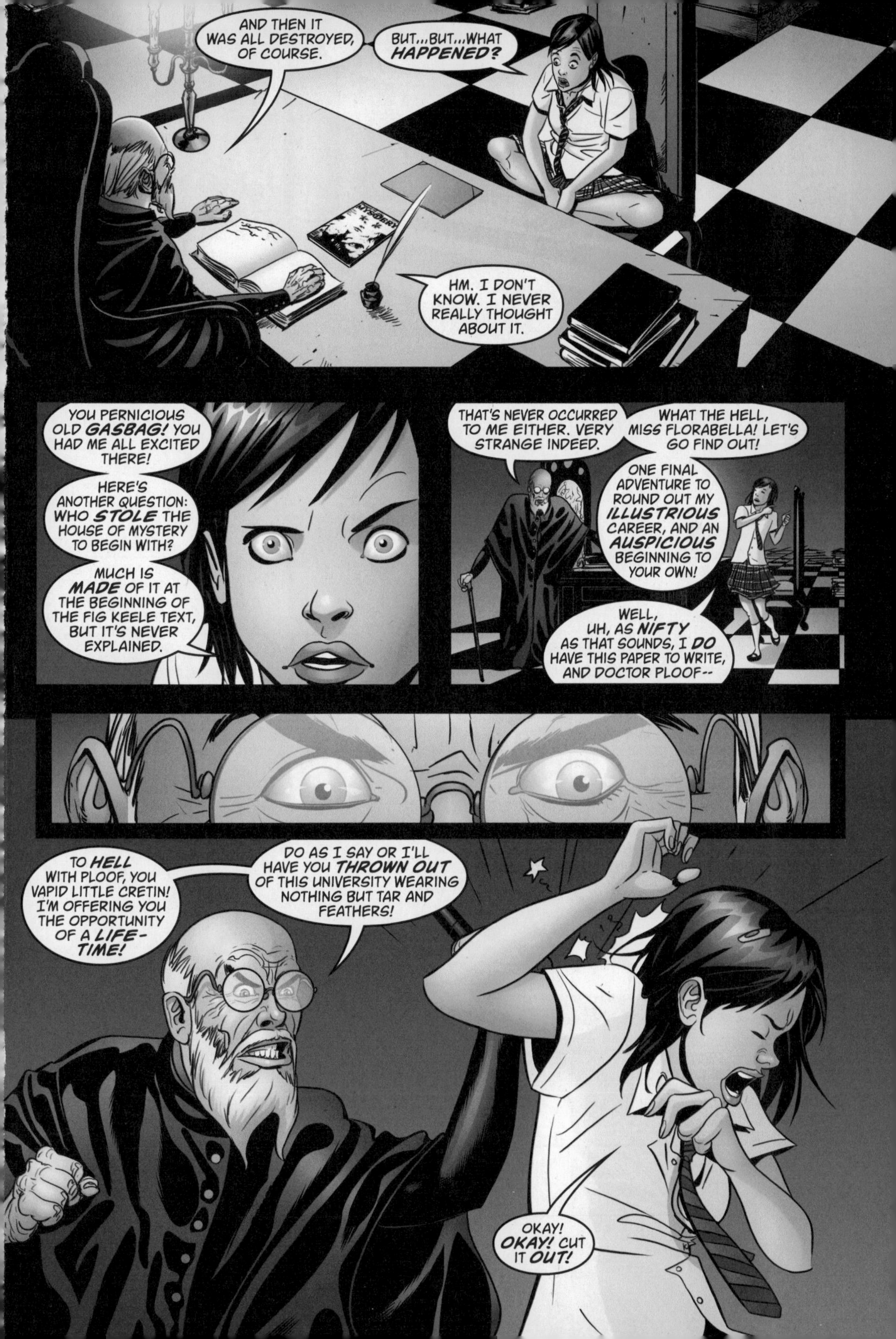
AND THEN IT WAS ALL DESTROYED, OF COURSE.
BUT...BUT...WHAT HAPPENED?
HM. I DON'T KNOW. I NEVER REALLY THOUGHT ABOUT IT.
YOU PERNICIOUS OLD GASBAG! YOU HAD ME ALL EXCITED THERE!
HERE'S ANOTHER QUESTION: WHO STOLE THE HOUSE OF MYSTERY TO BEGIN WITH?
MUCH IS MADE OF IT AT THE BEGINNING OF THE FIG KEELE TEXT, BUT IT'S NEVER EXPLAINED.
THAT'S NEVER OCCURRED TO ME EITHER. VERY STRANGE INDEED.
WHAT THE HELL, MISS FLORABELLA! LET'S GO FIND OUT!
ONE FINAL ADVENTURE TO ROUND OUT MY ILLUSTRIOUS CAREER, AND AN AUSPICIOUS BEGINNING TO YOUR OWN!
WELL, UH, AS NIFTY AS THAT SOUNDS, I DO HAVE THIS PAPER TO WRITE, AND DOCTOR PLOOF--
TO HELL WITH PLOOF, YOU VAPID LITTLE CRETIN! I'M OFFERING YOU THE OPPORTUNITY OF A LIFE-TIME!
DO AS I SAY OR I'LL HAVE YOU THROWN OUT OF THIS UNIVERSITY WEARING NOTHING BUT TAR AND FEATHERS!
OKAY! OKAY! CUT IT OUT!

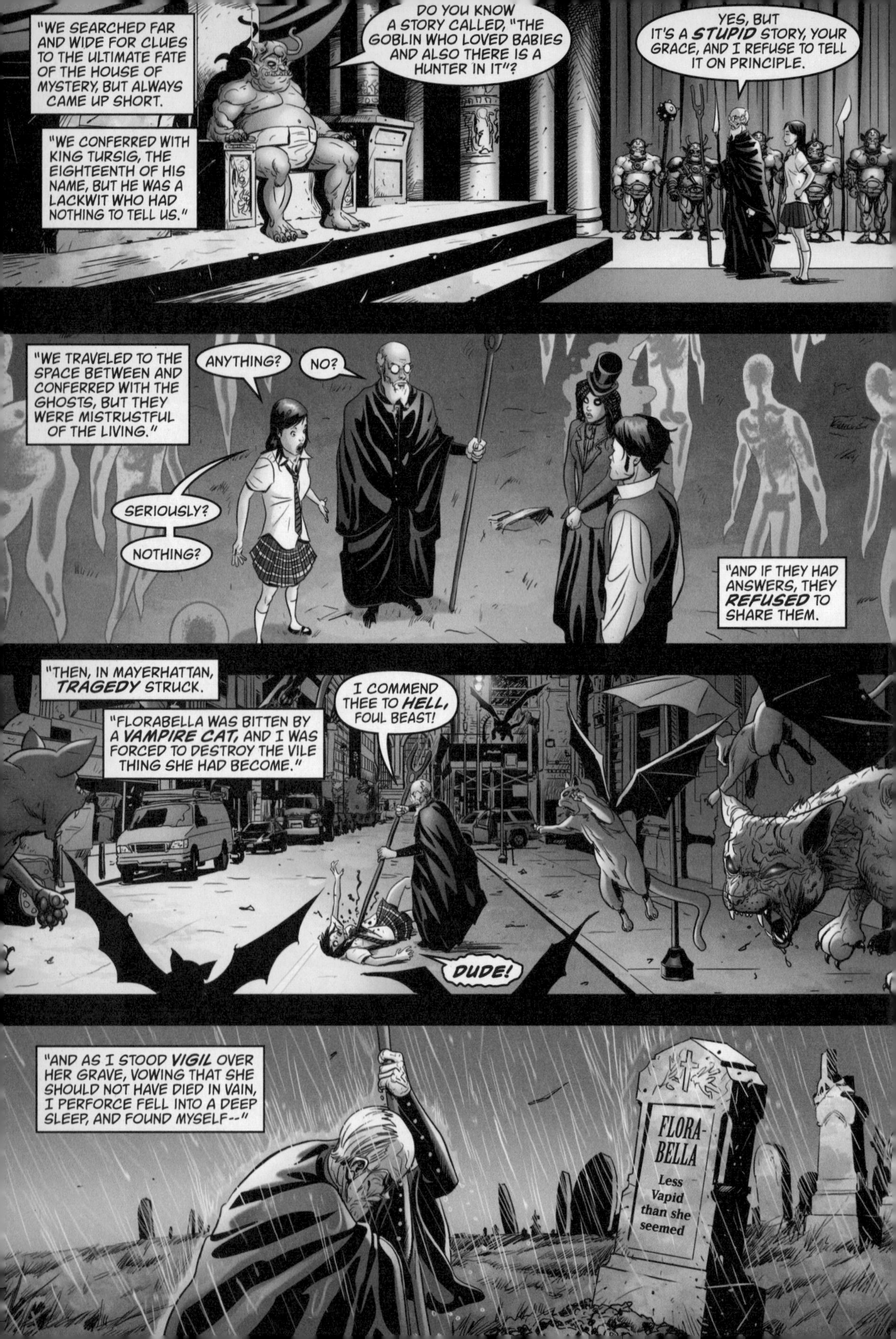
"WE SEARCHED FAR AND WIDE FOR CLUES TO THE ULTIMATE FATE OF THE HOUSE OF MYSTERY, BUT ALWAYS CAME UP SHORT.
"WE CONFERRED WITH KING TURSIG, THE EIGHTEENTH OF HIS NAME, BUT HE WAS A LACKWIT WHO HAD NOTHING TO TELL US."
DO YOU KNOW A STORY CALLED, "THE GOBLIN WHO LOVED BABIES AND ALSO THERE IS A HUNTER IN IT"?
YES, BUT IT'S A STUPID STORY, YOUR GRACE, AND I REFUSE TO TELL IT ON PRINCIPLE.
"WE TRAVELED TO THE SPACE BETWEEN AND CONFERRED WITH THE GHOSTS, BUT THEY WERE MISTRUSTFUL OF THE LIVING."
ANYTHING?
NO?
SERIOUSLY?
NOTHING?
"AND IF THEY HAD ANSWERS, THEY REFUSED TO SHARE THEM.
"THEN, IN MAYERHATTAN, TRAGEDY STRUCK.
"FLORABELLA WAS BITTEN BY A VAMPIRE CAT, AND I WAS FORCED TO DESTROY THE VILE THING SHE HAD BECOME."
I COMMEND THEE TO HELL, FOUL BEAST!
DUDE!
"AND AS I STOOD VIGIL OVER HER GRAVE, VOWING THAT SHE SHOULD NOT HAVE DIED IN VAIN, I PERFORCE FELL INTO A DEEP SLEEP, AND FOUND MYSELF--"
FLORA-BELLA
Less Vapid than she seemed

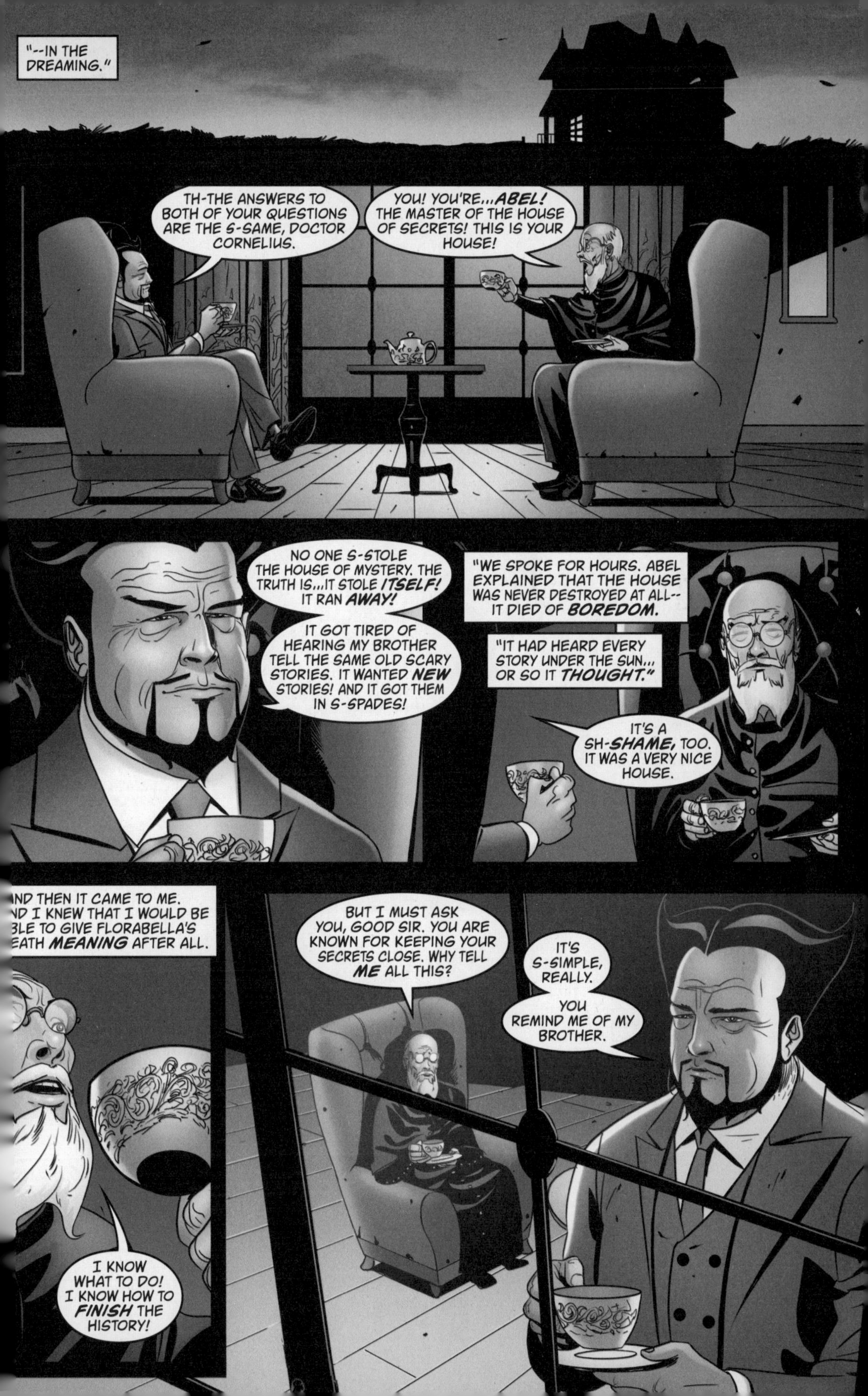
"--IN THE DREAMING."
TH-THE ANSWERS TO BOTH OF YOUR QUESTIONS ARE THE S-SAME, DOCTOR CORNELIUS.
YOU! YOU'RE...ABEL! THE MASTER OF THE HOUSE OF SECRETS! THIS IS YOUR HOUSE!
NO ONE S-STOLE THE HOUSE OF MYSTERY. THE TRUTH IS...IT STOLE ITSELF! IT RAN AWAY!
IT GOT TIRED OF HEARING MY BROTHER TELL THE SAME OLD SCARY STORIES. IT WANTED NEW STORIES! AND IT GOT THEM IN S-SPADES!
"WE SPOKE FOR HOURS. ABEL EXPLAINED THAT THE HOUSE WAS NEVER DESTROYED AT ALL-- IT DIED OF BOREDOM.
"IT HAD HEARD EVERY STORY UNDER THE SUN... OR SO IT THOUGHT."
IT'S A SH-SHAME, TOO. IT WAS A VERY NICE HOUSE.
ND THEN IT CAME TO ME. ND I KNEW THAT I WOULD BE BLE TO GIVE FLORABELLA'S EATH MEANING AFTER ALL.
I KNOW WHAT TO DO! I KNOW HOW TO FINISH THE HISTORY!
BUT I MUST ASK YOU, GOOD SIR. YOU ARE KNOWN FOR KEEPING YOUR SECRETS CLOSE. WHY TELL ME ALL THIS?
IT'S S-SIMPLE, REALLY.
YOU REMIND ME OF MY BROTHER.

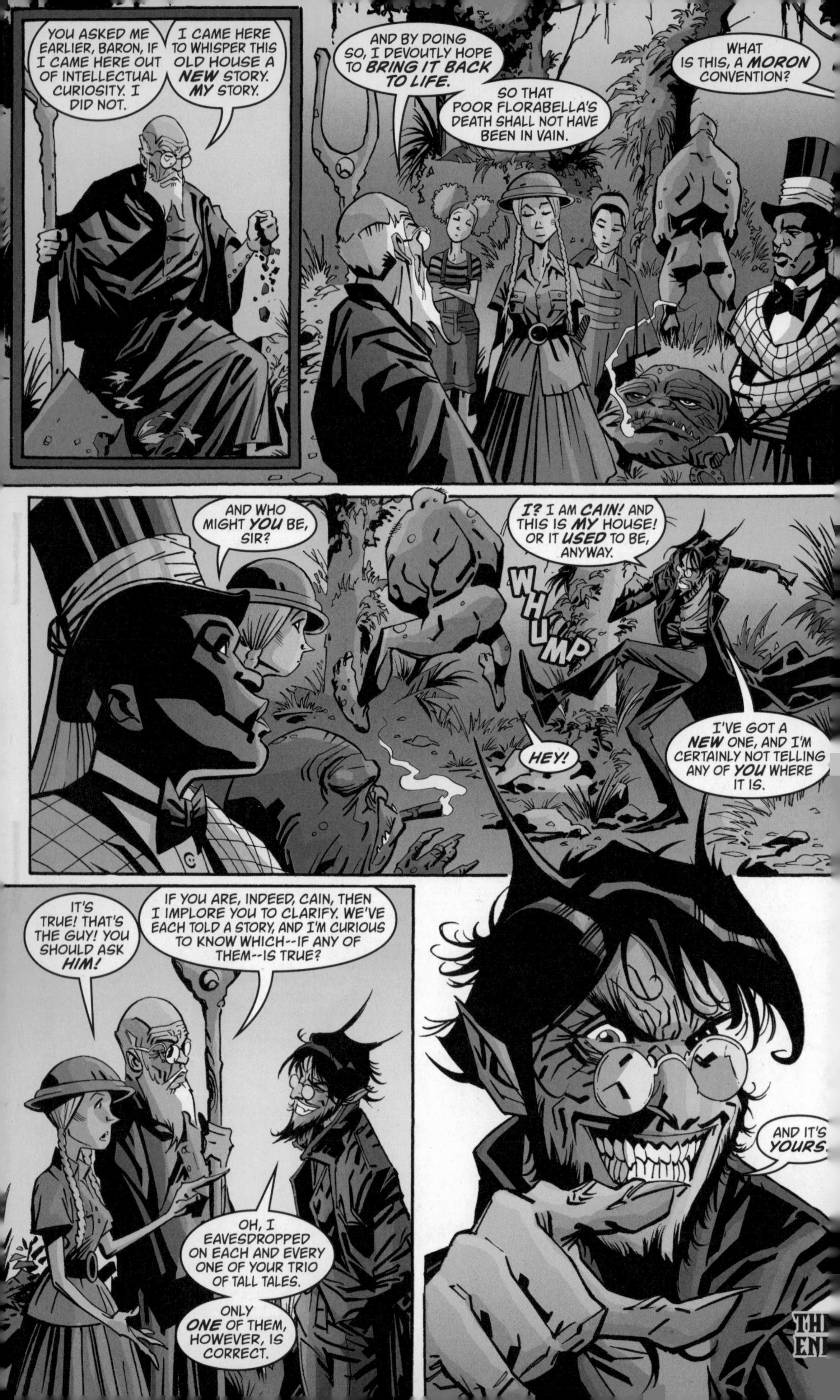
YOU ASKED ME EARLIER, BARON, IF I CAME HERE OUT OF INTELLECTUAL CURIOSITY. I DID NOT.
I CAME HERE TO WHISPER THIS OLD HOUSE A NEW STORY. MY STORY.
AND BY DOING SO, I DEVOUTLY HOPE TO BRING IT BACK TO LIFE.
SO THAT POOR FLORABELLA'S DEATH SHALL NOT HAVE BEEN IN VAIN.
WHAT IS THIS, A MORON CONVENTION?
AND WHO MIGHT YOU BE, SIR?
I? I AM CAIN! AND THIS IS MY HOUSE! OR IT USED TO BE, ANYWAY.
WHUMP
HEY!
I'VE GOT A NEW ONE, AND I'M CERTAINLY NOT TELLING ANY OF YOU WHERE IT IS.
IT'S TRUE! THAT'S THE GUY! YOU SHOULD ASK HIM!
IF YOU ARE, INDEED, CAIN, THEN I IMPLORE YOU TO CLARIFY. WE'VE EACH TOLD A STORY, AND I'M CURIOUS TO KNOW WHICH--IF ANY OF THEM--IS TRUE?
OH, I EAVESDROPPED ON EACH AND EVERY ONE OF YOUR TRIO OF TALL TALES.
ONLY ONE OF THEM, HOWEVER, IS CORRECT.
AND IT'S YOURS.
THE END

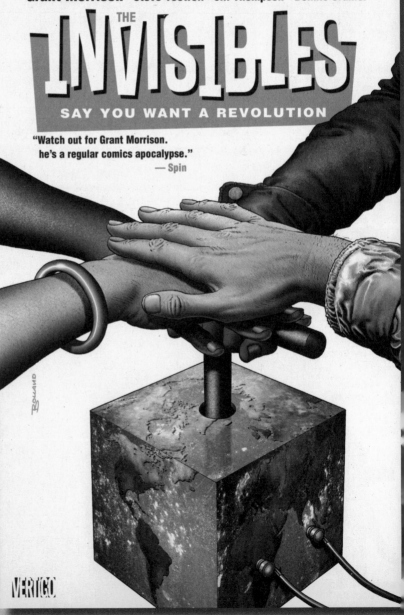